™

LUE GUIDE

HALLMARK
Keepsake Ornaments

Secondary Market Price Guide
& Collector Handbook

THIRD EDITION

HALLMARK
Keepsake Ornaments

This publication is *not* affiliated with Hallmark Cards, Inc. or any of its affiliates, subsidiaries, distributors or representatives. Any opinions expressed are solely those of the authors, and do not necessarily reflect those of Hallmark Cards, Inc. Product names and product designs are the property of Hallmark Cards, Inc., Kansas City, MO.

Front cover (left to right): "Frosty Friends" (20th edition in *Frosty Friends* Keepsake series, 1999); "The Cat in the Hat" (set/2, 1st edition in *Dr. Seuss® Books* Keepsake series, 1999).

Back cover (top to bottom): "Peter Rabbit™" (1st edition in *Beatrix Potter™* Spring Ornaments series, 1996); "1938 GARTON® Lincoln Zephyr" (LE-24,500, Kiddie Car Classics, 1997).

Managing Editor:	Jeff Mahony	Creative Director:	Joe T. Nguyen
Associate Editors:	Melissa A. Bennett	Production Supervisor:	Scott Sierakowski
	Jan Cronan	Senior Graphic Designers:	Lance Doyle
	Gia C. Manalio		Carole Mattia-Slater
	Paula Stuckart		Leanne Peters
Contributing Editor:	Mike Micciulla	Graphic Designers:	Jennifer J. Denis
Editorial Assistants:	Jennifer Filipek		Peter Dunbar
	Nicole LeGard Lenderking		Sean-Ryan Dudley
	Christina Levere		Kimberly Eastman
	Joan C. Wheal		Ryan Falis
Research Assistants:	Timothy R. Affleck		Jason Jasch
	Priscilla Berthiaume		David S. Maloney
	Heather N. Carreiro		David Ten Eyck
	Beth Hackett	Art Interns:	Janice Evert
	Victoria Puorro		Ali Leibenhaut
	Steven Shinkaruk		Jocelyn R. Parente
Web Reporters:	Samantha Bouffard		
	Ren Messina		

ISBN 1-888914-53-X

CheckerBee PUBLISHING
(formerly Collectors' Publishing)
306 Industrial Park Road • Middletown, CT 06457

collectorbee.com

TABLE OF CONTENTS

COLLECTOR'S
VALUE GUIDE™

TABLE OF CONTENTS

Renowned Hallmark expert Clara Johnson Scroggins has been collecting ornaments for over 30 years. She has written nine books and numerous articles on ornament collecting and is famous among fellow ornament fans for her ever-growing collection, as well as her holiday displays.

Hello again! I can't believe another year has come to a close, but it has! This last year was tremendous and many of you entered 1999 with fond memories of the fun we had during the 25th Anniversary of Hallmark Keepsake Ornaments. The convention held in August in Kansas City was a blast! Hallmark did such a wonderful job and I was so excited to see so many old friends, plus make a lot of new ones.

Even though the excitement of the 25th Anniversary has passed, 1999 is no time to slow down! It is time to look forward to – among other things – the six Artists On Tour events planned for the Summer and Fall. There will be pieces to win at these events, plus lots of good friends to celebrate your love of Hallmark with. So you don't want to miss it! I hope I will see you there!

Now that we are in the 26th year of Hallmark Keepsake Ornaments and facing a new millennium, there is no better time to be a collector. Ornaments are important to help commemorate a passing from the old to the new, and will help capture the excitement of this time of change in the year 2000 and beyond.

Clara

INTRODUCING THE COLLECTOR'S VALUE GUIDE

*W*elcome to the third edition of the Hallmark Keepsake Ornaments Collector's Value Guide™! This all-inclusive guide will provide you with everything you need to know about the ornaments that have grown from a holiday tradition into a popular year-round collectible.

The guide starts with a history of the company and is followed by an overview of the different types of Hallmark Ornaments and collectibles, including Spring Ornaments, Merry Miniatures and Kiddie Car Classics. Next, our *New Series Spotlight* offers a preview of the upcoming series for 1999. Catch an inside glimpse into the lives of the Keepsake artists through exclusive interviews with Patricia Andrews, Ken Crow and Nello Williams, followed by biographies on all of the Keepsake artists.

Then it's on to the Value Guide, where we provide you with full-color pictures and 1999 secondary market prices for every ornament produced since the line's debut in 1973. All the information on each piece, including stock number and issue price is here as well – all in an easy-to-use format.

In the guide, we'll also bring you to the company's 25th Anniversary Celebration, and introduce you to noted ornament expert, Clara Johnson Scroggins. And you won't want to miss our sections on the Hallmark Keepsake Ornament Collector's Club, tips on insuring your collectibles and ideas for displaying your collection!

So what are you waiting for? Make the holiday season every day and turn the page to enter the exciting world of Hallmark Keepsake Ornaments!

History

*W*hen people think of Hallmark, certain images come to mind: high-quality greeting cards, carefully-crafted, ornaments and heart-warming collectibles. Certainly you wouldn't imagine a pile of picture postcards in a shoe-box. Yet that's all 18-year-old Joyce Hall had when he

arrived at the YMCA in Kansas City, Missouri one chilly day in 1910. Now, almost 90 years later this entrepreneur and his family have capitalized on his dreams.

Starting a company at such a young age was no easy feat, but Hall recognized the success of illustrated postcards in the market-place and decided to distribute his collection. After sending hundreds of packets to Mid-western dealers, Hall started to see his vision grow – dealers were responding! While some kept the postcards without paying and some just sent them back, many actually sent checks and within a few months' time, Hall had amassed $200. Despite his initial success, Hall felt the real prosperity lay in higher quality cards and three years later when Hall combined these greeting cards with envelopes, he had a winner. From then on, the company known as Hall Brothers was well on its way.

By 1923, Joyce's two brothers, William and Rollie, joined the company, along with more than 120 employees and in the following years, the Hall Brothers firm changed the loca-tion of its headquarters several times to accom-modate its rapidly expanding employee and customer base. It wasn't until 1956 that a newly renamed Hallmark Cards, Inc. settled in

CLUBBIN' IT

In 1987, Hallmark introduced the Keepsake Ornament Collector's Club, which provides faithful fans of the holiday ornaments with special access to Hallmark news and prod-ucts.

Each year the club sends members exclusive Keepsake Ornaments in a membership kit. Members can also purchase special Club Edition ornaments – a must for any serious collec-tor. The club features a quarterly newsletter, early access to the Hallmark Keepsake Ornament Dream Book, notification of special events and decorating tips.

Today, there are more than 160,000 members in the club, many of whom have started their own local Keepsake Ornament Collector's Club chapters.

its current headquarters.

The 1950s marked a busy and exciting period in Hallmark's history, one that saw the company delve into different markets. Newly added festive gift wrap and colorful party decorations were a welcome change to what Joyce Hall referred to as "drab" and otherwise "limited" choices for consumers. And on Christmas Eve, 1951, with the presentation of "Amahl and the Night Visitors," Hallmark introduced The Hallmark Hall Of Fame, a series of dramatic television specials aimed at bringing social values to television programming. Over the years, these productions have had the honor of receiving numerous awards, including the first Emmy to be rewarded to a sponsor.

In 1966, Joyce handed down his responsibilities as Chief Executive Officer to his son Donald J. Hall who continues to maintain the strong business practices his father instilled in him. And the company itself has remained in a constant state of expansion. Adding to its growing success, Hallmark made several acquisitions, including the 1967 purchase of the jigsaw puzzle manufacturer, Springbok Editions and the 1984 purchase of Binney & Smith, the producer of Crayola Crayons®.

In 1968, Hallmark undertook another venture in hopes of bettering the community. Wishing to give back something to those who supported them, Hallmark turned an eyesore of abandoned parking lots and businesses in downtown Kansas City into a real jewel: The Crown Center. Today, this business mecca encompasses 85 acres of land and houses the new Visitor's Center where you can take a tour of 25 years of Hallmark history, as well as learn about the production process that has made those 25 years possible. And after your tour, you can take some time to relax by wandering through the complex's many shops, grabbing a bite to eat at its many restaurants, taking in some culture at one of its theaters or just resting in one of the complex's luxury hotels. Still under construction, The Crown Center is an entertainment mecca all within the heart of Kansas City.

In 1994, Hallmark added to its credits with the start of Hallmark Entertainment, Inc., a company dedicated to producing and distributing a number of family oriented television programs.

To date, Hallmark employs almost 20,000 people who own more than one-third of the corporation through the "Employee Profit Sharing and Ownership Program." Hallmark has incorporated the work of well-known artists such as Norman Rockwell and Salvador Dali into its line-up, and relies upon the skills of a diverse creative staff that includes painters, poets, photographers, calligraphers and sculptors, to name just a few.

The once one person, "out-of-a-shoe-box" business headed by Joyce Hall has grown step by step into one of the most profitable, and entertaining, companies in the industry.

THE GIVING TREE

Each year after the holidays, the Christmas tree in Hallmark's Crown Center is taken down and turned to mulch. The core of the tree is preserved and given to the Hallmark artisans to use in the creation of special ornaments known as "Mayor's Ornaments." The ornaments are later sold, with the the proceeds going to help the less-fortunate citizens of Kansas City.

OVERVIEW

*O*ver the years, Hallmark has dramatically changed the concept of Christmas decorations. No longer just a seasonal past-time, decorating the tree (and the tree is just one option) has become a way for passionate collectors to showcase their exquisite Hallmark Ornaments. Ornaments have become a way to preserve memories and traditions, to celebrate and mark life's memorable events and to show someone that you care. Whatever the occasion, whatever your need, Hallmark has an ornament!

In 1973, Hallmark introduced six decorated glass ball ornaments and 12 yarn figures. The yarn figures, which were only available for a limited time, sold for just over $1 each and started quite a craze. Since then, more than 4,000 Hallmark Ornaments have been produced!

KEEPSAKE ORNAMENTS

When you think of Hallmark Ornaments, you probably think of the line called Hallmark Keepsake Ornaments. Introduced in 1973, the line offered collectors something different: hand-crafted pieces made with materials such as cloth and wood.

The Keepsake Ornaments collection is large and eclectic. Whatever your reason for collecting, you're sure to find an ornament that suits your needs and your tastes. And based on the number of ornaments produced and the life of the line, you probably already have a few.

The possibilities within this collection are endless. Looking to capture a traditional holiday scene? Many pieces offer collectors a chance to steal a favorite moment of the holiday season, or things only dreamed about, and keep it forever. Some even offer the opportunity to travel the skies or battle the dark forces with STAR TREK™ or STAR WARS™ characters. Others pay tribute to pop culture icons such BARBIE™ and Dorothy from "The Wizard of Oz™."

With this plethora of ornaments, you would think that they can be found anywhere and everywhere. However, this isn't necessarily true. One of the most unique features of the Hallmark line is that the ornaments are only available for a limited amount of time, usually from early summer until Christmas. Another unique feature within the line is the collectible series. Sharing a common theme or design, the pieces in a series are released one per year, each referred to as an "edition." And as all good things must come to an end, so is the case with series. Whatever the reason for the ending of a series, Hallmark will announce its retirement in the "Dream Book," the annual full-color catalog that Hallmark issues to showcase that year's collection.

MAGIC ORNAMENTS

In 1984, Hallmark came out with the "Lighted Ornament Collection." This innovative series originally featured ornaments that glowed with soft light, but just two years later they were on the move – literally. Now, with the advent of animation, these magical ornaments became known as Keepsake Magic Ornaments. And in 1989, this magical experience became audible as well, with the addition of sound.

Beyond the mysteries of light and sound, Keepsake Magic Ornaments also offer collectors a myriad of themes, including their own set of series.

CROWN REFLECTIONS

Hallmark introduced Crown Reflections in 1998. The line is made up of blown glass, which is hand painted and styled after the traditional European ornaments that appeared more than a century ago. The precise attention to detail that the artists give to these pieces ensure their uniqueness and beauty.

With its second release, the line has almost doubled, incorporating many sets to its credit. Appearing are some American classics: including a plump sparkly snowman and a snow-covered church. There are also additions to the transportation genre: a "1950 Lionel® Santa Fe Diesel Locomotive" and a "1955 Murray® Ranch Wagon," and of course, the "U.S.S. Enterprise™ NCC-1701 STAR TREK™."

LASER CREATIONS ORNAMENTS

Always the innovator, in 1999, Hallmark debuted the Laser Creations ornaments line. To produce these ornaments, a pattern is cut on archival paper by a beam of laser light that is too small to be viewed by the human eye. The ornament is then assembled by hand and, once the product is complete, the delicate design reflects lights and shadows in a way that is truly unique.

The eight new pieces of this line include many themes. There is an angel, Santa's workshop and a Yuletide charm among other holiday sentiments. Each ornament captures the beauty and special spirit of the holidays, ensuring that this particular line will be an instant hit with collectors.

SHOWCASE ORNAMENTS

These metal and porcelain ornaments stood out when they were first introduced in 1993, as they featured a more traditional style that focused on religious and folk art scenes and were only available through Hallmark Gold Crown stores. The series is no longer active, although the style of its pieces is featured in some current ornamental designs.

MINIATURE ORNAMENTS

True to their name, these ornaments measure only a few inches high. Their size can range from 1/2" to 1-3/4" but just because they're small doesn't mean they fall short on the intricate detail and personality that characterize the rest of the Hallmark family of ornaments. Introduced in 1988, the Miniature Ornaments have been popular with collectors and in turn, difficult to find, especially since they are distributed in lesser quantities than other Keepsake ornaments.

The 1999 new releases number at about 30 and encompass a broad spectrum of artistic ideas, many of which borrow from popular culture. Collectors will easily recognize characters from LOONEY TUNES™, PEANUTS® and Dr. Suess®.

OTHER HALLMARK ORNAMENTS

Several ornaments have been produced in the past that do not necessarily belong in one particular line of the Hallmark Ornament Collection and they are listed under these additional categories:

Collector's Club Ornaments — In 1987, Hallmark introduced the Keepsake Ornament Collector's Club, as means of offering collectors another way to enjoy their collections.

A yearly Club membership includes a subscription to the Club newsletter, invitations to special events and the opportunity to purchase exclusive Club Edition ornaments. Often, these exclusive pieces are designed to complement series within the general line.

Premiere Exclusives — On July 17, Gold Crown stores will host the 7th National Keepsake Ornament Premiere Event which showcases the debut of the line's annual pieces. On this day only, collectors lucky enough to attend the event will have the opportunity to purchase the exclusive ornaments "Zebra Fantasy" and the Merry Miniatures' Madame Alexander®'s "Park Avenue Wendy & Alex The Bellhop."

Special Events — Throughout the year, Hallmark hosts various other special events at which collectors have the opportunity to meet the Hallmark artists, win prizes and purchase exclusive "event" ornaments.

Many events are on tap for 1999, including the Artists on Tour event which is slated to take place in various cities throughout the United States. And at Gold Crown stores, on October 9, more than 20 new Keepsake Ornaments will be introduced, while on November 13 and 14, the stores will host a Holiday Open House featuring the Millennium Princess BARBIE™ ornament, as well as much more.

SPRING ORNAMENTS

The arrival of Spring each year is certainly something to celebrate, and Hallmark makes it even more enjoyable with its Spring Ornament Collection. You'll find a palette of pastel colors and soft detail in this line of ornaments with animals and spring themes.

The line also contains pieces with Easter themes, as the line was originally called "Easter Ornaments" when it was introduced in 1991. However, as the themes broadened, so did the collection's name and it became known as

"Spring Ornaments." This popular line features some new themes, as well as a return to old childhood favorites, such as Winnie the Pooh.

MERRY MINIATURES

Merry Miniatures are very special figurines that date back almost as far as Hallmark's first ornaments. The line features animals such as cats, dogs and mice depicted in various scenes. Several of these pieces have the honor of having only been made available at special events such as this year's Ornament Premiere.

KIDDIE CAR CLASSICS

Kiddie Car Classics have been recognized as the best-selling, non-ornament series since their inception in 1992.

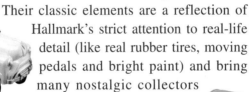

Their classic elements are a reflection of Hallmark's strict attention to real-life detail (like real rubber tires, moving pedals and bright paint) and bring many nostalgic collectors back to the days of childhood transportation. The 1999 Kiddie Car Classics introductions include some new modes of transportation to the line-up, including "1951 Hopalong Cassidy™ Velocipede" and a "1941 Garton® Field Ambulence."

You can classify your Kiddie Car Classics in a number of ways. The pieces are issued as either general releases or are limited in either Limited or Luxury Editions. In 1998 Hallmark introduced Numbered

Editions, which means pieces will be released in sequential production editions, with each edition containing 9,999 pieces.

The Kiddie Car Corner, introduced in 1997, has been growing rapidly and features accessories that allow you to turn your collection into a real community. New to the block are a billboard and fire station, complete with dalmatians. Each piece features great attention to detail and will make you feel as if you've stepped into a time machine and stepped out into days gone by.

OTHER HALLMARK COLLECTIBLES

In addition to Hallmark's roster are certain collectibles that have become as popular as the company's ornaments. These pieces can range from the ever-popular and elegant BARBIE™ COLLECTIBLES By Hallmark to die-cast metal trains in the Great

American Railways™ collection and the 1999 celebration of Legends In Flight. And further feeding the collector appetite are the School Days Lunch Boxes™, featuring animated scenes from popular television shows and movies from the 50s, 60s and 70s.

So whether you're looking to decorate a tree, take a walk down memory lane or celebrate 90s culture, Hallmark has your ornament. In the last 25 years Hallmark has built quite a remarkable reputation and has managed to become a forerunner in the collectibles market – position that is sure to last for the next 25 years and the next 25 years after that.

COLLECTIONS & "UNANNOUNCED" SERIES

In addition to official series, there are groupings of themed ornaments called collections. The pieces in these collections are often released during a single year with related pieces offered in subsequent years. Therefore, these groupings provide collectors with an "instantly" themed collection, yet one that has room to grow.

Some of the more popular collections include the Child's Age Collection, featuring bears celebrating the first five years of life; Looney Tunes™, featuring Bugs Bunny, Porky Pig, Elmer Fudd and all their friends; Mickey & Co., featuring Goofy, Donald, Minnie and of course Mickey; STAR TREK™, featuring both the original and next generations and Winnie the Pooh and all his Hundred Acre Wood buddies.

There are also "unannounced" series which are groupings of ornaments related by theme that are issued from year to year. These groupings give collectors the opportunity to slowly build their collection and provide collectors the pleasure of anticipating what might come out next.

These popular "not quite" series include Tonka® which constructed a name for itself in 1996; Mr. Potato Head® whose half-baked sense of style was introduced in 1997; Hot Wheels™ which drove into the line in 1998 and The Three Stooges™ which poked its way into the Hallmark family in 1998.

Whether an offical series or not, an instant collection or an annually growing one; themed ornaments provide another aspect to the fun of collecting.

*O*f all the Hallmark ornaments that are released each year, some of the most highly anticipated releases are those that belong to a series. Since 1978, Hallmark has released a number of new series each year, in almost every one of its different lines including Keepsake Ornaments, Magic Ornaments, Miniature Ornaments, Crown Reflections and even Spring Ornaments. Although the series are available for various lengths of time, most of the series last for a minimum of three years, with few exceptions having a shorter lifespan. *Here Comes Santa,* which is still current (and extremely popular), is the longest running series to date, with 21 pieces released since 1979. Another extremely popular series is the *Rocking Horse* series which debuted in 1981 and galloped into retirement in 1996.

Ornaments that are part of a series are often very popular and demand some of the highest values on the secondary market. The first edition in each series usually becomes the most coveted and therefore the most valuable as collectors often miss the first released pieces and want to make their collections as complete as possible. However, it's hard to tell which series will become the most popular. Here's a look at the first editions of the new 1999 series:

New Keepsake Series

Dr. Seuss® Books — A "cat in a hat," can you imagine that? Children of all ages have fallen in love with Dr. Seuss and his comical creatures, and now you can cherish them in this new series. This year's release, "The Cat in the Hat," is a set of two ornaments: the cat balancing on a ball, and the goldfish precariously perched atop a teapot!

Favorite Bible Stories — This series will highlight an inspirational Bible story every year in the form of a three-dimensional ornament. In this year's release, "David and Goliath," the giant threateningly towers off the page while the brave David battles him with his slingshot.

Gift Bearers — Every year, a poseable bear with a new holiday theme will make its appearance in the *Gift Bearers* series. This year's edition is a porcelain teddy dressed in a green vest and a cap topped with a gold star, who carries an ornament to help decorate the tree.

Harley-Davidson® Motorcycle Milestones —Motorcycle lovers will go "hog wild" for this new Hallmark series! Sculpted by Don Palmiter, each of these chrome masterpieces will represent a different Harley-Davidson® model. "Heritage Springer®" is the first in the series.

Joyful Santa — Each year, collectors can look forward to Santa Claus dressed in a distinctive costume. In the first piece of the series, Santa is robed in a red and white coat marked with a traditional African design.

Mischievous Kittens — Just as its name implies, this series will feature playful kittens who just can't seem to keep out of trouble! The first release portrays a playful black and white kitty who wants to "have dinner" with a wide-eyed goldfish!

Town and Country — This new series will spotlight buildings with a rural, small-town feel. The homey red and white "Farm House" is the first piece in this series and is made of pressed tin. This beautifully detailed piece was sculpted by Linda Scikman.

Winnie the Pooh and Christopher Robin, Too — This series will bring to life the tales of Winnie the Pooh and his friends from the Hundred Acre Wood. Pooh's playful personality is captured in the first piece in the series as he frolicks with Christopher Robin in "Playing With Pooh."

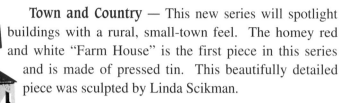

NEW MINIATURE SERIES

Holiday Flurries — Playful snowmen participate in a variety of wintertime activities in this series. The snowman making his debut in 1999 carries a pine tree and a gift, ready to help you start the holiday decorating!

LIONEL® 746 Norfolk and Western — A new set of trains will pull into your station each year, thanks to this new series. Collectors won't want to miss this year's edition, as no train is complete without its "Locomotive and Tender."

Miniature Harley-Davidson® Motorcycle — The second motorcycle series to debut in 1999, this group of die-cast metal bikes will replicate the look of real Harleys. "Electra-Glide®," the first bike to have an electric start, is the first model featured in this series.

Seaside Scenes — While there is no message in this bottle, there is a beautiful seaside scene. This series will feature a different coastal scene each year and for 1999, a lighthouse perches on the edge of a craggy cliff, ready to warn sailors of potential dangers.

The Wonders of Oz™ — Each year, this series will feature a different ornament depicting a scene from the classic film "The Wizard of Oz™." "Dorothy's Ruby Slippers" is this year's reminder that "there's no place like home!"

LAST CALL!

When Hallmark decides to retire a particular series, it lets collectors know in advance by designating the last piece as the "final" edition. The following 14 ornament series will end in 1999:

KEEPSAKE SERIES
The Clauses on Vacation
Dolls of the World
The Enchanted Memories Collection
Fabulous Decade
Hallmark Archives
Language of Flowers
Marilyn Monroe
Merry Olde Santa
Stock Car Champions
Thomas Kinkade

MAGIC SERIES
Journeys Into Space

MINIATURE SERIES
Centuries of Santa
Snowflake Ballet
Welcome Friends

Q & A With Hallmark Artists

*C*heckerBee Publishing recently asked three Hallmark Ornament artists to share a little bit about what it's like to spend their workday designing the famous ornaments that everyone loves! Read on to find out more about some of your favorite artists.

Patricia Andrews

CheckerBee Publishing: You began your career at Hallmark as an engraver. How did you make the switch to ornament artist?

Patricia Andrews: That was quite a year for me in '87 when I was accepted in Keepsakes. My job was eliminated a week after my 3-year-old son died. This kind of trauma removed all fear, allowing me to create a new life for myself. I do believe that for every door that is closed, God opens a new one. So I sat down with a block of Sculpey and taught myself how to sculpt. I used my son's face on two elves (crying most of the time) and I was hired on the spot. I have no regrets.

CP: You are married to fellow ornament artist, Dill Rhodus. What is it like to work together?

PA: Very natural! We've worked together since I came to Hallmark 23 years ago. We trust each other's opinions and frequently critique each other's work. This is particularly helpful when doing Star Wars™ characters together.

CP: You are known for the many BARBIE™ ornaments you have sculpted. Can you tell us how working with a cultural icon is different than creating an original design?

PA: When working with something like Barbie, I'm trying to match it exactly. The challenge comes in trying to duplicate her costumes and huge hair. With original designs, I am depending on my imagination and skills to project emotion. It is more satisfying for me (and a lot faster).

CP: How does it feel to help Barbie celebrate her 40th Anniversary?

PA: It immediately takes me back to when I was 7 years old and I first saw her. I remember a girlfriend bringing her Barbie to the playground on a sunny spring day in Orlando. I couldn't believe what I was seeing! She was this gorgeous, grown-up looking doll, with tiny hoop earrings, high heels and her own sunglasses! I fell in love. Happy birthday, Barbie!

CP: Speaking of anniversaries, last year you were selected to sculpt the limited "Angelic Flight" 25th Anniversary commemorative ornament. Can you tell us about this ornament and your experience at the convention in Kansas City?

PA: This ornament was inspired by an angel designed by Robert Haas. He is one of our premier artists at Hallmark and a personal friend. So I was honored when asked to do this. It also adds to my memories of this wonderful 25th Anniversary Celebration. Wow! What a time! I saw a lot of old friends and made a few new ones. The only bad part was having to write a speech and practice it. It made me very (uncharacteristically) nervous.

CP: You've worked on ornaments representing many famous American movie icons, such as Marilyn Monroe and Scarlett O'Hara. How do you pick the moments you choose to capture them?

PA: I love old movies, especially black and white ones. So when I had the opportunity to do some of the great stars, I was excited. I try to pick moments that I personally feel are strong. Sometimes it means playing a video frame by frame to catch that perfect second (Scarlett in the burgundy dress) and other times I concentrate on capturing a feeling (Scarlett in her BBQ dress).

CP: Your biography tells us that your most prized possession is your 1961 Barbie Doll. Other than Barbie, do you have any other collections?

PA: I guess my largest collection is my original sculpts and painted prototypes of the ornaments I've created through the years. I don't know why I save them, but I can't bear to throw them away.

CP: You were selected this year to sculpt "Angel of Hope," which will be part of Hallmark's Cards For The Cure campaign to help raise money for the Susan G. Komen Breast Cancer Foundation. Can you tell us about this honor, as well as how the ornament came about?

PA: I was thrilled to be involved with an important cause such as this. I hope my ornament does it justice. I wanted to portray the angel with quiet beauty and strength. Also, I was equally proud to be working for a company that will stand up and be counted as a major supporter. I am not surprised though. The Hall family is beyond generous when asked to help.

CP: Of all the ornaments you have sculpted, do you have a favorite?

PA: Yes, but it won't be out until next year!

CP: Collectors love creating trees and displays with Keepsake Ornaments. How do you decorate your house for the holidays?

PA: I usually take a week or two off before Christmas to get into the spirit. Working around Christmas all year round tends to keep you from realizing that the "real" season is here. I hit the craft stores and bring home way too many decorations. There's nothing like it to get in the mood. Then I cover the downstairs with all my "treasures." There have been years that I ran out of time to put everything up before Christmas so I continued for days after.

CP: Who has been the most influential person(s) in your career?

PA: My husband. He has been my greatest supporter and has always given me a strong kick in the pants when I get critical of myself.

Ken Crow

CheckerBee Publishing: Can you tell us how you got your start as a Hallmark Keepsake Ornament artist?

Ken Crow: I started at Hallmark doing gift wraps and greeting cards. I wanted to add more to my creativity, and sculpting was the way. My talents were recognized by the right people and the door was opened to me in Keepsakes. After 16 years, I am still finding new ways to express myself as a Keepsake artist.

CP: You've said your favorite ornament is "Our Little Blessings," which you modeled after your children. Can you tell us about this?

KC: Linda and I consider each of our children little gifts from God. Capturing a moment of their childhood in a Keepsake Ornament is wonderful. They are our little blessings. We can actually hold onto this moment in time forever. Someone a hundred years from now will enjoy this ornament with a smile just like we do now.

CP: You have created many of the Magic Ornaments; does the creative process differ from a general Keepsake Ornament?

KC: Yes, you must have an idea of engineering, lighting effects and animation. These elements along with the ability to transfer an idea into a sculpture can produce an ornament that is more than a general ornament – it's a Magic Ornament.

CP: We often see you with your plush companion, your crow. Can you tell us a little about him?

KC: My little stuffed crow is my key to fun. With him I can experience people and places in a more enjoyable way. I can take pictures of famous places and people with my own twist – and everyone seems to enjoy it – especially me.

CP: One of your designs for this year, "Jolly Locomotive," is constructed of die-cast metal, while last year's piece, "Cruising Into Christmas," was constructed of tin. Does the material being used for the ornament affect the way you sculpt?

KC: Yes. These ornaments require special design requirements. Tin requires flat artwork that will become stretched and distorted. Die-cast requires consideration of weight and assembly. Both add a greater feel to the Keepsake grouping of ornaments.

CP: The "Jazzy Jalopy" piece was also special because fellow artist Nello Williams provided the music and your co-workers provided the sound effects. Can you tell us about this experience?

KC: We had fun. Nello added a great creative touch by adding his own music that he had written. We rehearsed many times for just the right sound. It was fun with just the right amount of humor. What a neat production!

CP: Who has been the most influential person(s) in your career?

KC: Duane Unruh. He was the right person at the right time to help me throughout my 20 years at Hallmark. Thanks to him, I am a sculptor in Keepsakes. He is a great man in the lives of many people.

CP: Can you tell us a little about the ornament production process, from start to finish?

"Linda and I consider each of our children little gifts from God . . . Someone a hundred years from now will enjoy this ornament with a smile just like we do now. "

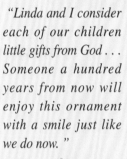

KC: All year I dream of new ornaments to make and I draw these ideas up for projects. When they are accepted, I will have about two weeks to sculpt one and then another week to paint it. Then it goes to a manufacturer. I won't see it again for maybe one or two years. Then, like an old friend, I see it once again in a Hallmark card shop.

CP: We spotted you at the Hallmark Keepsake Ornaments 25th Anniversary Convention. Do you have a favorite memory of the event that you could share with collectors?

KC: I greatly enjoyed performing with my Santa marionette. What would a celebration of Christmas ornaments be without Santa? He had to be there, and I am glad that I brought him.

CP: Collectors love creating trees and displays with Keepsake Ornaments. How do you decorate your house for the holidays?

KC: My wife, Linda, loves to decorate our house for Christmas. In fact, she decorates five trees, two fireplaces, our stairway, bookshelves and most other surfaces in our house. She is my biggest fan and I must say – I am hers! By the way, all of those decorations are Hallmark.

Q & A With Hallmark Artists

NELLO WILLIAMS

CHECKERBEE PUBLISHING: Can you tell us how you got your start as a Hallmark Keepsake Ornament artist?

NELLO WILLIAMS: I started designing ornaments as gifts for my friends and family after being inspired by a Keepsake Ornament, "Please Pause Here," I saw in the store. When I first interviewed with Hallmark, I was looking for a position as a card artist, but took one of these ornaments that I had done in also. While they liked my illustrations, they saw potential in that one piece and steered me in this direction.

CP: Your ornaments are known for their whimsical nature. Does this reflect an aspect of your personality?

NW: Oh, I'd like to think so. Actually, I think my best moments in life are when I can make people smile or laugh. As a child, I remember feeling good when I did something to make my mother grin, shake her head and say, "crazy kid!"

CP: Who do you ask for advice when developing an idea?

NW: Usually the real masters in the studio, people like Ed Seale, Ken Crow or Sue Tague. These people are just brilliant, and are always willing to help.

CP: It is obvious you have a deep love for what you do. What has been the best part about working for Hallmark and designing Keepsake Ornaments?

NW: It's a great feeling to go into a store and see something that I designed with my own two little hands. It's also great to get to meet the collectors at Artists On Tour. The really great thing, though, is that I get to work with some really creative and fun people every day.

CP: Of all the ornaments you have sculpted, do you have a favorite? Is there one that proved to be a challenge?

NW: I think the "Lion and Lamb" that was out in '97 is one of my favorites. I just love that concept on all its levels. The absolute most challenging thing I've done so far is the "1949 Cadillac Coupe deVille" out this year. Dealing with all the perfect symmetry and precision and doing it all by hand was certainly a challenge. I gained a real respect for Don Palmiter, who does that sort of thing all the time.

CP: You have a large collection of Buck Rogers and Flash Gordon memorabilia. How did you begin your collection?

NW: I started when I was doing the research for a rocket ornament that came out in '98. Just researching that brought back to me how much I had loved that sort of thing as a kid. After I found a few pieces for myself, other people have given, and keep giving, me more. It actually isn't terribly large, and it includes any space stuff in that "Golden Age" of sci-fi style. But, it does continue to grow.

CP: This year you sculpted "The Cat in the Hat," the first in the *Dr. Seuss Books®* series. How did you get to sculpt the piece and how did Hallmark decide which book the ornament would be from?

NW: We decided on "The Cat In The Hat" because it's probably the most recognized and beloved of the Dr. Seuss® books. I most likely got to do it because I did a Dr. Seuss character for the sculpture portfolio that I did to get the job with Keepsakes. I also did a "Cat In The Hat" piece that was used in some presentations before the ornament opportunity came up.

CP: At last year's 25th Anniversary Convention you composed and performed a special song, "A Collection Of

Memories," for collectors. Can you tell us a little about this and your love of music?

NW: My career choice other than an artist was to be a rock star. Though I think I made the right choice, I still love to do music. Having that love, I thought a song written especially for the collectors would be one thing that would make the Convention a little more special. It was a good way for me to combine two things I love doing.

CP: You also provided the music for Ken Crow's 1999 ornament, "Jazzy Jalopy." How did you get involved and what was it like to have other Keepsake Ornament artists help you with the sound effects?

NW: The sculpt was already done when they asked if anyone had any ideas for sounds for it. Being musical, I thought music would go great with it. I had this little Ragtime piece that we could put sound effects in. It's always more fun doing things like that as a group, so the more of us we could work in, we did. Though as musicians these other artists are rank amateurs! Amateurs, I tell you! Just kidding.

CP: Collectors love creating trees and displays with Keepsake Ornaments. How do you decorate your house for the holidays?

NW: Being a bachelor, I live in a pretty stereotypical bachelor pad. So, besides putting up a tree full of ornaments for the holidays, I do something really special: I tidy up the place.

CP: Who has been the most influential person(s) in your career?

NW: Certainly my original mentor, Ed Seale, has had a large influence. Others include Ken Crow and Duane Unruh (who I go to for sculpture technique and a lot of good old-fashioned fatherly advice).

*O*ne of the reasons that Hallmark is able to produce such a wide array of ornaments each year is because the company hires artists from a variety of different backgrounds. Here's a look at the 23 Keepsake Studio artists who bring each year's ornament designs to life:

PATRICIA ANDREWS

After working as an engraver for 11 years, Patricia Andrews joined the Keepsake Studio in 1987, on the same day that the Hallmark Keepsake Ornament Collector's Club started. An avid collector, Andrews admits that she is a member of the Club and keeps a sample of each ornament she creates.

Known as the "Barbie Lady" to many, Andrews' most recognized ornaments are based on childhood idols. She is the sculptor for several famous series, including *Holiday BARBIE*™, *Marilyn Monroe*™ and *Scarlett O'Hara*™. Her 1999 pieces include "40th Anniversary BARBIE™ Ornament," "Baby's First Christmas" and "Angel of Hope."

When she's not designing (or collecting) ornaments, Andrews enjoys gardening on the four acres of land she owns with her husband, fellow Keepsake artist Dill Rhodus.

NINA AUBÉ

Nina Aubé sat next to John "Collin" Francis when she joined the company as a Hallmark Specialty Artist in 1981. Watching Francis sculpt Merry Miniatures inspired Aubé to try her hand at sculpting. Her creations earned her the opportunity to sculpt more pieces, and she became a full-time member of the Keepsake Ornament Studio in 1994.

Aubé has since sculpted more than 100 Merry

Miniatures, as well as several Keepsake Ornaments. Her 1999 contributions include The Collegiate Collection, the first release in the *Mischievous Kittens* series, and "Best Pals," a piece inspired by her cockatiel, Opie.

Aubé enjoys going to flea markets, antique malls and toy shows to add to her own collections of dolls, toys and Hallmark Keepsake Ornaments. She also enjoys traveling and spending time with her friends, family and pets.

KATRINA BRICKER

Katrina Bricker knew in high school that she enjoyed sculpting, but did not know how she could apply her talent to a career. In college, she heard about the Keepsake Ornament Studio, and was determined to become an employee. Her goal was soon realized, as she was recruited into the Specialty Department straight out of college and joined the Keepsake Studio one year later, in 1995.

Family is an important part of Bricker's life. She lives with her husband, Paul, and their cocker spaniel, Molly. Bricker's devotion to family can be seen in her 1999 pieces, which include "Mom" and "Dad." Her other pieces include the "Max Rebo Band™" from the "Star Wars" movies.

ROBERT CHAD

Cartoons have had a major influence on Robert Chad's life. As a child, Chad would draw the comic figures while he watched them on television. Now, several years later, he has found a successful career by recreating many of those characters in his own sculptures.

A talented printmaker and animator, Chad loves to travel, listen to music and watch movies. He has sculpted several pieces for 1999, including a 12th edition to his *Mary's Angels* series, "Taz and the She-Devil," "Milk 'n' Cookies Express" and "Classic Batman™ and Robin™."

KEN CROW

Ken Crow stills remembers the first day he entered the Keepsake Ornament Studio in 1984. He recalls that he felt like a child entering Disneyland, and that his job hasn't lost any of its magic and excitement in the 15 years since he started as a Studio Artist.

In fact, Crow was raised in Long Beach, California, not far from Disneyland. And perhaps it was this exposure that led to his ability to "think as a child would think," when designing and sculpting ornaments; allowing him a whole new perspective on the world. At home with his wife and children, Crow enjoys dabbling in puppetry and, to this day, has a ventriloquist dummy named Jerry Mahoney that his parents gave him as a child.

Crow's contributions to the 1999 line include "Jazzy Jalopy" and "G.I. Joe®, Action Soldier™," among others.

JOANNE ESCHRICH

Originally from the Boston area, Joanne Eschrich planned to move to Kansas City, Missouri and work at Hallmark "just long enough to gain a little experience." Sixteen years later, she is happy to work as a Keepsake Ornament artist.

Having grown up on a farm with five siblings, Eschrich's favorite childhood memories are of skating, sledding and building igloos during the cold New England winters.

Eschrich joined the Keepsake Studio in 1996 and has

created several pieces for 1999, including "Son," "Daughter" and "Noah's Ark."

JOHN "COLLIN" FRANCIS

John "Collin" Francis was chosen in the early 1980s to sculpt a new line called Merry Miniatures for the Specialty department at Hallmark. In 1986, he was transferred to the Keepsake Ornament Studio, or "Trim-A-Home," department as it was called at the time.

Francis looks to his love of animals, the outdoors and his native Wyoming for inspiration in designing his pieces. He has five feeders in his backyard for the local birds, and again has taken up painting watercolors, a hobby which he enjoyed in years past.

Francis' contributions for 1999 include "Gordie Howe®" in the *Hockey Greats* series, and the third edition of *Lighthouse Greetings,* as well as "Park Avenue Wendy & Alex the Bellhop *Madame Alexander®*," a Merry Miniatures Premiere piece.

TAMMY HADDIX

When she was five years old, Tammy Haddix told her mother that she wanted to work as a Hallmark artist. That dream was fulfilled when Haddix was recruited directly from the Kansas City Art Institute during a campus visit. She began working on partyware, gift wrap and albums in the Specialty Department, but special assignments for the Keepsake Studio helped her to become a full-time Keepsake Artist in 1996.

When she's not sculpting, Haddix enjoys working on the house that she and her husband, Rick, built together. She also enjoys antiquing, gardening, and spending time with her husband and her son, Zachary.

In 1999, Haddix adds such ornaments as "Warm Welcome" and "Little Cloud Keeper" to her credits.

KRISTINA KLINE

When Kristina Kline first joined the Keepsake Ornament Studio as an intern in 1995, she felt like she was joining a family. She recalls that everyone was willing to share their tools and their experience with her, and made her feel right at home.

That sense of family is important to Kline, who counts religion and family among her most important values. So it is no surprise that the artist names a quilt that her mother made her and a pin that her father gave her among her most prized possessions. In her spare time, Kline enjoys baking, sewing and going to the movies.

Kline's 1999 pieces include "Outstanding Teacher," the NBA Collection and "Cocoa Break HERSHEY'S™."

TRACY LARSEN

Tracy Larsen, a native of the mountains in northern Utah, has worked for Hallmark since 1987. Originally a greeting card artist, he was invited to join the Keepsake Ornament Studio in 1995.

An illustrator from Brigham Young University, Larsen made the switch to three-dimensional art with great success. His 1997 debut – "Howdy Doody™" – was immensely popular and was named as one of ornament historian Clara Johnson Scroggins' top picks for the year.

Among Larsen's leisure activities, spending time with

his wife and four children takes top priority. He is actively involved in his church's youth activities and choir, and also enjoys painting. A sports fan, Larsen also coaches a Little League team.

Larsen's 1999 contributions include "David and Goliath," the first piece in the *Favorite Bible Stories* series, "Welcome to 2000;" "Larry, Moe and Curly The Three Stooges™ " and "Let It Snow!"

JOYCE LYLE

Introduced to the beauty of art through her brother Jerold, Joyce Lyle dreamed of being an art teacher while a student at Oklahoma State University. However, she married before finishing school, and soon was busy raising four sons and a daughter.

No stranger to a big family, Lyle was the only daughter in a family of six boys. Not surprisingly, her favorite movie is "The Sound of Music," a story which revolves around a large family with six children.

Lyle joined the Keepsake Studio in 1984, after working as a free lance artist for the company for many years. She enjoys being able to express herself in her work, and delights in the variety of ornaments she is able to create!

Lyle's work in 1999 includes pieces such as "Dorothy and Glinda, The Good Witch™ The Wizard of Oz™," "The Lollipop Guild™ The Wizard of Oz™" and the "For My Grandma" photoholder.

LYNN NORTON

After years of working as an engraver for
Hallmark, Lynn Norton was hired as a technical
artist in the Keepsake Studio in 1987. Some might
say that Norton is a "natural" for this position, as
he has been building models since the age of eight.
He claims that his love of "planes, trains and automobiles" is hereditary, and was passed on to him
through his grandfather, who once crafted a large-
scale model of a train engine.

Norton is thrilled that he is able to make a career
out of a hobby that he enjoys, and has designed many of
the pieces in the Star Trek™, Star Wars™ and LIONEL® train
collections. Among his 1999 contributions are "Runabout –
U.S.S. Rio Grande Star Trek: Deep Space Nine™'" and
"Curtiss R3C-2 Seaplane" in the *Sky's the Limit* series.

DON PALMITER

Don Palmiter has a long history with
Hallmark. Joining the company straight out of
high school, he originally worked as an engraver
before joining the Keepsake Studio in 1987. In
addition to his sculpting duties, Palmiter is the
primary design and research consultant for
Kiddie Car Classics and Sidewalk Cruisers.
Palmiter works with both collectors and
automotive authorities to choose the
pieces which will be produced each year –
and even sculpts them himself. Palmiter
also created the *Classic American Cars* ornament series, as
well as the new *Harley-Davidson® Motorcycle Milestones*
and the Miniature Ornament *Harley-Davidson® Motorcycle*
series for 1999.

In addition to a lifelong affection for classic automobiles, Palmiter enjoys interior decorating, going to antique malls and traveling. He also collects art glass, crystal and Guiseppe Armani sculptures, and enjoys spending time with his wife, Karol, and their family.

Sharon Pike

Sharon Pike recently returned to the Hallmark Keepsake Studio after a four-year hiatus, during which time she nursed a broken arm. She admits that during her time off she missed the Studio, where she has the opportunity to express herself and her ideas through the creation of new pieces.

Pike often incorporates her sense of humor into work, and especially enjoys sculpting animals. Many of her pieces are inspired by her cat, Skunk, who died recently at the age of 17. Pike also has a calico cat named C.C., who she says is her most prized possession.

Pike's 1999 contributions include "On Thin Ice" and the final edition of the *Fabulous Decade* series.

Dill Rhodus

In his 13 years with the Keepsake Studio, Dill Rhodus has sculpted a wide variety of pieces. He is most recognized for his sports pieces, which range from "Joe Montana" to "Jackie Robinson." He has also been instrumental in the creation of several Star Wars™ pieces. This year, Rhodus' work can be witnessed in the latest editions to his *Football Legends* and *At the Ballpark* series, as well as "Darth Vader's TIE Fighter" and "Chewbacca™."

Rhodus is a fan of sports and names golf as one of the few things he is truly passionate about. He also enjoys coaching his children's soccer teams and gardening with his wife, fellow Keepsake Artist Patricia Andrews, in their four-acre garden.

ANITA MARRA ROGERS

After three years of working part-time for the Keepsake Studio, Anita Marra Rogers became a full-time studio artist in 1987. She says that the moment she entered the Studio, she knew that sculpting was the career for her. In the 12 years since she joined the Studio, Rogers has proved herself to be a very talented sculptor who has a special talent for portraying cultural icons.

When she is not at work, Rogers enjoys spending time with her family. She is an avid "puzzler" and has an assortment of mind-boggling games. She also collects Longaberger baskets and pottery, as well as Hallmark Keepsake Ornaments.

Rogers contributions to 1999 include "Lieutenant Commander Worf™ Star Trek: Deep Space Nine™," "The Flash™" and "Russian Barbie™ Ornament," which is the final edition in the *Dolls of the World* series.

ED SEALE

A native of Canada, Ed Seale was raised in the wooded countryside of southern Ontario. While growing up, he held a variety of jobs, including working as a carpenter near his home during the summers and a boatbuilder in Florida in the winters.

Seale has always been good with his hands, so it was a natural progression for him to find a career where he could put this talent to use. He came to the Hallmark Keepsake Studio in 1980 and has since created several pieces in the popular *Frosty Friends* and *Heart Of Christmas* series.

In his spare time, Seale enjoys building boats and sailing in his catamaran, as well as photography and spending time with his grandchildren.

LINDA SICKMAN

Upon joining the company nearly 36 years ago, Linda Sickman worked in a variety of positions at Hallmark before finally settling down in the Keepsake Ornament Studio in 1976.

Over the years, Sickman has created several well-known pieces, and is credited with designing several popular series, including the *Rocking Horse* series, which lasted for 16 years. She is especially well-known for her work with pressed tin and has used the material to sculpt several ornaments including pieces from the *Tin Locomotive* and *Yuletide Central* series.

Her 1999 ornaments include "Farm House," the first piece in the *Town and Country* series; "Red Barn," which complements the *Town and Country* series and "Merry Motorcycle."

BOB SIEDLER

While artists are invited to join the Keepsake Studio in a number of different ways, few have applied the "noon doodle" method, which Bob Siedler used. Siedler, who worked in the sales promotion department for Hallmark, would create rough clay sculptures on his lunch break – which he called "noon doodles."

Soon the budding artist had a small collection of pieces and it was these "roughs" that eventually landed Siedler a job at the Keepsake Studio, where he has worked since 1982. Siedler, who sees each ornament as a "new challenge," finds his inspiration through observing people and their behavior.

This year, Siedler's ornaments include the second piece in the *Spotlight on Snoopy*™ series and the final piece in *The Clauses on Vacation* series.

SUE TAGUE

Immediately after Sue Tague's graduation from Syracuse University where she studied illustration and fine arts, this Long Island native took a job at Hallmark. Thirty-three years later, Sue Tague is still with Hallmark, and has worked in almost every artistic facet of the company.

After ten years of designing greeting cards, Tague moved into designing and sculpting three-dimensional products for Hallmark, as well as creating licensed characters for the Kid Biz department.

Tague joined the Keepsake Studio in 1994, although she had been creating Hallmark Ornaments for many years. She designed one of the first ball ornaments for Hallmark, and was instrumental in creating some of the first series and Merry Miniatures for the company.

In addition to creating ornaments, Tague enjoys making dolls and puppets, and even helped Hallmark introduce a line of plush toys called the "Family of Bears."

DUANE UNRUH

A born sculptor, Duane Unruh used to make his own toys when he was growing up during the Depression. As he grew older, he enjoyed wood-carving and wax sculpting, although he did not pursue a career in arts until after he completed a successful 24-year career as a high school coach.

Unruh has been with the Keepsake Studio since 1984, and was named a Senior Designer in 1994. He enjoys every aspect of creating ornaments, from the research to the finishing touches. While he enjoys creating every piece, Unruh admits that the sports pieces are the most dear to him.

In his spare time, Unruh enjoys caring for the 76 acres of wooded land he owns, and spending time with his wife of 45 years, Barbara, and his dog, Amber.

LaDENE VOTRUBA

LaDene Votruba, who came to the Keepsake Studio in 1983 after working in other Hallmark departments for ten years, finds it easy to come up with designs for new pieces. She finds inspiration in everything she does, from walking through her family's farm in Wilson, Kansas, to sifting through the books in her library.

While she enjoys every aspect of her work, Votruba (who is of Czechoslovakian descent) most enjoys creating holiday-themed pieces and pieces based on Beatrix Potter's fictional characters. She feels that she can relate to Potter's artwork, and hopes that her personal expressions of holiday sentiments will touch the hearts of collectors who share similar memories.

Votruba has numerous hobbies, some of which include antiquing, reading, watching movies, listening to music, studying history, shopping and making jewelry.

NELLO WILLIAMS

While working as an illustrator in Tucson, Arizona, Nello Williams enjoyed creating Christmas ornaments, which he would then give as gifts to family and friends. When he went for an interview with Hallmark's card division, he brought one of his handmade ornaments, which his interviewer noticed. That ornament eventually landed Williams an internship at the Hallmark Keepsake Studio, where he was given the opportunity to expand his talents.

Two of the designs he created during that internship were offered in the 1997 Hallmark Keepsake Ornament collection, and Williams is now a full-time Studio Artist. He is also a talented musician, and wrote and directed the music for the 1999 Magic Ornament "Jazzy Jalopy."

In 1999, Williams lends his talents to "The Cat in the Hat," the first in the *Dr. Seuss® Books* series, "1949 Cadillac® Coupe de Ville," and "Spellin' Santa."

*T*his section highlights the ten most valuable Hallmark Ornaments as determined by their secondary market values. Not surprisingly, most of these are first editions in collectible series. Are you lucky enough to have any of these coveted treasures?

SANTA'S MOTORCAR (1979)
1st in the *Here Comes Santa* series
#900QX1559
Original Price: $9
MARKET VALUE: $690

TIN LOCOMOTIVE (1982)
1st in the *Tin Locomotive* series
#1300QX4603
Original Price: $13
MARKET VALUE: $670

A COOL YULE (1980)
1st in the *Frosty Friends* series
#650QX1374
Original Price: $6.50
MARKET VALUE: $655

ROCKING HORSE (1981)
1st in the *Rocking Horse* series
#900QX4222
Original Price: $9
MARKET VALUE: $585

FROSTY FRIENDS (1981)
2nd in the *Frosty Friends* series
#800QX4335
Original Price: $8
MARKET VALUE: $495

**TRUEST JOYS OF
CHRISTMAS (1977)**
5th in the *Betsey Clark* series
#350QX2642
Original Price: $3.50
MARKET VALUE: **$450**

THE BELLSWINGER (1979)
1st in *The Bellringers* series
#1000QX1479
Original Price: $10
MARKET VALUE: **$410**

ROCKING HORSE (1982)
2nd in the *Rocking Horse* series
#1000QX5023
Original Price: $10
MARKET VALUE: **$405**

ANTIQUE TOYS (1978)
1st in the *Carrousel Series*
#600QX1463
Original Price: $6
MARKET VALUE: **$400**

CARDINALIS (1982)
1st in the *Holiday Wildlife series*
#700QX3133
Original Price: $7
MARKET VALUE: **$395**

How To Use Your Collector's Value Guide™

1. Locate your collectible in the Value Guide. The Value Guide section starts with Hallmark Keepsake Ornaments, which are divided into two sections: collectible series (listed in alphabetical order by series name) and the general ornaments (listed in reverse chronological order from 1999 to 1973). For each year, the general ornaments are grouped in the following categories: Keepsake, Magic, Crown Reflections, Showcase, Laser Creations, Miniature and miscellaneous. Spring Ornaments, Merry Miniatures and Kiddie Car Classics are listed in separate sections. An alphabetical index begins on page 333.

2. Fill in the amount you originally paid for the piece in the "Price Paid" column. To calculate the original retail price, make a note of the first 3 or 4 digits of the Hallmark stock number. A piece that has the stock number "495QSM8552," for example, would have a retail price of $4.95.

3. Record the current market value of your piece in the "Value of My Collection" column. An "N/E" indicates that the market value is not yet established.

4. Calculate the value of each page by adding the boxes in each column. Transfer these totals to the "Total Value Of My Collection" worksheets on pages 309-313. Next, add the totals together to calculate the total value of your collection!

①

African-American Holiday BARBIE™ (1st, 1998)
Handcrafted • ANDR
1595QX6936 • **Value $26**

AFRICAN-AMERICAN HOLIDAY BARBIE™		
	Price Paid	Value of My Collection
1.	15.95	26.00
ALL-AMERICAN TRUCKS		
2.		
3.		
4.		
5.		
6.		
ALL GOD'S CHILDREN®		
7.		
8.		
9.		
ART MASTERPIECE		
10.		
11.		
12.		
AT THE BALLPARK		
13.		
14.		
15.		
16.		
	15.95	26.00
	PENCIL TOTALS	

Keepsake Series

Since the line's introduction in 1973, the ornaments in the Hallmark Keepsake series have traditionally been some of the most popular pieces in the collection and 1999 promises to be no exception. Eight new series will be introduced this year, while 10 favorites will say goodbye with their final editions.

①

African-American Holiday BARBIE™ (1st & final, 1998)
Handcrafted • ANDR
1595QX6936 • **Value $26**

②

1956 Ford Truck (1st, 1995)
Handcrafted • PALM
1395QX5527 • **Value $38**

③

1955 Chevrolet Cameo (2nd, 1996)
Handcrafted • PALM
1395QX5241 • **Value $31**

④

1953 GMC (3rd, 1997)
Handcrafted • PALM
1395QX6105 • **Value $26**

⑤

1937 Ford V-8 (4th, 1998)
Handcrafted • PALM
1395QX6263 • **Value $23**

⑥ NEW!

1957 Dodge® Sweptside D100 (5th, 1999)
Handcrafted • PALM
1395QX6269 • **Value $13.95**

⑦

Christy (1st, 1996)
Handcrafted • N/A
1295QX5564 • **Value $26**

⑧

Nikki (2nd, set/2, 1997)
Handcrafted • N/A
1295QX6142 • **Value $23**

⑨

Ricky (3rd & final, 1998)
Handcrafted • N/A
1295QX6363 • **Value $19**

⑩

Madonna and Child and St. John (1st, 1984)
Bezeled Satin • MCGE
650QX3494 • **Value $21**

⑪

Madonna of the Pomegranate (2nd, 1985)
Bezeled Satin • MCGE
675QX3772 • **Value $19**

⑫

Madonna and Child with the Infant St. John (3rd & final, 1986)
Bezeled Satin • MCGE
675QX3506 • **Value $28**

⑬

Nolan Ryan (1st, 1996)
Handcrafted • RHOD
1495QXI5711 • **Value $37**

⑭

Hank Aaron (2nd, 1997)
Handcrafted • RHOD
1495QX6152 • **Value $28**

⑮

Cal Ripken Jr. (3rd, 1998)
Handcrafted • RHOD
1495QXI4033 • **Value $23**

⑯ NEW!

Ken Griffey Jr. (4th, 1999)
Handcrafted • RHOD
1495QXI4037 • **Value $14.95**

	Price Paid	Value of My Collection
AFRICAN-AMERICAN HOLIDAY BARBIE™		
1.		
ALL-AMERICAN TRUCKS		
2.		
3.		
4.		
5.		
6.		
ALL GOD'S CHILDREN®		
7.		
8.		
9.		
ART MASTERPIECE		
10.		
11.		
12.		
AT THE BALLPARK		
13.		
14.		
15.		
16.		
PENCIL TOTALS		

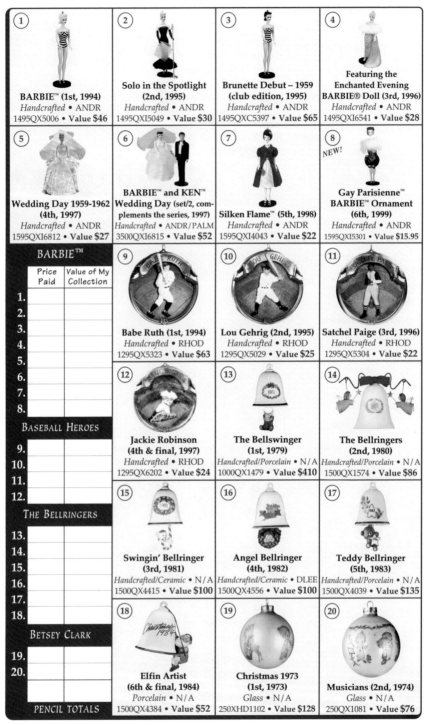

1

BARBIE™ (1st, 1994)
Handcrafted • ANDR
1495QX5006 • **Value $46**

2

Solo in the Spotlight
(2nd, 1995)
Handcrafted • ANDR
1495QXI5049 • **Value $30**

3

Brunette Debut – 1959
(club edition, 1995)
Handcrafted • ANDR
1495QXC5397 • **Value $65**

4

Featuring the
Enchanted Evening
BARBIE® Doll (3rd, 1996)
Handcrafted • ANDR
1495QXI6541 • **Value $28**

5

Wedding Day 1959-1962
(4th, 1997)
Handcrafted • ANDR
1595QXI6812 • **Value $27**

6

BARBIE™ and KEN™
Wedding Day (set/2, com-
plements the series, 1997)
Handcrafted • ANDR/PALM
3500QXI6815 • **Value $52**

7

Silken Flame™ (5th, 1998)
Handcrafted • ANDR
1595QXI4043 • **Value $22**

8

NEW!

Gay Parisienne™
BARBIE™ Ornament
(6th, 1999)
Handcrafted • ANDR
1595QXI5301 • **Value $15.95**

BARBIE™

	Price Paid	Value of My Collection
1.		
2.		
3.		
4.		
5.		
6.		
7.		
8.		

Baseball Heroes

9.		
10.		
11.		
12.		

The Bellringers

13.		
14.		
15.		
16.		
17.		
18.		

Betsey Clark

19.		
20.		

PENCIL TOTALS

9

Babe Ruth (1st, 1994)
Handcrafted • RHOD
1295QX5323 • **Value $63**

10

Lou Gehrig (2nd, 1995)
Handcrafted • RHOD
1295QX5029 • **Value $25**

11

Satchel Paige (3rd, 1996)
Handcrafted • RHOD
1295QX5304 • **Value $22**

12

Jackie Robinson
(4th & final, 1997)
Handcrafted • RHOD
1295QX6202 • **Value $24**

13

The Bellswinger
(1st, 1979)
Handcrafted/Porcelain • N/A
1000QX1479 • **Value $410**

14

The Bellringers
(2nd, 1980)
Handcrafted/Porcelain • N/A
1500QX1574 • **Value $86**

15

Swingin' Bellringer
(3rd, 1981)
Handcrafted/Ceramic • N/A
1500QX4415 • **Value $100**

16

Angel Bellringer
(4th, 1982)
Handcrafted/Ceramic • DLEE
1500QX4556 • **Value $100**

17

Teddy Bellringer
(5th, 1983)
Handcrafted/Porcelain • N/A
1500QX4039 • **Value $135**

18

Elfin Artist
(6th & final, 1984)
Porcelain • N/A
1500QX4384 • **Value $52**

19

Christmas 1973
(1st, 1973)
Glass • N/A
250XHD1102 • **Value $128**

20

Musicians (2nd, 1974)
Glass • N/A
250QX1081 • **Value $76**

1. Caroling Trio (3rd, 1975)
Glass • N/A
300QX1331 • **Value $70**

2. Christmas 1976 (4th, 1976)
Glass • N/A
300QX1951 • **Value $110**

3. Truest Joys of Christmas (5th, 1977)
Glass • N/A
350QX2642 • **Value $450**

4. Christmas Spirit (6th, 1978)
Satin • N/A
350QX2016 • **Value $62**

5. Holiday Fun (7th, 1979)
Satin • N/A
350QX2019 • **Value $42**

6. Joy-in-the-Air (8th, 1980)
Glass • N/A
400QX2154 • **Value $32**

7. Christmas 1981 (9th, 1981)
Glass • N/A
450QX8022 • **Value $32**

8. Joys of Christmas (10th, 1982)
Satin • N/A
450QX2156 • **Value $34**

9. Christmas Happiness (11th, 1983)
Glass • N/A
450QX2119 • **Value $31**

10. Days are Merry (12th, 1984)
Glass • N/A
500QX2494 • **Value $33**

11. Special Kind of Feeling (13th & final, 1985)
Glass • PIKE
500QX2632 • **Value $35**

12. Betsey Clark: Home For Christmas (1st, 1986)
Glass • PIKE
500QX2776 • **Value $35**

13. Betsey Clark: Home For Christmas (2nd, 1987)
Glass • PIKE
500QX2727 • **Value $25**

14. Betsey Clark: Home For Christmas (3rd, 1988)
Glass • PIKE
500QX2714 • **Value $23**

15. Betsey Clark: Home For Christmas (4th, 1989)
Glass • N/A
500QX2302 • **Value $36**

16. Betsey Clark: Home For Christmas (5th, 1990)
Glass • N/A
500QX2033 • **Value $24**

17. Betsey Clark: Home For Christmas (6th & final, 1991)
Glass • N/A
500QX2109 • **Value $30**

18. Betsey 's Country Christmas (1st, 1992)
Glass • N/A
500QX2104 • **Value $26**

19. Betsey 's Country Christmas (2nd, 1993)
Glass • N/A
500QX2062 • **Value $19**

20. Betsey 's Country Christmas (3rd & final, 1994)
Glass • N/A
500QX2403 • **Value $16**

BETSEY CLARK	Price Paid	Value of My Collection
1.		
2.		
3.		
4.		
5.		
6.		
7.		
8.		
9.		
10.		
11.		
BETSEY CLARK: HOME FOR CHRISTMAS		
12.		
13.		
14.		
15.		
16.		
17.		
BETSEY'S COUNTRY CHRISTMAS		
18.		
19.		
20.		
PENCIL TOTALS		

VALUE GUIDE — HALLMARK KEEPSAKE ORNAMENTS

(1) **Antique Toys (1st, 1978)** *Handcrafted* • N/A 600QX1463 • **Value $400**	**(2)** **Christmas Carrousel (2nd, 1979)** *Handcrafted* • N/A 650QX1467 • **Value $190**

(3) **Merry Carrousel (3rd, 1980)** *Handcrafted* • N/A 750QX1414 • **Value $172**

(4) **Skaters' Carrousel (4th, 1981)** *Handcrafted* • N/A 900QX4275 • **Value $90**

(5) **Snowman Carrousel (5th, 1982)** *Handcrafted* • SEAL 1000QX4783 • **Value $102**

(6) **Santa and Friends (6th & final, 1983)** *Handcrafted* • SICK 1100QX4019 • **Value $54**

(7) **Cat Naps (1st, 1994)** *Handcrafted* • RHOD 795QX5313 • **Value $40**

(8) **Cat Naps (2nd, 1995)** *Handcrafted* • RHOD 795QX5097 • **Value $26**

(9) **Cat Naps (3rd, 1996)** *Handcrafted* • RHOD 795QX5641 • **Value $20**

(10) **Cat Naps (4th, 1997)** *Handcrafted* • BRIC 895QX6205 • **Value $19**

(11) **Cat Naps (5th & final, 1998)** *Handcrafted* • BRIC 895QX6383 • **Value $20**

(12) **A Celebration Of Angels (1st, 1995)** *Handcrafted* • ANDR 1295QX5077 • **Value $26**

(13) **A Celebration Of Angels (2nd, 1996)** *Handcrafted* • ANDR 1295QX5634 • **Value $26**

(14) **A Celebration of Angels (3rd, 1997)** *Handcrafted* • ANDR 1395QX6175 • **Value $21**

(15) **A Celebration of Angels (4th & final, 1998)** *Handcrafted* • ANDR 1395QX6366 • **Value $21**

(16) **Christmas Kitty (1st, 1989)** *Porcelain* • RGRS 1475QX5445 • **Value $31**

(17) **Christmas Kitty (2nd, 1990)** *Porcelain* • RGRS 1475QX4506 • **Value $34**

(18) **Christmas Kitty (3rd & final, 1991)** *Porcelain* • RGRS 1475QX4377 • **Value $30**

	Price Paid	Value of My Collection
CARROUSEL SERIES		
1.		
2.		
3.		
4.		
5.		
6.		
CAT NAPS		
7.		
8.		
9.		
10.		
11.		
A CELEBRATION OF ANGELS		
12.		
13.		
14.		
15.		
CHRISTMAS KITTY		
16.		
17.		
18.		
PENCIL TOTALS		

VALUE GUIDE — HALLMARK KEEPSAKE ORNAMENTS

(1) St. Nicholas (1st, 1995)
Handcrafted • RGRS
1495QX5087 • **Value $30**

(2) Christkindl (2nd, 1996)
Handcrafted • VOTR
1495QX5631 • **Value $28**

(3) Kolyada
(3rd & final, 1997)
Handcrafted • VOTR
1495QX6172 • **Value $24**

(4) 1957 Corvette (1st, 1991)
Handcrafted • PALM
1275QX4319 • **Value $220**

(5) 1966 Mustang (2nd, 1992)
Handcrafted • PALM
1275QX4284 • **Value $55**

(6) 1956 Ford Thunderbird
(3rd, 1993)
Handcrafted • PALM
1275QX5275 • **Value $38**

(7) 1957 Chevrolet Bel Air
(4th, 1994)
Handcrafted • PALM
1295QX5422 • **Value $35**

(8) 1969 Chevrolet Camaro
(5th, 1995)
Handcrafted • PALM
1295QX5239 • **Value $24**

(9) 1958 Ford Edsel
Citation Convertible
(club edition, 1995)
Handcrafted • PALM
1295QXC4167 • **Value $78**

(10) 1959 Cadillac De Ville
(6th, 1996)
Handcrafted • PALM
1295QX5384 • **Value $30**

(11) 1969 Hurst Oldsmobile
442 (7th, 1997)
Handcrafted • PALM
1395QX6102 • **Value $26**

(12) 1970 Plymouth®
Hemi 'Cuda (8th, 1998)
Handcrafted • PALM
1395QX6256 • **Value $26**

(13) *NEW!* 1955 Chevrolet®
Nomad® Wagon
(9th, 1999)
Handcrafted • PALM
1395QX6367 • **Value $13.95**

(14) The Clauses on Vacation
(1st, 1997)
Handcrafted • SIED
1495QX6112 • **Value $27**

(15) The Clauses on Vacation
(2nd, 1998)
Handcrafted • SIED
1495QX6276 • **Value $22**

(16) *NEW!* The Clauses on Vacation
(3rd & final, 1999)
Handcrafted • SIED
1495QX6399 • **Value $14.95**

(17) British (1st, 1982)
Handcrafted • SICK
500QX4583 • **Value $135**

(18) Early American
(2nd, 1983)
Handcrafted • SICK
500QX4029 • **Value $51**

(19) Canadian Mountie
(3rd, 1984)
Handcrafted • SICK
500QX4471 • **Value $32**

(20) Scottish Highlander
(4th, 1985)
Handcrafted • SICK
550QX4715 • **Value $30**

CHRISTMAS VISITORS		
	Price Paid	Value of My Collection
1.		
2.		
3.		
CLASSIC AMERICAN CARS		
4.		
5.		
6.		
7.		
8.		
9.		
10.		
11.		
12.		
13.		
THE CLAUSES ON VACATION		
14.		
15.		
16.		
CLOTHESPIN SOLDIER		
17.		
18.		
19.		
20.		
PENCIL TOTALS		

(1) French Officer (5th, 1986)
Handcrafted • SICK
550QX4063 • **Value $30**

(2) Sailor (6th & final, 1987)
Handcrafted • SICK
550QX4807 • **Value $29**

(3) Light Shines at Christmas (1st, 1987)
Porcelain • VOTR
800QX4817 • **Value $68**

(4) Waiting for Santa (2nd, 1988)
Porcelain • VOTR
800QX4061 • **Value $45**

(5) Morning of Wonder (3rd, 1989)
Porcelain • VOTR
825QX4612 • **Value $29**

(6) Cookies for Santa (4th, 1990)
Porcelain • VOTR
875QX4436 • **Value $29**

(7) Let It Snow! (5th, 1991)
Porcelain • VOTR
875QX4369 • **Value $26**

(8) Sweet Holiday Harmony (6th & final, 1992)
Porcelain • VOTR
875QX4461 • **Value $25**

(9) Bright Journey (1st, 1989)
Handcrafted • SICK
875QX4352 • **Value $62**

(10) Bright Moving Colors (2nd, 1990)
Handcrafted • CROW
875QX4586 • **Value $48**

(11) Bright Vibrant Carols (3rd, 1991)
Handcrafted • CROW
975QX4219 • **Value $43**

(12) Bright Blazing Colors (4th, 1992)
Handcrafted • CROW
975QX4264 • **Value $40**

(13) Bright Shining Castle (5th, 1993)
Handcrafted • CROW
1075QX4422 • **Value $28**

(14) Bright Playful Colors (6th, 1994)
Handcrafted • CROW
1095QX5273 • **Value $30**

(15) Bright 'n' Sunny Tepee (7th, 1995)
Handcrafted • ANDR
1095QX5247 • **Value $23**

(16) Bright Flying Colors (8th, 1996)
Handcrafted • CROW
1095QX5391 • **Value $28**

(17) Bright Rocking Colors (9th, 1997)
Handcrafted • TAGU
1295QX6235 • **Value $25**

(18) Bright Sledding Colors (10th & final, 1998)
Handcrafted • TAGU
1295QX6166 • **Value $22**

(19) Native American BARBIE™ (1st, 1996)
Handcrafted • ANDR
1495QX5561 • **Value $30**

(20) Chinese BARBIE™ (2nd, 1997)
Handcrafted • RGRS
1495QX6162 • **Value $27**

CLOTHESPIN SOLDIER

	Price Paid	Value of My Collection
1.		
2.		

COLLECTOR'S PLATE

3.		
4.		
5.		
6.		
7.		
8.		

CRAYOLA® CRAYON

9.		
10.		
11.		
12.		
13.		
14.		
15.		
16.		
17.		
18.		

DOLLS OF THE WORLD

19.		
20.		

PENCIL TOTALS

(1) Mexican BARBIE™
(3rd, 1998)
Handcrafted • RGRS
1495QX6356 • **Value $25**

(2) NEW! Russian BARBIE™
Ornament
(4th & final, 1999)
Handcrafted • RGRS
1495QX6369 • **Value $14.95**

(3) NEW! The Cat in the Hat
(1st, 1999, set/2)
Handcrafted • WILL
1495QXI6457 • **Value $14.95**

(4) Cinderella (1st, 1997)
Handcrafted • CROW
1495QXD4045 • **Value $30**

(5) Walt Disney's *Snow White* (2nd, 1998)
Handcrafted • N/A
1495QXD4056 • **Value $25**

(6) NEW! Walt Disney's
Sleeping Beauty
(3rd & final, 1999)
Handcrafted • N/A
1495QXD4097 • **Value $14.95**

(7) Fabulous Decade
(1st, 1990)
Handcrafted/Brass • SEAL
775QX4466 • **Value $40**

(8) Fabulous Decade
(2nd, 1991)
Handcrafted/Brass • SEAL
775QX4119 • **Value $42**

(9) Fabulous Decade
(3rd, 1992)
Handcrafted/Brass • SEAL
775QX4244 • **Value $47**

(10) Fabulous Decade
(4th, 1993)
Handcrafted/Brass • PIKE
775QX4475 • **Value $24**

(11) Fabulous Decade
(5th, 1994)
Handcrafted/Brass • SEAL
795QX5263 • **Value $27**

(12) Fabulous Decade
(6th, 1995)
Handcrafted/Brass • SEAL
795QX5147 • **Value $22**

(13) Fabulous Decade
(7th, 1996)
Handcrafted/Brass • SEAL
795QX5661 • **Value $22**

(14) Fabulous Decade
(8th, 1997)
Handcrafted/Brass • PIKE
795QX6232 • **Value $17**

(15) Fabulous Decade
(9th, 1998)
Handcrafted/Brass • PIKE
795QX6393 • **Value $17**

(16) NEW! Fabulous Decade
(10th & final, 1999)
Handcrafted/Brass • PIKE
795QX6357 • **Value $7.95**

(17) NEW! David and Goliath
(1st, 1999)
Handcrafted • LARS
1395QX6447 • **Value $13.95**

DOLLS OF THE WORLD		
	Price Paid	Value of My Collection
1.		
2.		

DR. SEUSS® BOOKS

3.		

THE ENCHANTED MEMORIES COLLECTION

4.		
5.		
6.		

FABULOUS DECADE

7.		
8.		
9.		
10.		
11.		
12.		
13.		
14.		
15.		
16.		

FAVORITE BIBLE STORIES

17.		

PENCIL TOTALS

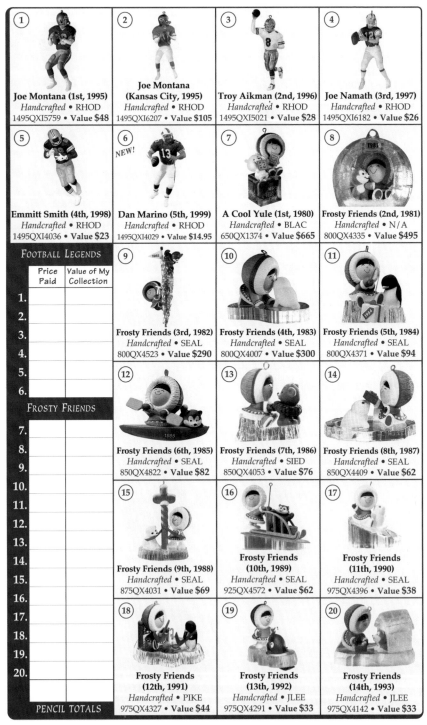

① Joe Montana (1st, 1995)
Handcrafted • RHOD
1495QXI5759 • **Value $48**

② Joe Montana (Kansas City, 1995)
Handcrafted • RHOD
1495QXI6207 • **Value $105**

③ Troy Aikman (2nd, 1996)
Handcrafted • RHOD
1495QXI5021 • **Value $28**

④ Joe Namath (3rd, 1997)
Handcrafted • RHOD
1495QXI6182 • **Value $26**

⑤ Emmitt Smith (4th, 1998)
Handcrafted • RHOD
1495QXI4036 • **Value $23**

⑥ NEW! Dan Marino (5th, 1999)
Handcrafted • RHOD
1495QXI4029 • **Value $14.95**

⑦ A Cool Yule (1st, 1980)
Handcrafted • BLAC
650QX1374 • **Value $665**

⑧ Frosty Friends (2nd, 1981)
Handcrafted • N/A
800QX4335 • **Value $495**

⑨ Frosty Friends (3rd, 1982)
Handcrafted • SEAL
800QX4523 • **Value $290**

⑩ Frosty Friends (4th, 1983)
Handcrafted • SEAL
800QX4007 • **Value $300**

⑪ Frosty Friends (5th, 1984)
Handcrafted • SEAL
800QX4371 • **Value $94**

⑫ Frosty Friends (6th, 1985)
Handcrafted • SEAL
850QX4822 • **Value $82**

⑬ Frosty Friends (7th, 1986)
Handcrafted • SIED
850QX4053 • **Value $76**

⑭ Frosty Friends (8th, 1987)
Handcrafted • SEAL
850QX4409 • **Value $62**

⑮ Frosty Friends (9th, 1988)
Handcrafted • SEAL
875QX4031 • **Value $69**

⑯ Frosty Friends (10th, 1989)
Handcrafted • SEAL
925QX4572 • **Value $62**

⑰ Frosty Friends (11th, 1990)
Handcrafted • SEAL
975QX4396 • **Value $38**

⑱ Frosty Friends (12th, 1991)
Handcrafted • PIKE
975QX4327 • **Value $44**

⑲ Frosty Friends (13th, 1992)
Handcrafted • JLEE
975QX4291 • **Value $33**

⑳ Frosty Friends (14th, 1993)
Handcrafted • JLEE
975QX4142 • **Value $33**

Football Legends

	Price Paid	Value of My Collection
1.		
2.		
3.		
4.		
5.		
6.		

Frosty Friends

7.		
8.		
9.		
10.		
11.		
12.		
13.		
14.		
15.		
16.		
17.		
18.		
19.		
20.		
PENCIL TOTALS		

Value Guide — Hallmark Keepsake Ornaments

1 Frosty Friends (complements the series, 1993)
Handcrafted • SEAL
2000QX5682 • **Value $48**

2 Frosty Friends (15th, 1994)
Handcrafted • SEAL
995QX5293 • **Value $32**

3 Frosty Friends (16th, 1995)
Handcrafted • SEAL
1095QX5169 • **Value $28**

4 Frosty Friends (17th, 1996)
Handcrafted • SEAL
1095QX5681 • **Value $24**

5 Frosty Friends (18th, 1997)
Handcrafted • SEAL
1095QX6255 • **Value $24**

6 Frosty Friends (19th, 1998)
Handcrafted • SEAL
1095QX6226 • **Value $23**

7 NEW! Frosty Friends (20th, 1999)
Handcrafted • SEAL
1295QX6297 • **Value $12.95**

8 NEW! Gift Bearers (1st, 1999)
Porcelain • TAGU
1295QX6437 • **Value $12.95**

9 St. Nicholas (1st, 1989)
Glass • VOTR
500QX2795 • **Value $26**

10 St. Lucia (2nd, 1990)
Glass • VOTR
500QX2803 • **Value $22**

11 Christkindl (3rd, 1991)
Glass • VOTR
500QX2117 • **Value $22**

12 Kolyada (4th, 1992)
Glass • VOTR
500QX2124 • **Value $21**

13 The Magi (5th & final, 1993)
Glass • VOTR
500QX2065 • **Value $22**

14 Greatest Story (1st, 1990)
Porcelain/Brass • VOTR
1275QX4656 • **Value $28**

15 Greatest Story (2nd, 1991)
Porcelain/Brass • VOTR
1275QX4129 • **Value $27**

16 Greatest Story (3rd & final, 1992)
Porcelain/Brass • VOTR
1275QX4251 • **Value $25**

17 Donald's Surprising Gift (1st, 1997)
Handcrafted • BRIC
1295QXD4025 • **Value $25**

18 Ready for Christmas (2nd, 1998)
Handcrafted • N/A
1295QXD4006 • **Value $20**

19 NEW! Minnie Trims the Tree (3rd & final, 1999)
Handcrafted • N/A
1295QXD4059 • **Value $12.95**

FROSTY FRIENDS		
	Price Paid	Value of My Collection
1.		
2.		
3.		
4.		
5.		
6.		
7.		
GIFT BEARERS		
8.		
THE GIFT BRINGERS		
9.		
10.		
11.		
12.		
13.		
GREATEST STORY		
14.		
15.		
16.		
HALLMARK ARCHIVES		
17.		
18.		
19.		
PENCIL TOTALS		

(1) Hark! It's Herald (1st, 1989)
Handcrafted • CROW
675QX4555 • **Value $28**

(2) Hark! It's Herald (2nd, 1990)
Handcrafted • CROW
675QX4463 • **Value $24**

(3) Hark! It's Herald (3rd, 1991)
Handcrafted • RGRS
675QX4379 • **Value $26**

(4) Hark! It's Herald (4th & final, 1992)
Handcrafted • JLEE
775QX4464 • **Value $22**

(5) NEW! Heritage Springer® (1st, 1999)
Die-Cast Metal • PALM
1495QXI8007 • **Value $14.95**

(6) Heart of Christmas (1st, 1990)
Handcrafted • SEAL
1375QX4726 • **Value $75**

(7) Heart of Christmas (2nd, 1991)
Handcrafted • SEAL
1375QX4357 • **Value $30**

(8) Heart of Christmas (3rd, 1992)
Handcrafted • SEAL
1375QX4411 • **Value $29**

(9) Heart of Christmas (4th, 1993)
Handcrafted • SEAL
1475QX4482 • **Value $27**

(10) Heart of Christmas (5th & final, 1994)
Handcrafted • SEAL
1495QX5266 • **Value $27**

(11) Heavenly Angels (1st, 1991)
Handcrafted • LYLE
775QX4367 • **Value $27**

(12) Heavenly Angels (2nd, 1992)
Handcrafted • LYLE
775QX4454 • **Value $30**

(13) Heavenly Angels (3rd & final, 1993)
Handcrafted • LYLE
775QX4945 • **Value $22**

(14) Santa's Motorcar (1st, 1979)
Handcrafted • MAHO
900QX1559 • **Value $690**

(15) Santa's Express (2nd, 1980)
Handcrafted • MAHO
1200QX1434 • **Value $215**

(16) Rooftop Deliveries (3rd, 1981)
Handcrafted • MAHO
1300QX4382 • **Value $325**

(17) Jolly Trolley (4th, 1982)
Handcrafted • SICK
1500QX4643 • **Value $150**

(18) Santa Express (5th, 1983)
Handcrafted • DLEE
1300QX4037 • **Value $290**

(19) Santa's Deliveries (6th, 1984)
Handcrafted • SICK
1300QX4324 • **Value $94**

Hark! It's Herald	Price Paid	Value of My Collection
1.		
2.		
3.		
4.		
Harley Davidson® Motorcycle Milestones		
5.		
Heart Of Christmas		
6.		
7.		
8.		
9.		
10.		
Heavenly Angels		
11.		
12.		
13.		
Here Comes Santa		
14.		
15.		
16.		
17.		
18.		
19.		
PENCIL TOTALS		

KEEPSAKE SERIES

(1) Santa's Fire Engine
(7th, 1985)
Handcrafted • SICK
1400QX4965 • **Value $69**

(2) Kringle's Kool Treats
(8th, 1986)
Handcrafted • SIED
1400QX4043 • **Value $75**

(3) Santa's Woody (9th, 1987)
Handcrafted • CROW
1400QX4847 • **Value $85**

(4) Kringle Koach
(10th, 1988)
Handcrafted • CROW
1400QX4001 • **Value $50**

(5) Christmas Caboose
(11th, 1989)
Handcrafted • CROW
1475QX4585 • **Value $54**

(6) Festive Surrey
(12th, 1990)
Handcrafted • SICK
1475QX4923 • **Value $45**

(7) Santa's Antique Car
(13th, 1991)
Handcrafted • SICK
1475QX4349 • **Value $56**

(8) Kringle Tours
(14th, 1992)
Handcrafted • SICK
1475QX4341 • **Value $37**

(9) Happy Haul-idays
(15th, 1993)
Handcrafted • SICK
1475QX4102 • **Value $35**

(10) Shopping With Santa
(complements the series, 1993)
Handcrafted • SICK
2400QX5675 • **Value $45**

(11) Makin' Tractor Tracks
(16th, 1994)
Handcrafted • SICK
1495QX5296 • **Value $55**

(12) Santa's Roadster
(17th, 1995)
Handcrafted • SICK
1495QX5179 • **Value $32**

(13) Santa's 4 x 4 (18th, 1996)
Handcrafted • SEAL
1495QX5684 • **Value $32**

(14) The Claus-Mobile
(19th, 1997)
Handcrafted • TAGU
1495QX6262 • **Value $26**

(15) Santa's Bumper Car
(20th, 1998)
Handcrafted • TAGU
1495QX6283 • **Value $22**

(16) NEW! Santa's Golf Cart
(21st, 1999)
Handcrafted • RHOD
1495QX6337 • **Value $14.95**

(17) Wayne Gretzky
(1st, 1997)
Handcrafted • UNRU
1595QXI6275 • **Value $33**

(18) Mario Lemieux
(2nd, 1998)
Handcrafted • FRAN
1595QXI6476 • **Value $24**

(19) NEW! Gordie Howe®
(3rd, 1999)
Handcrafted • FRAN
1595QXI4047 • **Value $15.95**

(20) Holiday BARBIE™
(1st, 1993)
Handcrafted • ANDR
1475QX5725 • **Value $170**

	HERE COMES SANTA	
	Price Paid	Value of My Collection
1.		
2.		
3.		
4.		
5.		
6.		
7.		
8.		
9.		
10.		
11.		
12.		
13.		
14.		
15.		
16.		
HOCKEY GREATS		
17.		
18.		
19.		
HOLIDAY BARBIE™		
20.		
PENCIL TOTALS		

(1) Holiday BARBIE™
(2nd, 1994)
Handcrafted • ANDR
1495QX5216 • **Value $56**

(2) Holiday BARBIE™
(3rd, 1995)
Handcrafted • ANDR
1495QXI5057 • **Value $37**

(3) Holiday BARBIE™
(4th, 1996)
Handcrafted • ANDR
1495QXI5371 • **Value $33**

(4) Holiday BARBIE™
(5th, 1997)
Handcrafted • ANDR
1595QXI6212 • **Value $25**

(5) Holiday BARBIE™
(6th & final, 1998)
Handcrafted • ANDR
1595QXI4023 • **Value $24**

(6) Based on the 1988 Happy
Holidays® BARBIE® Doll
(1st, club edition, 1996)
Handcrafted • ANDR
1495QXC4181 • **Value $60**

(7) Based on the 1989 Happy
Holidays® BARBIE® Doll
(2nd, club edition, 1997)
Handcrafted • ANDR
1595QXC5162 • **Value $42**

(8) Based on the 1990 Happy
Holidays® BARBIE® Doll
(3rd, club edition, 1998)
Handcrafted • ANDR
1595QXC4493 • **Value $40**

(9) NEW! Based on the 1991 Happy
Holidays® Barbie™ Doll
(4th, club edition, 1999)
Handcrafted • ANDR
1595QXC4507 • **Value $15.95**

(10) Holiday Heirloom
(1st, LE-34,600, 1987)
Crystal/Silver-Plated • UNRU
2500QX4857 • **Value $30**

(11) Holiday Heirloom
(2nd, club edition,
LE-34,600, 1988)
Crystal/Silver-Plated • N/A
2500QX4064 • **Value $34**

(12) Holiday Heirloom
(3rd & final, club
edition, LE-34,600, 1989)
Crystal/Silver-Plated • N/A
2500QXC4605 • **Value $38**

(13) Cardinalis (1st, 1982)
Wood • N/A
700QX3133 • **Value $395**

(14) Black-Capped
Chickadees (2nd, 1983)
Wood • N/A
700QX3099 • **Value $75**

(15) Ring-Necked Pheasant
(3rd, 1984)
Wood • N/A
725QX3474 • **Value $32**

(16) California Partridge
(4th, 1985)
Wood • N/A
750QX3765 • **Value $32**

(17) Cedar Waxwing
(5th, 1986)
Wood • N/A
750QX3216 • **Value $30**

(18) Snow Goose (6th, 1987)
Wood • VOTR
750QX3717 • **Value $26**

(19) Purple Finch
(7th & final, 1988)
Wood • N/A
775QX3711 • **Value $28**

HOLIDAY BARBIE™

	Price Paid	Value of My Collection
1.		
2.		
3.		
4.		
5.		

HOLIDAY BARBIE™ – COLLECTOR'S CLUB

6.		
7.		
8.		
9.		

HOLIDAY HEIRLOOM

10.		
11.		
12.		

HOLIDAY WILDLIFE

13.		
14.		
15.		
16.		
17.		
18.		
19.		

PENCIL TOTALS

Value Guide — Hallmark Keepsake Ornaments

(1) Shaquille O'Neal (1st, 1995)
Handcrafted • N/A
1495QXI5517 • **Value $42**

(2) Larry Bird (2nd, 1996)
Handcrafted • N/A
1495QXI5014 • **Value $32**

(3) Magic Johnson (3rd, 1997)
Handcrafted • N/A
1495QXI6832 • **Value $25**

(4) Grant Hill (4th, 1998)
Handcrafted • UNRU
1495QXI6846 • **Value $22**

(5) NEW! Scottie Pippen (5th, 1999)
Handcrafted • UNRU
1495QXI4177 • **Value $14.95**

(6) NEW! Joyful Santa (1st, 1999)
Handcrafted • CHAD
1495QX6949 • **Value $14.95**

(7) Murray® "Champion" (1st, 1994)
Die-Cast Metal • PALM
1395QX5426 • **Value $72**

(8) Murray® Fire Truck (2nd, 1995)
Die-Cast Metal • PALM
1395QX5027 • **Value $33**

(9) Murray® Airplane (3rd, 1996)
Die-Cast Metal • PALM
1395QX5364 • **Value $28**

(10) 1937 Steelcraft Auburn by Murray® (club edition, 1996)
Die-Cast Metal • PALM
1595QXC4174 • **Value $57**

(11) Murray® Dump Truck (4th, 1997)
Die-Cast Metal • PALM
1395QX6195 • **Value $25**

(12) 1937 Steelcraft Airflow by Murray® (club edition, 1997)
Die-Cast Metal • PALM
1595QXC5185 • **Value $50**

(13) 1955 Murray® Tractor and Trailer (5th, 1998)
Die-Cast Metal • PALM
1695QX6376 • **Value $27**

(14) 1935 Steelcraft by Murray® (club edition, 1998)
Die-Cast Metal • PALM
1595QXC4496 • **Value $40**

(15) NEW! 1968 Murray® Jolly Roger Flagship (6th, 1999)
Die-Cast Metal • PALM
1395QX6279 • **Value $13.95**

(16) NEW! 1939 Garton® Ford Station Wagon (7th, club edition, 1999)
Die-Cast Metal • PALM
1595QXC4509 • **Value $15.95**

(17) Pansy (1st, 1996)
Handcrafted • TAGU
1595QK1171 • **Value $55**

(18) Snowdrop Angel (2nd, 1997)
Handcrafted • TAGU
1595QX1095 • **Value $30**

(19) Iris Angel (3rd, 1998)
Handcrafted • TAGU
1595QX6156 • **Value $23**

(20) NEW! Rose Angel (4th & final, 1999)
Handcrafted • TAGU
1595QX6289 • **Value $15.95**

HOOP STARS

	Price Paid	Value of My Collection
1.		
2.		
3.		
4.		
5.		

JOYFUL SANTA

6.		

KIDDIE CAR CLASSICS

7.		
8.		
9.		
10.		
11.		
12.		
13.		
14.		
15.		
16.		

THE LANGUAGE OF FLOWERS

17.		
18.		
19.		
20.		

PENCIL TOTALS

1
700E Hudson Steam Locomotive (1st, 1996)
Die-Cast Metal • N/A
1895QX5531 • **Value $66**

2
1950 Santa Fe F3 Diesel Locomotive (2nd, 1997)
Die-Cast Metal • N/A
1895QX6145 • **Value $40**

3
Pennsylvania GG-1 Locomotive (3rd, 1998)
Die-Cast Metal • N/A
1895QX6346 • **Value $30**

4
NEW!
746 Norfolk and Western Steam Locomotive (4th, 1999)
Die-Cast Metal • N/A
1895QX6377 • **Value $18.95**

5
Cinderella – 1995 (1st, 1996)
Handcrafted • FRAN
1495QX6311 • **Value $42**

6
Little Red Riding Hood – 1991 (2nd, 1997)
Handcrafted • FRAN
1495QX6155 • **Value $32**

7
Mop Top Wendy (3rd, 1998)
Handcrafted • FRAN
1495QX6353 • **Value $26**

8
NEW!
Red Queen – Alice in Wonderland (4th, 1999)
Handcrafted • FRAN
1495QX6379 • **Value $14.95**

LIONEL® Train

	Price Paid	Value of My Collection
1.		
2.		
3.		
4.		

Madame Alexander®

5.		
6.		
7.		
8.		

Madame Alexander® Holiday Angels

9.		
10.		

Majestic Wilderness

11.		
12.		
13.		

Marilyn Monroe

14.		
15.		
16.		

Mary's Angels

17.		
18.		

PENCIL TOTALS

9
Glorious Angel (1st, 1998)
Handcrafted • FRAN
1495QX6493 • **Value $27**

10
NEW!
Angel of The Nativity (2nd, 1999)
Handcrafted • FRAN
1495QX6419 • **Value $14.95**

11
Snowshoe Rabbits in Winter Mark Newman (1st, 1997)
Handcrafted • N/A
1295QX5694 • **Value $32**

12
Timber Wolves at Play Mark Newman (2nd, 1998)
Handcrafted • N/A
1295QX6273 • **Value $22**

13
NEW!
Curious Raccoons Mark Newman (3rd, 1999)
Handcrafted • N/A
1295QX6287 • **Value $12.95**

14
Marilyn Monroe (1st, 1997)
Handcrafted • ANDR
1495QX5704 • **Value $28**

15
Marilyn Monroe (2nd, 1998)
Handcrafted • ANDR
1495QX6333 • **Value $23**

16
NEW!
Marilyn Monroe (3rd & final, 1999)
Handcrafted • ANDR
1495QX6389 • **Value $14.95**

17
Buttercup (1st, 1988)
Handcrafted • CHAD
500QX4074 • **Value $46**

18
Bluebell (2nd, 1989)
Handcrafted • CHAD
575QX4545 • **Value $92**

1

Rosebud (3rd, 1990)
Handcrafted • CHAD
575QX4423 • **Value $43**

2

Iris (4th, 1991)
Handcrafted • CHAD
675QX4279 • **Value $44**

3

Lily (5th, 1992)
Handcrafted • CHAD
675QX4274 • **Value $57**

4

Ivy (6th, 1993)
Handcrafted • CHAD
675QX4282 • **Value $28**

5

Jasmine (7th, 1994)
Handcrafted • CHAD
695QX5276 • **Value $24**

6

Camellia (8th, 1995)
Handcrafted • CHAD
695QX5149 • **Value $21**

7

Violet (9th, 1996)
Handcrafted • CHAD
695QX5664 • **Value $19**

8

Daisy (10th, 1997)
Handcrafted • CHAD
795QX6242 • **Value $17**

9

Daphne (11th, 1998)
Handcrafted • CHAD
795QX6153 • **Value $14**

10 NEW!

Heather (12th, 1999)
Handcrafted • CHAD
795QX6329 • **Value $7.95**

11

**Merry Olde Santa
(1st, 1990)**
Handcrafted • SEAL
1475QX4736 • **Value $84**

12

**Merry Olde Santa
(2nd, 1991)**
Handcrafted • JLEE
1475QX4359 • **Value $90**

13

**Merry Olde Santa
(3rd, 1992)**
Handcrafted • UNRU
1475QX4414 • **Value $38**

14

**Merry Olde Santa
(4th, 1993)**
Handcrafted • RGRS
1475QX4842 • **Value $37**

15

**Merry Olde Santa
(5th, 1994)**
Handcrafted • CHAD
1495QX5256 • **Value $33**

16

**Merry Olde Santa
(6th, 1995)**
Handcrafted • ANDR
1495QX5139 • **Value $30**

17

**Merry Olde Santa
(7th, 1996)**
Handcrafted • CROW
1495QX5654 • **Value $27**

18

**Merry Olde Santa
(8th, 1997)**
Handcrafted • LYLE
1495QX6225 • **Value $28**

19

**Merry Olde Santa
(9th, 1998)**
Handcrafted • UNRU
1595QX6386 • **Value $23**

20 NEW!

**Merry Olde Santa
(10th & final, 1999)**
Handcrafted • RHOD
1595QX6359 • **Value $15.95**

MARY'S ANGELS		
	Price Paid	Value of My Collection
1.		
2.		
3.		
4.		
5.		
6.		
7.		
8.		
9.		
10.		
MERRY OLDE SANTA		
11.		
12.		
13.		
14.		
15.		
16.		
17.		
18.		
19.		
20.		
PENCIL TOTALS		

VALUE GUIDE — HALLMARK KEEPSAKE ORNAMENTS

(1) Bandleader Mickey (1st, 1997)
Handcrafted • SIED
1395QXD4022 • **Value $25**

(2) Minnie Plays the Flute (2nd, 1998)
Handcrafted • N/A
1395QXD4106 • **Value $22**

(3) NEW! Donald Plays the Cymbals (3rd, 1999)
Handcrafted • N/A
1395QXD4057 • **Value $13.95**

(4) Miniature Crèche (1st, 1985)
Wood/Straw • SEAL
875QX4825 • **Value $32**

(5) Miniature Crèche (2nd, 1986)
Porcelain • SEAL
900QX4076 • **Value $62**

(6) Miniature Crèche (3rd, 1987)
Brass • SEAL
900QX4819 • **Value $36**

(7) Miniature Crèche (4th, 1988)
Acrylic • UNRU
850QX4034 • **Value $33**

(8) Miniature Crèche (5th & final, 1989)
Handcrafted • RGRS
925QX4592 • **Value $23**

(9) NEW! Mischievous Kittens (1st, 1999)
Handcrafted • AUBE
995QX6427 • **Value $9.95**

(10) Humpty Dumpty (1st, 1993)
Handcrafted • SEAL/VOTR
1375QX5282 • **Value $42**

(11) Hey Diddle, Diddle (2nd, 1994)
Handcrafted • SEAL
1395QX5213 • **Value $43**

(12) Jack and Jill (3rd, 1995)
Handcrafted • SEAL/VOTR
1395QX5099 • **Value $27**

(13) Mary Had a Little Lamb (4th, 1996)
Handcrafted • SEAL/VOTR
1395QX5644 • **Value $27**

(14) Little Boy Blue (5th & final, 1997)
Handcrafted • SEAL/VOTR
1395QX6215 • **Value $24**

(15) Merry Mistletoe Time (1st, 1986)
Handcrafted • UNRU
1300QX4026 • **Value $107**

(16) Home Cooking (2nd, 1987)
Handcrafted • UNRU
1325QX4837 • **Value $68**

(17) Shall We Dance (3rd, 1988)
Handcrafted • UNRU
1300QX4011 • **Value $55**

(18) Holiday Duet (4th, 1989)
Handcrafted • UNRU
1325QX4575 • **Value $52**

(19) Popcorn Party (5th, 1990)
Handcrafted • UNRU
1375QX4393 • **Value $72**

MICKEY'S HOLIDAY PARADE		
	Price Paid	Value of My Collection
1.		
2.		
3.		
MINIATURE CRÈCHE		
4.		
5.		
6.		
7.		
8.		
MISCHIEVOUS KITTENS		
9.		
MOTHER GOOSE		
10.		
11.		
12.		
13.		
14.		
MR. AND MRS. CLAUS		
15.		
16.		
17.		
18.		
19.		
PENCIL TOTALS		

VALUE GUIDE — HALLMARK KEEPSAKE ORNAMENTS

(1) **Checking His List**
(6th, 1991)
Handcrafted • UNRU
1375QX4339 • **Value $46**

(2) **Gift Exchange**
(7th, 1992)
Handcrafted • UNRU
1475QX4294 • **Value $39**

(3) **A Fitting Moment**
(8th, 1993)
Handcrafted • FRAN
1475QX4202 • **Value $38**

(4) **A Handwarming**
Present (9th, 1994)
Handcrafted • UNRU
1495QX5283 • **Value $35**

(5) **Christmas Eve Kiss**
(10th & final, 1995)
Handcrafted • UNRU
1495QX5157 • **Value $29**

(6) **Santa's Visitors**
(1st, 1980)
Cameo • N/A
650QX3061 • **Value $240**

(7) **The Carolers (2nd, 1981)**
Cameo • N/A
850QX5115 • **Value $50**

(8) **Filling the Stockings**
(3rd, 1982)
Cameo • N/A
850QX3053 • **Value $33**

(9) **Dress Rehearsal**
(4th, 1983)
Cameo • N/A
750QX3007 • **Value $38**

(10) **Caught Napping**
(5th, 1984)
Cameo • MCGE
750QX3411 • **Value $36**

(11) **Jolly Postman (6th, 1985)**
Cameo • MCGE
750QX3745 • **Value $35**

(12) **Checking Up (7th, 1986)**
Cameo • PIKE
775QX3213 • **Value $28**

(13) **The Christmas Dance**
(8th, 1987)
Cameo • PALM
775QX3707 • **Value $24**

(14) **And to All a Good**
Night (9th & final, 1988)
Cameo • N/A
775QX3704 • **Value $26**

(15) **Victorian Dollhouse**
(1st, 1984)
Handcrafted • DLEE
1300QX4481 • **Value $212**

(16) **Old-Fashioned Toy**
Shop (2nd, 1985)
Handcrafted • DLEE
1375QX4975 • **Value $136**

(17) **Christmas Candy**
Shoppe (3rd, 1986)
Handcrafted • DLEE
1375QX4033 • **Value $295**

(18) **House on Main St.**
(4th, 1987)
Handcrafted • DLEE
1400QX4839 • **Value $82**

(19) **Hall Bro's Card Shop**
(5th, 1988)
Handcrafted • DLEE
1450QX4014 • **Value $66**

(20) **U.S. Post Office**
(6th, 1989)
Handcrafted • DLEE
1425QX4582 • **Value $70**

MR. AND MRS. CLAUS

	Price Paid	Value of My Collection
1.		
2.		
3.		
4.		
5.		

NORMAN ROCKWELL

6.		
7.		
8.		
9.		
10.		
11.		
12.		
13.		
14.		

NOSTALGIC HOUSES AND SHOPS

15.		
16.		
17.		
18.		
19.		
20.		
PENCIL TOTALS		

VALUE GUIDE – HALLMARK KEEPSAKE ORNAMENTS

(1) Holiday Home
(7th, 1990)
Handcrafted • DLEE
1475QX4696 • **Value $74**

(2) Fire Station (8th, 1991)
Handcrafted • DLEE
1475QX4139 • **Value $67**

(3) Five and Ten Cent Store (9th, 1992)
Handcrafted • DLEE
1475QX4254 • **Value $41**

(4) Cozy Home (10th, 1993)
Handcrafted • DLEE
1475QX4175 • **Value $44**

(5) Tannenbaum's Dept. Store (complements the series, 1993)
Handcrafted • DLEE
2600QX5612 • **Value $55**

(6) Neighborhood Drugstore (11th, 1994)
Handcrafted • DLEE
1495QX5286 • **Value $36**

(7) Town Church (12th, 1995)
Handcrafted • PALM
1495QX5159 • **Value $30**

(8) Accessories for Nostalgic Houses and Shops (set/3, 1995)
Handcrafted • JLEE
895QX5089 • **Value $16**

(9) Victorian Painted Lady (13th, 1996)
Handcrafted • PALM
1495QX5671 • **Value $29**

(10) Cafe (14th, 1997)
Handcrafted • PALM
1695QX6245 • **Value $28**

(11) Grocery Store (15th, 1998)
Handcrafted • PALM
1695QX6266 • **Value $25**

(12) Halls Station (complements the series, 1998)
Handcrafted • PALM
2500QX6833 • **Value $40**

(13) NEW! House on Holly Lane (16th, 1999)
Handcrafted • PALM
1695QX6349 • **Value $16.95**

(14) Pony Express Rider (1st, 1998)
Handcrafted • UNRU
1395QX6323 • **Value $22**

(15) NEW! Prospector (2nd, 1999)
Handcrafted • UNRU
1395QX6317 • **Value $13.95**

(16) Owliver (1st, 1992)
Handcrafted • SIED
775QX4544 • **Value $21**

(17) Owliver (2nd, 1993)
Handcrafted • SIED
775QX5425 • **Value $20**

(18) Owliver (3rd & final, 1994)
Handcrafted • SIED
795QX5226 • **Value $20**

(19) Italy (1st, 1991)
Handcrafted • SICK
1175QX5129 • **Value $27**

(20) Spain (2nd, 1992)
Handcrafted • SICK
1175QX5174 • **Value $23**

NOSTALGIC HOUSES AND SHOPS	Price Paid	Value of My Collection
1.		
2.		
3.		
4.		
5.		
6.		
7.		
8.		
9.		
10.		
11.		
12.		
13.		
THE OLD WEST		
14.		
15.		
OWLIVER		
16.		
17.		
18.		
PEACE ON EARTH		
19.		
20.		
PENCIL TOTALS		

VALUE GUIDE — HALLMARK KEEPSAKE ORNAMENTS

(1) Poland (3rd & final, 1993)
Handcrafted • SICK
1175QX5242 • **Value $25**

(2) The PEANUTS® Gang (1st, 1993)
Handcrafted • RHOD
975QX5315 • **Value $57**

(3) The PEANUTS® Gang (2nd, 1994)
Handcrafted • BISH
995QX5203 • **Value $26**

(4) The PEANUTS® Gang (3rd, 1995)
Handcrafted • SIED
995QX5059 • **Value $27**

(5) The PEANUTS® Gang (4th & final, 1996)
Handcrafted • FRAN
995QX5381 • **Value $19**

(6) A Pony for Christmas (1st, 1998)
Handcrafted • SICK
1095QX6316 • **Value $21**

(7) NEW! A Pony for Christmas (2nd, 1999)
Handcrafted • SICK
1095QX6299 • **Value $10.95**

(8) Cinnamon Teddy (1st, 1983)
Porcelain • DUTK
700QX4289 • **Value $80**

(9) Cinnamon Bear (2nd, 1984)
Porcelain • N/A
700QX4541 • **Value $53**

(10) Porcelain Bear (3rd, 1985)
Porcelain • DUTK
750QX4792 • **Value $60**

(11) Porcelain Bear (4th, 1986)
Porcelain • N/A
775QX4056 • **Value $42**

(12) Porcelain Bear (5th, 1987)
Porcelain • N/A
775QX4427 • **Value $40**

(13) Porcelain Bear (6th, 1988)
Porcelain • PIKE
800QX4044 • **Value $40**

(14) Porcelain Bear (7th, 1989)
Porcelain • PIKE
875QX4615 • **Value $34**

(15) Porcelain Bear (8th & final, 1990)
Porcelain • N/A
875QX4426 • **Value $34**

(16) Puppy Love (1st, 1991)
Handcrafted/Brass • RGRS
775QX5379 • **Value $63**

(17) Puppy Love (2nd, 1992)
Handcrafted/Brass • RGRS
775QX4484 • **Value $40**

(18) Puppy Love (3rd, 1993)
Handcrafted/Brass • RGRS
775QX5045 • **Value $27**

(19) Puppy Love (4th, 1994)
Handcrafted/Brass • RGRS
795QX5253 • **Value $22**

	Price Paid	Value of My Collection
PEACE ON EARTH		
1.		
THE PEANUTS® GANG		
2.		
3.		
4.		
5.		
A PONY FOR CHRISTMAS		
6.		
7.		
PORCELAIN BEAR		
8.		
9.		
10.		
11.		
12.		
13.		
14.		
15.		
PUPPY LOVE		
16.		
17.		
18.		
19.		
PENCIL TOTALS		

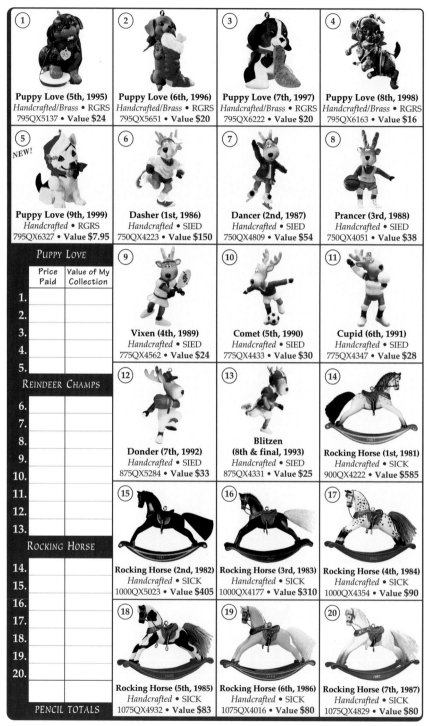

① Puppy Love (5th, 1995)
Handcrafted/Brass • RGRS
795QX5137 • **Value $24**

② Puppy Love (6th, 1996)
Handcrafted/Brass • RGRS
795QX5651 • **Value $20**

③ Puppy Love (7th, 1997)
Handcrafted/Brass • RGRS
795QX6222 • **Value $20**

④ Puppy Love (8th, 1998)
Handcrafted/Brass • RGRS
795QX6163 • **Value $16**

⑤ NEW! Puppy Love (9th, 1999)
Handcrafted • RGRS
795QX6327 • **Value $7.95**

⑥ Dasher (1st, 1986)
Handcrafted • SIED
750QX4223 • **Value $150**

⑦ Dancer (2nd, 1987)
Handcrafted • SIED
750QX4809 • **Value $54**

⑧ Prancer (3rd, 1988)
Handcrafted • SIED
750QX4051 • **Value $38**

⑨ Vixen (4th, 1989)
Handcrafted • SIED
775QX4562 • **Value $24**

⑩ Comet (5th, 1990)
Handcrafted • SIED
775QX4433 • **Value $30**

⑪ Cupid (6th, 1991)
Handcrafted • SIED
775QX4347 • **Value $28**

⑫ Donder (7th, 1992)
Handcrafted • SIED
875QX5284 • **Value $33**

⑬ Blitzen (8th & final, 1993)
Handcrafted • SIED
875QX4331 • **Value $25**

⑭ Rocking Horse (1st, 1981)
Handcrafted • SICK
900QX4222 • **Value $585**

⑮ Rocking Horse (2nd, 1982)
Handcrafted • SICK
1000QX5023 • **Value $405**

⑯ Rocking Horse (3rd, 1983)
Handcrafted • SICK
1000QX4177 • **Value $310**

⑰ Rocking Horse (4th, 1984)
Handcrafted • SICK
1000QX4354 • **Value $90**

⑱ Rocking Horse (5th, 1985)
Handcrafted • SICK
1075QX4932 • **Value $83**

⑲ Rocking Horse (6th, 1986)
Handcrafted • SICK
1075QX4016 • **Value $80**

⑳ Rocking Horse (7th, 1987)
Handcrafted • SICK
1075QX4829 • **Value $80**

Puppy Love

	Price Paid	Value of My Collection
1.		
2.		
3.		
4.		
5.		

Reindeer Champs

6.		
7.		
8.		
9.		
10.		
11.		
12.		
13.		

Rocking Horse

14.		
15.		
16.		
17.		
18.		
19.		
20.		

PENCIL TOTALS

(1) Rocking Horse (8th, 1988)
Handcrafted • SICK
1075QX4024 • **Value $65**

(2) Rocking Horse (9th, 1989)
Handcrafted • SICK
1075QX4622 • **Value $57**

(3) Rocking Horse (10th, 1990)
Handcrafted • SICK
1075QX4646 • **Value $92**

(4) Rocking Horse (11th, 1991)
Handcrafted • SICK
1075QX4147 • **Value $45**

(5) Rocking Horse (12th, 1992)
Handcrafted • SICK
1075QX4261 • **Value $42**

(6) Rocking Horse (13th, 1993)
Handcrafted • SICK
1075QX4162 • **Value $37**

(7) Rocking Horse (14th, 1994)
Handcrafted • SICK
1095QX5016 • **Value $27**

(8) Rocking Horse (15th, 1995)
Handcrafted • SICK
1095QX5167 • **Value $25**

(9) Pewter Rocking Horse (15th Anniversary Edition, 1995)
Pewter • SICK
2000QX6167 • **Value $39**

(10) Rocking Horse (16th & final, 1996)
Handcrafted • SICK
1095QX5674 • **Value $24**

(11) Donald and Daisy in Venice (1st, 1998)
Handcrafted • LARS
1495QXD4103 • **Value $23**

(12) NEW! Mickey and Minnie in Paradise (2nd, 1999)
Handcrafted • N/A
1495QXD4049 • **Value $14.95**

(13) Scarlett O'Hara™ (1st, 1997)
Handcrafted • ANDR
1495QX6125 • **Value $29**

(14) Scarlett O'Hara™ (2nd, 1998)
Handcrafted • ANDR
1495QX6336 • **Value $22**

(15) NEW! Scarlett O'Hara™ (3rd, 1999)
Handcrafted • ANDR
1495QX6397 • **Value $14.95**

(16) The Flight at Kitty Hawk (1st, 1997)
Handcrafted • NORT
1495QX5574 • **Value $32**

(17) 1917 Curtiss JN-4D "Jenny" (2nd, 1998)
Handcrafted • NORT
1495QX6286 • **Value $23**

(18) NEW! Curtiss R3C-2 Seaplane (3rd, 1999)
Handcrafted • NORT
1495QX6387 • **Value $14.95**

(19) Ice Hockey Holiday (1st, 1979)
Handcrafted • N/A
800QX1419 • **Value $140**

Rocking Horse		
	Price Paid	Value of My Collection
1.		
2.		
3.		
4.		
5.		
6.		
7.		
8.		
9.		
10.		
Romantic Vacations		
11.		
12.		
Scarlett O'Hara™		
13.		
14.		
15.		
Sky's The Limit		
16.		
17.		
18.		
Snoopy® And Friends		
19.		
Pencil Totals		

(1) Ski Holiday (2nd, 1980) *Handcrafted* • FRAN 900QX1541 • **Value $140**	**(2)** SNOOPY® and Friends (3rd, 1981) *Handcrafted* • FRAN 1200QX4362 • **Value $135**	**(3)** SNOOPY® and Friends (4th, 1982) *Handcrafted* • SEAL 1300QX4803 • **Value $105**	**(4)** Santa SNOOPY® (5th & final, 1983) *Handcrafted* • SICK 1300QX4169 • **Value $95**
(5) Snow Buddies (1st, 1998) *Handcrafted* • HADD 795QX6853 • **Value $21**	**(6)** NEW! Snow Buddies (2nd, 1999) *Handcrafted* • HADD 795QX6319 • **Value $7.95**	**(7)** Joe Cool (1st, 1998) *Handcrafted* • SIED 995QX6453 • **Value $20**	**(8)** NEW! Famous Flying Ace (2nd, 1999) *Handcrafted* • SIED 995QX6409 • **Value $9.95**

SNOOPY® AND FRIENDS

	Price Paid	Value of My Collection
1.		
2.		
3.		
4.		

SNOW BUDDIES

(9) Luke Skywalker™ (1st, 1997) *Handcrafted* • RHOD 1395QXI5484 • **Value $33**	**(10)** Princess Leia™ (2nd, 1998) *Handcrafted* • RHOD 1395QXI4026 • **Value $27**	**(11)** NEW! Han Solo™ (3rd, 1999) *Handcrafted* • ANDR 1395QXI4007 • **Value $13.95**	

	Price Paid	Value of My Collection
5.		
6.		

SPOTLIGHT ON SNOOPY

(12) Jeff Gordon (1st, 1997) *Handcrafted* • SEAL 1595QXI6165 • **Value $38**	**(13)** Richard Petty (2nd, 1998) *Handcrafted* • SEAL 1595QXI4143 • **Value $29**	**(14)** NEW! Bill Elliott (3rd & final, 1999) *Handcrafted* • SEAL 1595QXI4039 • **Value $15.95**	

	Price Paid	Value of My Collection
7.		
8.		

STAR WARS™

	Price Paid	Value of My Collection
9.		
10.		
11.		

STOCK CAR CHAMPIONS

(15) Mouse in a Thimble (1st, 1978, re-issued in 1979) *Handcrafted* • N/A 250QX1336 • **Value $290**	**(16)** A Christmas Salute (2nd, 1979, re-issued in 1980) *Handcrafted* • N/A 300QX1319 • **Value $175**	**(17)** Mouse in a Thimble (1979, re-issued from 1978) *Handcrafted* • N/A 300QX1336 • **Value $290**	

	Price Paid	Value of My Collection
12.		
13.		
14.		

THIMBLE SERIES

(18) Thimble Elf (3rd, 1980) *Handcrafted* • N/A 400QX1321 • **Value $175**	

	Price Paid	Value of My Collection
15.		
16.		
17.		
18.		

PENCIL TOTALS

Keepsake Series

1. A Christmas Salute
(1980, re-issued from 1979)
Handcrafted • N/A
400QX1319 • **Value $175**

2. Thimble Angel (4th, 1981)
Handcrafted • N/A
450QX4135 • **Value $154**

3. Thimble Mouse
(5th, 1982)
Handcrafted • N/A
500QX4513 • **Value $77**

4. Thimble Elf (6th, 1983)
Handcrafted • N/A
500QX4017 • **Value $39**

5. Thimble Angel (7th, 1984)
Handcrafted • N/A
500QX4304 • **Value $60**

6. Thimble Santa (8th, 1985)
Handcrafted • SIED
550QX4725 • **Value $37**

7. Thimble Partridge
(9th, 1986)
Handcrafted • N/A
575QX4066 • **Value $26**

8. Thimble Drummer
(10th, 1987)
Handcrafted • SIED
575QX4419 • **Value $28**

9. Thimble Snowman
(11th, 1988)
Handcrafted • SIED
575QX4054 • **Value $24**

10. Thimble Puppy
(12th & final, 1989)
Handcrafted • RGRS
575QX4552 • **Value $28**

11. Victorian Christmas
Thomas Kinkade, Painter
of Light™ (1st, 1997)
Porcelain • SEAL
1095QXI6135 • **Value $26**

12. Victorian Christmas II,
Thomas Kinkade, Painter
of Light™ (2nd, 1998)
Ceramic • N/A
1095QX61343 • **Value $26**

13. NEW!
Victorian Christmas III
Thomas Kinkade,
Painter of Light™
(3rd & final, 1999)
Ceramic • N/A
1095QX6407 • **Value $10.95**

14. Tin Locomotive (1st, 1982)
Pressed Tin • SICK
1300QX4603 • **Value $670**

15. Tin Locomotive (2nd, 1983)
Pressed Tin • SICK
1300QX4049 • **Value $295**

16. Tin Locomotive (3rd, 1984)
Pressed Tin • SICK
1400QX4404 • **Value $92**

17. Tin Locomotive (4th, 1985)
Pressed Tin • SICK
1475QX4972 • **Value $86**

18. Tin Locomotive (5th, 1986)
Pressed Tin • SICK
1475QX4036 • **Value $82**

19. Tin Locomotive (6th, 1987)
Pressed Tin • SICK
1475QX4849 • **Value $68**

20. Tin Locomotive (7th, 1988)
Pressed Tin • SICK
1475QX4004 • **Value $56**

Thimble Series

	Price Paid	Value of My Collection
1.		
2.		
3.		
4.		
5.		
6.		
7.		
8.		
9.		
10.		

Thomas Kinkade

11.		
12.		
13.		

Tin Locomotive

14.		
15.		
16.		
17.		
18.		
19.		
20.		
PENCIL TOTALS		

(1) Tin Locomotive
(8th & final, 1989)
Pressed Tin • SICK
1475QX4602 • **Value $60**

(2) Tobin Fraley Carousel
(1st, 1992)
Porcelain/Brass • FRAL
2800QX4891 • **Value $58**

(3) Tobin Fraley Carousel
(2nd, 1993)
Porcelain/Brass • FRAL
2800QX5502 • **Value $47**

(4) Tobin Fraley Carousel
(3rd, 1994)
Porcelain/Brass • FRAL
2800QX5223 • **Value $58**

(5) Tobin Fraley Carousel
(4th & final, 1995)
Porcelain • FRAL
2800QX5069 • **Value $50**

(6) NEW! Farm House (1st, 1999)
Pressed Tin • SICK
1595QX6439 • **Value $15.95**

(7) NEW! Red Barn (complements the series, 1999)
Pressed Tin • SICK
1595QX6947 • **Value $15.95**

(8) The Fireman (1st, 1995)
Die-Cast Metal • CROW
1695QK1027 • **Value $42**

(9) Uncle Sam (2nd, 1996)
Die-Cast Metal • CROW
1695QK1084 • **Value $34**

(10) Santa Claus
(3rd & final, 1997)
Die-Cast Metal • CROW
1695QX1215 • **Value $24**

(11) Partridge in a Pear Tree
(1st, 1984)
Acrylic • N/A
600QX3484 • **Value $292**

(12) Two Turtle Doves
(2nd, 1985)
Acrylic • PIKE
650QX3712 • **Value $75**

(13) Three French Hens
(3rd, 1986)
Acrylic • VOTR
650QX3786 • **Value $48**

(14) Four Colly Birds
(4th, 1987)
Acrylic • PIKE
650QX3709 • **Value $38**

(15) Five Golden Rings
(5th, 1988)
Acrylic • PIKE
650QX3714 • **Value $28**

(16) Six Geese A-Laying
(6th, 1989)
Acrylic • N/A
675QX3812 • **Value $23**

(17) Seven Swans
A-Swimming (7th, 1990)
Acrylic • N/A
675QX3033 • **Value $28**

(18) Eight Maids A-Milking
(8th, 1991)
Acrylic • N/A
675QX3089 • **Value $28**

(19) Nine Ladies Dancing
(9th, 1992)
Acrylic • PYDA
675QX3031 • **Value $25**

	Price Paid	Value of My Collection
Tin Locomotive		
1.		
Tobin Fraley Carousel		
2.		
3.		
4.		
5.		
Town and Country		
6.		
7.		
Turn-of-the-Century Parade		
8.		
9.		
10.		
The Twelve Days Of Christmas		
11.		
12.		
13.		
14.		
15.		
16.		
17.		
18.		
19.		
Pencil Totals		

1

**Ten Lords A-Leaping
(10th, 1993)**
Acrylic • CHAD
675QX3012 • **Value $25**

2

**Eleven Pipers Piping
(11th, 1994)**
Acrylic • N/A
695QX3183 • **Value $18**

3

**Twelve Drummers
Drumming
(12th & final, 1995)**
Acrylic • N/A
695QX3009 • **Value $18**

4

**U.S. Christmas Stamps
(1st, 1993)**
Enamel/Copper • SICK
1075QX5292 • **Value $27**

5

**U.S. Christmas Stamps
(2nd, 1994)**
Enamel/Copper • N/A
1095QX5206 • **Value $26**

6

**U.S. Christmas Stamps
(3rd & final, 1995)**
Enamel/Copper • N/A
1095QX5067 • **Value $23**

7

**Cruella de Vil
Walt Disney's 101
Dalmatians (1st, 1998)**
Handcrafted • ESCH
1495QXD4063 • **Value $24**

8

NEW!

**Snow White's Jealous
Queen (2nd, 1999)**
Handcrafted • N/A
1495QXD4089 • **Value $14.95**

9

Feliz Navidad (1st, 1985)
Handcrafted • DLEE
975QX4902 • **Value $95**

10

**Vrolyk Kerstfeest
(2nd, 1986)**
Handcrafted • SIED
1000QX4083 • **Value $67**

11

**Mele Kalikimaka
(3rd, 1987)**
Handcrafted • DLEE
1000QX4827 • **Value $33**

12

Joyeux Noël (4th, 1988)
Handcrafted • DLEE
1000QX4021 • **Value $35**

13

**Fröhliche Weihnachten
(5th, 1989)**
Handcrafted • DLEE
1075QX4625 • **Value $33**

14

**Nollaig Shona
(6th & final, 1990)**
Handcrafted • DLEE
1075QX4636 • **Value $30**

15

**A Visit From Piglet
(1st, 1998)**
Handcrafted • N/A
1395QXD4086 • **Value $23**

16

NEW!

Honey Time (2nd, 1999)
Handcrafted • N/A
1395QXD4129 • **Value $13.95**

17

NEW!

**Playing With Pooh
(1st, 1999)**
Handcrafted • N/A
1395QXD4197 • **Value $13.95**

THE TWELVE DAYS OF CHRISTMAS	Price Paid	Value of My Collection
1.		
2.		
3.		
U.S. CHRISTMAS STAMPS		
4.		
5.		
6.		
UNFORGETTABLE VILLAINS		
7.		
8.		
WINDOWS OF THE WORLD		
9.		
10.		
11.		
12.		
13.		
14.		
WINNIE THE POOH		
15.		
16.		
WINNIE THE POOH AND CHRISTOPHER ROBIN, TOO		
17.		
PENCIL TOTALS		

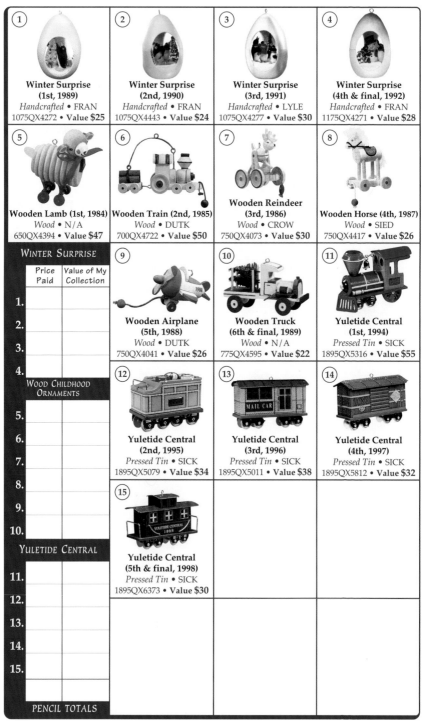

Winter Surprise (1st, 1989)
Handcrafted • FRAN
1075QX4272 • **Value $25**

Winter Surprise (2nd, 1990)
Handcrafted • FRAN
1075QX4443 • **Value $24**

Winter Surprise (3rd, 1991)
Handcrafted • LYLE
1075QX4277 • **Value $30**

Winter Surprise (4th & final, 1992)
Handcrafted • FRAN
1175QX4271 • **Value $28**

Wooden Lamb (1st, 1984)
Wood • N/A
650QX4394 • **Value $47**

Wooden Train (2nd, 1985)
Wood • DUTK
700QX4722 • **Value $50**

Wooden Reindeer (3rd, 1986)
Wood • CROW
750QX4073 • **Value $30**

Wooden Horse (4th, 1987)
Wood • SIED
750QX4417 • **Value $26**

Wooden Airplane (5th, 1988)
Wood • DUTK
750QX4041 • **Value $26**

Wooden Truck (6th & final, 1989)
Wood • N/A
775QX4595 • **Value $22**

Yuletide Central (1st, 1994)
Pressed Tin • SICK
1895QX5316 • **Value $55**

Yuletide Central (2nd, 1995)
Pressed Tin • SICK
1895QX5079 • **Value $34**

Yuletide Central (3rd, 1996)
Pressed Tin • SICK
1895QX5011 • **Value $38**

Yuletide Central (4th, 1997)
Pressed Tin • SICK
1895QX5812 • **Value $32**

Yuletide Central (5th & final, 1998)
Pressed Tin • SICK
1895QX6373 • **Value $30**

Winter Surprise

	Price Paid	Value of My Collection
1.		
2.		
3.		
4.		

Wood Childhood Ornaments

5.		
6.		
7.		
8.		
9.		
10.		

Yuletide Central

11.		
12.		
13.		
14.		
15.		
Pencil Totals		

Magic Series

There have been nine Magic collectible series since the ornaments featuring light, sound and motion debuted in 1985. The "Candlelight Services" and "Lighthouse Greetings" series each welcome one new piece in 1999, while this year marks the final addition to the "Journeys Into Space" series.

(1)

The Stone Church
(1st, 1998)
Handcrafted • SEAL
1895QLX7636 • **Value $44**

(2)
NEW!

Colonial Church
(2nd, 1999)
Handcrafted • SEAL
1895QLX7387 • **Value $18.95**

(3)

Chris Mouse (1st, 1985)
Handcrafted • SIED
1250QLX7032 • **Value $92**

(4)

Chris Mouse Dreams
(2nd, 1986)
Handcrafted • DUTK
1300QLX7056 • **Value $83**

(5)

Chris Mouse Glow
(3rd, 1987)
Handcrafted • SIED
1100QLX7057 • **Value $64**

(6)

Chris Mouse Star
(4th, 1988)
Handcrafted • SIED
875QLX7154 • **Value $63**

(7)

Chris Mouse Cookout
(5th, 1989)
Handcrafted • RGRS
950QLX7225 • **Value $63**

(8)

Chris Mouse Wreath
(6th, 1990)
Handcrafted • RGRS
1000QLX7296 • **Value $46**

(9)

Chris Mouse Mail
(7th, 1991)
Handcrafted • SIED
1000QLX7207 • **Value $40**

(10)

Chris Mouse Tales
(8th, 1992)
Handcrafted • RGRS
1200QLX7074 • **Value $30**

(11)

Chris Mouse Flight
(9th, 1993)
Handcrafted • RGRS
1200QLX7152 • **Value $32**

(12)

Chris Mouse Jelly
(10th, 1994)
Handcrafted • RGRS
1200QLX7393 • **Value $28**

(13)

Chris Mouse Tree
(11th, 1995)
Handcrafted • RGRS
1250QLX7307 • **Value $27**

(14)

Chris Mouse Inn
(12th, 1996)
Handcrafted • SIED
1450QLX7371 • **Value $28**

(15)

Chris Mouse Luminaria
(13th & final, 1997)
Handcrafted • SIED
1495QLX7525 • **Value $26**

MAGIC SERIES

	Price Paid	Value of My Collection
CANDLELIGHT SERVICES		
1.		
2.		
CHRIS MOUSE		
3.		
4.		
5.		
6.		
7.		
8.		
9.		
10.		
11.		
12.		
13.		
14.		
15.		
PENCIL TOTALS		

(1) The Nutcracker Ballet – Sugarplum Fairy (1st, 1986)
Handcrafted • N/A
1750QLX7043 • **Value $82**

(2) A Christmas Carol (2nd, 1987)
Handcrafted • N/A
1600QLX7029 • **Value $70**

(3) Night Before Christmas (3rd, 1988)
Handcrafted • DLEE
1500QLX7161 • **Value $41**

(4) Little Drummer Boy (4th, 1989)
Handcrafted • DLEE
1350QLX7242 • **Value $40**

(5) The Littlest Angel (5th & final, 1990)
Handcrafted • FRAN
1400QLX7303 • **Value $48**

(6) Forest Frolics (1st, 1989)
Handcrafted • PIKE
2450QLX7282 • **Value $88**

(7) Forest Frolics (2nd, 1990)
Handcrafted • PIKE
2500QLX7236 • **Value $72**

(8) Forest Frolics (3rd, 1991)
Handcrafted • PIKE
2500QLX7219 • **Value $68**

(9) Forest Frolics (4th, 1992)
Handcrafted • PIKE
2800QLX7254 • **Value $62**

(10) Forest Frolics (5th, 1993)
Handcrafted • PIKE
2500QLX7165 • **Value $52**

(11) Forest Frolics (6th, 1994)
Handcrafted • PIKE
2800QLX7436 • **Value $58**

(12) Forest Frolics (7th & final, 1995)
Handcrafted • PIKE
2800QLX7299 • **Value $48**

(13) Freedom 7 (1st, 1996)
Handcrafted • SEAL
2400QLX7524 • **Value $52**

(14) Friendship 7 (2nd, 1997)
Handcrafted • SEAL
2400QLX7532 • **Value $46**

(15) Apollo Lunar Module (3rd, 1998)
Handcrafted • N/A
2400QLX7543 • **Value $38**

(16) NEW! Lunar Rover Vehicle (4th & final, 1999)
Handcrafted • SEAL
2400QLX7377 • **Value $24**

(17) Lighthouse Greetings (1st, 1997)
Handcrafted • FRAN
2400QLX7442 • **Value $60**

(18) Lighthouse Greetings (2nd, 1998)
Handcrafted • FRAN
2400QLX7536 • **Value $40**

(19) NEW! Lighthouse Greetings (3rd, 1999)
Handcrafted • FRAN
2400QLX7379 • **Value $24**

Christmas Classics

	Price Paid	Value of My Collection
1.		
2.		
3.		
4.		
5.		

Forest Frolics

6.		
7.		
8.		
9.		
10		
11.		
12.		

Journeys Into Space

13.		
14.		
15.		
16.		

Lighthouse Greetings

17.		
18.		
19.		

PENCIL TOTALS

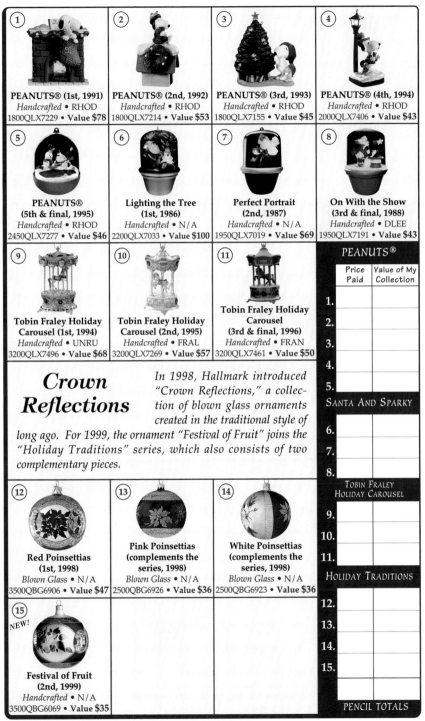

MAGIC/CROWN

① PEANUTS® (1st, 1991)
Handcrafted • RHOD
1800QLX7229 • **Value $78**

② PEANUTS® (2nd, 1992)
Handcrafted • RHOD
1800QLX7214 • **Value $53**

③ PEANUTS® (3rd, 1993)
Handcrafted • RHOD
1800QLX7155 • **Value $45**

④ PEANUTS® (4th, 1994)
Handcrafted • RHOD
2000QLX7406 • **Value $43**

⑤ PEANUTS® (5th & final, 1995)
Handcrafted • RHOD
2450QLX7277 • **Value $46**

⑥ Lighting the Tree (1st, 1986)
Handcrafted • N/A
2200QLX7033 • **Value $100**

⑦ Perfect Portrait (2nd, 1987)
Handcrafted • N/A
1950QLX7019 • **Value $69**

⑧ On With the Show (3rd & final, 1988)
Handcrafted • DLEE
1950QLX7191 • **Value $43**

⑨ Tobin Fraley Holiday Carousel (1st, 1994)
Handcrafted • UNRU
3200QLX7496 • **Value $68**

⑩ Tobin Fraley Holiday Carousel (2nd, 1995)
Handcrafted • FRAL
3200QLX7269 • **Value $57**

⑪ Tobin Fraley Holiday Carousel (3rd & final, 1996)
Handcrafted • FRAN
3200QLX7461 • **Value $50**

Crown Reflections

In 1998, Hallmark introduced "Crown Reflections," a collection of blown glass ornaments created in the traditional style of long ago. For 1999, the ornament "Festival of Fruit" joins the "Holiday Traditions" series, which also consists of two complementary pieces.

⑫ Red Poinsettias (1st, 1998)
Blown Glass • N/A
3500QBG6906 • **Value $47**

⑬ Pink Poinsettias (complements the series, 1998)
Blown Glass • N/A
2500QBG6926 • **Value $36**

⑭ White Poinsettias (complements the series, 1998)
Blown Glass • N/A
2500QBG6923 • **Value $36**

⑮ NEW! Festival of Fruit (2nd, 1999)
Handcrafted • N/A
3500QBG6069 • **Value $35**

PEANUTS®

	Price Paid	Value of My Collection
1.		
2.		
3.		
4.		
5.		

SANTA AND SPARKY

6.		
7.		
8.		

TOBIN FRALEY HOLIDAY CAROUSEL

9.		
10.		
11.		

HOLIDAY TRADITIONS

12.		
13.		
14.		
15.		

PENCIL TOTALS

Miniature Series

There are five new Miniature collectible series for 1999 ("Holiday Flurries," "Lionel® 746 Norfolk and Western," "Harley-Davidson® Motorcycle," "Seaside Scenes" and "The Wonders Of Oz"), bringing the total number of series since 1988 to 32. Of the 13 series that are current, three will close this year.

① **Alice in Wonderland (1st, 1995)**
Handcrafted • ANDR
675QXM4777 • **Value $18**

② **Mad Hatter (2nd, 1996)**
Handcrafted • ANDR
675QXM4074 • **Value $16**

③ **White Rabbit (3rd, 1997)**
Handcrafted • ANDR
695QXM4142 • **Value $14**

④ **Cheshire Cat (4th & final, 1998)**
Handcrafted • ANDR
695QXM4186 • **Value $12**

⑤ **Antique Tractors (1st, 1997)**
Die-Cast Metal • SICK
695QXM4185 • **Value $18**

⑥ **Antique Tractors (2nd, 1998)**
Die-Cast Metal • SICK
695QXM4166 • **Value $13**

⑦ NEW! **Antique Tractors (3rd, 1999)**
Die-Cast Metal • SICK
695QXM4567 • **Value $6.95**

⑧ **The Bearymores (1st, 1992)**
Handcrafted • RGRS
575QXM5544 • **Value $21**

⑨ **The Bearymores (2nd, 1993)**
Handcrafted • RGRS
575QXM5125 • **Value $18**

⑩ **The Bearymores (3rd & final, 1994)**
Handcrafted • RGRS
575QXM5133 • **Value $16**

⑪ **Centuries of Santa (1st, 1994)**
Handcrafted • SICK
600QXM5153 • **Value $27**

⑫ **Centuries of Santa (2nd, 1995)**
Handcrafted • SICK
575QXM4789 • **Value $20**

⑬ **Centuries of Santa (3rd, 1996)**
Handcrafted • SICK
575QXM4091 • **Value $15**

⑭ **Centuries of Santa (4th, 1997)**
Handcrafted • SICK
595QXM4295 • **Value $13**

⑮ **Centuries of Santa (5th, 1998)**
Handcrafted • SICK
595QXM4206 • **Value $11**

⑯ NEW! **Centuries of Santa (6th & final, 1999)**
Handcrafted • SICK
595QXM4589 • **Value $5.95**

ALICE IN WONDERLAND

	Price Paid	Value of My Collection
1.		
2.		
3.		
4.		

ANTIQUE TRACTORS

5.		
6.		
7.		

THE BEARYMORES

8.		
9.		
10.		

CENTURIES OF SANTA

11.		
12.		
13.		
14.		
15.		
16.		

PENCIL TOTALS

Value Guide — Hallmark Keepsake Ornaments

1 Christmas Bells
(1st, 1995)
Handcrafted/Metal • SEAL
475QXM4007 • **Value $20**

2 Christmas Bells
(2nd, 1996)
Handcrafted/Metal • SEAL
475QXM4071 • **Value $16**

3 Christmas Bells
(3rd, 1997)
Handcrafted/Metal • SEAL
495QXM4162 • **Value $13**

4 Christmas Bells
(4th, 1998)
Handcrafted/Metal • SEAL
495QXM4196 • **Value $11**

5 NEW! Christmas Bells
(5th, 1999)
Handcrafted/Metal • SEAL
495QXM4489 • **Value $4.95**

6 NEW! Holiday Flurries
(1st, 1999)
Handcrafted • SICK
695QXM4547 • **Value $6.95**

7 Kittens in Toyland
(1st, 1988)
Handcrafted • CROW
500QXM5621 • **Value $27**

8 Kittens in Toyland
(2nd, 1989)
Handcrafted • CROW
450QXM5612 • **Value $21**

9 Kittens in Toyland
(3rd, 1990)
Handcrafted • CROW
450QXM5736 • **Value $21**

10 Kittens in Toyland
(4th, 1991)
Handcrafted • CROW
450QXM5639 • **Value $18**

11 Kittens in Toyland
(5th & final, 1992)
Handcrafted • CROW
450QXM5391 • **Value $18**

12 The Kringles (1st, 1989)
Handcrafted • RGRS
600QXM5625 • **Value $31**

13 The Kringles (2nd, 1990)
Handcrafted • RGRS
600QXM5753 • **Value $28**

14 The Kringles (3rd, 1991)
Handcrafted • RGRS
600QXM5647 • **Value $26**

15 The Kringles (4th, 1992)
Handcrafted • RGRS
600QXM5381 • **Value $21**

16 The Kringles
(5th & final, 1993)
Handcrafted • RGRS
575QXM5135 • **Value $17**

17 NEW! Locomotive and Tender
(1st, 1999, set/2)
Die-Cast Metal • SEAL
1095QXM4549 • **Value $10.95**

	Price Paid	Value of My Collection
CHRISTMAS BELLS		
1.		
2.		
3.		
4.		
5.		
HOLIDAY FLURRIES		
6.		
KITTENS IN TOYLAND		
7.		
8.		
9.		
10.		
11.		
THE KRINGLES		
12.		
13.		
14.		
15.		
16.		
LIONEL® 746 NORFOLK AND WESTERN		
17.		
PENCIL TOTALS		

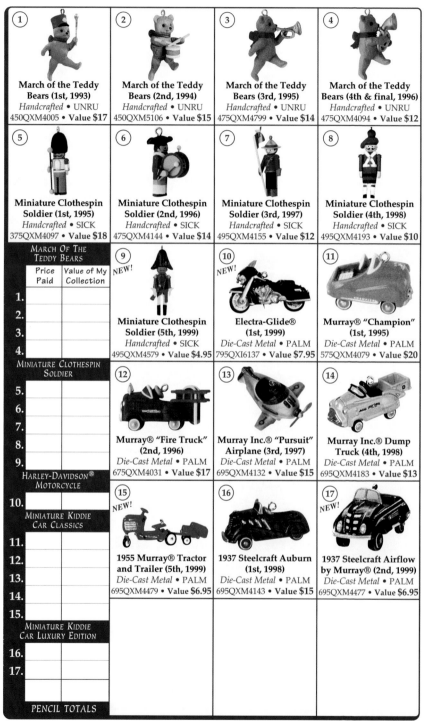

1. March of the Teddy Bears (1st, 1993)
Handcrafted • UNRU
450QXM4005 • **Value $17**

2. March of the Teddy Bears (2nd, 1994)
Handcrafted • UNRU
450QXM5106 • **Value $15**

3. March of the Teddy Bears (3rd, 1995)
Handcrafted • UNRU
475QXM4799 • **Value $14**

4. March of the Teddy Bears (4th & final, 1996)
Handcrafted • UNRU
475QXM4094 • **Value $12**

5. Miniature Clothespin Soldier (1st, 1995)
Handcrafted • SICK
375QXM4097 • **Value $18**

6. Miniature Clothespin Soldier (2nd, 1996)
Handcrafted • SICK
475QXM4144 • **Value $14**

7. Miniature Clothespin Soldier (3rd, 1997)
Handcrafted • SICK
495QXM4155 • **Value $12**

8. Miniature Clothespin Soldier (4th, 1998)
Handcrafted • SICK
495QXM4193 • **Value $10**

9. NEW! Miniature Clothespin Soldier (5th, 1999)
Handcrafted • SICK
495QXM4579 • **Value $4.95**

10. NEW! Electra-Glide® (1st, 1999)
Die-Cast Metal • PALM
795QXI6137 • **Value $7.95**

11. Murray® "Champion" (1st, 1995)
Die-Cast Metal • PALM
575QXM4079 • **Value $20**

12. Murray® "Fire Truck" (2nd, 1996)
Die-Cast Metal • PALM
675QXM4031 • **Value $17**

13. Murray Inc.® "Pursuit" Airplane (3rd, 1997)
Die-Cast Metal • PALM
695QXM4132 • **Value $15**

14. Murray Inc.® Dump Truck (4th, 1998)
Die-Cast Metal • PALM
695QXM4183 • **Value $13**

15. NEW! 1955 Murray® Tractor and Trailer (5th, 1999)
Die-Cast Metal • PALM
695QXM4479 • **Value $6.95**

16. 1937 Steelcraft Auburn (1st, 1998)
Die-Cast Metal • PALM
695QXM4143 • **Value $15**

17. NEW! 1937 Steelcraft Airflow by Murray® (2nd, 1999)
Die-Cast Metal • PALM
695QXM4477 • **Value $6.95**

March Of The Teddy Bears

	Price Paid	Value of My Collection
1.		
2.		
3.		
4.		

Miniature Clothespin Soldier

5.		
6.		
7.		
8.		
9.		

Harley-Davidson® Motorcycle

10.		

Miniature Kiddie Car Classics

11.		
12.		
13.		
14.		
15.		

Miniature Kiddie Car Luxury Edition

16.		
17.		

PENCIL TOTALS

1. The Nativity (1st, 1998)
Pewter • UNRU
995QXM4156 • **Value $17**

2. NEW! The Nativity (2nd, 1999)
Pewter • UNRU
995QXM4497 • **Value $9.95**

3. Nature's Angels (1st, 1990)
Handcrafted/Brass • SEAL
450QXM5733 • **Value $25**

4. Nature's Angels (2nd, 1991)
Handcrafted/Brass • PIKE
450QXM5657 • **Value $22**

5. Nature's Angels (3rd, 1992)
Handcrafted/Brass • PIKE
450QXM5451 • **Value $20**

6. Nature's Angels (4th, 1993)
Handcrafted/Brass • ANDR
450QXM5122 • **Value $17**

7. Nature's Angels (5th, 1994)
Handcrafted/Brass • VOTR
450QXM5126 • **Value $14**

8. Nature's Angels (6th, 1995)
Handcrafted/Brass • ANDR
475QXM4809 • **Value $14**

9. Nature's Angels (7th & final, 1996)
Handcrafted/Brass • PIKE
475QXM4111 • **Value $12**

10. The Night Before Christmas (1st, 1992, w/display house)
Handcrafted • UNRU
1375QXM5541 • **Value $32**

11. The Night Before Christmas (2nd, 1993)
Handcrafted • UNRU
450QXM5115 • **Value $20**

12. The Night Before Christmas (3rd, 1994)
Handcrafted • UNRU
450QXM5123 • **Value $16**

13. The Night Before Christmas (4th, 1995)
Handcrafted • UNRU
475QXM4807 • **Value $19**

14. The Night Before Christmas (5th & final, 1996)
Handcrafted • UNRU
575QXM4104 • **Value $14**

15. Locomotive (1st, 1989)
Handcrafted • SICK
850QXM5762 • **Value $47**

16. Coal Car (2nd, 1990)
Handcrafted • SICK
850QXM5756 • **Value $35**

17. Passenger Car (3rd, 1991)
Handcrafted • SICK
850QXM5649 • **Value $50**

18. Box Car (4th, 1992)
Handcrafted • SICK
700QXM5441 • **Value $24**

19. Flatbed Car (5th, 1993)
Handcrafted • SICK
700QXM5105 • **Value $24**

20. Stock Car (6th, 1994)
Handcrafted • SICK
700QXM5113 • **Value $21**

THE NATIVITY	Price Paid	Value of My Collection
1.		
2.		
NATURE'S ANGELS		
3.		
4.		
5.		
6.		
7.		
8.		
9.		
THE NIGHT BEFORE CHRISTMAS		
10.		
11.		
12.		
13.		
14.		
NOEL R.R.		
15.		
16.		
17.		
18.		
19.		
20.		
PENCIL TOTALS		

MINIATURE SERIES

(1) Milk Tank Car (7th, 1995)
Handcrafted • SICK
675QXM4817 • **Value $19**

(2) Cookie Car (8th, 1996)
Handcrafted • SICK
675QXM4114 • **Value $17**

(3) Candy Car (9th, 1997)
Handcrafted • SICK
695QXM4175 • **Value $14**

(4) Caboose (10th & final, 1998)
Handcrafted • SICK
695QXM4216 • **Value $13**

(5) Noel R.R. Locomotive 1989-1998 (Anniversary Edition, 1998)
Pewter • SICK
1095QXM4286 • **Value $19**

(6) The Nutcracker Ballet (1st, 1996, w/display stage)
Handcrafted • VOTR
1475QXM4064 • **Value $27**

(7) Herr Drosselmeyer (2nd, 1997)
Handcrafted • VOTR
595QXM4135 • **Value $12**

(8) Nutcracker (3rd, 1998)
Handcrafted • VOTR
595QXM4146 • **Value $12**

(9) NEW! Mouse King (4th, 1999)
Handcrafted • VOTR
595QXM4487 • **Value $5.95**

(10) Nutcracker Guild (1st, 1994)
Handcrafted • SICK
575QXM5146 • **Value $20**

(11) Nutcracker Guild (2nd, 1995)
Handcrafted • SICK
575QXM4787 • **Value $17**

(12) Nutcracker Guild (3rd, 1996)
Handcrafted • SICK
575QXM4084 • **Value $14**

(13) Nutcracker Guild (4th, 1997)
Handcrafted • SICK
695QXM4165 • **Value $13**

(14) Nutcracker Guild (5th, 1998)
Handcrafted • SICK
695QXM4203 • **Value $12**

(15) NEW! Nutcracker Guild (6th, 1999)
Handcrafted • SICK
695QXM4587 • **Value $6.95**

(16) Family Home (1st, 1988)
Handcrafted • DLEE
850QXM5634 • **Value $44**

(17) Sweet Shop (2nd, 1989)
Handcrafted • JLEE
850QXM5615 • **Value $29**

(18) School (3rd, 1990)
Handcrafted • JLEE
850QXM5763 • **Value $24**

(19) Inn (4th, 1991)
Handcrafted • JLEE
850QXM5627 • **Value $26**

(20) Church (5th, 1992)
Handcrafted • JLEE
700QXM5384 • **Value $32**

NOEL R.R.

	Price Paid	Value of My Collection
1.		
2.		
3.		
4.		
5.		

THE NUTCRACKER BALLET

6.		
7.		
8.		
9.		

NUTCRACKER GUILD

10.		
11.		
12.		
13.		
14.		
15.		

OLD ENGLISH VILLAGE

16.		
17.		
18.		
19.		
20.		

PENCIL TOTALS

VALUE GUIDE – HALLMARK KEEPSAKE ORNAMENTS

① Toy Shop (6th, 1993)
Handcrafted • JLEE
700QXM5132 • **Value $19**

② Hat Shop (7th, 1994)
Handcrafted • ANDR
700QXM5143 • **Value $20**

③ Tudor House (8th, 1995)
Handcrafted • JLEE
675QXM4819 • **Value $17**

④ Village Mill (9th, 1996)
Handcrafted • RHOD
675QXM4124 • **Value $15**

⑤ Village Depot (10th & final, 1997)
Handcrafted • LARS
695QXM4182 • **Value $13**

⑥ On the Road (1st, 1993)
Pressed Tin • SICK
575QXM4002 • **Value $20**

⑦ On the Road (2nd, 1994)
Pressed Tin • SICK
575QXM5103 • **Value $17**

⑧ On the Road (3rd, 1995)
Pressed Tin • SICK
575QXM4797 • **Value $15**

⑨ On the Road (4th, 1996)
Pressed Tin • SICK
575QXM4101 • **Value $13**

⑩ On the Road (5th, 1997)
Pressed Tin • SICK
595QXM4172 • **Value $13**

⑪ On the Road (6th & final, 1998)
Pressed Tin • SICK
595QXM4213 • **Value $11**

⑫ Penguin Pal (1st, 1988)
Handcrafted • SIED
375QXM5631 • **Value $27**

⑬ Penguin Pal (2nd, 1989)
Handcrafted • N/A
450QXM5602 • **Value $21**

⑭ Penguin Pal (3rd, 1990)
Handcrafted • N/A
450QXM5746 • **Value $18**

⑮ Penguin Pal (4th & final, 1991)
Handcrafted • SIED
450QXM5629 • **Value $17**

⑯ Rocking Horse (1st, 1988)
Handcrafted • SICK
450QXM5624 • **Value $47**

⑰ Rocking Horse (2nd, 1989)
Handcrafted • SICK
450QXM5605 • **Value $33**

⑱ Rocking Horse (3rd, 1990)
Handcrafted • SICK
450QXM5743 • **Value $29**

⑲ Rocking Horse (4th, 1991)
Handcrafted • SICK
450QXM5637 • **Value $29**

⑳ Rocking Horse (5th, 1992)
Handcrafted • SICK
450QXM5454 • **Value $24**

OLD ENGLISH VILLAGE		
	Price Paid	Value of My Collection
1.		
2.		
3.		
4.		
5.		

ON THE ROAD		
6.		
7.		
8.		
9.		
10.		
11.		

PENGUIN PAL		
12.		
13.		
14.		
15.		

ROCKING HORSE		
16.		
17.		
18.		
19.		
20.		
PENCIL TOTALS		

(1) Rocking Horse
(6th, 1993)
Handcrafted • SICK
450QXM5112 • **Value $18**

(2) Rocking Horse
(7th, 1994)
Handcrafted • SICK
450QXM5116 • **Value $18**

(3) Rocking Horse
(8th, 1995)
Handcrafted • SICK
450QXM4827 • **Value $19**

(4) Rocking Horse
(9th, 1996)
Handcrafted • SICK
475QXM4121 • **Value $15**

(5) Rocking Horse
(10th & final, 1997)
Handcrafted • SICK
495QXM4302 • **Value $13**

(6) Santa's Little Big Top
(1st, 1995)
Handcrafted • CROW
675QXM4779 • **Value $20**

(7) Santa's Little Big Top
(2nd, 1996)
Handcrafted • CROW
675QXM4081 • **Value $15**

(8) Santa's Little Big Top
(3rd & final, 1997)
Handcrafted • CROW
695QXM4152 • **Value $13**

(9) NEW!
Seaside Scenes
(1st, 1999)
Handcrafted • SEAL
795QXM4649 • **Value $7.95**

(10) Snowflake Ballet
(1st, 1997)
Handcrafted • ANDR
595QXM4192 • **Value $16**

(11) Snowflake Ballet
(2nd, 1998)
Handcrafted • ANDR
595QXM4173 • **Value $12**

(12) NEW!
Snowflake Ballet
(3rd & final, 1999)
Handcrafted • ANDR
595QXM4569 • **Value $5.95**

(13) Teddy-Bear Style
(1st, 1997)
Handcrafted • UNRU
595QXM4215 • **Value $14**

(14) Teddy-Bear Style
(2nd, 1998)
Handcrafted • UNRU
595QXM4176 • **Value $11**

(15) NEW!
Teddy-Bear Style
(3rd, 1999)
Handcrafted • UNRU
595QXM4499 • **Value $5.95**

(16) Thimble Bells
(1st, 1990)
Porcelain • PYDA
600QXM5543 • **Value $24**

(17) Thimble Bells
(2nd, 1991)
Porcelain • PYDA
600QXM5659 • **Value $22**

ROCKING HORSE

	Price Paid	Value of My Collection
1.		
2.		
3.		
4.		
5.		

SANTA'S LITTLE BIG TOP

6.		
7.		
8.		

SEASIDE SCENES

9.		

SNOWFLAKE BALLET

10.		
11.		
12.		

TEDDY-BEAR STYLE

13.		
14.		
15.		

THIMBLE BELLS

16.		
17.		

PENCIL TOTALS

VALUE GUIDE – HALLMARK KEEPSAKE ORNAMENTS

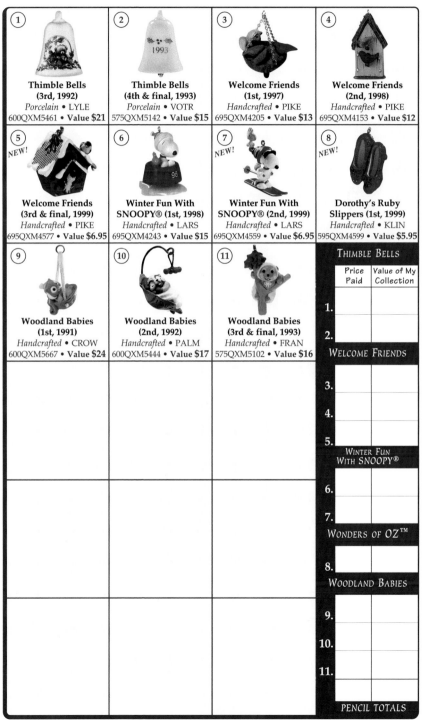

(1) **Thimble Bells**
(3rd, 1992)
Porcelain • LYLE
600QXM5461 • **Value $21**

(2) **Thimble Bells**
(4th & final, 1993)
Porcelain • VOTR
575QXM5142 • **Value $15**

(3) **Welcome Friends**
(1st, 1997)
Handcrafted • PIKE
695QXM4205 • **Value $13**

(4) **Welcome Friends**
(2nd, 1998)
Handcrafted • PIKE
695QXM4153 • **Value $12**

(5) NEW! **Welcome Friends**
(3rd & final, 1999)
Handcrafted • PIKE
695QXM4577 • **Value $6.95**

(6) **Winter Fun With**
SNOOPY® (1st, 1998)
Handcrafted • LARS
695QXM4243 • **Value $15**

(7) NEW! **Winter Fun With**
SNOOPY® (2nd, 1999)
Handcrafted • LARS
695QXM4559 • **Value $6.95**

(8) NEW! **Dorothy's Ruby**
Slippers (1st, 1999)
Handcrafted • KLIN
595QXM4599 • **Value $5.95**

(9) **Woodland Babies**
(1st, 1991)
Handcrafted • CROW
600QXM5667 • **Value $24**

(10) **Woodland Babies**
(2nd, 1992)
Handcrafted • PALM
600QXM5444 • **Value $17**

(11) **Woodland Babies**
(3rd & final, 1993)
Handcrafted • FRAN
575QXM5102 • **Value $16**

THIMBLE BELLS	Price Paid	Value of My Collection
1.		
2.		
WELCOME FRIENDS		
3.		
4.		
5.		
WINTER FUN WITH SNOOPY®		
6.		
7.		
WONDERS OF OZ™		
8.		
WOODLAND BABIES		
9.		
10.		
11.		
PENCIL TOTALS		

1999

With 213 pieces being added to the Keepsake collection in 1999, there is sure to be an ornament for everyone! Two new lines join the Hallmark Keepsake family this year: Laser Creations, a series of ornaments cut by laser light; and Legends of Flight, a group of die-cast model airplanes. See the collectible series section for more 1999 ornaments.

(1)
1949 Cadillac® Coupe deVille
Die-Cast Metal• WILL
1495QX6429 • **Value $14.95**

(2)
40th Anniversary BARBIE® Ornament
Handcrafted • ANDR
1595QXI8049 • **Value $15.95**

(3)
Adding the Best Part
Handcrafted • CROW
795QX6569 • **Value $7.95**

(4)
PHOTO UNAVAILABLE
African-American Millennium Princess BARBIE® Ornament
Handcrafted • RGRS
1595QXI6449 • **Value $15.95**

(5)
All Sooted Up
Handcrafted • KLIN
995QX6837 • **Value $9.95**

(6)
Angel in Disguise
Handcrafted • AUBE
895QX6629 • **Value $8.95**

(7)
Angel of Hope
Porcelain • ANDR
1495QXI6339 • **Value $14.95**

(8)
Angel Song
Handcrafted • VOTR
1895QX6939 • **Value $18.95**

(9)
Baby Mickey's Sweet Dreams
Handcrafted • N/A
1095QXD4087 • **Value $10.95**

(10)
Baby's First Christmas
Handcrafted • HADD
795QX6649 • **Value $7.95**

(11)
Baby's First Christmas
Handcrafted • FRAN
795QX6667 • **Value $7.95**

(12)
Baby's First Christmas
Handcrafted • VOTR
895QX6657 • **Value $8.95**

(13)
Baby's First Christmas
Porcelain • TAGU
995QX6659 • **Value $9.95**

(14)
Baby's First Christmas
Handcrafted • ANDR
1895QX6647 • **Value $18.95**

(15)
Baby's Second Christmas
Handcrafted • FRAN
795QX6669 • **Value $7.95**

(16)
Balthasar – The Magi (to be re-issued in 2000)
Porcelain • LYLE
1295QX6819 • **Value $12.95**

(17)
BARBIE® Doll Dreamhouse™ Playhouse Ornament
Handcrafted • ANDR
1495QXI8047 • **Value $14.95**

General Keepsake		
	Price Paid	Value of My Collection
1.		
2.		
3.		
4.		
5.		
6.		
7.		
8.		
9.		
10.		
11.		
12.		
13.		
14.		
15.		
16.		
17.		
PENCIL TOTALS		

1. Best Pals
Handcrafted • AUBE
1895QX6879 • **Value $18.95**

2. Bowling's a Ball
Handcrafted • KLIN
795QX6577 • **Value $7.95**

3. Caspar – The Magi
(to be re-issued in 2000)
Porcelain • LYLE
1295QX8039 • **Value $12.95**

4. Chewbacca™
Handcrafted • RHOD
1495QXI4009 • **Value $14.95**

5. Child of Wonder
Handcrafted • UNRU
1495QX6817 • **Value $14.95**

6. Child's Fifth Christmas
Handcrafted • CROW
795QX6679 • **Value $7.95**

7. Child's Fourth Christmas
Handcrafted • CROW
795QX6687 • **Value $7.95**

8. Child's Third Christmas
Handcrafted • CROW
795QX6677 • **Value $7.95**

9. The Christmas Story
Handcrafted • UNRU
2200QX6897 • **Value $22**

10. Clownin' Around
CRAYOLA® Crayon
Handcrafted • TAGU
1095QX6487 • **Value $10.95**

11. Cocoa Break
HERSHEY's™
Handcrafted • KLIN
1095QX8009 • **Value $10.95**

12. Counting On Success
Handcrafted • PIKE
795QX6707 • **Value $7.95**

13. Cross of Hope
Pewter/Lead Crystal • UNRU
995QX6557 • **Value $9.95**

14. Dad
Pressed Tin • BRIC
895QX6719 • **Value $8.95**

15. Dance for the Season
Handcrafted • ESCH
995QX6587 • **Value $9.95**

16. Daughter
Handcrafted • ESCH
895QX6729 • **Value $8.95**

17. Dorothy and Glinda, the Good Witch™
Handcrafted • LYLE
2400QX6509 • **Value $24**

18. Dumbo's First Flight
Handcrafted • N/A
1395QXD4117 • **Value $13.95**

19. Episode I: Figural
PHOTO UNAVAILABLE
Handcrafted • RHOD
1495QXI4187 • **Value $14.95**

20. Episode I: Ship
PHOTO UNAVAILABLE
Handcrafted • WEBB
1895QXI7613 • **Value $18.95**

1999

General Keepsake

	Price Paid	Value of My Collection
1.		
2.		
3.		
4.		
5.		
6.		
7.		
8.		
9.		
10.		
11.		
12.		
13.		
14.		
15.		
16.		
17.		
18.		
19.		
20.		
PENCIL TOTALS		

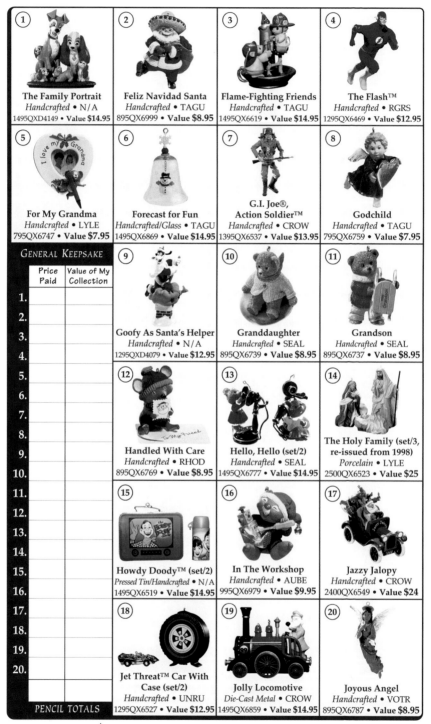

1. The Family Portrait
Handcrafted • N/A
1495QXD4149 • **Value $14.95**

2. Feliz Navidad Santa
Handcrafted • TAGU
895QX6999 • **Value $8.95**

3. Flame-Fighting Friends
Handcrafted • TAGU
1495QX6619 • **Value $14.95**

4. The Flash™
Handcrafted • RGRS
1295QX6469 • **Value $12.95**

5. For My Grandma
Handcrafted • LYLE
795QX6747 • **Value $7.95**

6. Forecast for Fun
Handcrafted/Glass • TAGU
1495QX6869 • **Value $14.95**

7. G.I. Joe®,
Action Soldier™
Handcrafted • CROW
1395QX6537 • **Value $13.95**

8. Godchild
Handcrafted • TAGU
795QX6759 • **Value $7.95**

9. Goofy As Santa's Helper
Handcrafted • N/A
1295QXD4079 • **Value $12.95**

10. Granddaughter
Handcrafted • SEAL
895QX6739 • **Value $8.95**

11. Grandson
Handcrafted • SEAL
895QX6737 • **Value $8.95**

12. Handled With Care
Handcrafted • RHOD
895QX6769 • **Value $8.95**

13. Hello, Hello (set/2)
Handcrafted • SEAL
1495QX6777 • **Value $14.95**

14. The Holy Family (set/3,
re-issued from 1998)
Porcelain • LYLE
2500QX6523 • **Value $25**

15. Howdy Doody™ (set/2)
Pressed Tin/Handcrafted • N/A
1495QX6519 • **Value $14.95**

16. In The Workshop
Handcrafted • AUBE
995QX6979 • **Value $9.95**

17. Jazzy Jalopy
Handcrafted • CROW
2400QX6549 • **Value $24**

18. Jet Threat™ Car With
Case (set/2)
Handcrafted • UNRU
1295QX6527 • **Value $12.95**

19. Jolly Locomotive
Die-Cast Metal • CROW
1495QX6859 • **Value $14.95**

20. Joyous Angel
Handcrafted • VOTR
895QX6787 • **Value $8.95**

GENERAL KEEPSAKE

	Price Paid	Value of My Collection
1.		
2.		
3.		
4.		
5.		
6.		
7.		
8.		
9.		
10.		
11.		
12.		
13.		
14.		
15.		
16.		
17.		
18.		
19.		
20.		
PENCIL TOTALS		

(1) **A Joyous Christmas** *Glass* • N/A 595QX6827 • **Value $5.95**	**(2)** **King Malh – Third King** *Handcrafted* • ANDR 1395QX6797 • **Value $13.95**	**(3)** **Kringle's Whirligig** *Handcrafted* • CROW 1295QX6847 • **Value $12.95**	**(4)** **Larry, Moe, and Curly (set/3)** *Handcrafted* • LARS 3000QX6499 • **Value $30**
(5) **Lieutenant Commander Worf™** *Handcrafted* • RGRS 1495QXI4139 • **Value $14.95**	**(6)** **Little Cloud Keeper** *Porcelain* • HADD 1695QX6877 • **Value $16.95**	**(7)** **The Lollipop Guild™ (set/3)** *Handcrafted* • LYLE 1995QX8029 • **Value $19.95**	**(8)** **"Lucy Gets In Pictures"** *Handcrafted* • VOTR 1395QX6547 • **Value $13.95**

1999

(9) **Mary's Bears** *Handcrafted* • TAGU 1295QX5569 • **Value $12.95**	**(10)** **Melchoir – The Magi (to be re-issued in 2000)** *Porcelain* • LYLE 1295QX6819 • **Value $12.95**	**(11)** **Merry Motorcycle** *Pressed Tin* • SICK 895QX6637 • **Value $8.95**	

GENERAL KEEPSAKE

	Price Paid	Value of My Collection
1.		
2.		
3.		
4.		
5.		
6.		
7.		
8.		
9.		
10.		
11.		
12.		
13.		
14.		
15.		
16.		
17.		
18.		
19.		
20.		
PENCIL TOTALS		

(12) **Military on Parade** *Handcrafted* • CROW 1095QX6639 • **Value $10.95**	**(13)** **Milk 'n' Cookies Express** *Handcrafted* • CHAD 895QX6839 • **Value $8.95**	**(14)** PHOTO UNAVAILABLE **Millennium Princess BARBIE® Ornament** *Handcrafted* • RGRS 1595QXI4019 • **Value $15.95**
(15) **Millennium Snowman** *Handcrafted* • SEAL 895QX8059 • **Value $8.95**	**(16)** **Mom** *Pressed Tin* • BRIC 895QX6717 • **Value $8.95**	**(17)** **Mom and Dad** *Handcrafted* • SEAL 995QX6709 • **Value $9.95**
(18) **Mother and Daughter** *Precious Metal* • VOTR 895QX6757 • **Value $8.95**	**(19)** **Muhammad Ali** *Handcrafted* • UNRU 1495QXI4147 • **Value $14.95**	**(20)** **A Musician of Note** *Handcrafted* • HADD 795QX6567 • **Value $7.95**

(1) My Sister, My Friend
Handcrafted • TAGU
995QX6749 • **Value $9.95**

(2) New Home
Handcrafted • SEAL
995QX6347 • **Value $9.95**

(3) Noah's Ark
Handcrafted • ESCH
1295QX6809 • **Value $12.95**

(4) North Pole Mr. Potato Head™
Handcrafted • N/A
1095QX8027 • **Value $10.95**

(5) North Pole Star
Handcrafted • CHAD
895QX6589 • **Value $8.95**

(6) On Thin Ice
Handcrafted • PIKE
1095QX6489 • **Value $10.95**

(7) Our Christmas Together
Handcrafted • KLIN
995QX6689 • **Value $9.95**

(8) Our First Christmas Together
Acrylic • VOTR
795QX3207 • **Value $7.95**

(9) Our First Christmas Together
Handcrafted • TAGU
895QX6697 • **Value $8.95**

(10) Our First Christmas Together
Handcrafted • UNRU
2200QX6699 • **Value $22**

(11) Outstanding Teacher
Handcrafted • KLIN
895QX6627 • **Value $8.95**

(12) Pepé LePew and Penelope
Handcrafted • CHAD
1295QX6507 • **Value $12.95**

(13) Piano Player Mickey
Handcrafted • N/A
2400QXD7389 • **Value $24**

(14) Pinocchio and Geppetto
Handcrafted • N/A
1695QXD4107 • **Value $16.95**

(15) Playful Snowman
Handcrafted • SICK
1295QX6867 • **Value $12.95**

(16) The Poky Little Puppy™ (w/book)
Handcrafted • VOTR
1195QX6479 • **Value $11.95**

(17) Praise the Day
Handcrafted • TAGU
1495QX6799 • **Value $14.95**

(18) Presents From Pooh
Handcrafted • N/A
1495QXD4093 • **Value $14.95**

(19) Reel Fun
Handcrafted • TAGU
1095QX6609 • **Value $10.95**

(20) Rhett Butler™
Handcrafted • ANDR
1295QX6467 • **Value $12.95**

GENERAL KEEPSAKE

	Price Paid	Value of My Collection
1.		
2.		
3.		
4.		
5.		
6.		
7.		
8.		
9.		
10.		
11.		
12.		
13.		
14.		
15.		
16.		
17.		
18.		
19.		
20.		
PENCIL TOTALS		

Value Guide — Hallmark Keepsake Ornaments

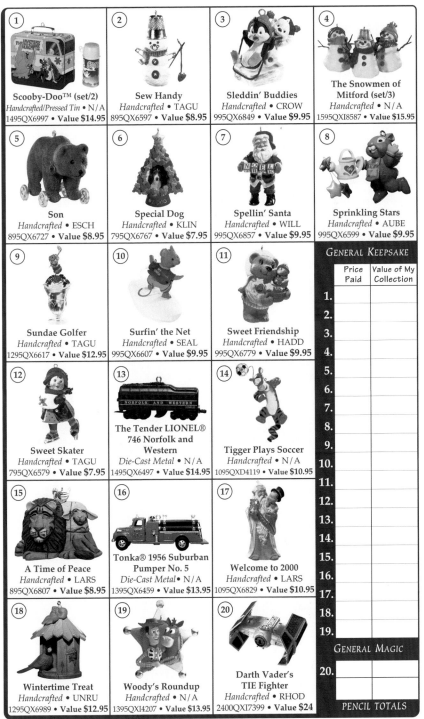

1. Scooby-Doo™ (set/2)
Handcrafted/Pressed Tin • N/A
1495QX6997 • **Value $14.95**

2. Sew Handy
Handcrafted • TAGU
895QX6597 • **Value $8.95**

3. Sleddin' Buddies
Handcrafted • CROW
995QX6849 • **Value $9.95**

4. The Snowmen of Mitford (set/3)
Handcrafted • N/A
1595QXI8587 • **Value $15.95**

5. Son
Handcrafted • ESCH
895QX6727 • **Value $8.95**

6. Special Dog
Handcrafted • KLIN
795QX6767 • **Value $7.95**

7. Spellin' Santa
Handcrafted • WILL
995QX6857 • **Value $9.95**

8. Sprinkling Stars
Handcrafted • AUBE
995QX6599 • **Value $9.95**

9. Sundae Golfer
Handcrafted • TAGU
1295QX6617 • **Value $12.95**

10. Surfin' the Net
Handcrafted • SEAL
995QX6607 • **Value $9.95**

11. Sweet Friendship
Handcrafted • HADD
995QX6779 • **Value $9.95**

12. Sweet Skater
Handcrafted • TAGU
795QX6579 • **Value $7.95**

13. The Tender LIONEL® 746 Norfolk and Western
Die-Cast Metal • N/A
1495QX6497 • **Value $14.95**

14. Tigger Plays Soccer
Handcrafted • N/A
1095QXD4119 • **Value $10.95**

15. A Time of Peace
Handcrafted • LARS
895QX6807 • **Value $8.95**

16. Tonka® 1956 Suburban Pumper No. 5
Die-Cast Metal • N/A
1395QX6459 • **Value $13.95**

17. Welcome to 2000
Handcrafted • LARS
1095QX6829 • **Value $10.95**

18. Wintertime Treat
Handcrafted • UNRU
1295QX6989 • **Value $12.95**

19. Woody's Roundup
Handcrafted • N/A
1395QXI4207 • **Value $13.95**

20. Darth Vader's TIE Fighter
Handcrafted • RHOD
2400QXI7399 • **Value $24**

	Price Paid	Value of My Collection
General Keepsake		
1.		
2.		
3.		
4.		
5.		
6.		
7.		
8.		
9.		
10.		
11.		
12.		
13.		
14.		
15.		
16.		
17.		
18.		
19.		
General Magic		
20.		
Pencil Totals		

1999

1
Let It Snow!
Porcelain • LARS
1895QLX7427 • **Value $18.95**

2
Runabout – U.S.S. Rio Grande
Handcrafted • NORT
2400QXI7593 • **Value $24**

3
Warm Welcome
Handcrafted • HADD
1695QLX7417 • **Value $16.95**

4
1950 LIONEL® Santa Fe F3 Diesel Locomotive
Blown Glass • N/A
3500QBG6119 • **Value $35**

5
1955 Murray® Ranch Wagon
Blown Glass • N/A
3500QBG6077 • **Value $35**

6
Childhood Treasures (set/3)
Blown Glass • N/A
3000QBG4237 • **Value $30**

7
Frankincense (re-issued from 1998)
Blown Glass • N/A
2200QBG6896 • **Value $22**

8
Frosty Friends
Blown Glass • N/A
3500QBG6067 • **Value $35**

9
Gold (re-issued from 1998)
Blown Glass • N/A
2200QBG6836 • **Value $22**

10
Harvest of Grapes
Blown Glass • N/A
2500QBG6047 • **Value $25**

11
The Holy Family
Blown Glass • N/A
3000QBG6127 • **Value $30**

12
Jolly Snowman
Blown Glass • N/A
2000QBG6059 • **Value $20**

13
Myrrh (re-issued from 1998)
Blown Glass • N/A
2200QBG6893 • **Value $22**

14
U.S.S. Enterprise™ NCC-1701
Blown Glass • N/A
2500QBG6117 • **Value $25**

15
Village Church
Blown Glass • N/A
3000QBG6057 • **Value $30**

16
Yummy Memories (set/8)
Blown Glass • N/A
4500QBG6049 • **Value $45**

17
Angelic Messenger
Archival Paper • N/A
795QLZ4287 • **Value $7.95**

18
Christmas In Bloom
Archival Paper • N/A
895QLZ4257 • **Value $8.95**

19
Don't Open Till 2000
Archival Paper • N/A
895QLZ4289 • **Value $8.95**

20
Inside Santa's Workshop
Archival Paper • N/A
895QLZ4239 • **Value $8.95**

	Price Paid	Value of My Collection
General Magic		
1.		
2.		
3.		
General Crown Reflections		
4.		
5.		
6.		
7.		
8.		
9.		
10.		
11.		
12.		
13.		
14.		
15.		
16.		
General Laser Creations		
17.		
18.		
19.		
20.		
Pencil Totals		

VALUE GUIDE — HALLMARK KEEPSAKE ORNAMENTS

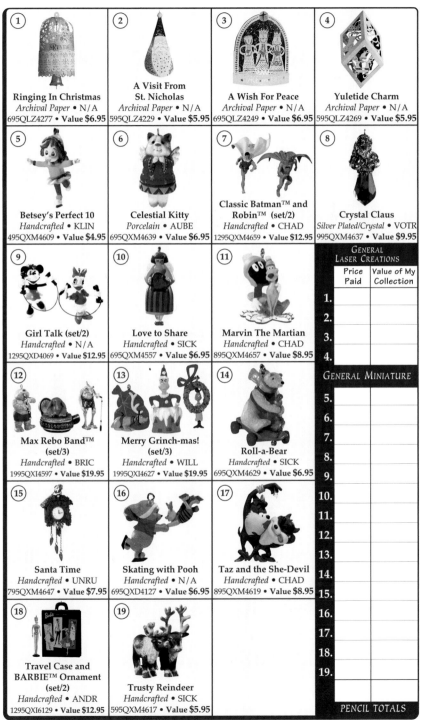

(1) Ringing In Christmas
Archival Paper • N/A
695QLZ4277 • **Value $6.95**

(2) A Visit From St. Nicholas
Archival Paper • N/A
595QLZ4229 • **Value $5.95**

(3) A Wish For Peace
Archival Paper • N/A
695QLZ4249 • **Value $6.95**

(4) Yuletide Charm
Archival Paper • N/A
595QLZ4269 • **Value $5.95**

(5) Betsey's Perfect 10
Handcrafted • KLIN
495QXM4609 • **Value $4.95**

(6) Celestial Kitty
Porcelain • AUBE
695QXM4639 • **Value $6.95**

(7) Classic Batman™ and Robin™ (set/2)
Handcrafted • CHAD
1295QXM4659 • **Value $12.95**

(8) Crystal Claus
Silver Plated/Crystal • VOTR
995QXM4637 • **Value $9.95**

(9) Girl Talk (set/2)
Handcrafted • N/A
1295QXD4069 • **Value $12.95**

(10) Love to Share
Handcrafted • SICK
695QXM4557 • **Value $6.95**

(11) Marvin The Martian
Handcrafted • CHAD
895QXM4657 • **Value $8.95**

(12) Max Rebo Band™ (set/3)
Handcrafted • BRIC
1995QXI4597 • **Value $19.95**

(13) Merry Grinch-mas! (set/3)
Handcrafted • WILL
1995QXI4627 • **Value $19.95**

(14) Roll-a-Bear
Handcrafted • SICK
695QXM4629 • **Value $6.95**

(15) Santa Time
Handcrafted • UNRU
795QXM4647 • **Value $7.95**

(16) Skating with Pooh
Handcrafted • N/A
695QXD4127 • **Value $6.95**

(17) Taz and the She-Devil
Handcrafted • CHAD
895QXM4619 • **Value $8.95**

(18) Travel Case and BARBIE™ Ornament (set/2)
Handcrafted • ANDR
1295QXI6129 • **Value $12.95**

(19) Trusty Reindeer
Handcrafted • SICK
595QXM4617 • **Value $5.95**

1999

GENERAL LASER CREATIONS	Price Paid	Value of My Collection
1.		
2.		
3.		
4.		

GENERAL MINIATURE		
5.		
6.		
7.		
8.		
9.		
10.		
11.		
12.		
13.		
14.		
15.		
16.		
17.		
18.		
19.		
PENCIL TOTALS		

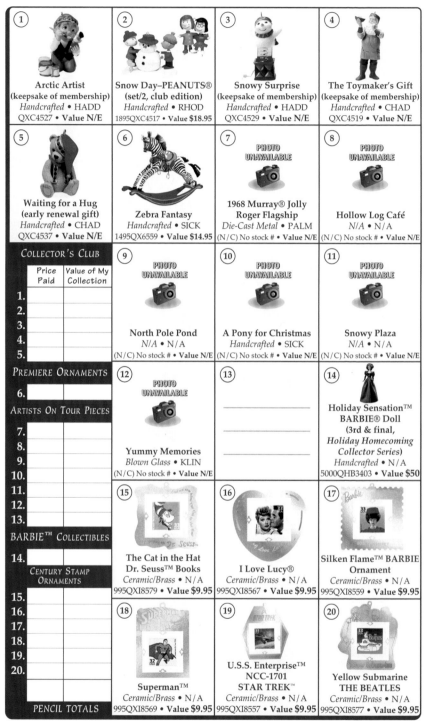

① Arctic Artist
(keepsake of membership)
Handcrafted • HADD
QXC4527 • **Value N/E**

② Snow Day–PEANUTS®
(set/2, club edition)
Handcrafted • RHOD
1895QXC4517 • **Value $18.95**

③ Snowy Surprise
(keepsake of membership)
Handcrafted • HADD
QXC4529 • **Value N/E**

④ The Toymaker's Gift
(keepsake of membership)
Handcrafted • CHAD
QXC4519 • **Value N/E**

⑤ Waiting for a Hug
(early renewal gift)
Handcrafted • CHAD
QXC4537 • **Value N/E**

⑥ Zebra Fantasy
Handcrafted • SICK
1495QX6559 • **Value $14.95**

**⑦ 1968 Murray® Jolly
Roger Flagship**
Die-Cast Metal • PALM
(N/C) No stock # • **Value N/E**

⑧ Hollow Log Café
N/A • N/A
(N/C) No stock # • **Value N/E**

⑨ North Pole Pond
N/A • N/A
(N/C) No stock # • **Value N/E**

⑩ A Pony for Christmas
Handcrafted • SICK
(N/C) No stock # • **Value N/E**

⑪ Snowy Plaza
N/A • N/A
(N/C) No stock # • **Value N/E**

⑫ Yummy Memories
Blown Glass • KLIN
(N/C) No stock # • **Value N/E**

⑬

**⑭ Holiday Sensation™
BARBIE® Doll
(3rd & final,
*Holiday Homecoming
Collector Series*)**
Handcrafted • N/A
5000QHB3403 • **Value $50**

**⑮ The Cat in the Hat
Dr. Seuss™ Books**
Ceramic/Brass • N/A
995QXI8579 • **Value $9.95**

⑯ I Love Lucy®
Ceramic/Brass • N/A
995QXI8567 • **Value $9.95**

**⑰ Silken Flame™ BARBIE
Ornament**
Ceramic/Brass • N/A
995QXI8559 • **Value $9.95**

⑱ Superman™
Ceramic/Brass • N/A
995QXI8569 • **Value $9.95**

**⑲ U.S.S. Enterprise™
NCC-1701
STAR TREK™**
Ceramic/Brass • N/A
995QXI8557 • **Value $9.95**

**⑳ Yellow Submarine
THE BEATLES**
Ceramic/Brass • N/A
995QXI8577 • **Value $9.95**

COLLECTOR'S CLUB

	Price Paid	Value of My Collection
1.		
2.		
3.		
4.		
5.		

PREMIERE ORNAMENTS

6.		

ARTISTS ON TOUR PIECES

7.		
8.		
9.		
10.		
11.		
12.		
13.		

BARBIE™ COLLECTIBLES

14.		

CENTURY STAMP ORNAMENTS

15.		
16.		
17.		
18.		
19.		
20.		

PENCIL TOTALS

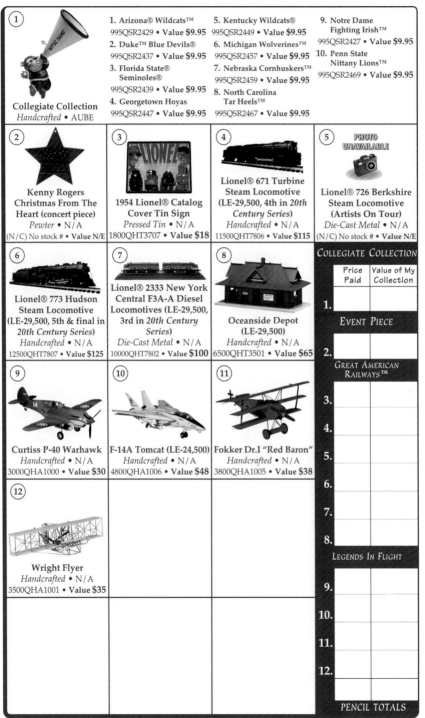

(1) Collegiate Collection
Handcrafted • AUBE

1. Arizona® Wildcats™
995QSR2429 • **Value $9.95**
2. Duke™ Blue Devils®
995QSR2437 • **Value $9.95**
3. Florida State®
Seminoles®
995QSR2439 • **Value $9.95**
4. Georgetown Hoyas
995QSR2447 • **Value $9.95**

5. Kentucky Wildcats®
995QSR2449 • **Value $9.95**
6. Michigan Wolverines™
995QSR2457 • **Value $9.95**
7. Nebraska Cornhuskers™
995QSR2459 • **Value $9.95**
8. North Carolina
Tar Heels™
995QSR2467 • **Value $9.95**

9. Notre Dame
Fighting Irish™
995QSR2427 • **Value $9.95**
10. Penn State
Nittany Lions™
995QSR2469 • **Value $9.95**

(2) Kenny Rogers
Christmas From The
Heart (concert piece)
Pewter • N/A
(N/C) No stock # • **Value N/E**

(3) 1954 Lionel® Catalog
Cover Tin Sign
Pressed Tin • N/A
1800QHT3707 • **Value $18**

(4) Lionel® 671 Turbine
Steam Locomotive
(LE-29,500, 4th in *20th
Century Series*)
Handcrafted • N/A
11500QHT7806 • **Value $115**

(5) PHOTO UNAVAILABLE
Lionel® 726 Berkshire
Steam Locomotive
(Artists On Tour)
Die-Cast Metal • N/A
(N/C) No stock # • **Value N/E**

1999

(6) Lionel® 773 Hudson
Steam Locomotive
(LE-29,500, 5th & final in
20th Century Series)
Handcrafted • N/A
12500QHT7807 • **Value $125**

(7) Lionel® 2333 New York
Central F3A-A Diesel
Locomotives (LE-29,500,
3rd in *20th Century
Series*)
Die-Cast Metal • N/A
10000QHT7802 • **Value $100**

(8) Oceanside Depot
(LE-29,500)
Handcrafted • N/A
6500QHT3501 • **Value $65**

(9) Curtiss P-40 Warhawk
Handcrafted • N/A
3000QHA1000 • **Value $30**

(10) F-14A Tomcat (LE-24,500)
Handcrafted • N/A
4800QHA1006 • **Value $48**

(11) Fokker Dr.I "Red Baron"
Handcrafted • N/A
3800QHA1005 • **Value $38**

(12) Wright Flyer
Handcrafted • N/A
3500QHA1001 • **Value $35**

COLLEGIATE COLLECTION		
	Price Paid	Value of My Collection
1.		
EVENT PIECE		
2.		
GREAT AMERICAN RAILWAYS™		
3.		
4.		
5.		
6.		
7.		
8.		
LEGENDS IN FLIGHT		
9.		
10.		
11.		
12.		
PENCIL TOTALS		

Value Guide — Hallmark Keepsake Ornaments

NBA Collection (10 assorted)
Handcrafted • KLIN

1. Charlotte Hornets™
1095QSR1057 • Value **$10.95**
2. Chicago Bulls™
1095QSR1019 • Value **$10.95**
3. Detroit Pistons™
1095QSR1027 • Value **$10.95**
4. Houston Rockets™
1095QSR1029 • Value **$10.95**
5. Indiana Pacers™
1095QSR1037 • Value **$10.95**
6. Los Angeles Lakers™
1095QSR1039 • Value **$10.95**
7. New York Knicks™
1095QSR1047 • Value **$10.95**
8. Orlando Magic™
1095QSR1059 • Value **$10.95**
9. Seattle SuperSonics™
1095QSR1067 • Value **$10.95**
10. Utah Jazz™
1095QSR1069 • Value **$10.95**

NFL Collection (15 assorted)
Handcrafted • HADD

1. Carolina Panthers™
1095QSR5217 • Value **$10.95**
2. Chicago Bears™
1095QSR5219 • Value **$10.95**
3. Dallas Cowboys™
1095QSR5227 • Value **$10.95**
4. Denver Broncos™
1095QSR5229 • Value **$10.95**
5. Green Bay Packers™
1095QSR5237 • Value **$10.95**
6. Kansas City Chiefs™
1095QSR5197 • Value **$10.95**
7. Miami Dolphins™
1095QSR5239 • Value **$10.95**
8. Minnesota Vikings™
1095QSR5247 • Value **$10.95**
9. New England Patriots™
1095QSR5279 • Value **$10.95**
10. New York Giants™
1095QSR5249 • Value **$10.95**
11. Oakland Raiders™
1095QSR5257 • Value **$10.95**
12. Philadelphia Eagles™
1095QSR5259 • Value **$10.95**
13. Pittsburgh Steelers™
1095QSR5267 • Value **$10.95**
14. San Francisco 49ers™
1095QSR5269 • Value **$10.95**
15. Washington Redskins™
1095QSR5277 • Value **$10.95**

1950s Donald Duck
Pressed Tin • N/A
1095QHM8806 • Value **$10.95**

1960s Mickey's School Days
Pressed Tin • N/A
1095QHM8804 • Value **$10.95**

1960s Star Trek™
Pressed Tin • N/A
1095QHM8810 • Value **$10.95**

1962 Barbie™
Pressed Tin • N/A
1095QHM8807 • Value **$10.95**

1970s Snow White
Pressed Tin • N/A
1095QHM8814 • Value **$10.95**

1973 Super Friends™
Pressed Tin • N/A
1095QHM8815 • Value **$10.95**

1977 Star Wars™
Pressed Tin • N/A
1095QHM8817 • Value **$10.95**

1980 Peanuts®
Pressed Tin • N/A
1095QHM8812 • Value **$10.95**

A Charlie Brown Christmas
Pressed Tin • N/A
N/A • Value **$10.95**

Looney Tunes Rodeo
Pressed Tin • N/A
1095QHM8805 • Value **$10.95**

Scooby-Doo™
Pressed Tin • N/A
1095QHM8818 • Value **$10.95**

	Price Paid	Value of My Collection
NBA Collection		
1.		
NFL Collection		
2.		
School Days Lunch Boxes		
3.		
4.		
5.		
6.		
7.		
8.		
9.		
10.		
11.		
12.		
13.		
PENCIL TOTALS		

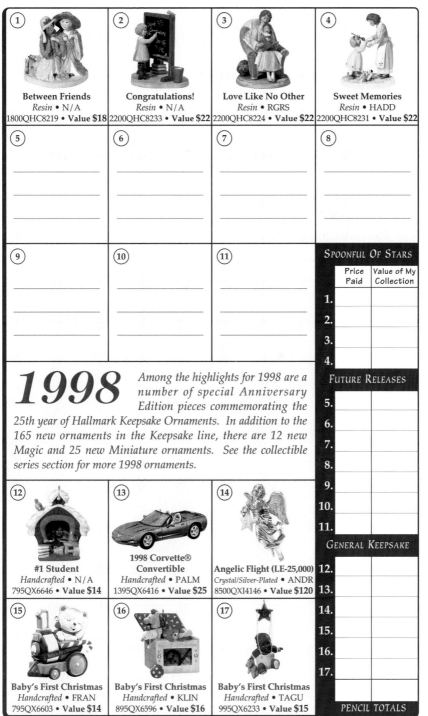

(1)
Between Friends
Resin • N/A
1800QHC8219 • **Value $18**

(2)
Congratulations!
Resin • N/A
2200QHC8233 • **Value $22**

(3)
Love Like No Other
Resin • RGRS
2200QHC8224 • **Value $22**

(4)
Sweet Memories
Resin • HADD
2200QHC8231 • **Value $22**

(5)

(6)

(7)

(8)

(9)

(10)

(11)

1998

Among the highlights for 1998 are a number of special Anniversary Edition pieces commemorating the 25th year of Hallmark Keepsake Ornaments. In addition to the 165 new ornaments in the Keepsake line, there are 12 new Magic and 25 new Miniature ornaments. See the collectible series section for more 1998 ornaments.

(12)
#1 Student
Handcrafted • N/A
795QX6646 • **Value $14**

(13)
**1998 Corvette®
Convertible**
Handcrafted • PALM
1395QX6416 • **Value $25**

(14)
Angelic Flight (LE-25,000)
Crystal/Silver-Plated • ANDR
8500QXI4146 • **Value $120**

(15)
Baby's First Christmas
Handcrafted • FRAN
795QX6603 • **Value $14**

(16)
Baby's First Christmas
Handcrafted • KLIN
895QX6596 • **Value $16**

(17)
Baby's First Christmas
Handcrafted • TAGU
995QX6233 • **Value $15**

Spoonful Of Stars

	Price Paid	Value of My Collection
1.		
2.		
3.		
4.		

Future Releases

5.		
6.		
7.		
8.		
9.		
10.		
11.		

General Keepsake

12.		
13.		
14.		
15.		
16.		
17.		

Pencil Totals

1998

① Baby's First Christmas
Handcrafted • ESCH
995QX6586 • **Value $15**

② Baby's Second Christmas
Handcrafted • CROW
795QX6606 • **Value $15**

③ Boba Fett™
Handcrafted • RHOD
1495QXI4053 • **Value $27**

④ Bouncy Baby-sitter
Handcrafted • SIED
1295QXD4096 • **Value $22**

⑤ Bugs Bunny
Handcrafted • CHAD
1395QX6443 • **Value $22**

⑥ Building a Snowman
Handcrafted • SIED
1495QXD4133 • **Value $26**

⑦ Buzz Lightyear
Handcrafted • CROW
1495QXD4066 • **Value $28**

⑧ Captain Kathryn Janeway™
Handcrafted • RGRS
1495QXI4046 • **Value $28**

⑨ Catch of the Season
Handcrafted • SEAL
1495QX6786 • **Value $22**

⑩ Chatty Chipmunk
Handcrafted • CROW
995QX6716 • **Value $16**

⑪ Checking Santa's Files
Handcrafted • TAGU
895QX6806 • **Value $15**

⑫ A Child Is Born
Handcrafted • VOTR
1295QX6176 • **Value $18**

⑬ Child's Fifth Christmas
Handcrafted • CROW
795QX6623 • **Value $13**

⑭ Child's Fourth Christmas
Handcrafted • CROW
795QX6616 • **Value $13**

⑮ Child's Third Christmas
Handcrafted • CROW
795QX6613 • **Value $14**

⑯ A Christmas Eve Story Becky Kelly
Handcrafted • TAGU
1395QXD6873 • **Value $22**

⑰ Christmas Request
Handcrafted • FRAN
1495QX6193 • **Value $23**

⑱ Christmas Sleigh Ride
Die-Cast Metal • CROW
1295QX6556 • **Value $23**

⑲ Cinderella's Coach
Handcrafted • WILL
1495QXD4083 • **Value $21**

⑳ Compact Skater
Handcrafted • TAGU
995QX6766 • **Value $16**

General Keepsake	Price Paid	Value of My Collection
1.		
2.		
3.		
4.		
5.		
6.		
7.		
8.		
9.		
10.		
11.		
12.		
13.		
14.		
15.		
16.		
17.		
18.		
19.		
20.		
PENCIL TOTALS		

1

Country Home
Marjolein Bastin
Handcrafted • FRAN
1095QX5172 • **Value $20**

2

Cross of Peace
Metal • KLIN
995QX6856 • **Value $16**

3

Cruising into Christmas
Handcrafted/Tin • CROW
1695QX6196 • **Value $28**

4

Dad
Handcrafted • KLIN
895QX6663 • **Value $16**

5

Daughter
Handcrafted • AUBE
895QX6673 • **Value $15**

6

Daydreams
Handcrafted • BRIC
1395QXD4136 • **Value $22**

7

Decorating
Maxine-Style
Handcrafted • N/A
1095QXE6883 • **Value $19**

8

Downhill Dash
Handcrafted • CROW
1395QX6776 • **Value $20**

9

Fancy Footwork
Handcrafted • VOTR
895QX6536 • **Value $16**

10

Feliz Navidad
Handcrafted • CHAD
895QX6173 • **Value $17**

11

Flik
Handcrafted • N/A
1295QXD4153 • **Value $25**

12

Forever Friends Bear
Handcrafted • PIKE
895QX6303 • **Value $15**

13

Friend of My Heart
(set/2)
Handcrafted • SEAL
1495QX6723 • **Value $21**

14

Future Ballerina
Handcrafted • TAGU
795QX6756 • **Value $13**

15

Gifted Gardener
Handcrafted • CHAD
795QX6736 • **Value $13**

16

Godchild
Handcrafted • CHAD
795QX6703 • **Value $13**

17

Good Luck Dice
Handcrafted • HADD
995QX6813 • **Value $14**

18

Goofy Soccer Star
Handcrafted • CHAD
1095QXD4123 • **Value $18**

19

Granddaughter
Handcrafted • FRAN
795QX6683 • **Value $14**

20

Grandma's Memories
Handcrafted • KLIN
895QX6686 • **Value $15**

1998

GENERAL KEEPSAKE		
	Price Paid	Value of My Collection
1.		
2.		
3.		
4.		
5.		
6.		
7.		
8.		
9.		
10.		
11.		
12.		
13.		
14.		
15.		
16.		
17.		
18.		
19.		
20.		
PENCIL TOTALS		

(1)
Grandson
Handcrafted • FRAN
795QX6676 • **Value $14**

(2)
The Grinch
Handcrafted • CHAD
1395QXI6466 • **Value $48**

(3)
Guardian Friend
Handcrafted • LYLE
895QX6543 • **Value $17**

(4)
Heavenly Melody
Handcrafted • VOTR
1895QX6576 • **Value $29**

(5)
Holiday Camper
Handcrafted • SEAL
1295QX6783 • **Value $19**

(6)
Holiday Decorator
Handcrafted • WILL
1395QX6566 • **Value $20**

(7)
The Holy Family
(re-issued in 1999, set/3)
Porcelain • LYLE
2500QX6523 • **Value $46**

(8)
Hot Wheels™
Handcrafted • CROW
1395QX6436 • **Value $22**

(9)
Iago, Abu and the Genie
Handcrafted • WILL
1295QXD4076 • **Value $20**

(10)
Joe Montana
Notre Dame
Handcrafted • UNRU
1495QXI6843 • **Value $22**

(11)
Journey To Bethlehem
Handcrafted • UNRU
1695QX6223 • **Value $28**

(12)
Joyful Messenger
Handcrafted/Silver-Plated • LYLE
1895QXI6733 • **Value $27**

(13)
King Kharoof–
Second King
Handcrafted • ANDR
1295QX6186 • **Value $25**

(14)
Larry, Moe, and Curly
The Three Stooges™
(set/3)
Handcrafted • LARS
2700QX6503 • **Value $45**

(15)
Madonna and Child
Handcrafted • RGRS
1295QX6516 • **Value $22**

(16)
Make-Believe Boat
Handcrafted • ESCH
1295QXD4113 • **Value $22**

(17)
Maxine
Handcrafted • PIKE
995QX6446 • **Value $17**

(18)
Memories of Christmas
Glass • LARS
595QX2406 • **Value $10**

(19)
Merry Chime
Handcrafted/Brass • CROW
995QX6692 • **Value $17**

(20)
The Mickey and
Minnie Handcar
Handcrafted • WILL
1495QXD4116 • **Value $23**

GENERAL KEEPSAKE	Price Paid	Value of My Collection
1.		
2.		
3.		
4.		
5.		
6.		
7.		
8.		
9.		
10.		
11.		
12.		
13.		
14.		
15.		
16.		
17.		
18.		
19.		
20.		
PENCIL TOTALS		

1	2	3	4
Mickey's Favorite Reindeer	**Miracle in Bethlehem**	**Mistletoe Fairy**	**Mom**
Handcrafted • LARS	*Handcrafted* • SEAL	*Handcrafted* • ESCH	*Handcrafted* • KLIN
1395QXD4013 • **Value $20**	1295QX6513 • **Value $22**	1295QX6216 • **Value $20**	895QX6656 • **Value $14**

5	6	7	8
Mom and Dad	**Mother and Daughter**	**Mrs. Potato Head®**	**Mulan, Mushu and Cri-Kee (set/2)**
Handcrafted • KLIN	*Porcelain* • VOTR	*Handcrafted* • N/A	*Handcrafted* • N/A
995QX6653 • **Value $15**	895QX6696 • **Value $14**	1095QX6886 • **Value $20**	1495QXD4156 • **Value $24**

1998

9	10	11	GENERAL KEEPSAKE
Munchkinland™ Mayor and Coroner (set/2)	**National Salute**	**New Arrival**	
Handcrafted • LYLE	*Handcrafted* • RHOD	*Porcelain* • VOTR	
1395QX6463 • **Value $27**	895QX6293 • **Value $15**	1895QX6306 • **Value $27**	

	Price Paid	Value of My Collection
1.		
2.		
3.		
4.		
5.		
6.		
7.		
8.		
9.		
10.		
11.		
12.		
13.		
14.		
15.		
16.		
17.		
18.		
19.		
20.		
PENCIL TOTALS		

12	13	14
New Home	**Nick's Wish List**	**Night Watch**
Handcrafted • SEAL	*Handcrafted* • ANDR	*Handcrafted* • SIED
995QX6713 • **Value $15**	895QX6863 • **Value $16**	995QX6725 • **Value $18**

15	16	17
North Pole Reserve	**Our First Christmas Together**	**Our First Christmas Together**
Handcrafted • SEAL	*Acrylic* • VOTR	*Brass/Porcelain* • VOTR
1095QX6803 • **Value $20**	795QX3193 • **Value $13**	1895QX6643 • **Value $14**

18	19	20
Our First Christmas Together	**OUR SONG**	**Peekaboo Bears**
Handcrafted • TAGU	*Ceramic* • N/A	*Handcrafted* • CROW
895QX6636 • **Value $25**	995QX6183 • **Value $16**	1295QX6563 • **Value $23**

1 A Perfect Match
Handcrafted • RHOD
1095QX6633 • **Value $17**

2 Polar Bowler
Handcrafted • ESCH
795QX6746 • **Value $15**

3 Princess Aurora (set/2)
Handcrafted • BRIC
1295QXD4126 • **Value $25**

4 Purr-fect Little Deer
Handcrafted • PIKE
795QX6526 • **Value $13**

5 Puttin' Around
Handcrafted • RHOD
895QX6763 • **Value $14**

6 Rocket to Success
Handcrafted • PIKE
895QX6793 • **Value $14**

7 Runaway Toboggan (set/2)
Handcrafted • N/A
1695QXD4003 • **Value $26**

8 Santa's Deer Friend
Handcrafted • CHAD
2400QX6583 • **Value $33**

9 Santa's Flying Machine
Handcrafted/Tin • SEAL
1695QX6573 • **Value $25**

10 Santa's Hidden Surprise
Ceramic • N/A
1495QX6913 • **Value $23**

11 "Sew" Gifted
Handcrafted • TAGU
795QX6743 • **Value $14**

12 Simba & Nala
Handcrafted • N/A
1395QXD4073 • **Value $24**

13 Sister to Sister
Handcrafted • PIKE
895QX6693 • **Value $15**

14 Soaring With Angels
Handcrafted • SICK
1695QX6213 • **Value $28**

15 Son
Handcrafted • AUBE
895QX6666 • **Value $15**

16 Special Dog
Handcrafted • N/A
795QX6706 • **Value $13**

17 Spoonful of Love
Handcrafted • TAGU
895QX6796 • **Value $14**

18 Superman™
Pressed Tin • N/A
1295QX6423 • **Value $20**

19 Surprise Catch
Handcrafted • FRAN
795QX6753 • **Value $14**

20 Sweet Rememberings
Handcrafted • TAGU
895QX6876 • **Value $16**

General Keepsake

	Price Paid	Value of My Collection
1.		
2.		
3.		
4.		
5.		
6.		
7.		
8.		
9.		
10.		
11.		
12.		
13.		
14.		
15.		
16.		
17.		
18.		
19.		
20.		
PENCIL TOTALS		

VALUE GUIDE — HALLMARK KEEPSAKE ORNAMENTS

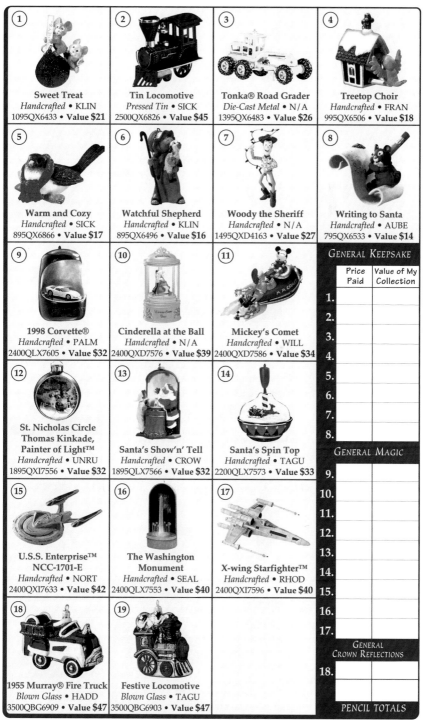

1
Sweet Treat
Handcrafted • KLIN
1095QX6433 • **Value $21**

2
Tin Locomotive
Pressed Tin • SICK
2500QX6826 • **Value $45**

3
Tonka® Road Grader
Die-Cast Metal • N/A
1395QX6483 • **Value $26**

4
Treetop Choir
Handcrafted • FRAN
995QX6506 • **Value $18**

5
Warm and Cozy
Handcrafted • SICK
895QX6866 • **Value $17**

6
Watchful Shepherd
Handcrafted • KLIN
895QX6496 • **Value $16**

7
Woody the Sheriff
Handcrafted • N/A
1495QXD4163 • **Value $27**

8
Writing to Santa
Handcrafted • AUBE
795QX6533 • **Value $14**

9
1998 Corvette®
Handcrafted • PALM
2400QLX7605 • **Value $32**

10
Cinderella at the Ball
Handcrafted • N/A
2400QXD7576 • **Value $39**

11
Mickey's Comet
Handcrafted • WILL
2400QXD7586 • **Value $34**

12
**St. Nicholas Circle
Thomas Kinkade,
Painter of Light™**
Handcrafted • UNRU
1895QXI7556 • **Value $32**

13
Santa's Show'n' Tell
Handcrafted • CROW
1895QLX7566 • **Value $32**

14
Santa's Spin Top
Handcrafted • TAGU
2200QLX7573 • **Value $33**

15
**U.S.S. Enterprise™
NCC-1701-E**
Handcrafted • NORT
2400QXI7633 • **Value $42**

16
**The Washington
Monument**
Handcrafted • SEAL
2400QLX7553 • **Value $40**

17
X-wing Starfighter™
Handcrafted • RHOD
2400QXI7596 • **Value $40**

18
1955 Murray® Fire Truck
Blown Glass • HADD
3500QBG6909 • **Value $47**

19
Festive Locomotive
Blown Glass • TAGU
3500QBG6903 • **Value $47**

1998

GENERAL KEEPSAKE

	Price Paid	Value of My Collection
1.		
2.		
3.		
4.		
5.		
6.		
7.		
8.		

GENERAL MAGIC

9.		
10.		
11.		
12.		
13.		
14.		
15.		
16.		
17.		

GENERAL CROWN REFLECTIONS

18.		

PENCIL TOTALS

1
Frankincense
(re-issued in 1999)
Blown Glass • LARS
2200QBG6896 • **Value $22**

2
Frosty Friends (set/2)
Blown Glass • SEAL
4800QBG6907 • **Value $60**

3
Gold (re-issued in 1999)
Blown Glass • LARS
2200QBG6836 • **Value $22**

4
Myrrh
(re-issued in 1999)
Blown Glass • LARS
2200QBG6893 • **Value $22**

5
Sugarplum Cottage
Blown Glass • HADD
3500QBG6917 • **Value $47**

6
Sweet Memories (set/8)
Blown Glass • KLIN
4500QBG6933 • **Value $60**

7
Angel Chime
Die-Cast Metal • TAGU
895QXM4283 • **Value $14**

8
Betsey's Prayer
Handcrafted • KLIN
495QXM4263 • **Value $9**

GENERAL CROWN REFLECTIONS		
	Price Paid	Value of My Collection
1.		
2.		
3.		
4.		
5.		
6.		
GENERAL MINIATURE		
7.		
8.		
9.		
10.		
11.		
12.		
13.		
14.		
15.		
16.		
17.		
18.		
19.		
COLLECTOR'S CLUB		
20.		
PENCIL TOTALS		

9
"Coca-Cola" Time
Handcrafted • UNRU
695QXM4296 • **Value $12**

10
Ewoks™ (set/3)
Handcrafted • BRIC
1695QXI4223 • **Value $27**

11
Fishy Surprise
Handcrafted • ESCH
695QXM4276 • **Value $12**

12
Glinda, The Good Witch™ &
Wicked Witch of the
West™ (set/2)
Handcrafted • LYLE
1495QXM4233 • **Value $24**

13
Holly-Jolly Jig
Handcrafted • TAGU
695QXM4266 • **Value $12**

14
Peaceful Pandas
Handcrafted • SICK
595QXM4253 • **Value $12**

15
Pixie Parachute
Handcrafted • ESCH
495QXM4256 • **Value $10**

16
Sharing Joy
Handcrafted • N/A
495QXM4273 • **Value $10**

17
Singin' in the Rain™
(set/2)
Handcrafted • ANDR
1095QXM4303 • **Value $18**

18
Superman™ (set/2)
Handcrafted • CHAD
1095QXM4313 • **Value $17**

19
Tree Trimmin' Time
(set/3)
Handcrafted • N/A
1995QXD4236 • **Value $29**

20
Follow the Leader
(club edition, set/2)
Handcrafted • SIED
1695QXC4503 • **Value $34**

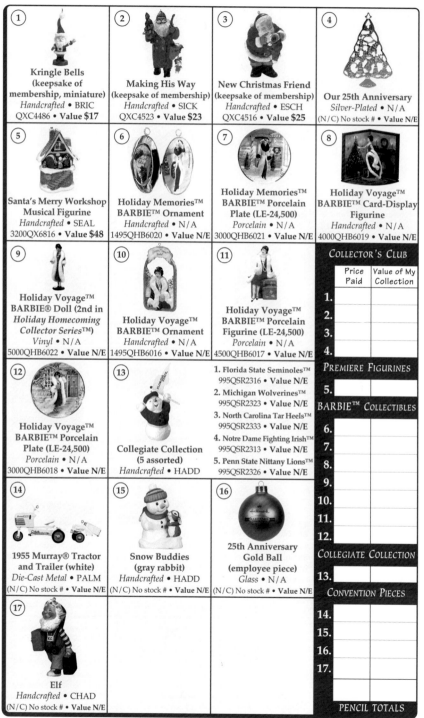

1
Kringle Bells
(keepsake of membership, miniature)
Handcrafted • BRIC
QXC4486 • **Value $17**

2
Making His Way
(keepsake of membership)
Handcrafted • SICK
QXC4523 • **Value $23**

3
New Christmas Friend
(keepsake of membership)
Handcrafted • ESCH
QXC4516 • **Value $25**

4
Our 25th Anniversary
Silver-Plated • N/A
(N/C) No stock # • **Value N/E**

5
Santa's Merry Workshop Musical Figurine
Handcrafted • SEAL
3200QX6816 • **Value $48**

6
Holiday Memories™ BARBIE™ Ornament
Handcrafted • N/A
1495QHB6020 • **Value N/E**

7
Holiday Memories™ BARBIE™ Porcelain Plate (LE-24,500)
Porcelain • N/A
3000QHB6021 • **Value N/E**

8
Holiday Voyage™ BARBIE™ Card-Display Figurine
Handcrafted • N/A
4000QHB6019 • **Value N/E**

9
Holiday Voyage™ BARBIE® Doll (2nd in *Holiday Homecoming Collector Series™)*
Vinyl • N/A
5000QHB6022 • **Value N/E**

10
Holiday Voyage™ BARBIE™ Ornament
Handcrafted • N/A
1495QHB6016 • **Value N/E**

11
Holiday Voyage™ BARBIE™ Porcelain Figurine (LE-24,500)
Porcelain • N/A
4500QHB6017 • **Value N/E**

12
Holiday Voyage™ BARBIE™ Porcelain Plate (LE-24,500)
Porcelain • N/A
3000QHB6018 • **Value N/E**

13
Collegiate Collection (5 assorted)
Handcrafted • HADD

1. Florida State Seminoles™
995QSR2316 • **Value N/E**
2. Michigan Wolverines™
995QSR2323 • **Value N/E**
3. North Carolina Tar Heels™
995QSR2333 • **Value N/E**
4. Notre Dame Fighting Irish™
995QSR2313 • **Value N/E**
5. Penn State Nittany Lions™
995QSR2326 • **Value N/E**

14
1955 Murray® Tractor and Trailer (white)
Die-Cast Metal • PALM
(N/C) No stock # • **Value N/E**

15
Snow Buddies (gray rabbit)
Handcrafted • HADD
(N/C) No stock # • **Value N/E**

16
25th Anniversary Gold Ball (employee piece)
Glass • N/A
(N/C) No stock # • **Value N/E**

17
Elf
Handcrafted • CHAD
(N/C) No stock # • **Value N/E**

1998

COLLECTOR'S CLUB	Price Paid	Value of My Collection
1.		
2.		
3.		
4.		
PREMIERE FIGURINES		
5.		
BARBIE™ COLLECTIBLES		
6.		
7.		
8.		
9.		
10.		
11.		
12.		
COLLEGIATE COLLECTION		
13.		
CONVENTION PIECES		
14.		
15.		
16.		
17.		
PENCIL TOTALS		

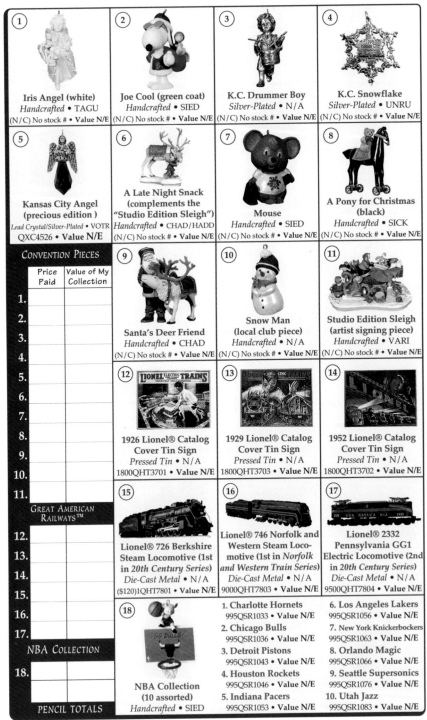

1. Iris Angel (white)
Handcrafted • TAGU
(N/C) No stock # • **Value N/E**

2. Joe Cool (green coat)
Handcrafted • SIED
(N/C) No stock # • **Value N/E**

3. K.C. Drummer Boy
Silver-Plated • N/A
(N/C) No stock # • **Value N/E**

4. K.C. Snowflake
Silver-Plated • UNRU
(N/C) No stock # • **Value N/E**

5. Kansas City Angel (precious edition)
Lead Crystal/Silver-Plated • VOTR
QXC4526 • **Value N/E**

6. A Late Night Snack (complements the "Studio Edition Sleigh")
Handcrafted • CHAD/HADD
(N/C) No stock # • **Value N/E**

7. Mouse
Handcrafted • SIED
(N/C) No stock # • **Value N/E**

8. A Pony for Christmas (black)
Handcrafted • SICK
(N/C) No stock # • **Value N/E**

9. Santa's Deer Friend
Handcrafted • CHAD
(N/C) No stock # • **Value N/E**

10. Snow Man (local club piece)
Handcrafted • N/A
(N/C) No stock # • **Value N/E**

11. Studio Edition Sleigh (artist signing piece)
Handcrafted • VARI
(N/C) No stock # • **Value N/E**

12. 1926 Lionel® Catalog Cover Tin Sign
Pressed Tin • N/A
1800QHT3701 • **Value N/E**

13. 1929 Lionel® Catalog Cover Tin Sign
Pressed Tin • N/A
1800QHT3703 • **Value N/E**

14. 1952 Lionel® Catalog Cover Tin Sign
Pressed Tin • N/A
1800QHT3702 • **Value N/E**

15. Lionel® 726 Berkshire Steam Locomotive (1st in *20th Century Series*)
Die-Cast Metal • N/A
($120)1QHT7801 • **Value N/E**

16. Lionel® 746 Norfolk and Western Steam Locomotive (1st in *Norfolk and Western Train Series*)
Die-Cast Metal • N/A
9000QHT7803 • **Value N/E**

17. Lionel® 2332 Pennsylvania GG1 Electric Locomotive (2nd in *20th Century Series*)
Die-Cast Metal • N/A
9500QHT7804 • **Value N/E**

18. NBA Collection (10 assorted)
Handcrafted • SIED

1. Charlotte Hornets
995QSR1033 • **Value N/E**
2. Chicago Bulls
995QSR1036 • **Value N/E**
3. Detroit Pistons
995QSR1043 • **Value N/E**
4. Houston Rockets
995QSR1046 • **Value N/E**
5. Indiana Pacers
995QSR1053 • **Value N/E**
6. Los Angeles Lakers
995QSR1056 • **Value N/E**
7. New York Knickerbockers
995QSR1063 • **Value N/E**
8. Orlando Magic
995QSR1066 • **Value N/E**
9. Seattle Supersonics
995QSR1076 • **Value N/E**
10. Utah Jazz
995QSR1083 • **Value N/E**

Convention Pieces

	Price Paid	Value of My Collection
1.		
2.		
3.		
4.		
5.		
6.		
7.		
8.		
9.		
10.		
11.		

Great American Railways™

12.		
13.		
14.		
15.		

NBA Collection

16.		
17.		
18.		

PENCIL TOTALS

1. Carolina Panthers™
995QSR5026 • **Value N/E**
2. Chicago Bears™
995QSR5033 • **Value N/E**
3. Dallas Cowboys™
995QSR5046 • **Value N/E**
4. Denver Broncos™
995QSR5053 • **Value N/E**
5. Green Bay Packers™
995QSR5063 • **Value N/E**

6. Kansas City Chiefs™
995QSR5013 • **Value N/E**
7. Miami Dolphins™
995QSR5096 • **Value N/E**
8. Minnesota Vikings™
995QSR5126 • **Value N/E**
9. New York Giants™
995QSR5143 • **Value N/E**
10. Oakland Raiders™
995QSR5086 • **Value N/EE**

11. Philadelphia Eagles™
995QSR5153 • **Value N/E**
12. Pittsburgh Steelers™
995QSR5163 • **Value N/E**
13. St. Louis Rams™
995QSR5093 • **Value N/E**
14. San Francisco 49ers™
995QSR5173 • **Value N/E**
15. Washington Redskins™
995QSR5186 • **Value N/E**

NFL Collection
(15 assorted)
Handcrafted • FRAN

1997

1950s HOWDY DOODY™
Pressed Tin • N/A
1950QHM8801 • **Value N/E**

1950s Lone Ranger™
Pressed Tin • N/A
1950QHM8802 • **Value N/E**

1950s SUPERMAN™
Pressed Tin • N/A
1950QHM8803 • **Value N/E**

1970s Hot Wheels™
Pressed Tin • N/A
1950QHM8813 • **Value N/E**

Christmas Caring
Resin • BRIC
1800QHC8251 • **Value N/E**

Dreams and Wishes
Resin • VOTR
2500QHC8250 • **Value N/E**

Splendid Days
Resin • TAGU
1800QHC8216 • **Value N/E**

Thoughtful Ways
Resin • HADD/TAGU
1800QHC8215 • **Value N/E**

Together Days
Resin • BRIC
1800QHC8217 • **Value N/E**

1997

Highlights for 1997 included a new collection of Disney ornaments, as well as several ornaments based on the STAR WARS *movies. The 1997 collection featured 144 Keepsake ornaments, 17 Magic ornaments and 36 Miniature ornaments. See the collectible series section for more 1997 ornaments.*

1997 Corvette
Handcrafted • PALM
1395QXI6455 • **Value $28**

All-Round Sports Fan
Handcrafted • WILL
895QX6392 • **Value $28**

All-Weather Walker
Handcrafted • WILL
895QX6415 • **Value $18**

NFL Collection		
	Price Paid	Value of My Collection
1.		
School Days Lunch Boxes		
2.		
3.		
4.		
5.		
Spoonful of Stars		
6.		
7.		
8.		
9.		
10.		
General Keepsake		
11.		
12.		
13.		
Pencil Totals		

(1) Angel Friend
Handcrafted • FRAN
1495QX6762 • **Value $26**

(2) Ariel, The Little Mermaid
Handcrafted • BRIC
1295QXI4072 • **Value $23**

(3) Baby's First Christmas
Handcrafted • N/A
795QX6482 • **Value $21**

(4) Baby's First Christmas
Handcrafted • CROW
795QX6495 • **Value $25**

(5) Baby's First Christmas
Handcrafted • VOTR
995QX6485 • **Value $21**

(6) Baby's First Christmas
Handcrafted • ANDR
995QX6492 • **Value $20**

(7) Baby's First Christmas
Porcelain • VOTR
1495QX6535 • **Value $24**

(8) Baby's Second Christmas
Handcrafted • CROW
795QX6502 • **Value $19**

(9) Biking Buddies
Handcrafted • PALM
1295QX6682 • **Value $22**

(10) Book of the Year
Handcrafted • BRIC
795QX6645 • **Value $17**

(11) Breezin' Along
Handcrafted • SEAL
895QX6722 • **Value $19**

(12) Bucket Brigade
Handcrafted • FRAN
895QX6382 • **Value $17**

(13) Catch of the Day
Handcrafted • TAGU
995QX6712 • **Value $18**

(14) Child's Fifth Christmas
Handcrafted • CROW
795QX6515 • **Value $16**

(15) Child's Fourth Christmas
Handcrafted • CROW
795QX6512 • **Value $16**

(16) Child's Third Christmas
Handcrafted • CROW
795QX6505 • **Value $17**

(17) Christmas Checkup
Handcrafted • SIED
795QX6385 • **Value $17**

(18) Classic Cross
Precious Metal • VOTR
1395QX6805 • **Value $20**

(19) Clever Camper
Handcrafted • CHAD
795QX6445 • **Value $18**

(20) Commander Data™
Handcrafted • RGRS
1495QXI6345 • **Value $27**

	Price Paid	Value of My Collection
General Keepsake		
1.		
2.		
3.		
4.		
5.		
6.		
7.		
8.		
9.		
10.		
11.		
12.		
13.		
14.		
15.		
16.		
17.		
18.		
19.		
20.		
PENCIL TOTALS		

1. Cycling Santa
Handcrafted • WILL
1495QX6425 • **Value $26**

2. Dad
Handcrafted • SIED
895QX6532 • **Value $19**

3. Daughter
Pressed Tin • BRIC
795QX6612 • **Value $18**

4. Downhill Run
Handcrafted • CROW
995QX6705 • **Value $22**

5. Dr. Leonard H. McCoy™
Handcrafted • RGRS
1495QXI6352 • **Value $27**

6. Elegance on Ice
Handcrafted • LYLE
995QX6432 • **Value $20**

7. Expressly for Teacher
Handcrafted • TAGU
795QX6375 • **Value $16**

8. Feliz Navidad
Handcrafted • SEAL
895QX6665 • **Value $30**

9. Friendship Blend
Handcrafted • SEAL
995QX6655 • **Value $21**

10. Garden Bouquet
Handcrafted • LYLE
1495QX6752 • **Value $30**

11. Gift of Friendship
Porcelain • N/A
1295QXE6835 • **Value $20**

12. Godchild
Handcrafted • BRIC
795QX6662 • **Value $16**

13. God's Gift of Love
Porcelain • LYLE
1695QX6792 • **Value $30**

14. Goofy's Ski Adventure
Handcrafted • CHAD
1295QXD4042 • **Value $22**

15. Granddaughter
Handcrafted • TAGU
795QX6622 • **Value $18**

16. Grandma
Handcrafted • PIKE
895QX6625 • **Value $16**

17. Grandson
Handcrafted • TAGU
795QX6615 • **Value $18**

18. Gus & Jaq, Cinderella
Handcrafted • CROW
1295QXD4052 • **Value $26**

19. Heavenly Song
Acrylic • VOTR
1295QX6795 • **Value $23**

20. Hercules
Handcrafted • WILL
1295QXI4005 • **Value $22**

General Keepsake

	Price Paid	Value of My Collection
1.		
2.		
3.		
4.		
5.		
6.		
7.		
8.		
9.		
10.		
11.		
12.		
13.		
14.		
15.		
16.		
17.		
18.		
19.		
20.		
PENCIL TOTALS		

1997

VALUE GUIDE – HALLMARK KEEPSAKE ORNAMENTS

(1) Honored Guests
Handcrafted • FRAN
1495QX6745 • **Value $30**

(2) Howdy Doody™
Handcrafted • LARS
1295QX6272 • **Value $28**

(3) The Incredible Hulk®
Handcrafted • N/A
1295QX5471 • **Value $22**

(4) Jasmine & Aladdin, Aladdin & the King of Thieves
Handcrafted • RGRS
1495QXD4062 • **Value $24**

(5) Jingle Bell Jester
Handcrafted • PIKE
995QX6695 • **Value $21**

(6) Juggling Stars
Handcrafted • TAGU
995QX6595 • **Value $20**

(7) King Noor–First King
Handcrafted • ANDR
1295QX6552 • **Value $27**

(8) Leading The Way
Handcrafted • SICK
1695QX6782 • **Value $30**

(9) Lion and Lamb
Handcrafted • WILL
795QX6602 • **Value $20**

(10) The Lone Ranger™
Pressed Tin • N/A
1295QX6265 • **Value $36**

(11) Love to Sew
Handcrafted • TAGU
795QX6435 • **Value $19**

(12) Madonna del Rosario
Handcrafted • SICK
1295QX6545 • **Value $24**

(13) Marbles Champion
Handcrafted • UNRU
1095QX6342 • **Value $21**

(14) Meadow Snowman
Pressed Tin • SICK
1295QX6715 • **Value $30**

(15) Megara and Pegasus
Handcrafted • CROW
1695QXI4012 • **Value $29**

(16) Michigan J. Frog
Handcrafted • CHAD
995QX6332 • **Value $23**

(17) Mickey's Long Shot
Handcrafted • SIED
1095QXD6412 • **Value $22**

(18) Mickey's Snow Angel
Handcrafted • SIED
995QXD4035 • **Value $20**

(19) Miss Gulch
Handcrafted • LYLE
1395QX6372 • **Value $27**

(20) Mom
Handcrafted • SIED
895QX6525 • **Value $18**

GENERAL KEEPSAKE

	Price Paid	Value of My Collection
1.		
2.		
3.		
4.		
5.		
6.		
7.		
8.		
9.		
10.		
11.		
12.		
13.		
14.		
15.		
16.		
17.		
18.		
19.		
20.		
PENCIL TOTALS		

1 Mom and Dad
Handcrafted • SIED
995QX6522 • **Value $19**

2 Mr. Potato Head®
Handcrafted • SIED
1095QX6335 • **Value $25**

3 Nativity Tree
Handcrafted • UNRU
1495QX6575 • **Value $31**

4 New Home
Handcrafted • PIKE
895QX6652 • **Value $18**

5 New Pair of Skates
Handcrafted • LARS
1395QXD4032 • **Value $24**

6 The Night Before Christmas
Handcrafted • CROW
2400QX5721 • **Value $42**

7 Our Christmas Together
Pewter • N/A
1695QX6475 • **Value $23**

8 Our First Christmas Together
Acrylic • N/A
795QX3182 • **Value $17**

9 Our First Christmas Together
Handcrafted • PIKE
895QX6472 • **Value $24**

10 Our First Christmas Together
Handcrafted • SEAL
1095QX6465 • **Value $19**

11 Phoebus & Esmeralda, The Hunchback of Notre Dame
Handcrafted • CROW
1495QXD6344 • **Value $23**

12 Playful Shepherd
Handcrafted • TAGU
995QX6592 • **Value $22**

13 Porcelain Hinged Box
Porcelain • VOTR
1495QX6772 • **Value $32**

14 Praise Him
Handcrafted • SICK
895QX6542 • **Value $19**

15 Prize Topiary
Handcrafted • SEAL
1495QX6675 • **Value $25**

16 Sailor Bear
Handcrafted • UNRU
1495QX6765 • **Value $23**

17 Santa Mail
Handcrafted • WILL
1095QX6702 • **Value $22**

18 Santa's Friend
Handcrafted • UNRU
1295QX6685 • **Value $25**

19 Santa's Magical Sleigh
Handcrafted • UNRU
2400QX6672 • **Value $40**

20 Santa's Merry Path
Handcrafted • SICK
1695QX6785 • **Value $32**

1997

General Keepsake

	Price Paid	Value of My Collection
1.		
2.		
3.		
4.		
5.		
6.		
7.		
8.		
9.		
10.		
11.		
12.		
13.		
14.		
15.		
16.		
17.		
18.		
19.		
20.		
PENCIL TOTALS		

Value Guide — Hallmark Keepsake Ornaments

(1) Santa's Polar Friend *Handcrafted* • CHAD 1695QX6755 • **Value $32**	**(2)** Santa's Ski Adventure *Handcrafted* • CHAD 1295QX6422 • **Value $24**	**(3)** Sister to Sister *Handcrafted* • PIKE 995QX6635 • **Value $20**	**(4)** Snow Bowling *Handcrafted* • WILL 695QX6395 • **Value $17**
(5) Snow White, Anniversary Edition (set/2) *Handcrafted* • ESCH 1695QXD4055 • **Value $32**	**(6)** Snowgirl *Handcrafted* • TAGU 795QX6562 • **Value $18**	**(7)** Son *Pressed Tin* • BRIC 795QX6605 • **Value $16**	**(8)** Special Dog *Handcrafted* • BRIC 795QX6632 • **Value $17**

General Keepsake

	Price Paid	Value of My Collection
1.		
2.		
3.		
4.		
5.		
6.		
7.		
8.		
9.		
10.		
11.		
12.		
13.		
14.		
15.		
16.		
17.		
18.		
19.		
20.		
PENCIL TOTALS		

(9) The Spirit of Christmas *Handcrafted* • LARS 995QX6585 • **Value $20**	**(10)** Stealing a Kiss *Handcrafted* • TAGU 1495QX6555 • **Value $27**	**(11)** Sweet Discovery *Handcrafted* • SICK 1195QX6325 • **Value $23**
(12) Sweet Dreamer *Handcrafted* • BRIC 695QX6732 • **Value $16**	**(13)** Swinging in the Snow *Handcrafted/Glass* • TAGU 1295QX6775 • **Value $22**	**(14)** Taking A Break *Handcrafted* • UNRU 1495QX6305 • **Value $28**
(15) Timon & Pumbaa, The Lion King *Handcrafted* • WILL 1295QXD4065 • **Value $21**	**(16)** Tomorrow's Leader *Ceramic* • N/A 995QX6452 • **Value $18**	**(17)** Tonka® Mighty Front Loader *Die-Cast Metal* • N/A 1395QX6362 • **Value $27**
(18) Two-Tone, 101 Dalmatians *Handcrafted* • CHAD 995QXD4015 • **Value $19**	**(19)** Waitin' on Santa – Winnie the Pooh *Handcrafted* • SIED 1295QXD6365 • **Value $26**	**(20)** What a Deal! *Handcrafted* • PIKE 895QX6442 • **Value $17**

VALUE GUIDE — HALLMARK KEEPSAKE ORNAMENTS

(1) Yoda™ *Handcrafted* • BRIC 995QXI6355 • **Value $37**	**(2)** Darth Vader™ *Handcrafted* • RHOD 2400QXI7531 • **Value $42**	**(3)** Decorator Taz *Handcrafted* • CHAD 3000QLX7502 • **Value $48**	**(4)** Glowing Angel *Handcrafted* • VOTR 1895QLX7435 • **Value $30**
(5) Holiday Serenade *Handcrafted* • FRAN 2400QLX7485 • **Value $38**	**(6)** Joy to the World *Handcrafted* • TAGU 1495QLX7512 • **Value $28**	**(7)** The Lincoln Memorial *Handcrafted* • SEAL 2400QLX7522 • **Value $43**	**(8)** Madonna and Child *Handcrafted* • LYLE 1995QLX7425 • **Value $36**

1997

(9) Motorcycle Chums *Handcrafted* • SEAL 2400QLX7495 • **Value $42**	**(10)** Santa's Secret Gift *Handcrafted* • CHAD 2400QLX7455 • **Value $39**	**(11)** Santa's Showboat *Handcrafted* • CROW 4200QLX7465 • **Value $70**
(12) SNOOPY Plays Santa *Handcrafted* • RGRS 2200QLX7475 • **Value $37**	**(13)** Teapot Party *Handcrafted* • TAGU 1895QLX7482 • **Value $36**	**(14)** U.S.S. Defiant™ *Handcrafted* • NORT 2400QXI7481 • **Value $40**
(15) The Warmth of Home *Handcrafted* • LARS 1895QXI7545 • **Value $32**	**(16)** C-3PO™ and R2-D2™ (set/2) *Handcrafted* • RHOD 1295QXI4265 • **Value $27**	**(17)** Casablanca™ (set/3) *Handcrafted* • ANDR 1995QXM4272 • **Value $32**
(18) Future Star *Handcrafted* • PIKE 595QXM4232 • **Value $13**	**(19)** Gentle Giraffes *Handcrafted* • SICK 595QXM4221 • **Value $13**	**(20)** He Is Born *Handcrafted* • VOTR 795QXM4235 • **Value $17**

GENERAL KEEPSAKE

	Price Paid	Value of My Collection
1.		

GENERAL MAGIC

2.		
3.		
4.		
5.		
6.		
7.		
8.		
9.		
10.		
11.		
12.		
13.		
14.		
15.		

GENERAL MINIATURE

16.		
17.		
18.		
19.		
20.		
PENCIL TOTALS		

VALUE GUIDE — HALLMARK KEEPSAKE ORNAMENTS

1. Heavenly Music
Handcrafted • TAGU
595QXM4292 • **Value $11**

2. Home Sweet Home
Handcrafted • SEAL
595QXM4222 • **Value $13**

3. Honey of a Gift– Winnie the Pooh
Handcrafted • LARS
695QXD4255 • **Value $16**

4. Ice Cold Coca-Cola®
Handcrafted • CHAD
695QXM4252 • **Value $15**

5. King of the Forest (set/4)
Handcrafted • RGRS
2400QXM4262 • **Value $43**

6. Miniature 1997 Corvette
Handcrafted • PALM
695QXI4322 • **Value $14**

7. Our Lady of Guadalupe
Pewter • CHAD
895QXM4275 • **Value $16**

8. Peppermint Painter
Handcrafted • TAGU
495QXM4312 • **Value $12**

9. Polar Buddies
Handcrafted • FRAN
495QXM4332 • **Value $12**

10. Seeds of Joy
Handcrafted • TAGU
695QXM4242 • **Value $13**

11. Sew Talented
Handcrafted • SEAL
595QXM4195 • **Value $13**

12. Shutterbug
Handcrafted • TAGU
595QXM4212 • **Value $14**

13. Snowboard Bunny
Handcrafted • TAGU
495QXM4315 • **Value $12**

14. Tiny Home Improvers (set/6)
Handcrafted • SEAL
2900QXM4282 • **Value $42**

15. Victorian Skater
Handcrafted • UNRU
595QXM4305 • **Value $12**

16. Away to the Window
(keepsake of membership)
Handcrafted • WILL
QXC5135 • **Value $20**

17. Farmer's Market, Tender Touches (club edition)
Handcrafted • SEAL
1500QXC5182 • **Value $29**

18. Happy Christmas to All!
(keepsake of membership)
Handcrafted • WILL
QXC5132 • **Value $22**

19. Jolly Old Santa
(keepsake of membership, miniature)
Handcrafted • WILL
QXC5145 • **Value $17**

20. Ready for Santa
(keepsake of membership, miniature)
Handcrafted • WILL
QXC5142 • **Value $12**

GENERAL MINIATURE

	Price Paid	Value of My Collection
1.		
2.		
3.		
4.		
5.		
6.		
7.		
8.		
9.		
10.		
11.		
12.		
13.		
14.		
15.		

COLLECTOR'S CLUB

	Price Paid	Value of My Collection
16.		
17.		
18.		
19.		
20.		
PENCIL TOTALS		

1.
The Perfect Tree, Tender Touches
Handcrafted • SEAL
1500QX6572 • **Value $24**

2.
1953 GMC (green)
Handcrafted • PALM
(N/C) No stock # • **Value N/E**

3.
First Class Thank You
Handcrafted • RGRS
(N/C) No stock # • **Value N/E**

4.
Mrs. Claus's Story
Handcrafted • ESCH/KLIN
($14.95) No stock # • **Value $25**

5.
Murray® Dump Truck (orange)
Die-Cast Metal • PALM
(N/C) No stock # • **Value N/E**

6.
PHOTO UNAVAILABLE
Murray Inc.® "Pursuit" Airplane (miniature, tan)
Die-Cast Metal • PALM
(N/C) No stock # • **Value N/E**

7.
Santa's Magical Sleigh (silver runners)
Handcrafted • UNRU
(N/C) No stock # • **Value N/E**

8.
Trimming Santa's Tree (set/2)
Handcrafted • VARI
6000QXC5175 • **Value $80**

9.
BARBIE™ Lapel Pin (re-issued from 1996)
Handcrafted • N/A
495XLP3544 • **Value N/E**

10.
Holiday BARBIE™ Stocking Hanger (re-issued from 1996)
Handcrafted • N/A
1995XSH3101 • **Value N/E**

11.
Holiday Traditions™ BARBIE® Doll (1st in Holiday Homecoming Collector Series™)
Vinyl • N/A
5000QHB3402 • **Value N/E**

12.
Holiday Traditions™ BARBIE™ Ornament
Handcrafted • N/A
1495QHB6002 • **Value $19**

13.
Holiday Traditions™ BARBIE™ Porcelain Figurine
Porcelain • N/A
4500QHB6001 • **Value N/E**

14.
Holiday Traditions™ BARBIE™ Porcelain Plate
Porcelain • N/A
3000QHB6003 • **Value N/E**

15.
Victorian Elegance™ BARBIE™ Ornament
Handcrafted • N/A
1495QHB6004 • **Value $20**

16.
Victorian Elegance™ BARBIE™ Porcelain Plate
Porcelain • N/A
3000QHB6005 • **Value N/E**

17.
CHICAGO BULLS
NBA COLLECTION (10 assorted)
Ceramic • N/A

1. Charlotte Hornets™
995QSR1222 • **Value N/E**
2. Chicago Bulls™
995QSR1232 • **Value N/E**
3. Detroit Pistons™
995QSR1242 • **Value N/E**
4. Houston Rockets™
995QSR1245 • **Value N/E**
5. Indiana Pacers™
995QSR1252 • **Value N/E**
6. Los Angeles Lakers™
995QSR1262 • **Value N/E**
7. New York Knickerbockers™
995QSR1272 • **Value N/E**
8. Orlando Magic™
995QSR1282 • **Value N/E**
9. Phoenix Suns™
995QSR1292 • **Value N/E**
10. Seattle Supersonics™
995QSR1295 • **Value N/E**

	Price Paid	Value of My Collection
PREMIERE ORNAMENTS		
1.		
ARTISTS ON TOUR PIECES		
2.		
3.		
4.		
5.		
6.		
7.		
8.		
BARBIE™ COLLECTIBLES		
9.		
10.		
11.		
12.		
13.		
14.		
15.		
16.		
NBA COLLECTION		
17.		
PENCIL TOTALS		

1997

Value Guide – Hallmark Keepsake Ornaments

NFL COLLECTION
(30 assorted)
Handcrafted • SIED

	1. Arizona Cardinals™ 995QSR5505 • Value N/E	11. Green Bay Packers™ 995QSR5372 • Value N/E	21. New York Jets™ 995QSR5495 • Value N/E

1. Arizona Cardinals™ 995QSR5505 • Value N/E
2. Atlanta Falcons™ 995QSR5305 • Value N/E
3. Baltimore Ravens™ 995QSR5352 • Value N/E
4. Buffalo Bills™ 995QSR5312 • Value N/E
5. Carolina Panthers™ 995QSR5315 • Value N/E
6. Chicago Bears™ 995QSR5322 • Value N/E
7. Cincinnati Bengals™ 995QSR5325 • Value N/E
8. Dallas Cowboys™ 995QSR5355 • Value N/E
9. Denver Broncos™ 995QSR5362 • Value N/E
10. Detroit Lions™ 995QSR5365 • Value N/E
11. Green Bay Packers™ 995QSR5372 • Value N/E
12. Houston Oilers™ 995QSR5375 • Value N/E
13. Indianapolis Colts™ 995QSR5411 • Value N/E
14. Jacksonville Jaguars™ 995QSR5415 • Value N/E
15. Kansas City Chiefs™ 995QSR5302 • Value N/E
16. Miami Dolphins™ 995QSR5472 • Value N/E
17. Minnesota Vikings™ 995QSR5475 • Value N/E
18. New England Patriots™ 995QSR5482 • Value N/E
19. New Orleans Saints™ 995QSR5485 • Value N/E
20. New York Giants™ 995QSR5492 • Value N/E
21. New York Jets™ 995QSR5495 • Value N/E
22. Oakland Raiders™ 995QSR5422 • Value N/E
23. Philadelphia Eagles™ 995QSR5502 • Value N/E
24. Pittsburgh Steelers™ 995QSR5512 • Value N/E
25. St. Louis Rams™ 995QSR5425 • Value N/E
26. San Diego Chargers™ 995QSR5515 • Value N/E
27. San Francisco 49ers™ 995QSR5522 • Value N/E
28. Seattle Seahawks™ 995QSR5525 • Value N/E
29. Tampa Bay Buccaneers™ 995QSR5532 • Value N/E
30. Washington Redskins™ 995QSR5535 • Value N/E

1996

Hallmark introduced several ornaments and collectibles commemorating the Centennial Olympic Games in Atlanta, Georgia in 1996. Overall, there were 135 Keepsake ornaments in the collection, as well as 23 Magic, 13 Showcase and 34 Miniature ornaments. See the collectible series section for more 1996 ornaments.

NFL COLLECTION

	Price Paid	Value of My Collection
1.		
2.		
3.		
4.		
5.		
6.		
7.		
8.		
9.		
10.		
PENCIL TOTALS		

GENERAL KEEPSAKE

(2) **101 Dalmatians** *Handcrafted* • N/A 1295QXI6544 • Value **$23**

(3) **Antlers Aweigh!** *Handcrafted* • CHAD 995QX5901 • Value **$21**

(4) **Apple for Teacher** *Handcrafted* • AUBE 795QX6121 • Value **$13**

(5) **Baby's First Christmas** *Handcrafted* • SEAL 795QX5761 • Value **$21**

(6) **Baby's First Christmas** *Handcrafted* • CROW 795QX5764 • Value **$21**

(7) **Baby's First Christmas** *Handcrafted* • ANDR 995QX5754 • Value **$22**

(8) **Baby's First Christmas** *Porcelain* • N/A 1095QX5751 • Value **$22**

(9) **Baby's First Christmas** *Porcelain* • VOTR 1895QX5744 • Value **$30**

(10) **Baby's Second Christmas** *Handcrafted* • CROW 795QX5771 • Value **$19**

114   *1997 Collection / 1996 Collection*

① Bounce Pass
Handcrafted • SIED
795QX6031 • **Value $15**

② Bowl 'em Over
Handcrafted • SIED
795QX6014 • **Value $14**

③ Child Care Giver
Handcrafted • SIED
895QX6071 • **Value $16**

④ Child's Fifth Christmas
Handcrafted • RHOD
695QX5784 • **Value $17**

⑤ Child's Fourth Christmas
Handcrafted • CROW
795QX5781 • **Value $17**

⑥ Child's Third Christmas
Handcrafted • CROW
795QX5774 • **Value $17**

⑦ Christmas Joy
Handcrafted • UNRU
1495QX6241 • **Value $26**

⑧ Christmas Snowman
Handcrafted • UNRU
995QX6214 • **Value $20**

⑨ Close-Knit Friends
Handcrafted • BRIC
995QX5874 • **Value $17**

⑩ Come All Ye Faithful
Handcrafted • CROW
1295QX6244 • **Value $23**

⑪ Commander William T. Riker™
Handcrafted • RGRS
1495QXI5551 • **Value $26**

⑫ Dad
Handcrafted • SIED
795QX5831 • **Value $17**

⑬ Daughter
Handcrafted • PALM
895QX6077 • **Value $19**

⑭ Esmeralda and Djali
Handcrafted • CROW
1495QXI6351 • **Value $22**

⑮ Evergreen Santa
Handcrafted • LYLE
2200QX5714 • **Value $40**

⑯ Fan-tastic Season
Handcrafted • CHAD
995QX5924 • **Value $21**

⑰ Feliz Navidad
Handcrafted • SICK
995QX6304 • **Value $21**

⑱ Foghorn Leghorn and Henery Hawk (set/2)
Handcrafted • CHAD
1395QX5444 • **Value $23**

⑲ Glad Tidings
Handcrafted • LYLE
1495QX6231 • **Value $28**

⑳ Goal Line Glory (set/2)
Handcrafted • SEAL
1295QX6001 • **Value $24**

1996

GENERAL KEEPSAKE

	Price Paid	Value of My Collection
1.		
2.		
3.		
4.		
5.		
6.		
7.		
8.		
9.		
10.		
11.		
12.		
13.		
14.		
15.		
16.		
17.		
18.		
19.		
20.		
PENCIL TOTALS		

(1) Godchild
Handcrafted • RGRS
895QX5841 • **Value $16**

(2) Granddaughter
Handcrafted • RGRS
795QX5697 • **Value $16**

(3) Grandma
Handcrafted • VOTR
895QX5844 • **Value $18**

(4) Grandpa
Handcrafted • VOTR
895QX5851 • **Value $18**

(5) Grandson
Handcrafted • RGRS
795QX5699 • **Value $16**

(6) Growth of a Leader
Ceramic • N/A
995QX5541 • **Value $17**

(7) Happy Holi-doze
Handcrafted • RHOD
995QX5904 • **Value $19**

(8) Hearts Full of Love
Handcrafted • RHOD
995QX5814 • **Value $20**

(9) High Style
Handcrafted • CHAD
895QX6064 • **Value $19**

(10) Hillside Express
Handcrafted • AUBE
1295QX6134 • **Value $22**

(11) Holiday Haul
Handcrafted • SICK
1495QX6201 • **Value $31**

(12) Hurrying Downstairs
Handcrafted • FRAN
895QX6074 • **Value $18**

(13) I Dig Golf
Handcrafted • RHOD
1095QX5891 • **Value $19**

(14) Invitation to the Games (set/2)
Ceramic • MCGE
1495QXE5511 • **Value $25**

(15) It's A Wonderful Life™
Handcrafted • CROW
1495QXI6531 • **Value $33**

(16) IZZY™ – The Mascot
Handcrafted • PALM
995QXE5724 • **Value $17**

(17) Jackpot Jingle
Handcrafted • SIED
995QX5911 • **Value $18**

(18) Jolly Wolly Ark
Handcrafted • CROW
1295QX6221 • **Value $25**

(19) Kindly Shepherd
Handcrafted • ANDR
1295QX6274 • **Value $24**

(20) Laverne, Victor and Hugo
Handcrafted • CROW
1295QXI6354 • **Value $20**

GENERAL KEEPSAKE	Price Paid	Value of My Collection
1.		
2.		
3.		
4.		
5.		
6.		
7.		
8.		
9.		
10.		
11.		
12.		
13.		
14.		
15.		
16.		
17.		
18.		
19.		
20.		
PENCIL TOTALS		

VALUE GUIDE — HALLMARK KEEPSAKE ORNAMENTS

① Lighting the Way
Handcrafted • CHAD
1295QX6124 • **Value $22**

② A Little Song and Dance
Handcrafted • CROW
995QX6211 • **Value $18**

③ Little Spooners
Handcrafted • UNRU
1295QX5504 • **Value $22**

④ Madonna and Child
Tin • SICK
1295QX6324 • **Value $19**

⑤ Making His Rounds
Handcrafted • FRAN
1495QX6271 • **Value $24**

⑥ Marvin the Martian
Handcrafted • CHAD
1095QX5451 • **Value $24**

⑦ Matchless Memories
Handcrafted • CROW
995QX6061 • **Value $18**

⑧ Maxine
Handcrafted • PIKE
995QX6224 • **Value $25**

⑨ Merry Carpoolers
Handcrafted • CROW
1495QX5884 • **Value $25**

⑩ Mom
Handcrafted • LYLE
795QX5824 • **Value $17**

⑪ Mom and Dad
Handcrafted • RHOD
995QX5821 • **Value $17**

⑫ Mom-to-Be
Handcrafted • UNRU
795QX5791 • **Value $16**

⑬ Mr. Spock
Handcrafted • RGRS
1495QXI5544 • **Value $32**

⑭ New Home
Handcrafted • SEAL
895QX5881 • **Value $20**

⑮ Olive Oyl and Swee' Pea
Handcrafted • CHAD
1095QX5481 • **Value $23**

⑯ Olympic Triumph
Handcrafted • SEAL
1095QXE5731 • **Value $19**

⑰ On My Way
Handcrafted • TAGU
795QX5861 • **Value $14**

⑱ Our Christmas Together
Handcrafted • PALM
1895QX5794 • **Value $35**

⑲ Our Christmas Together Photo Holder
Handcrafted • CROW
895QX5804 • **Value $17**

⑳ Our First Christmas Together
Acrylic • VOTR
695QX3051 • **Value $16**

	GENERAL KEEPSAKE	
	Price Paid	Value of My Collection
1.		
2.		
3.		
4.		
5.		
6.		
7.		
8.		
9.		
10.		
11.		
12.		
13.		
14.		
15.		
16.		
17.		
18.		
19.		
20.		
	PENCIL TOTALS	

1996

(1) Our First Christmas Together
Handcrafted • PALM
995QX5811 • **Value $21**

(2) Our First Christmas Together Collector's Plate
Porcelain • N/A
1095QX5801 • **Value $22**

(3) Parade of Nations
Porcelain • N/A
1095QXE5741 • **Value $20**

(4) Peppermint Surprise
Handcrafted • PIKE
795QX6234 • **Value $18**

(5) Percy the Small Engine – No. 6
Handcrafted • RHOD
995QX6314 • **Value $21**

(6) PEZ® Snowman
Handcrafted • N/A
795QX6534 • **Value $16**

(7) Polar Cycle
Handcrafted • UNRU
1295QX6034 • **Value $22**

(8) Prayer for Peace
Handcrafted • LYLE
795QX6261 • **Value $17**

(9) Precious Child
Handcrafted • VOTR
895QX6251 • **Value $17**

(10) Pup-Tenting
Handcrafted • PALM
795QX6011 • **Value $16**

(11) Quasimodo
Handcrafted • CROW
995QXI6341 • **Value $17**

(12) Regal Cardinal
Handcrafted • FRAN
995QX6204 • **Value $22**

(13) Sew Sweet
Handcrafted • AUBE
895QX5921 • **Value $17**

(14) Sister to Sister
Handcrafted • LYLE
995QX5834 • **Value $19**

(15) Son
Handcrafted • PALM
895QX6079 • **Value $18**

(16) Special Dog
Handcrafted • TAGU
795QX5864 • **Value $17**

(17) SPIDER-MAN™
Handcrafted • CHAD
1295QX5757 • **Value $26**

(18) Star of the Show
Handcrafted • AUBE
895QX6004 • **Value $19**

(19) Tamika
Handcrafted • BRIC
795QX6301 • **Value $16**

General Keepsake

	Price Paid	Value of My Collection
1.		
2.		
3.		
4.		
5.		
6.		
7.		
8.		
9.		
10.		
11.		
12.		
13.		
14.		
15.		
16.		
17.		
18.		
19.		
PENCIL TOTALS		

VALUE GUIDE — HALLMARK KEEPSAKE ORNAMENTS

1. Tender Lovin' Care
Handcrafted • SEAL
795QX6114 • **Value $17**

2. Thank You, Santa
Handcrafted • BRIC
795QX5854 • **Value $15**

3. This Big!
Handcrafted • SEAL
995QX5914 • **Value $18**

4. Time for a Treat
Handcrafted • SICK
1195QX5464 • **Value $23**

5. Tonka® Mighty Dump Truck
Die-Cast Metal • N/A
1395QX6321 • **Value $32**

6. A Tree for SNOOPY
Handcrafted • SIED
895QX5507 • **Value $18**

7. Welcome Guest
Handcrafted • UNRU
1495QX5394 • **Value $27**

8. Welcome Him
Handcrafted • TAGU
895QX6264 • **Value $18**

9. Winnie the Pooh and Piglet
Handcrafted • SIED
1295QX5454 • **Value $33**

10. Witch of the West
Handcrafted • LYLE
1395QX5554 • **Value $30**

11. WONDER WOMAN™
Handcrafted • RGRS
1295QX5941 • **Value $25**

12. Woodland Santa
Pressed Tin • SICK
1295QX6131 • **Value $24**

13. Yogi Bear™ and Boo Boo™
Handcrafted • RGRS
1295QX5521 • **Value $24**

14. Yuletide Cheer
Handcrafted • VOTR
795QX6054 • **Value $16**

15. Ziggy®
Handcrafted • CHAD
995QX6524 • **Value $23**

16. Baby's First Christmas
Handcrafted • FRAN
2200QLX7404 • **Value $39**

17. Chicken Coop Chorus
Handcrafted • CROW
2450QLX7491 • **Value $44**

18. Emerald City
Handcrafted • CROW
3200QLX7454 • **Value $66**

19. Father Time
Handcrafted • CHAD
2450QLX7391 • **Value $47**

20. THE JETSONS™
Handcrafted • CROW
2800QLX7411 • **Value $52**

	Price Paid	Value of My Collection
GENERAL KEEPSAKE		
1.		
2.		
3.		
4.		
5.		
6.		
7.		
8.		
9.		
10.		
11.		
12.		
13.		
14.		
15.		
GENERAL MAGIC		
16.		
17.		
18.		
19.		
20.		
PENCIL TOTALS		

1996

1 Jukebox Party
Handcrafted • PALM
2450QLX7339 • **Value $54**

2 Let Us Adore Him
Handcrafted • LYLE
1650QLX7381 • **Value $34**

3 Lighting the Flame
Handcrafted • UNRU
2800QXE7444 • **Value $45**

4 Millennium Falcon™
Handcrafted • N/A
2400QLX7474 • **Value $48**

5 North Pole Volunteers
Handcrafted • SEAL
4200QLX7471 • **Value $79**

6 Over the Rooftops
Handcrafted • SEAL
1450QLX7374 • **Value $28**

7 PEANUTS®
Handcrafted • CHAD
1850QLX7394 • **Value $42**

8 Pinball Wonder
Handcrafted • CROW
2800QLX7451 • **Value $49**

9 Sharing a Soda
Handcrafted • CROW
2450QLX7424 • **Value $43**

10 Slippery Day
Handcrafted • SIED
2450QLX7414 • **Value $50**

11 STAR TREK®, 30 Years
(set/2, w/display base)
Handcrafted • NORT/RHOD
4500QXI7534 • **Value $81**

12 The Statue of Liberty
Handcrafted • SEAL
2450QLX7421 • **Value $43**

13 Treasured Memories
Handcrafted • SICK
1850QLX7384 • **Value $37**

14 U.S.S. Voyager™
Handcrafted • NORT
2400QXI7544 • **Value $50**

15 Video Party
Handcrafted • SIED
2800QLX7431 • **Value $47**

16 Carmen
Cookie Jar Friends
Porcelain • RGRS
1595QK1164 • **Value $25**

17 Clyde
Cookie Jar Friends
Porcelain • AUBE
1595QK1161 • **Value $21**

18 Caroling Angel
Folk Art Americana
Handcrafted/Copper • SICK
1695QK1134 • **Value $30**

19 Mrs. Claus
Folk Art Americana
Handcrafted/Copper • SICK
1895QK1204 • **Value $30**

20 Santa's Gifts
Folk Art Americana
Handcrafted/Copper • SICK
1895QK1124 • **Value $35**

General Magic

	Price Paid	Value of My Collection
1.		
2.		
3.		
4.		
5.		
6.		
7.		
8.		
9.		
10.		
11.		
12.		
13.		
14.		
15.		

General Showcase

	Price Paid	Value of My Collection
16.		
17.		
18.		
19.		
20.		
Pencil Totals		

Value Guide — Hallmark Keepsake Ornaments

1. Balthasar (Frankincense)
Magi Bells
Porcelain • VOTR
1395QK1174 • **Value $25**

2. Caspar (Myrrh)
Magi Bells
Porcelain • VOTR
1395QK1184 • **Value $25**

3. Melchoir (Gold)
Magi Bells
Porcelain • VOTR
1395QK1181 • **Value $25**

4. The Birds' Christmas Tree
Nature's Sketchbook
Handcrafted • UNRU
1895QK1114 • **Value $28**

5. Christmas Bunny
Nature's Sketchbook
Handcrafted • FRAN
1895QK1104 • **Value $38**

6. The Holly Basket
Nature's Sketchbook
Handcrafted • LYLE
1895QK1094 • **Value $30**

7. Madonna and Child
Sacred Masterworks
Handcrafted • SICK
1595QK1144 • **Value $28**

8. Praying Madonna
Sacred Masterworks
Handcrafted • SICK
1595QK1154 • **Value $27**

9. African Elephants
Handcrafted • SICK
575QXM4224 • **Value $17**

10. Baby Sylvester
Handcrafted • PALM
575QXM4154 • **Value $16**

11. Baby Tweety
Handcrafted • PALM
575QXM4014 • **Value $25**

12. A Child's Gifts
Handcrafted • ANDR
675QXM4234 • **Value $13**

13. Christmas Bear
Handcrafted • SEAL
475QXM4241 • **Value $14**

14. Cloisonné Medallion
Cloisonné • MCGE
975QXE4041 • **Value $19**

15. Cool Delivery
Coca-Cola®
Handcrafted • PIKE
575QXM4021 • **Value $15**

16. GONE WITH THE
WIND™ (set/3)
Handcrafted • ANDR
1995QXM4211 • **Value $37**

17. Hattie Chapeau
Handcrafted • RHOD
475QXM4251 • **Value $11**

18. Joyous Angel
Handcrafted • ANDR
475QXM4231 • **Value $10**

19. Long Winter's Nap
Handcrafted • ANDR
575QXM4244 • **Value $13**

20. Message for Santa
Handcrafted • SEAL
675QXM4254 • **Value $13**

1996

General Showcase

	Price Paid	Value of My Collection
1.		
2.		
3.		
4.		
5.		
6.		
7.		
8.		

General Miniature

9.		
10.		
11.		
12.		
13.		
14.		
15.		
16.		
17.		
18.		
19.		
20.		

PENCIL TOTALS

VALUE GUIDE — HALLMARK KEEPSAKE ORNAMENTS

(1) O Holy Night (set/4)
Handcrafted • RHOD
2450QXM4204 • **Value $33**

(2) Peaceful Christmas
Handcrafted • UNRU
475QXM4214 • **Value $13**

(3) Sparkling Crystal Angel
Lead Crystal/Silver • VOTR
975QXM4264 • **Value $21**

(4) Tiny Christmas Helpers (set/6)
Handcrafted • SEAL
2900QXM4261 • **Value $46**

(5) A Tree for WOODSTOCK
Handcrafted • SIED
575QXM4767 • **Value $17**

(6) The Vehicles of STAR WARS™ (set/3)
Handcrafted • RHOD
1995QXM4024 • **Value $39**

(7) Winnie the Pooh and Tigger
Handcrafted • SIED
975QXM4044 • **Value $24**

(8) Airmail for Santa (gift membership bonus)
Handcrafted • RGRS
QXC4194 • **Value $22**

(9) Holiday Bunny (early renewal piece, miniature)
Handcrafted • FRAN
QXC4191 • **Value $17**

(10) Rudolph the Red-Nosed Reindeer® (keepsake of membership, magic)
Handcrafted • SIED
QXC7341 • **Value $25**

(11) Rudolph®'s Helper (keepsake of membership, miniature)
Handcrafted • SIED
QXC4171 • **Value $17**

(12) Santa (keepsake of membership)
Handcrafted • SIED
QXC4164 • **Value $23**

(13) The Wizard of OZ™ (club edition)
Handcrafted • RGRS
1295QXC4161 • **Value $52**

(14) "Get Hooked On Collecting" Starter Set (book with "Filled With Memories" ornament)
Handcrafted • N/A
799XPR837 • **Value N/E**

(15) Welcome Sign, Tender Touches
Handcrafted • SEAL
1500QX6331 • **Value $25**

(16) 1955 Chevrolet Cameo (red)
Handcrafted • PALM
(N/C) No stock # • **Value N/E**

(17) Gold Rocking Horse (miniature)
Handcrafted • SICK
($12.95) No stock # • **Value $42**

(18) Murray® Airplane (tan)
Die-Cast Metal • PALM
(N/C) No stock # • **Value N/E**

(19) Murray® Fire Truck (miniature, white)
Die-Cast Metal • PALM
(N/C) No stock # • **Value N/E**

(20) Santa's Toy Shop (set/2, artist signing piece)
Handcrafted • VARI
6000QXC4201 • **Value $122**

	Price Paid	Value of My Collection
GENERAL MINIATURE		
1.		
2.		
3.		
4.		
5.		
6.		
7.		
COLLECTOR'S CLUB		
8.		
9.		
10.		
11.		
12.		
13.		
PREMIERE ORNAMENTS		
14.		
15.		
ARTISTS ON TOUR PIECES		
16.		
17.		
18.		
19.		
20.		
PENCIL TOTALS		

1. Toy Shop Santa
Handcrafted • UNRU
($14.95) No stock # • **Value $38**

2. BARBIE™ Lapel Pin
(re-issued in 1997)
Handcrafted • N/A
495XLP3544 • **Value $4.95**

3. Holiday BARBIE™
Stocking Hanger
(re-issued in 1997)
Handcrafted • N/A
1995XSH3101 • **Value $35**

4. Yuletide Romance ™
BARBIE® Doll
(3rd & final in series)
Vinyl • N/A
5000QHX3401 • **Value $100**

5. Reindeer Rooters
Handcrafted • CROW
(N/C) No stock # • **Value N/E**

6. Golden Age
Batman and Robin™
"The Dynamic Duo™"
Handcrafted • UNRU
7000QHF3103 • **Value N/E**

7. Golden Age
Superman™ "Man of
Steel™" (LE-14,500)
Handcrafted • N/A
8000QHF3101 • **Value N/E**

8. Golden Age Wonder
Woman™ "Champion
of Freedom"
Handcrafted • RGRS
3500QHF3107 • **Value N/E**

1996

9. Modern Era Batman™
"Guardian of
Gotham City™"
Handcrafted • CHAD
5500QHF3104 • **Value N/E**

10. Modern Era Robin™
"World's Bravest
Teenager"
Handcrafted • CHAD
4000QHF3105 • **Value N/E**

11. Modern Era
Superman™ "In A
Single Bound"
Handcrafted • N/A
6000QHF3102 • **Value N/E**

ARTISTS ON TOUR PIECES

	Price Paid	Value of My Collection
1.		

BARBIE™ COLLECTIBLES

2.		
3.		
4.		

CLUB TOUR ORNAMENT

5.		

D.C. SUPER HEROES FIGURINES

6.		
7.		
8.		
9.		
10.		
11.		
12.		

NFL COLLECTION

13.		
14.		

PENCIL TOTALS

12. Modern Era Wonder
Woman™ "Warrior of
Strength and Wisdom"
Handcrafted • RGRS
3500QHF3106 • **Value N/E**

1. Buffalo Bills™
595BIL2035 • **Value $10**
2. Carolina Panthers™
(re-issued from 1995)
595PNA2035 • **Value $10**
3. Chicago Bears™
(re-issued from 1995)
595BRS2035 • **Value $10**
4. Dallas Cowboys™
(re-issued from 1995)
595COW2035 • **Value $10**
5. Green Bay Packers™
595PKR2035 • **Value $10**
6. Kansas City Chiefs™
(re-issued from 1995)
595CHF2035 • **Value $10**
7. Los Angeles Raiders™
(re-issued from 1995)
595RDR2035 • **Value $10**

8. Minnesota Vikings™
(re-issued from 1995)
595VIK2035 • **Value $10**
9. New England Patriots™
(re-issued from 1995)
595NEP2035 • **Value $10**
10. Philadelphia Eagles™
(re-issued from 1995)
595EAG2035 • **Value $10**
11. Pittsburgh Steelers™
595PIT2035 • **Value $10**
12. St. Louis Rams™
595RAM2035 • **Value $10**
13. San Francisco 49ers™
595FOR2035 • **Value $10**
14. Washington Redskins™
(re-issued from 1995)
595RSK2035 • **Value $10**

13. NFL COLLECTION
(14 assorted)
Glass • N/A

14. NFL COLLECTION
(30 assorted)
Handcrafted • UNRU

1. Arizona Cardinals™
995QSR6484 • **Value $15**
2. Atlanta Falcons™
995QSR6364 • **Value $15**
3. Browns™
995QSR6391 • **Value $15**
4. Buffalo Bills™
995QSR6371 • **Value $15**
5. Carolina Panthers™
995QSR6374 • **Value $15**
6. Chicago Bears™
995QSR6381 • **Value $15**

7. Cincinnati Bengals™
995QSR6384 • **Value $15**
8. Dallas Cowboys™
995QSR6394 • **Value $15**
9. Denver Broncos™
995QSR6411 • **Value $15**
10. Detroit Lions™
995QSR6414 • **Value $15**
11. Green Bay Packers™
995QSR6421 • **Value $15**
12. Indianapolis Colts™
995QSR6431 • **Value $15**

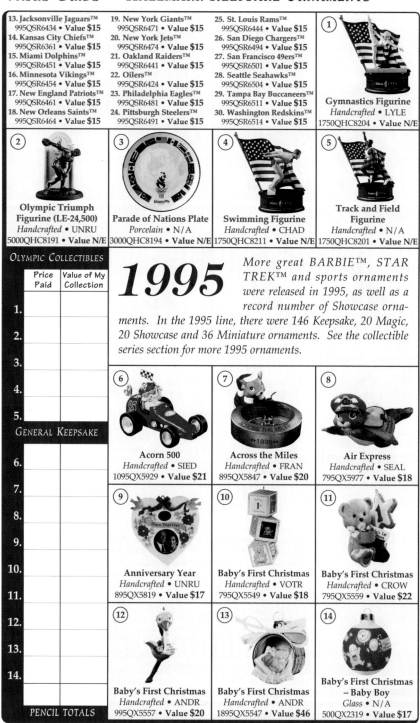

13. Jacksonville Jaguars™
995QSR6434 • Value $15
14. Kansas City Chiefs™
995QSR6361 • Value $15
15. Miami Dolphins™
995QSR6451 • Value $15
16. Minnesota Vikings™
995QSR6454 • Value $15
17. New England Patriots™
995QSR6461 • Value $15
18. New Orleans Saints™
995QSR6464 • Value $15

19. New York Giants™
995QSR6471 • Value $15
20. New York Jets™
995QSR6474 • Value $15
21. Oakland Raiders™
995QSR6441 • Value $15
22. Oilers™
995QSR6424 • Value $15
23. Philadelphia Eagles™
995QSR6481 • Value $15
24. Pittsburgh Steelers™
995QSR6491 • Value $15

25. St. Louis Rams™
995QSR6444 • Value $15
26. San Diego Chargers™
995QSR6494 • Value $15
27. San Francisco 49ers™
995QSR6501 • Value $15
28. Seattle Seahawks™
995QSR6504 • Value $15
29. Tampa Bay Buccaneers™
995QSR6511 • Value $15
30. Washington Redskins™
995QSR6514 • Value $15

①
Gymnastics Figurine
Handcrafted • LYLE
1750QHC8204 • **Value N/E**

②
Olympic Triumph Figurine (LE-24,500)
Handcrafted • UNRU
5000QHC8191 • **Value N/E**

③
Parade of Nations Plate
Porcelain • N/A
3000QHC8194 • **Value N/E**

④
Swimming Figurine
Handcrafted • CHAD
1750QHC8211 • **Value N/E**

⑤
Track and Field Figurine
Handcrafted • N/A
1750QHC8201 • **Value N/E**

1995

More great BARBIE™, STAR TREK™ and sports ornaments were released in 1995, as well as a record number of Showcase ornaments. In the 1995 line, there were 146 Keepsake, 20 Magic, 20 Showcase and 36 Miniature ornaments. See the collectible series section for more 1995 ornaments.

OLYMPIC COLLECTIBLES

	Price Paid	Value of My Collection
1.		
2.		
3.		

GENERAL KEEPSAKE

4.		
5.		
6.		
7.		
8.		
9.		
10.		
11.		
12.		
13.		
14.		

PENCIL TOTALS

⑥
Acorn 500
Handcrafted • SIED
1095QX5929 • **Value $21**

⑦
Across the Miles
Handcrafted • FRAN
895QX5847 • **Value $20**

⑧
Air Express
Handcrafted • SEAL
795QX5977 • **Value $18**

⑨
Anniversary Year
Handcrafted • UNRU
895QX5819 • **Value $17**

⑩
Baby's First Christmas
Handcrafted • VOTR
795QX5549 • **Value $18**

⑪
Baby's First Christmas
Handcrafted • CROW
795QX5559 • **Value $22**

⑫
Baby's First Christmas
Handcrafted • ANDR
995QX5557 • **Value $20**

⑬
Baby's First Christmas
Handcrafted • ANDR
1895QX5547 • **Value $46**

⑭
Baby's First Christmas – Baby Boy
Glass • N/A
500QX2319 • **Value $17**

①
Baby's First Christmas
– Baby Girl
Glass • N/A
500QX2317 • **Value $17**

②
Baby's Second
Christmas
Handcrafted • CROW
795QX5567 • **Value $23**

③
Barrel-Back Rider
Handcrafted • FRAN
995QX5189 • **Value $23**

④
Batmobile
Handcrafted • PALM
1495QX5739 • **Value $26**

⑤
Betty and Wilma
Handcrafted • RHOD
1495QX5417 • **Value $23**

⑥
Beverly and Teddy
Handcrafted • UNRU
2175QX5259 • **Value $32**

⑦
Bingo Bear
Handcrafted • VOTR
795QX5919 • **Value $18**

⑧
Bobbin' Along
Handcrafted • CROW
895QX5879 • **Value $29**

⑨
Brother
Handcrafted • LYLE
695QX5679 • **Value $14**

⑩
Bugs Bunny
Handcrafted • CHAD
895QX5019 • **Value $21**

⑪
Captain James T. Kirk
Handcrafted • RGRS
1395QXI5539 • **Value $27**

⑫
Captain Jean-Luc Picard
Handcrafted • RGRS
1395QXI5737 • **Value $28**

⑬
Captain John Smith
and Meeko
Handcrafted • CROW
1295QXI6169 • **Value $20**

⑭
Catch the Spirit
Handcrafted • SIED
795QX5899 • **Value $19**

⑮
Child's Fifth Christmas
Handcrafted • RHOD
695QX5637 • **Value $17**

⑯
Child's Fourth Christmas
Handcrafted • FRAN
695QX5629 • **Value $19**

⑰
Child's Third Christmas
Handcrafted • CROW
795QX5627 • **Value $19**

⑱
Christmas Fever
Handcrafted • AUBE
795QX5967 • **Value $17**

⑲
Christmas Morning
Handcrafted • FRAN
1095QX5997 • **Value $18**

⑳
Christmas Patrol
Handcrafted • ANDR
795QX5959 • **Value $19**

1995

GENERAL KEEPSAKE

	Price Paid	Value of My Collection
1.		
2.		
3.		
4.		
5.		
6.		
7.		
8.		
9.		
10.		
11.		
12.		
13.		
14.		
15.		
16.		
17.		
18.		
19.		
20.		
PENCIL TOTALS		

VALUE GUIDE — HALLMARK KEEPSAKE ORNAMENTS

1
Colorful World
Handcrafted • CROW
1095QX5519 • **Value $27**

2
Cows of Bali
Handcrafted • ANDR
895QX5999 • **Value $18**

3
Dad
Handcrafted • SIED
795QX5649 • **Value $16**

4
Dad-to-Be
Handcrafted • RHOD
795QX5667 • **Value $14**

5
Daughter
Handcrafted • PALM
695QX5677 • **Value $18**

6
Delivering Kisses
Handcrafted • SICK
1095QX4107 • **Value $24**

7
Dream On
Handcrafted • FRAN
1095QX6007 • **Value $21**

8
Dudley the Dragon
Handcrafted • PIKE
1095QX6209 • **Value $21**

9
Faithful Fan
Handcrafted • SIED
895QX5897 • **Value $18**

10
Feliz Navidad
Handcrafted • RHOD
795QX5869 • **Value $20**

11
For My Grandma
Handcrafted • PALM
695QX5729 • **Value $15**

12
Forever Friends Bear
Handcrafted • BRWN
895QX5258 • **Value $22**

13
Friendly Boost
Handcrafted • PALM
895QX5827 • **Value $21**

14
GARFIELD®
Handcrafted • N/A
1095QX5007 • **Value $26**

15
Glinda, Witch of the North
Handcrafted • LYLE
1395QX5749 • **Value $36**

16
Godchild
Handcrafted/Brass • PALM
795QX5707 • **Value $20**

17
Godparent
Glass • VOTR
500QX2417 • **Value $13**

18
Gopher Fun
Handcrafted • SIED
995QX5887 • **Value $18**

19
Grandchild's First Christmas
Handcrafted • FRAN
795QX5777 • **Value $16**

20
Granddaughter
Handcrafted • RGRS
695QX5779 • **Value $17**

GENERAL KEEPSAKE

	Price Paid	Value of My Collection
1.		
2.		
3.		
4.		
5.		
6.		
7.		
8.		
9.		
10.		
11.		
12.		
13.		
14.		
15.		
16.		
17.		
18.		
19.		
20.		
PENCIL TOTALS		

1. Grandmother
Handcrafted • ANDR
795QX5767 • **Value $20**

2. Grandpa
Handcrafted • CROW
895QX5769 • **Value $18**

3. Grandparents
Glass • LYLE
500QX2419 • **Value $13**

4. Grandson
Handcrafted • RGRS
695QX5787 • **Value $17**

5. Happy Wrappers (set/2)
Handcrafted • CROW
1095QX6037 • **Value $21**

6. Heaven's Gift (set/2)
Handcrafted • ANDR
2000QX6057 • **Value $44**

7. Hockey Pup
Handcrafted • CROW
995QX5917 • **Value $23**

8. Important Memo
Handcrafted • SICK
895QX5947 • **Value $17**

9. In a Heartbeat
Handcrafted • ANDR
895QX5817 • **Value $20**

10. In Time With Christmas
Handcrafted • CROW
1295QX6049 • **Value $24**

11. Joy to the World
Handcrafted • ANDR
895QX5867 • **Value $21**

12. LEGO® Fireplace With Santa
Handcrafted • CROW
1095QX4769 • **Value $25**

13. Lou Rankin Bear
Handcrafted • SIED
995QX4069 • **Value $22**

14. The Magic School Bus™
Handcrafted • RHOD
1095QX5849 • **Value $20**

15. Mary Engelbreit
Glass • N/A
500QX2409 • **Value $16**

16. Merry RV
Handcrafted • PALM
1295QX6027 • **Value $26**

17. Mom
Handcrafted • SIED
795QX5647 • **Value $18**

18. Mom and Dad
Handcrafted • RGRS
995QX5657 • **Value $25**

19. Mom-to-Be
Handcrafted • RHOD
795QX5659 • **Value $16**

20. Muletide Greetings
Handcrafted • CHAD
795QX6009 • **Value $17**

1995

General Keepsake

	Price Paid	Value of My Collection
1.		
2.		
3.		
4.		
5.		
6.		
7.		
8.		
9.		
10.		
11.		
12.		
13.		
14.		
15.		
16.		
17.		
18.		
19.		
20.		
PENCIL TOTALS		

(1) New Home
Handcrafted • ANDR
895QX5839 • **Value $18**

(2) North Pole 911
Handcrafted • SEAL
1095QX5957 • **Value $22**

(3) Number One Teacher
Handcrafted • SEAL
795QX5949 • **Value $17**

(4) The Olympic Spirit
Centennial Games
Atlanta 1996
Acrylic • N/A
795QX3169 • **Value $20**

(5) On the Ice
Handcrafted • CROW
795QX6047 • **Value $21**

(6) Our Christmas Together
Handcrafted • LYLE
995QX5809 • **Value $19**

(7) Our Family
Handcrafted • CHAD
795QX5709 • **Value $17**

(8) Our First Christmas
Together
Acrylic • LYLE
695QX3177 • **Value $17**

(9) Our First Christmas
Together
Handcrafted • SIED
895QX5799 • **Value $22**

(10) Our First Christmas
Together
Handcrafted • SEAL
895QX5807 • **Value $20**

(11) Our First Christmas
Handcrafted • LYLE
1695QX5797 • **Value $30**

(12) Our Little Blessings
Handcrafted • CROW
1295QX5209 • **Value $26**

(13) Packed With Memories
Handcrafted • SEAL
795QX5639 • **Value $19**

(14) Percy, Flit and Meeko
Handcrafted • CROW
995QXI6179 • **Value $21**

(15) Perfect Balance
Handcrafted • SIED
795QX5927 • **Value $18**

(16) PEZ® Santa
Handcrafted • FRAN
795QX5267 • **Value $20**

(17) Pocahontas
Handcrafted • CROW
1295QXI6177 • **Value $22**

(18) Pocahontas and Captain
John Smith
Handcrafted • CROW
1495QXI6197 • **Value $25**

(19) Polar Coaster
Handcrafted • CROW
895QX6117 • **Value $23**

(20) Popeye®
Handcrafted • CHAD
1095QX5257 • **Value $27**

GENERAL KEEPSAKE

	Price Paid	Value of My Collection
1.		
2.		
3.		
4.		
5.		
6.		
7.		
8.		
9.		
10.		
11.		
12.		
13.		
14.		
15.		
16.		
17.		
18.		
19.		
20.		
PENCIL TOTALS		

VALUE GUIDE — HALLMARK KEEPSAKE ORNAMENTS

(1) Refreshing Gift
Handcrafted • UNRU
1495QX4067 • **Value $30**

(2) Rejoice!
Handcrafted • LYLE
1095QX5987 • **Value $24**

(3) Roller Whiz
Handcrafted • SEAL
795QX5937 • **Value $19**

(4) Santa In Paris
Handcrafted • SICK
895QX5877 • **Value $26**

(5) Santa's Serenade
Handcrafted • CROW
895QX6017 • **Value $19**

(6) Santa's Visitors
Glass • N/A
500QX2407 • **Value $17**

(7) Simba, Pumbaa and Timon
Handcrafted • CROW
1295QX6159 • **Value $20**

(8) Sister
Handcrafted • LYLE
695QX5687 • **Value $15**

(9) Sister to Sister
Handcrafted • VOTR
895QX5689 • **Value $18**

(10) Ski Hound
Handcrafted • RHOD
895QX5909 • **Value $19**

(11) Son
Handcrafted • PALM
695QX5669 • **Value $18**

(12) Special Cat
Handcrafted • CHAD
795QX5717 • **Value $17**

(13) Special Dog
Handcrafted • CHAD
795QX5719 • **Value $17**

(14) Surfin' Santa
Handcrafted • CROW
995QX6019 • **Value $25**

(15) Sylvester and Tweety (set/2)
Handcrafted • CHAD
1395QX5017 • **Value $27**

(16) Takin' a Hike
Handcrafted • FRAN
795QX6029 • **Value $19**

(17) Tennis, Anyone?
Handcrafted • AUBE
795QX5907 • **Value $19**

(18) Thomas the Tank Engine – No. 1
Handcrafted • RHOD
995QX5857 • **Value $30**

(19) Three Wishes
Handcrafted • ANDR
795QX5979 • **Value $21**

(20) Two for Tea
Handcrafted • JLEE
995QX5829 • **Value $30**

1995

	General Keepsake	
	Price Paid	Value of My Collection
1.		
2.		
3.		
4.		
5.		
6.		
7.		
8.		
9.		
10.		
11.		
12.		
13.		
14.		
15.		
16.		
17.		
18.		
19.		
20.		
PENCIL TOTALS		

1. Vera the Mouse
Porcelain • N/A
895QX5537 • **Value $18**

2. Waiting Up for Santa
Handcrafted • PALM
895QX6106 • **Value $17**

3. Water Sports (set/2)
Handcrafted • SIED
1495QX6039 • **Value $34**

4. Wheel of Fortune®
Handcrafted • SICK
1295QX6187 • **Value $26**

5. Winnie the Pooh and Tigger
Handcrafted • SIED
1295QX5009 • **Value $34**

6. The Winning Play
Handcrafted • SIED
795QX5889 • **Value $22**

7. Baby's First Christmas
Handcrafted • CROW
2200QLX7317 • **Value $38**

8. Coming to See Santa
Handcrafted • PALM
3200QLX7369 • **Value $62**

9. Fred and Dino
Handcrafted • RHOD
2800QLX7289 • **Value $52**

10. Friends Share Fun
Handcrafted • RGRS
1650QLX7349 • **Value $34**

11. Goody Gumballs!
Handcrafted • SIED
1250QLX7367 • **Value $32**

12. Headin' Home
Handcrafted • JLEE
2200QLX7327 • **Value $44**

13. Holiday Swim
Handcrafted • RGRS
1850QLX7319 • **Value $37**

14. Jumping for Joy
Handcrafted • FRAN
2800QLX7347 • **Value $54**

15. My First HOT WHEELS™
Handcrafted • CROW
2800QLX7279 • **Value $50**

16. Romulan Warbird™
Handcrafted • NORT
2400QXI7267 • **Value $42**

17. Santa's Diner
Handcrafted • VOTR
2450QLX7337 • **Value $35**

18. Space Shuttle
Handcrafted • CROW
2450QLX7396 • **Value $43**

19. Superman™
Handcrafted • CHAD
2800QLX7309 • **Value $51**

20. Victorian Toy Box
Handcrafted • LYLE
4200QLX7357 • **Value $63**

	Price Paid	Value of My Collection
General Keepsake		
1.		
2.		
3.		
4.		
5.		
6.		
General Magic		
7.		
8.		
9.		
10.		
11.		
12.		
13.		
14.		
15.		
16.		
17.		
18.		
19.		
20.		
PENCIL TOTALS		

1.
Wee Little Christmas
Handcrafted • CROW
2200QLX7329 • **Value $44**

2.
Winnie the Pooh
Too Much Hunny
Handcrafted • SIED
2450QLX7297 • **Value $52**

3.
Angel of Light
All Is Bright
Handcrafted • ANDR
1195QK1159 • **Value $23**

4.
Gentle Lullaby
All Is Bright
Handcrafted • ANDR
1195QK1157 • **Value $23**

5.
Carole
Angel Bells
Porcelain • VOTR
1295QK1147 • **Value $28**

6.
Joy
Angel Bells
Porcelain • VOTR
1295QK1137 • **Value $32**

7.
Noelle
Angel Bells
Porcelain • VOTR
1295QK1139 • **Value $25**

8.
Fetching the Firewood
Folk Art Americana
Handcrafted • SICK
1595QK1057 • **Value $36**

9.
Fishing Party
Folk Art Americana
Handcrafted • SICK
1595QK1039 • **Value $35**

10.
Guiding Santa
Folk Art Americana
Handcrafted • SICK
1895QK1037 • **Value $48**

11.
Learning to Skate
Folk Art Americana
Handcrafted • SICK
1495QK1047 • **Value $38**

12.
Away in a Manger
Holiday Enchantment
Porcelain • N/A
1395QK1097 • **Value $27**

13.
Following the Star
Holiday Enchantment
Porcelain • VOTR
1395QK1099 • **Value $27**

14.
Cozy Cottage Teapot
Invitation To Tea
Handcrafted • ANDR
1595QK1127 • **Value $28**

15.
European Castle Teapot
Invitation To Tea
Handcrafted • ANDR
1595QK1129 • **Value $28**

16.
Victorian Home Teapot
Invitation To Tea
Handcrafted • ANDR
1595QK1119 • **Value $33**

17.
Backyard Orchard
Nature's Sketchbook
Handcrafted • FRAN
1895QK1069 • **Value $32**

18.
Christmas Cardinal
Nature's Sketchbook
Handcrafted • LYLE
1895QK1077 • **Value $42**

19.
Raising a Family
Nature's Sketchbook
Handcrafted • LYLE
1895QK1067 • **Value $32**

20.
Violets and Butterflies
Nature's Sketchbook
Handcrafted • LYLE
1695QK1079 • **Value $32**

1995

	Price Paid	Value of My Collection
General Magic		
1.		
2.		
General Showcase		
3.		
4.		
5.		
6.		
7.		
8.		
9.		
10.		
11.		
12.		
13.		
14.		
15.		
16.		
17.		
18.		
19.		
20.		
PENCIL TOTALS		

① Jolly Santa
Symbols Of Christmas
Handcrafted • ANDR
1595QK1087 • **Value $28**

② Sweet Song
Symbols Of Christmas
Handcrafted • ANDR
1595QK1089 • **Value $28**

③ Baby's First Christmas
Handcrafted • SEAL
475QXM4027 • **Value $13**

④ Calamity Coyote
Handcrafted • RGRS
675QXM4467 • **Value $15**

⑤ Christmas Wishes
Handcrafted • SEAL
375QXM4087 • **Value $16**

⑥ Cloisonné Partridge
Cloisonné • VOTR
975QXM4017 • **Value $19**

⑦ Downhill Double
Handcrafted • PALM
475QXM4837 • **Value $12**

⑧ Friendship Duet
Handcrafted • UNRU
475QXM4019 • **Value $13**

⑨ Furrball
Handcrafted • RGRS
575QXM4459 • **Value $15**

⑩ Grandpa's Gift
Handcrafted • RGRS
575QXM4829 • **Value $13**

⑪ Heavenly Praises
Handcrafted • ANDR
575QXM4037 • **Value $13**

⑫ Joyful Santa
Handcrafted • UNRU
475QXM4089 • **Value $12**

⑬ Little Beeper
Handcrafted • RGRS
575QXM4469 • **Value $15**

⑭ Merry Walruses
Handcrafted • SICK
575QXM4057 • **Value $21**

⑮ A Moustershire Christmas (set/4)
Handcrafted • RHOD
2450QXM4839 • **Value $42**

⑯ Pebbles and Bamm-Bamm
Handcrafted • RHOD
975QXM4757 • **Value $17**

⑰ Playful Penguins
Handcrafted • SICK
575QXM4059 • **Value $22**

⑱ Precious Creations
Handcrafted • SICK
975QXM4077 • **Value $19**

⑲ Santa's Visit
Handcrafted • CROW
775QXM4047 • **Value $19**

⑳ The Ships of STAR TREK® (set/3)
Handcrafted • N/A
1995QXI4109 • **Value $29**

GENERAL SHOWCASE

	Price Paid	Value of My Collection
1.		
2.		

GENERAL MINIATURE

3.		
4.		
5.		
6.		
7.		
8.		
9.		
10.		
11.		
12.		
13.		
14.		
15.		
16.		
17.		
18.		
19.		
20.		
PENCIL TOTALS		

(1) **Starlit Nativity** *Handcrafted* • UNRU 775QXM4039 • **Value $19**	**(2)** **Sugarplum Dreams** *Handcrafted* • CROW 475QXM4099 • **Value $14**	**(3)** **Tiny Treasures (set/6)** *Handcrafted* • SEAL 2900QXM4009 • **Value $47**	**(4)** **Tunnel of Love** *Handcrafted* • CROW 475QXM4029 • **Value $13**
(5) **Cinderella's Stepsisters** (gift membership bonus, Merry Miniature) *Handcrafted* • PIKE 375QXC4159 • **Value $48**	**(6)** **Collecting Memories** (keepsake of membership) *Handcrafted* • SIED QXC4117 • **Value $22**	**(7)** **Cool Santa** (keepsake of membership, miniature) *Handcrafted* • FRAN QXC4457 • **Value $16**	**(8)** **Cozy Christmas** (early renewal gift, miniature) *Handcrafted* • FRAN QXC4119 • **Value $18**

1995

(9) **Fishing For Fun** (keepsake of membership) *Handcrafted* • SEAL QXC5207 • **Value $22**	**(10)** **A Gift From Rodney** (keepsake of membership, miniature) *Handcrafted* • SICK QXC4129 • **Value $15**	**(11)** **Home From The Woods** (club edition) *Handcrafted* • SICK 1595QXC1059 • **Value $55**	

(12) **May Flower** (club edition, Easter sidekick) *Handcrafted* • SIED 495QXC8246 • **Value $50**	**(13)** **Happy Holidays** *Handcrafted* • VOTR 295QX6307 • **Value $14**

(14) **Hooked On Collecting –** **1995 – Ornament Premiere** *Handcrafted* • PALM (N/C) No stock # • **Value $10**

(15) **Wish List** *Handcrafted* • SEAL 1500QX5859 • **Value $25**	**(16)** **Charlie Brown** *A Charlie Brown Christmas* *Handcrafted* • SIED 395QRP4207 • **Value $26**	**(17)** **Linus** *A Charlie Brown Christmas* *Handcrafted* • RGRS 395QRP4217 • **Value $20**
(18) **Lucy** *A Charlie Brown Christmas* *Handcrafted* • SIED 395QRP4209 • **Value $20**	**(19)** **SNOOPY** *A Charlie Brown Christmas* *Handcrafted* • RGRS 395QRP4219 • **Value $26**	**(20)** **WOODSTOCK w/tree and snowbase** *A Charlie Brown Christmas* *Handcrafted* • RGRS 395QRP4227 • **Value $17**

GENERAL MINIATURE

	Price Paid	Value of My Collection
1.		
2.		
3.		
4.		

COLLECTOR'S CLUB

5.		
6.		
7.		
8.		
9.		
10.		
11.		
12.		

PREMIERE ORNAMENTS

13.		
14.		
15.		

REACH ORNAMENTS

16.		
17.		
18.		
19.		
20.		
PENCIL TOTALS		

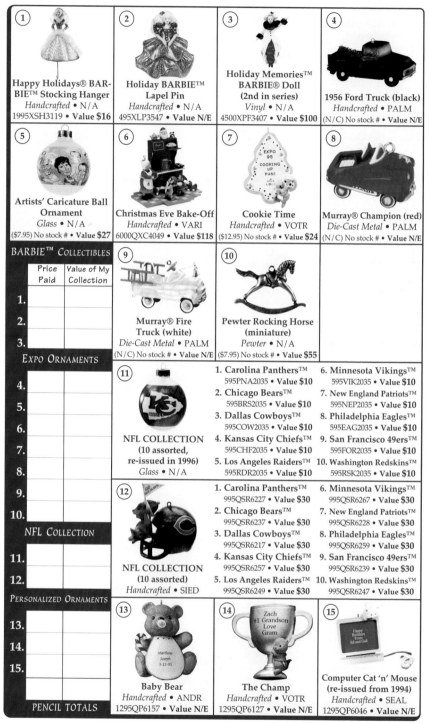

1 Happy Holidays® BARBIE™ Stocking Hanger
Handcrafted • N/A
1995XSH3119 • **Value $16**

2 Holiday BARBIE™ Lapel Pin
Handcrafted • N/A
495XLP3547 • **Value N/E**

3 Holiday Memories™ BARBIE® Doll (2nd in series)
Vinyl • N/A
4500XPF3407 • **Value $100**

4 1956 Ford Truck (black)
Handcrafted • PALM
(N/C) No stock # • **Value N/E**

5 Artists' Caricature Ball Ornament
Glass • N/A
($7.95) No stock # • **Value $27**

6 Christmas Eve Bake-Off
Handcrafted • VARI
6000QXC4049 • **Value $118**

7 Cookie Time
Handcrafted • VOTR
($12.95) No stock # • **Value $24**

8 Murray® Champion (red)
Die-Cast Metal • PALM
(N/C) No stock # • **Value N/E**

BARBIE™ COLLECTIBLES

	Price Paid	Value of My Collection
1.		
2.		
3.		

EXPO ORNAMENTS

4.		
5.		
6.		
7.		
8.		
9.		
10.		

NFL COLLECTION

| 11. | | |
| 12. | | |

PERSONALIZED ORNAMENTS

13.		
14.		
15.		

PENCIL TOTALS

9 Murray® Fire Truck (white)
Die-Cast Metal • PALM
(N/C) No stock # • **Value N/E**

10 Pewter Rocking Horse (miniature)
Pewter • N/A
($7.95) No stock # • **Value $55**

11 NFL COLLECTION (10 assorted, re-issued in 1996)
Glass • N/A

1. Carolina Panthers™ 595PNA2035 • **Value $10**
2. Chicago Bears™ 595BRS2035 • **Value $10**
3. Dallas Cowboys™ 595COW2035 • **Value $10**
4. Kansas City Chiefs™ 595CHF2035 • **Value $10**
5. Los Angeles Raiders™ 595RDR2035 • **Value $10**
6. Minnesota Vikings™ 595VIK2035 • **Value $10**
7. New England Patriots™ 595NEP2035 • **Value $10**
8. Philadelphia Eagles™ 595EAG2035 • **Value $10**
9. San Francisco 49ers™ 595FOR2035 • **Value $10**
10. Washington Redskins™ 595RSK2035 • **Value $10**

12 NFL COLLECTION (10 assorted)
Handcrafted • SIED

1. Carolina Panthers™ 995QSR6227 • **Value $30**
2. Chicago Bears™ 995QSR6237 • **Value $30**
3. Dallas Cowboys™ 995QSR6217 • **Value $30**
4. Kansas City Chiefs™ 995QSR6257 • **Value $30**
5. Los Angeles Raiders™ 995QSR6249 • **Value $30**
6. Minnesota Vikings™ 995QSR6267 • **Value $30**
7. New England Patriots™ 995QSR6228 • **Value $30**
8. Philadelphia Eagles™ 995QSR6259 • **Value $30**
9. San Francisco 49ers™ 995QSR6239 • **Value $30**
10. Washington Redskins™ 995QSR6247 • **Value $30**

13 Baby Bear
Handcrafted • ANDR
1295QP6157 • **Value N/E**

14 The Champ
Handcrafted • VOTR
1295QP6127 • **Value N/E**

15 Computer Cat 'n' Mouse (re-issued from 1994)
Handcrafted • SEAL
1295QP6046 • **Value N/E**

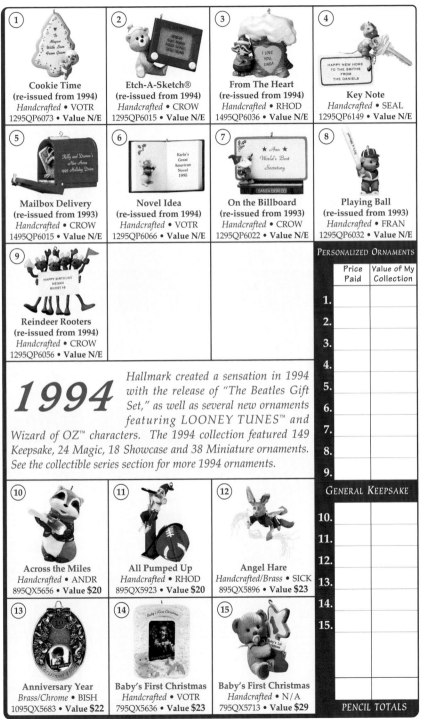

1 Cookie Time
(re-issued from 1994)
Handcrafted • VOTR
1295QP6073 • **Value N/E**

2 Etch-A-Sketch®
(re-issued from 1994)
Handcrafted • CROW
1295QP6015 • **Value N/E**

3 From The Heart
(re-issued from 1994)
Handcrafted • RHOD
1495QP6036 • **Value N/E**

4 Key Note
Handcrafted • SEAL
1295QP6149 • **Value N/E**

5 Mailbox Delivery
(re-issued from 1993)
Handcrafted • CROW
1495QP6015 • **Value N/E**

6 Novel Idea
(re-issued from 1994)
Handcrafted • VOTR
1295QP6066 • **Value N/E**

7 On the Billboard
(re-issued from 1993)
Handcrafted • CROW
1295QP6022 • **Value N/E**

8 Playing Ball
(re-issued from 1993)
Handcrafted • FRAN
1295QP6032 • **Value N/E**

9 Reindeer Rooters
(re-issued from 1994)
Handcrafted • CROW
1295QP6056 • **Value N/E**

1994

Hallmark created a sensation in 1994 with the release of "The Beatles Gift Set," as well as several new ornaments featuring LOONEY TUNES™ and Wizard of OZ™ characters. The 1994 collection featured 149 Keepsake, 24 Magic, 18 Showcase and 38 Miniature ornaments. See the collectible series section for more 1994 ornaments.

10 Across the Miles
Handcrafted • ANDR
895QX5656 • **Value $20**

11 All Pumped Up
Handcrafted • RHOD
895QX5923 • **Value $20**

12 Angel Hare
Handcrafted/Brass • SICK
895QX5896 • **Value $23**

13 Anniversary Year
Brass/Chrome • BISH
1095QX5683 • **Value $22**

14 Baby's First Christmas
Handcrafted • VOTR
795QX5636 • **Value $23**

15 Baby's First Christmas
Handcrafted • N/A
795QX5713 • **Value $29**

	Price Paid	Value of My Collection
PERSONALIZED ORNAMENTS		
1.		
2.		
3.		
4.		
5.		
6.		
7.		
8.		
9.		
GENERAL KEEPSAKE		
10.		
11.		
12.		
13.		
14.		
15.		
PENCIL TOTALS		

1994

(1) Baby's First Christmas
Handcrafted • SEAL
1295QX5743 • **Value $28**

(2) Baby's First Christmas
Porcelain/Brass • UNRU
1895QX5633 • **Value $33**

(3) Baby's First Christmas
– Baby Boy
Glass • N/A
500QX2436 • **Value $17**

(4) Baby's First Christmas
– Baby Girl
Glass • N/A
500QX2433 • **Value $17**

(5) Baby's Second
Christmas
Handcrafted • CROW
795QX5716 • **Value $23**

(6) Barney™
Handcrafted • RHOD
995QX5966 • **Value $25**

(7) Batman
Handcrafted • CHAD
1295QX5853 • **Value $28**

(8) The Beatles Gift Set
Handcrafted • RGRS
4800QX5373 • **Value $100**

GENERAL KEEPSAKE

	Price Paid	Value of My Collection
1.		
2.		
3.		
4.		
5.		
6.		
7.		
8.		
9.		
10.		
11.		
12.		
13.		
14.		
15.		
16.		
17.		
18.		
19.		
20.		
PENCIL TOTALS		

(9) Big Shot
Handcrafted • SIED
795QX5873 • **Value $19**

(10) Brother
Handcrafted • PIKE
695QX5516 • **Value $17**

(11) Busy Batter
Handcrafted • SIED
795QX5876 • **Value $19**

(12) Candy Caper
Handcrafted • ANDR
895QX5776 • **Value $22**

(13) Caring Doctor
Handcrafted • RGRS
895QX5823 • **Value $19**

(14) Champion Teacher
Handcrafted • SIED
695QX5836 • **Value $17**

(15) Cheers To You!
Handcrafted/Brass • CROW
1095QX5796 • **Value $27**

(16) Cheery Cyclists
Handcrafted • CROW
1295QX5786 • **Value $27**

(17) Child Care Giver
Handcrafted • VOTR
795QX5906 • **Value $16**

(18) Child's Fifth Christmas
Handcrafted • RHOD
695QX5733 • **Value $19**

(19) Child's Fourth
Christmas
Handcrafted • FRAN
695QX5726 • **Value $20**

(20) Child's Third Christmas
Handcrafted • FRAN
695QX5723 • **Value $20**

(1) **Coach** *Handcrafted* • UNRU 795QX5933 • **Value $17**	**(2)** **Cock-a-Doodle Christmas** *Handcrafted* • VOTR 895QX5396 • **Value $27**

(3) **Colors of Joy** *Handcrafted* • SEAL 795QX5893 • **Value $20**

(4) **The Cowardly Lion** *Handcrafted* • ANDR 995QX5446 • **Value $42**

(5) **Dad** *Handcrafted* • RGRS 795QX5463 • **Value $17**

(6) **Dad-to-Be** *Handcrafted* • PIKE 795QX5473 • **Value $17**

(7) **Daffy Duck** *Handcrafted* • PALM 895QX5415 • **Value $22**

(8) **Daisy Days** *Handcrafted* • CHAD 995QX5986 • **Value $21**

(9) **Daughter** *Handcrafted* • ANDR 695QX5623 • **Value $18**

(10) **Dear Santa Mouse (set/2)** *Handcrafted* • CROW 1495QX5806 • **Value $30**

(11) **Dorothy and Toto** *Handcrafted* • LYLE 1095QX5433 • **Value $80**

(12) **Extra-Special Delivery** *Handcrafted* • CROW 795QX5833 • **Value $19**

(13) **Feelin' Groovy** *Handcrafted* • N/A 795QX5953 • **Value $26**

(14) **A Feline of Christmas** *Handcrafted* • ANDR 895QX5816 • **Value $32**

(15) **Feliz Navidad** *Handcrafted* • RGRS 895QX5793 • **Value $22**

(16) **Follow the Sun** *Handcrafted* • CROW 895QX5846 • **Value $19**

(17) **For My Grandma** *Handcrafted* • DLEE 695QX5613 • **Value $17**

(18) **Fred and Barney** *Handcrafted* • RHOD 1495QX5003 • **Value $34**

(19) **Friendly Push** *Handcrafted* • SIED 895QX5686 • **Value $20**

(20) **Friendship Sundae** *Handcrafted* • SICK 1095QX4766 • **Value $26**

GENERAL KEEPSAKE		
	Price Paid	Value of My Collection
1.		
2.		
3.		
4.		
5.		
6.		
7.		
8.		
9.		
10.		
11.		
12.		
13.		
14.		
15.		
16.		
17.		
18.		
19.		
20.		
PENCIL TOTALS		

1994

(1) GARFIELD
Handcrafted • N/A
1295QX5753 • **Value $32**

(2) Gentle Nurse
Handcrafted • LYLE
695QX5973 • **Value $22**

(3) Godchild
Handcrafted • RGRS
895QX4453 • **Value $24**

(4) Godparent
Glass • N/A
500QX2423 • **Value $21**

(5) Grandchild's First Christmas
Handcrafted • UNRU
795QX5676 • **Value $19**

(6) Granddaughter
Handcrafted • PIKE
695QX5523 • **Value $18**

(7) Grandmother
Handcrafted • ANDR
795QX5673 • **Value $18**

(8) Grandpa
Handcrafted • UNRU
795QX5616 • **Value $21**

(9) Grandparents
Glass • N/A
500QX2426 • **Value $16**

(10) Grandson
Handcrafted • PIKE
695QX5526 • **Value $18**

(11) Happy Birthday, Jesus
Handcrafted • LYLE
1295QX5423 • **Value $30**

(12) Harvest Joy
Handcrafted • CHAD
995QX5993 • **Value $20**

(13) Hearts in Harmony
Porcelain • ANDR
1095QX4406 • **Value $24**

(14) Helpful Shepherd
Handcrafted • CHAD
895QX5536 • **Value $22**

(15) Holiday Patrol
Handcrafted • RHOD
895QX5826 • **Value $18**

(16) Ice Show
Handcrafted • ANDR
795QX5946 • **Value $20**

(17) In the Pink
Handcrafted • ANDR
995QX5763 • **Value $23**

(18) It's a Strike
Handcrafted • SIED
895QX5856 • **Value $20**

(19) Jingle Bell Band
Handcrafted • CROW
1095QX5783 • **Value $31**

(20) Joyous Song
Handcrafted • ANDR
895QX4473 • **Value $20**

GENERAL KEEPSAKE

	Price Paid	Value of My Collection
1.		
2.		
3.		
4.		
5.		
6.		
7.		
8.		
9.		
10.		
11.		
12.		
13.		
14.		
15.		
16.		
17.		
18.		
19.		
20.		
PENCIL TOTALS		

1

Jump-along Jackalope
Handcrafted • FRAN
895QX5756 • **Value $18**

2

Keep on Mowin'
Handcrafted • SIED
895QX5413 • **Value $17**

3

Kickin' Roo
Handcrafted • SIED
795QX5916 • **Value $17**

4

Kitty's Catamaran
Handcrafted • SEAL
1095QX5416 • **Value $21**

5

Kringle's Kayak
Handcrafted • SEAL
795QX5886 • **Value $22**

6

Lou Rankin Seal
Handcrafted • BISH
995QX5456 • **Value $22**

7

Lucinda and Teddy
Handcrafted/Fabric • UNRU
2175QX4813 • **Value $40**

8

Magic Carpet Ride
Handcrafted • SEAL
795QX5883 • **Value $23**

9

Making It Bright
Handcrafted • RHOD
895QX5403 • **Value $20**

10

Mary Engelbreit
Glass • N/A
500QX2416 • **Value $19**

11

Merry Fishmas
Handcrafted • PALM
895QX5913 • **Value $22**

12

Mistletoe Surprise (set/2)
Handcrafted • SEAL
1295QX5996 • **Value $32**

13

Mom
Handcrafted • RGRS
795QX5466 • **Value $18**

14

Mom and Dad
Handcrafted • SIED
995QX5666 • **Value $23**

15

Mom-to-Be
Handcrafted • PIKE
795QX5506 • **Value $18**

16

Mufasa and Simba
Handcrafted • CROW
1495QX5406 • **Value $30**

17

Nephew
Handcrafted • FRAN
795QX5546 • **Value $17**

18

New Home
Handcrafted • ANDR
895QX5663 • **Value $22**

19

Niece
Handcrafted • FRAN
795QX5543 • **Value $17**

20

Norman Rockwell Art
Glass • LYLE
500QX2413 • **Value $18**

1994

GENERAL KEEPSAKE

	Price Paid	Value of My Collection
1.		
2.		
3.		
4.		
5.		
6.		
7.		
8.		
9.		
10.		
11.		
12.		
13.		
14.		
15.		
16.		
17.		
18.		
19.		
20.		
PENCIL TOTALS		

①
Open-and-Shut Holiday
Handcrafted • SIED
995QX5696 • **Value $22**

②
Our Christmas Together
Handcrafted • RGRS
995QX4816 • **Value $22**

③
Our Family
Handcrafted • ANDR
795QX5576 • **Value $19**

④
Our First Christmas
Together
Acrylic • VOTR
695QX3186 • **Value $17**

⑤
Our First Christmas
Together
Brass/Fabric • ANDR
1895QX5706 • **Value $29**

⑥
Our First Christmas
Together
Handcrafted • PALM
895QX5653 • **Value $21**

⑦
Our First Christmas
Together
Handcrafted • BISH
995QX5643 • **Value $25**

⑧
Out of This World
Teacher
Handcrafted • UNRU
795QX5766 • **Value $20**

⑨
Practice Makes Perfect
Handcrafted • PALM
895QX5863 • **Value $18**

⑩
Red Hot Holiday
Handcrafted • RGRS
795QX5843 • **Value $19**

⑪
Reindeer Pro
Handcrafted • RHOD
795QX5926 • **Value $20**

⑫
Relaxing Moment
Handcrafted • FRAN
1495QX5356 • **Value $33**

⑬
Road Runner and
Wile E. Coyote
Handcrafted • CHAD
1295QX5602 • **Value $29**

⑭
Santa's LEGO® Sleigh
Handcrafted • CROW
1095QX5453 • **Value $33**

⑮
The Scarecrow
Handcrafted • UNRU
995QX5436 • **Value $48**

⑯
Secret Santa
Handcrafted • UNRU
795QX5736 • **Value $19**

⑰
A Sharp Flat
Handcrafted • CROW
1095QX5773 • **Value $25**

⑱
Simba and Nala (set/2)
Handcrafted • CROW
1295QX5303 • **Value $30**

⑲
Sister
Handcrafted • PIKE
695QX5513 • **Value $19**

⑳
Sister to Sister
Handcrafted • RHOD
995QX5533 • **Value $26**

GENERAL KEEPSAKE		
	Price Paid	Value of My Collection
1.		
2.		
3.		
4.		
5.		
6.		
7.		
8.		
9.		
10.		
11.		
12.		
13.		
14.		
15.		
16.		
17.		
18.		
19.		
20.		
PENCIL TOTALS		

1.
Son
Handcrafted • ANDR
695QX5626 • **Value $17**

2.
Special Cat
Acrylic • RHOD
795QX5606 • **Value $17**

3.
Special Dog
Handcrafted • RHOD
795QX5603 • **Value $17**

4.
Speedy Gonzales
Handcrafted • PALM
895QX5343 • **Value $22**

5.
Stamp of Approval
Handcrafted • SICK
795QX5703 • **Value $18**

6.
Sweet Greeting (set/2)
Handcrafted • PALM
1095QX5803 • **Value $24**

7.
The Tale of Peter Rabbit
BEATRIX POTTER
Glass • N/A
500QX2443 • **Value $19**

8.
Tasmanian Devil
Handcrafted • PALM
895QX5605 • **Value $56**

1994

9.
Thick 'n' Thin
Handcrafted • RGRS
1095QX5693 • **Value $22**

10.
Thrill a Minute
Handcrafted • SIED
895QX5866 • **Value $20**

11.
Time of Peace
Handcrafted • ANDR
795QX5813 • **Value $18**

12.
Timon and Pumbaa
Handcrafted • CROW
895QX5366 • **Value $23**

13.
The Tin Man
Handcrafted • UNRU
995QX5443 • **Value $45**

14.
Tou Can Love
Handcrafted • RGRS
895QX5646 • **Value $21**

15.
Tulip Time
Handcrafted • CHAD
995QX5983 • **Value $20**

16.
Winnie the Pooh
and Tigger
Handcrafted • SIED
1295QX5746 • **Value $37**

17.
Yosemite Sam
Handcrafted • PALM
895QX5346 • **Value $20**

18.
Yuletide Cheer
Handcrafted • CHAD
995QX5976 • **Value $21**

19.
Away in a Manger
Handcrafted • LYLE
1600QLX7383 • **Value $40**

20.
Baby's First Christmas
Handcrafted • FRAN
2000QLX7466 • **Value $44**

GENERAL KEEPSAKE		
	Price Paid	Value of My Collection
1.		
2.		
3.		
4.		
5.		
6.		
7.		
8.		
9.		
10.		
11.		
12.		
13.		
14.		
15.		
16.		
17.		
18.		
GENERAL MAGIC		
19.		
20.		
PENCIL TOTALS		

1

Barney™
Handcrafted • N/A
2400QLX7506 • **Value $48**

2

Candy Cane Lookout
Handcrafted • FRAN
1800QLX7376 • **Value $74**

3

Conversations With Santa
Handcrafted • SEAL
2800QLX7426 • **Value $58**

4

Country Showtime
Handcrafted • SICK
2200QLX7416 • **Value $47**

5

The Eagle Has Landed
Handcrafted • SEAL
2400QLX7486 • **Value $54**

6

Feliz Navidad
Handcrafted • CROW
2800QLX7433 • **Value $64**

7

Gingerbread Fantasy
Handcrafted • PALM
4400QLX7382 • **Value $95**

8

Klingon Bird of Prey™
Handcrafted • NORT
2400QLX7386 • **Value $50**

9

Kringle Trolley
Handcrafted • CROW
2000QLX7413 • **Value $44**

10

Maxine
Handcrafted • SICK
2000QLX7503 • **Value $49**

11

Peekaboo Pup
Handcrafted • RGRS
2000QLX7423 • **Value $45**

12

Rock Candy Miner
Handcrafted • SIED
2000QLX7403 • **Value $37**

13

Santa's Sing-Along
Handcrafted • CROW
2400QLX7473 • **Value $55**

14

Simba, Sarabi and Mufasa
Handcrafted • CROW
2000QLX7516 • **Value $40**

15

Simba, Sarabi and Mufasa (recalled due to defective sound)
Handcrafted • CROW
3200QLX7513 • **Value $68**

16

Very Merry Minutes
Handcrafted • VOTR
2400QLX7443 • **Value $47**

17

White Christmas
Handcrafted • DLEE
2800QLX7463 • **Value $62**

18

Winnie the Pooh Parade
Handcrafted • CROW
3200QLX7493 • **Value $70**

19

Home for the Holidays
Christmas Lights
Porcelain • PALM
1575QK1123 • **Value $20**

20

Moonbeams
Christmas Lights
Porcelain • ANDR
1575QK1116 • **Value $20**

General Magic

	Price Paid	Value of My Collection
1.		
2.		
3.		
4.		
5.		
6.		
7.		
8.		
9.		
10.		
11.		
12.		
13.		
14.		
15.		
16.		
17.		
18.		

General Showcase

19.		
20.		
PENCIL TOTALS		

1. Mother and Child
Christmas Lights
Porcelain • RGRS
1575QK1126 • **Value $20**

2. Peaceful Village
Christmas Lights
Porcelain • CHAD
1575QK1106 • **Value $20**

3. Catching 40 Winks
Folk Art Americana
Handcrafted • SICK
1675QK1183 • **Value $33**

4. Going to Town
Folk Art Americana
Handcrafted • SICK
1575QK1166 • **Value $33**

5. Racing Through the Snow
Folk Art Americana
Handcrafted • SICK
1575QK1173 • **Value $45**

6. Rarin' to Go
Folk Art Americana
Handcrafted • SICK
1575QK1193 • **Value $37**

7. Roundup Time
Folk Art Americana
Handcrafted • SICK
1675QK1176 • **Value $30**

8. Dapper Snowman
Holiday Favorites
Porcelain • VOTR
1375QK1053 • **Value $20**

9. Graceful Fawn
Holiday Favorites
Porcelain • VOTR
1175QK1033 • **Value $20**

10. Jolly Santa
Holiday Favorites
Porcelain • VOTR
1375QK1046 • **Value $26**

11. Joyful Lamb
Holiday Favorites
Porcelain • VOTR
1175QK1036 • **Value $20**

12. Peaceful Dove
Holiday Favorites
Porcelain • VOTR
1175QK1043 • **Value $20**

13. Silver Bells
Old-World Silver
Silver-Plated • UNRU
2475QK1026 • **Value $28**

14. Silver Bows
Old-World Silver
Silver-Plated • PALM
2475QK1023 • **Value $28**

15. Silver Poinsettia
Old-World Silver
Silver-Plated • UNRU
2475QK1006 • **Value $32**

16. Silver Snowflakes
Old-World Silver
Silver-Plated • UNRU
2475QK1016 • **Value $28**

17. Babs Bunny
Handcrafted • PALM
575QXM4116 • **Value $16**

18. Baby's First Christmas
Handcrafted • LYLE
575QXM4003 • **Value $16**

19. Baking Tiny Treats (set/6)
Handcrafted • SEAL
2900QXM4033 • **Value $63**

20. Beary Perfect Tree
Handcrafted • BISH
475QXM4076 • **Value $14**

1994

GENERAL SHOWCASE

	Price Paid	Value of My Collection
1.		
2.		
3.		
4.		
5.		
6.		
7.		
8.		
9.		
10.		
11.		
12.		
13.		
14.		
15.		
16.		

GENERAL MINIATURE

17.		
18.		
19.		
20.		
PENCIL TOTALS		

1. Buster Bunny
Handcrafted • PALM
575QXM5163 • **Value $14**

2. Corny Elf
Handcrafted • RHOD
450QXM4063 • **Value $12**

3. Cute as a Button
Handcrafted • CROW
375QXM4103 • **Value $15**

4. Dazzling Reindeer
Handcrafted • VOTR
975QXM4026 • **Value $22**

5. Dizzy Devil
Handcrafted • PALM
575QXM4133 • **Value $16**

6. Friends Need Hugs
Handcrafted • LYLE
450QXM4016 • **Value $14**

7. Graceful Carousel Horse
Pewter • BISH
775QXM4056 • **Value $19**

8. Hamton
Handcrafted • PALM
575QXM4126 • **Value $15**

9. Have a Cookie
Handcrafted • DLEE
575QXM5166 • **Value $15**

10. Hearts A-Sail
Handcrafted • BISH
575QXM4006 • **Value $14**

11. Jolly Visitor
Handcrafted • SICK
575QXM4053 • **Value $15**

12. Jolly Wolly Snowman
Handcrafted • VOTR
375QXM4093 • **Value $14**

13. Journey to Bethlehem
Handcrafted • LYLE
575QXM4036 • **Value $18**

14. Just My Size
Handcrafted • BISH
375QXM4086 • **Value $12**

15. Love Was Born
Handcrafted • SICK
450QXM4043 • **Value $15**

16. Melodic Cherub
Handcrafted • RGRS
375QXM4066 • **Value $11**

17. A Merry Flight
Handcrafted • CROW
575QXM4073 • **Value $14**

18. Mom
Handcrafted • RGRS
450QXM4013 • **Value $14**

19. Noah's Ark (set/3)
Handcrafted • SICK
2450QXM4106 • **Value $60**

20. Plucky Duck
Handcrafted • PALM
575QXM4123 • **Value $14**

General Miniature

	Price Paid	Value of My Collection
1.		
2.		
3.		
4.		
5.		
6.		
7.		
8.		
9.		
10.		
11.		
12.		
13.		
14.		
15.		
16.		
17.		
18.		
19.		
20.		
PENCIL TOTALS		

VALUE GUIDE — HALLMARK KEEPSAKE ORNAMENTS

(1) Pour Some More
Handcrafted • CHAD
575QXM5156 • **Value $14**

(2) Scooting Along
Handcrafted • FRAN
675QXM5173 • **Value $16**

(3) Sweet Dreams
Handcrafted • CROW
300QXM4096 • **Value $13**

(4) Tea With Teddy
Handcrafted • RGRS
725QXM4046 • **Value $18**

(5) First Hello
(gift membership bonus)
Handcrafted • RGRS
QXC4846 • **Value N/E**

(6) Happy Collecting
(early renewal piece,
Merry Miniature)
Handcrafted • N/A
QXC4803 • **Value $34**

(7) Holiday Pursuit
(keepsake of membership)
Handcrafted • FRAN
QXC4823 • **Value $30**

(8) Jolly Holly Santa
(club edition)
Handcrafted • LYLE
2200QXC4833 • **Value $52**

(9) Majestic Deer
(club edition)
Porcelain/Pewter • UNRU
2500QXC4836 • **Value $54**

(10) On Cloud Nine
(club edition)
Handcrafted • DLEE
1200QXC4853 • **Value $35**

(11) Sweet Bouquet
(keepsake of
membership, miniature)
Handcrafted • N/A
QXC4806 • **Value $30**

(12) Tilling Time
(Easter sidekick gift)
Handcrafted • SEAL
QXC8256 • **Value $62**

(13) Collector's Survival Kit
Premiere '94
Handcrafted • RGRS
(N/C) No stock # • **Value $22**

(14) Eager for Christmas
Handcrafted • SEAL
1500QX5336 • **Value $30**

(15) The Country Church
Sarah, Plain and Tall
Handcrafted • BAUR
795XPR9450 • **Value $22**

(16) The Hays Train Station
Sarah, Plain and Tall
Handcrafted • BAUR
795XPR9452 • **Value $22**

**(17) Mrs. Parkley's
General Store**
Sarah, Plain and Tall
Handcrafted • BAUR
795XPR9451 • **Value $22**

(18) Sarah's Maine Home
Sarah, Plain and Tall
Handcrafted • BAUR
795XPR9454 • **Value $24**

(19) Sarah's Prairie Home
Sarah, Plain and Tall
Handcrafted • BAUR
795XPR9453 • **Value $22**

**(20) Victorian Elegance™
BARBIE® Doll**
(1st in series)
Vinyl • N/A
4000XPF3546 • **Value $95**

GENERAL MINIATURE

	Price Paid	Value of My Collection
1.		
2.		
3.		
4.		

COLLECTOR'S CLUB

5.		
6.		
7.		
8.		
9.		
10.		
11.		
12.		

PREMIERE ORNAMENTS

13.		
14.		

REACH FIGURINES

15.		
16.		
17.		
18.		
19.		

BARBIE™ COLLECTIBLES

20.		

PENCIL TOTALS

1. Golden Bows
Gold-Plated • PALM
($10.00) No stock # • **Value $20**

2. Golden Dove of Peace
Gold-Plated • PALM
($10.00) No stock # • **Value $20**

3. Golden Poinsettia
Gold-Plated • UNRU
($10.00) No stock # • **Value $20**

4. Golden Santa
Gold-Plated • UNRU
($10.00) No stock # • **Value $20**

5. Golden Sleigh
Gold-Plated • PALM
($10.00) No stock # • **Value $20**

6. Golden Stars and Holly
Gold-Plated • PALM
($10.00) No stock # • **Value $20**

7. Mrs. Claus' Cupboard
(w/ miniature ornaments)
Handcrafted • N/A
5500QXC4843 • **Value N/E**

8. Baby Block Photoholder
(re-issued from 1993)
Handcrafted • FRAN
1495QP6035 • **Value N/E**

9. Computer Cat 'n' Mouse
(re-issued in 1995)
Handcrafted • SEAL
1295QP6046 • **Value N/E**

10. Cookie Time
(re-issued in 1995)
Handcrafted • VOTR
1295QP6073 • **Value N/E**

11. Etch-A-Sketch®
(re-issued in 1995)
Handcrafted • CROW
1295QP6006 • **Value N/E**

12. Festive Album Photoholder
(re-issued from 1993)
Handcrafted • VOTR
1295QP6025 • **Value N/E**

13. From The Heart
(re-issued in 1995)
Handcrafted • RHOD
1495QP6036 • **Value N/E**

14. Goin' Fishin'
Handcrafted • PALM
1495QP6023 • **Value N/E**

15. Going Golfin'
(re-issued from 1993)
Handcrafted • PALM
1295QP6012 • **Value N/E**

16. Holiday Hello
Handcrafted • SIED
2495QXR6116 • **Value $44**

17. Mailbox Delivery
(re-issued from 1993)
Handcrafted • CROW
1495QP6015 • **Value N/E**

18. Novel Idea
(re-issued in 1995)
Handcrafted • VOTR
1295QP6066 • **Value N/E**

19. On the Billboard
(re-issued from 1993)
Handcrafted • CROW
1295QP6022 • **Value N/E**

20. Playing Ball
(re-issued from 1993)
Handcrafted • FRAN
1295QP6032 • **Value N/E**

Expo Ornaments

	Price Paid	Value of My Collection
1.		
2.		
3.		
4.		
5.		
6.		
7.		

Personalized Ornaments

8.		
9.		
10.		
11.		
12.		
13.		
14.		
15.		
16.		
17.		
18.		
19.		
20.		
PENCIL TOTALS		

1

SOUTHWEST EAGLES PEP CLUB

Reindeer Rooters
(re-issued in 1995)
Handcrafted • CROW
1295QP6056 • **Value N/E**

2

Ho! Ho! Ho! Merry Christmas, Shelby

Santa Says
(re-issued from 1993)
Handcrafted • SEAL
1495QP6005 • **Value N/E**

1993

The 20th anniversary of Keepsake Ornaments was celebrated in 1993 with four special ornaments, including "Glowing Pewter Wreath" and pieces to complement three popular collectible series. Overall, there were 141 Keepsake, 21 Magic, 19 Showcase and 36 Miniature ornaments. See the collectible series section for more 1993 ornaments.

3

Across the Miles

Across the Miles
Handcrafted • FRAN
875QX5912 • **Value $20**

1993

4

Anniversary Year Photoholder
Brass/Chrome • LYLE
975QX5972 • **Value $20**

5

Apple for Teacher
Handcrafted • SEAL
775QX5902 • **Value $16**

6

Baby's First Christmas
Handcrafted • CROW
775QX5525 • **Value $29**

7

Baby's First Christmas
Handcrafted • ANDR
1075QX5515 • **Value $23**

8

Baby's First Christmas

Baby's First Christmas
Silver-Plated • PALM
1875QX5512 • **Value $38**

9

Baby's First Christmas – Baby Boy
Glass • VOTR
475QX2105 • **Value $17**

10

Baby's First Christmas – Baby Girl
Glass • VOTR
475QX2092 • **Value $17**

11

Baby's First Christmas Photoholder
Handcrafted/Lace • RGRS
775QX5522 • **Value $23**

12

Baby's Second Christmas
Handcrafted • FRAN
675QX5992 • **Value $22**

13

MASTERPIECE

Beary Gifted
Handcrafted • CROW
775QX5762 • **Value $19**

14

Big on Gardening
Handcrafted • VOTR
975QX5842 • **Value $17**

15

Big Roller
Handcrafted • SIED
875QX5352 • **Value $19**

(1) **Bird-Watcher** *Handcrafted* • JLEE 975QX5252 • **Value $18**	**(2)** **Bowling for ZZZs** *Handcrafted* • FRAN 775QX5565 • **Value $17**	**(3)** **Brother** *Handcrafted* • RGRS 675QX5542 • **Value $14**	**(4)** **Bugs Bunny** *Handcrafted* • SICK 875QX5412 • **Value $27**
(5) **Caring Nurse** *Handcrafted* • FRAN 675QX5785 • **Value $19**	**(6)** **A Child's Christmas** *Handcrafted* • FRAN 975QX5882 • **Value $23**	**(7)** **Child's Fifth Christmas** *Handcrafted* • RHOD 675QX5222 • **Value $17**	**(8)** **Child's Fourth Christmas** *Handcrafted* • FRAN 675QX5215 • **Value $16**

GENERAL KEEPSAKE

	Price Paid	Value of My Collection	
1.			**(9)** **Child's Third Christmas** *Handcrafted* • FRAN 675QX5995 • **Value $17**
2.			
3.			
4.			
5.			**(12)** **Coach** *Handcrafted* • PALM 675QX5935 • **Value $15**
6.			
7.			
8.			
9.			
10.			
11.			**(15)** **Dad-to-Be** *Handcrafted* • JLEE 675QX5532 • **Value $14**
12.			
13.			
14.			
15.			
16.			
17.			**(18)** **Dunkin' Roo** *Handcrafted* • SIED 775QX5575 • **Value $17**
18.			
19.			
20.			
PENCIL TOTALS			

Additional ornaments:

(10) **Christmas Break** *Handcrafted* • SEAL 775QX5825 • **Value $24**	**(11)** **Clever Cookie** *Handcrafted/Tin* • SICK 775QX5662 • **Value $25**
(13) **Curly 'n' Kingly** *Handcrafted/Brass* • CROW 1075QX5285 • **Value $23**	**(14)** **Dad** *Handcrafted* • JLEE 775QX5855 • **Value $19**
(16) **Daughter** *Handcrafted* • VOTR 675QX5872 • **Value $21**	**(17)** **Dickens Caroler Bell – Lady Daphne** *Porcelain* • CHAD 2175QX5505 • **Value $43**
(19) **Eeyore** *Handcrafted* • SIED 975QX5712 • **Value $24**	**(20)** **Elmer Fudd** *Handcrafted* • LYLE 875QX5495 • **Value $20**

VALUE GUIDE — HALLMARK KEEPSAKE ORNAMENTS

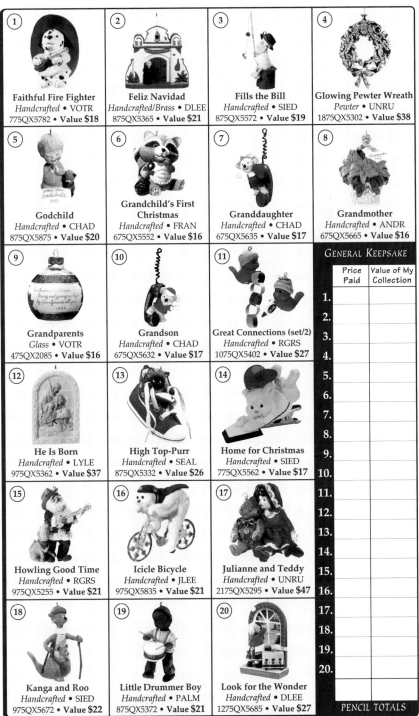

№	Name	Details	Code • Value
1	**Faithful Fire Fighter**	*Handcrafted* • VOTR	775QX5782 • **Value $18**
2	**Feliz Navidad**	*Handcrafted/Brass* • DLEE	875QX5365 • **Value $21**
3	**Fills the Bill**	*Handcrafted* • SIED	875QX5572 • **Value $19**
4	**Glowing Pewter Wreath**	*Pewter* • UNRU	1875QX5302 • **Value $38**
5	**Godchild**	*Handcrafted* • CHAD	875QX5875 • **Value $20**
6	**Grandchild's First Christmas**	*Handcrafted* • FRAN	675QX5552 • **Value $16**
7	**Granddaughter**	*Handcrafted* • CHAD	675QX5635 • **Value $17**
8	**Grandmother**	*Handcrafted* • ANDR	675QX5665 • **Value $16**
9	**Grandparents**	*Glass* • VOTR	475QX2085 • **Value $16**
10	**Grandson**	*Handcrafted* • CHAD	675QX5632 • **Value $17**
11	**Great Connections (set/2)**	*Handcrafted* • RGRS	1075QX5402 • **Value $27**
12	**He Is Born**	*Handcrafted* • LYLE	975QX5362 • **Value $37**
13	**High Top-Purr**	*Handcrafted* • SEAL	875QX5332 • **Value $26**
14	**Home for Christmas**	*Handcrafted* • SIED	775QX5562 • **Value $17**
15	**Howling Good Time**	*Handcrafted* • RGRS	975QX5255 • **Value $21**
16	**Icicle Bicycle**	*Handcrafted* • JLEE	975QX5835 • **Value $21**
17	**Julianne and Teddy**	*Handcrafted* • UNRU	2175QX5295 • **Value $47**
18	**Kanga and Roo**	*Handcrafted* • SIED	975QX5672 • **Value $22**
19	**Little Drummer Boy**	*Handcrafted* • PALM	875QX5372 • **Value $21**
20	**Look for the Wonder**	*Handcrafted* • DLEE	1275QX5685 • **Value $27**

1993

GENERAL KEEPSAKE

	Price Paid	Value of My Collection
1.		
2.		
3.		
4.		
5.		
6.		
7.		
8.		
9.		
10.		
11.		
12.		
13.		
14.		
15.		
16.		
17.		
18.		
19.		
20.		
	PENCIL TOTALS	

VALUE GUIDE — HALLMARK KEEPSAKE ORNAMENTS

#	Name	Material	Item / Value
1	**Lou Rankin Polar Bear**	*Handcrafted* • RHOD	975QX5745 • **Value $28**
2	**Makin' Music**	*Handcrafted/Brass* • SEAL	975QX5325 • **Value $19**
3	**Making Waves**	*Handcrafted* • PALM	975QX5775 • **Value $29**
4	**Mary Engelbreit**	*Glass* • N/A	500QX2075 • **Value $18**
5	**Maxine**	*Handcrafted* • SICK	875QX5385 • **Value $28**
6	**Mom**	*Handcrafted* • JLEE	775QX5852 • **Value $19**
7	**Mom and Dad**	*Handcrafted* • PALM	975QX5845 • **Value $19**
8	**Mom-to-Be**	*Handcrafted* • JLEE	675QX5535 • **Value $17**
9	**Nephew**	*Handcrafted* • RGRS	675QX5735 • **Value $13**
10	**New Home**	*Enamel/Metal* • PALM	775QX5905 • **Value $28**
11	**Niece**	*Handcrafted* • RGRS	675QX5732 • **Value $13**
12	**On Her Toes**	*Handcrafted* • ANDR	875QX5265 • **Value $24**
13	**One-Elf Marching Band**	*Handcrafted/Brass* • CHAD	1275QX5342 • **Value $28**
14	**Our Christmas Together**	*Handcrafted* • DLEE	1075QX5942 • **Value $24**
15	**Our Family Photoholder**	*Handcrafted* • UNRU	775QX5892 • **Value $19**
16	**Our First Christmas Together**	*Acrylic* • ANDR	675QX3015 • **Value $18**
17	**Our First Christmas Together**	*Brass/Silver-Plated* • RGRS	1875QX5955 • **Value $40**
18	**Our First Christmas Together**	*Handcrafted* • LYLE	975QX5642 • **Value $18**
19	**Our First Christmas Together Photoholder**	*Handcrafted* • UNRU	875QX5952 • **Value $18**
20	**Owl**	*Handcrafted* • SIED	975QX5695 • **Value $21**

GENERAL KEEPSAKE

	Price Paid	Value of My Collection
1.		
2.		
3.		
4.		
5.		
6.		
7.		
8.		
9.		
10.		
11.		
12.		
13.		
14.		
15.		
16.		
17.		
18.		
19.		
20.		
PENCIL TOTALS		

(1) PEANUTS®
Glass • N/A
500QX2072 • **Value $26**

(2) Peek-a-Boo Tree
Handcrafted • CROW
1075QX5245 • **Value $25**

(3) Peep Inside
Handcrafted • DLEE
1375QX5322 • **Value $27**

(4) People Friendly
Handcrafted • SEAL
875QX5932 • **Value $19**

(5) Perfect Match
Handcrafted • SIED
875QX5772 • **Value $19**

(6) The Pink Panther
Handcrafted • PALM
1275QX5755 • **Value $23**

(7) Playful Pals
Handcrafted • RGRS
1475QX5742 • **Value $30**

(8) Popping Good Times
(set/2)
Handcrafted • CHAD
1475QX5392 • **Value $30**

(9) Porky Pig
Handcrafted • ANDR
875QX5652 • **Value $20**

(10) Putt-Putt Penguin
Handcrafted • JLEE
975QX5795 • **Value $22**

(11) Quick as a Fox
Handcrafted • CROW
875QX5792 • **Value $19**

(12) Rabbit
Handcrafted • SIED
975QX5702 • **Value $22**

(13) Ready for Fun
Handcrafted/Tin • LYLE
775QX5124 • **Value $17**

(14) Room for One More
Handcrafted • CROW
875QX5382 • **Value $48**

(15) Silvery Noel
Silver-Plated • LYLE
1275QX5305 • **Value $34**

(16) Sister
Handcrafted • RGRS
675QX5545 • **Value $20**

(17) Sister to Sister
Handcrafted • SEAL
975QX5885 • **Value $52**

(18) Smile! It's Christmas Photoholder
Handcrafted • SEAL
975QX5335 • **Value $21**

(19) Snow Bear Angel
Handcrafted • JLEE
775QX5355 • **Value $19**

(20) Snowbird
Handcrafted • JLEE
775QX5765 • **Value $19**

1993

GENERAL KEEPSAKE		
	Price Paid	Value of My Collection
1.		
2.		
3.		
4.		
5.		
6.		
7.		
8.		
9.		
10.		
11.		
12.		
13.		
14.		
15.		
16.		
17.		
18.		
19.		
20.		
PENCIL TOTALS		

VALUE GUIDE — HALLMARK KEEPSAKE ORNAMENTS

(1) **Snowy Hideaway** *Handcrafted* • FRAN 975QX5312 • **Value $22**	(2) **Son** *Handcrafted* • VOTR 675QX5865 • **Value $20**	(3) **Special Cat Photoholder** *Handcrafted/Brass* • VOTR 775QX5235 • **Value $14**	(4) **Special Dog Photoholder** *Handcrafted/Brass* • VOTR 775QX5962 • **Value $14**
(5) **Star of Wonder** *Handcrafted* • LYLE 675QX5982 • **Value $38**	(6) **Star Teacher Photoholder** *Handcrafted* • ANDR 575QX5645 • **Value $14**	(7) **Strange and Wonderful Love** *Handcrafted* • SICK 875QX5965 • **Value $19**	(8) **Superman™** *Handcrafted* • CHAD 1275QX5752 • **Value $46**

GENERAL KEEPSAKE

	Price Paid	Value of My Collection
1.		
2.		
3.		
4.		
5.		
6.		
7.		
8.		
9.		
10.		
11.		
12.		
13.		
14.		
15.		
16.		
17.		
18.		
19.		
20.		
PENCIL TOTALS		

(9) **The Swat Team (set/2)** *Handcrafted/Yarn* • ANDR 1275QX5395 • **Value $30**	(10) **Sylvester and Tweety** *Handcrafted* • PALM 975QX5405 • **Value $30**	(11) **That's Entertainment** *Handcrafted* • SIED 875QX5345 • **Value $21**
(12) **Tigger and Piglet** *Handcrafted* • SIED 975QX5705 • **Value $47**	(13) **Tin Airplane** *Pressed Tin* • SICK 775QX5622 • **Value $28**	(14) **Tin Blimp** *Pressed Tin* • SICK 775QX5625 • **Value $18**
(15) **Tin Hot Air Balloon** *Pressed Tin* • SICK 775QX5615 • **Value $21**	(16) **To My Grandma Photoholder** *Handcrafted* • DLEE 775QX5555 • **Value $17**	(17) **Top Banana** *Handcrafted* • RGRS 775QX5925 • **Value $18**
(18) **Wake-Up Call** *Handcrafted* • UNRU 875QX5262 • **Value $20**	(19) **Warm and Special Friends** *Handcrafted/Metal* • VOTR 1075QX5895 • **Value $26**	(20) **Water Bed Snooze** *Handcrafted* • JLEE 975QX5375 • **Value $22**

1
Winnie the Pooh
Handcrafted • SIED
975QX5715 • **Value $35**

2
Baby's First Christmas
Handcrafted • FRAN
2200QLX7365 • **Value $43**

3
Bells Are Ringing
Handcrafted • CROW
2800QLX7402 • **Value $64**

4
Dog's Best Friend
Handcrafted • JLEE
1200QLX7172 • **Value $25**

5
Dollhouse Dreams
Handcrafted • CROW
2200QLX7372 • **Value $48**

6
Home on the Range
Handcrafted • SICK
3200QLX7395 • **Value $67**

7
The Lamplighter
Handcrafted • PALM
1800QLX7192 • **Value $42**

8
Last Minute Shopping
Handcrafted • VOTR
2800QLX7385 • **Value $63**

9
Messages of Christmas
Handcrafted • SIED
3500QLX7476 • **Value $46**

10
North Pole Merrython
Handcrafted • SEAL
2500QLX7392 • **Value $55**

11
Our First Christmas Together
Handcrafted • CHAD
2000QLX7355 • **Value $44**

12
Radio News Flash
Handcrafted • DLEE
2200QLX7362 • **Value $50**

13
Raiding the Fridge
Handcrafted • RGRS
1600QLX7185 • **Value $38**

14
Road Runner and Wile E. Coyote™
Handcrafted • CHAD
3000QLX7415 • **Value $75**

15
Santa's Snow-Getter
Handcrafted • CROW
1800QLX7352 • **Value $42**

16
Santa's Workshop
Handcrafted • SIED
2800QLX7375 • **Value $62**

17
Song of the Chimes
Handcrafted/Brass • ANDR
2500QLX7405 • **Value $56**

18
U.S.S. Enterprise™ THE NEXT GENERATION™
Handcrafted • NORT
2400QLX7412 • **Value $53**

19
Winnie the Pooh
Handcrafted • SIED
2400QLX7422 • **Value $50**

1993

GENERAL KEEPSAKE	Price Paid	Value of My Collection
1.		
GENERAL MAGIC		
2.		
3.		
4.		
5.		
6.		
7.		
8.		
9.		
10.		
11.		
12.		
13.		
14.		
15.		
16.		
17.		
18.		
19.		
PENCIL TOTALS		

1

Angel in Flight
Folk Art Americana
Handcrafted • SICK
1575QK1052 • **Value $54**

2

Polar Bear Adventure
Folk Art Americana
Handcrafted • SICK
1500QK1055 • **Value $68**

3

Riding in the Woods
Folk Art Americana
Handcrafted • SICK
1575QK1065 • **Value $70**

4

Riding the Wind
Folk Art Americana
Handcrafted • SICK
1575QK1045 • **Value $60**

5

Santa Claus
Folk Art Americana
Handcrafted • SICK
1675QK1072 • **Value $210**

6

Angelic Messengers
Holiday Enchantment
Porcelain • VOTR
1375QK1032 • **Value $38**

7

Bringing Home the Tree
Holiday Enchantment
Porcelain • CHAD
1375QK1042 • **Value $35**

8

Journey to the Forest
Holiday Enchantment
Porcelain • N/A
1375QK1012 • **Value $32**

GENERAL SHOWCASE		
	Price Paid	Value of My Collection
1.		
2.		
3.		
4.		
5.		
6.		
7.		
8.		
9.		
10.		
11.		
12.		
13.		
14.		
15.		
16.		
17.		
18.		
19.		
PENCIL TOTALS		

9

The Magi
Holiday Enchantment
Porcelain • N/A
1375QK1025 • **Value $35**

10

Visions of Sugarplums
Holiday Enchantment
Porcelain • N/A
1375QK1005 • **Value $35**

11

Silver Dove of Peace
Old-World Silver
Silver-Plated • PALM
2475QK1075 • **Value $36**

12

Silver Santa
Old-World Silver
Silver-Plated • UNRU
2475QK1092 • **Value $50**

13

Silver Sleigh
Old-World Silver
Silver-Plated • PALM
2475QK1082 • **Value $37**

14

Silver Stars and Holly
Old-World Silver
Silver-Plated • PALM
2475QK1085 • **Value $36**

15

Christmas Feast
Portraits in Bisque
Porcelain • PIKE
1575QK1152 • **Value $34**

16

Joy of Sharing
Portraits in Bisque
Porcelain • LYLE
1575QK1142 • **Value $34**

17

Mistletoe Kiss
Portraits in Bisque
Porcelain • PIKE
1575QK1145 • **Value $33**

18

**Norman Rockwell
– Filling the Stockings**
Portraits in Bisque
Porcelain • DUTK
1575QK1155 • **Value $36**

19

**Norman Rockwell
– Jolly Postman**
Portraits in Bisque
Porcelain • DUTK
1575QK1162 • **Value $36**

1. Baby's First Christmas
Handcrafted • VOTR
575QXM5145 • **Value $12**

2. Cheese Please
Handcrafted • SIED
375QXM4072 • **Value $10**

3. Christmas Castle
Handcrafted • SEAL
575QXM4085 • **Value $13**

4. Cloisonné Snowflake
Cloisonné/Brass • VOTR
975QXM4012 • **Value $20**

5. Country Fiddling
Handcrafted • FRAN
375QXM4062 • **Value $12**

6. Crystal Angel
Crystal/Gold-Plated • PALM
975QXM4015 • **Value $55**

7. Ears to Pals
Handcrafted • ANDR
375QXM4075 • **Value $9**

8. Grandma
Handcrafted • SEAL
450QXM5162 • **Value $13**

9. I Dream of Santa
Handcrafted • SICK
375QXM4055 • **Value $13**

10. Into the Woods
Handcrafted • SEAL
375QXM4045 • **Value $10**

11. Learning to Skate
Handcrafted • CHAD
300QXM4122 • **Value $10**

12. Lighting a Path
Handcrafted • CHAD
300QXM4115 • **Value $10**

13. Merry Mascot
Handcrafted • SIED
375QXM4042 • **Value $11**

14. Mom
Handcrafted • ANDR
450QXM5155 • **Value $14**

15. Monkey Melody
Handcrafted • SICK
575QXM4092 • **Value $15**

16. North Pole Fire Truck
Handcrafted • PALM
475QXM4105 • **Value $14**

17. Pear-Shaped Tones
Handcrafted • LYLE
375QXM4052 • **Value $10**

18. Pull Out a Plum
Handcrafted • FRAN
575QXM4095 • **Value $14**

19. Refreshing Flight
Handcrafted • CHAD
575QXM4112 • **Value $15**

20. 'Round the Mountain
Handcrafted • CROW
725QXM4025 • **Value $19**

1993

GENERAL MINIATURE

	Price Paid	Value of My Collection
1.		
2.		
3.		
4.		
5.		
6.		
7.		
8.		
9.		
10.		
11.		
12.		
13.		
14.		
15.		
16.		
17.		
18.		
19.		
20.		
PENCIL TOTALS		

VALUE GUIDE — HALLMARK KEEPSAKE ORNAMENTS

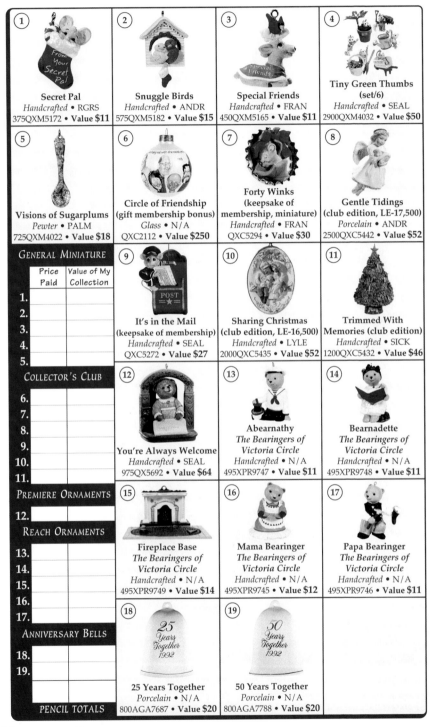

(1) Secret Pal
Handcrafted • RGRS
375QXM5172 • **Value $11**

(2) Snuggle Birds
Handcrafted • ANDR
575QXM5182 • **Value $15**

(3) Special Friends
Handcrafted • FRAN
450QXM5165 • **Value $11**

(4) Tiny Green Thumbs (set/6)
Handcrafted • SEAL
2900QXM4032 • **Value $50**

(5) Visions of Sugarplums
Pewter • PALM
725QXM4022 • **Value $18**

(6) Circle of Friendship (gift membership bonus)
Glass • N/A
QXC2112 • **Value $250**

(7) Forty Winks (keepsake of membership, miniature)
Handcrafted • FRAN
QXC5294 • **Value $30**

(8) Gentle Tidings (club edition, LE-17,500)
Porcelain • ANDR
2500QXC5442 • **Value $52**

GENERAL MINIATURE

	Price Paid	Value of My Collection
1.		
2.		
3.		
4.		
5.		

COLLECTOR'S CLUB

6.		
7.		
8.		
9.		
10.		
11.		

PREMIERE ORNAMENTS

12.		

REACH ORNAMENTS

13.		
14.		
15.		
16.		
17.		

ANNIVERSARY BELLS

18.		
19.		

PENCIL TOTALS

(9) It's in the Mail (keepsake of membership)
Handcrafted • SEAL
QXC5272 • **Value $27**

(10) Sharing Christmas (club edition, LE-16,500)
Handcrafted • LYLE
2000QXC5435 • **Value $52**

(11) Trimmed With Memories (club edition)
Handcrafted • SICK
1200QXC5432 • **Value $46**

(12) You're Always Welcome
Handcrafted • SEAL
975QX5692 • **Value $64**

(13) Abearnathy
The Bearingers of Victoria Circle
Handcrafted • N/A
495XPR9747 • **Value $11**

(14) Bearnadette
The Bearingers of Victoria Circle
Handcrafted • N/A
495XPR9748 • **Value $11**

(15) Fireplace Base
The Bearingers of Victoria Circle
Handcrafted • N/A
495XPR9749 • **Value $14**

(16) Mama Bearinger
The Bearingers of Victoria Circle
Handcrafted • N/A
495XPR9745 • **Value $12**

(17) Papa Bearinger
The Bearingers of Victoria Circle
Handcrafted • N/A
495XPR9746 • **Value $11**

(18) 25 Years Together
Porcelain • N/A
800AGA7687 • **Value $20**

(19) 50 Years Together
Porcelain • N/A
800AGA7788 • **Value $20**

1. Our First Anniversary
Porcelain • N/A
1000AGA7865 • **Value $20**

2. Our Fifth Anniversary
Porcelain • N/A
1000AGA7866 • **Value $20**

3. Our Tenth Anniversary
Porcelain • N/A
1000AGA7867 • **Value $20**

4. 25 Years Together
Porcelain • N/A
1000AGA7686 • **Value $20**

5. 40 Years Together
Porcelain • N/A
1000AGA7868 • **Value $20**

6. 50 Years Together
Porcelain • N/A
1000AGA7787 • **Value $20**

7. Santa's Favorite Stop
Handcrafted • VARI
5500QXC4125 • **Value $350**

8. Baby's Christening
Handcrafted • N/A
1200BBY2917 • **Value $18**

9. Baby's Christening Photoholder
Silver-Plated • N/A
1000BBY1335 • **Value $15**

10. Baby's First Christmas
Handcrafted • N/A
1200BBY2918 • **Value $17**

11. Baby's First Christmas
Handcrafted • N/A
1400BBY2919 • **Value $20**

12. Baby's First Christmas Photoholder
Silver-Plated • N/A
1000BBY1470 • **Value $15**

13. Granddaughter's First Christmas
Handcrafted • N/A
1400BBY2802 • **Value $18**

14. Grandson's First Christmas
Handcrafted • N/A
1400BBY2801 • **Value $18**

15. K.C. Angel
Silver-Plated • N/A
(N/C) No stock # • **Value $500**

16. Baby Block Photoholder (re-issued in 1994)
Handcrafted • FRAN
1475QP6035 • **Value N/E**

17. Cool Snowman
Glass • N/A
875QP6052 • **Value N/E**

18. Festive Album Photoholder (re-issued in 1994)
Handcrafted • VOTR
1275QP6025 • **Value N/E**

19. Filled With Cookies
Handcrafted • RGRS
1275QP6042 • **Value N/E**

20. Going Golfin' (re-issued in 1994)
Handcrafted • PALM
1275QP6012 • **Value N/E**

1993

	Price Paid	Value of My Collection
ANNIVERSARY ORNAMENTS		
1.		
2.		
3.		
4.		
5.		
6.		
ARTISTS ON TOUR PIECES		
7.		
BABY ORNAMENTS		
8.		
9.		
10.		
11.		
12.		
13.		
14.		
CONVENTION ORNAMENTS		
15.		
PERSONALIZED ORNAMENTS		
16.		
17.		
18.		
19.		
20.		
PENCIL TOTALS		

(1) Here's Your Fortune *Handcrafted* • SEAL 1075QP6002 • **Value N/E**	**(2)** Mailbox Delivery (re-issued in 1994 and 1995) *Handcrafted* • CROW 1475QP6015 • **Value N/E**	**(3)** On the Billboard (re-issued in 1994 and 1995) *Handcrafted* • CROW 1275QP6022 • **Value N/E**	**(4)** PEANUTS® *Glass* • N/A 900QP6045 • **Value N/E**
(5) Playing Ball (re-issued in 1994 and 1995) *Handcrafted* • FRAN 1275QP6032 • **Value N/E**	**(6)** Reindeer in the Sky *Glass* • N/A 875QP6055 • **Value N/E**	**(7)** Santa Says (re-issued in 1994) *Handcrafted* • SEAL 1475QP6005 • **Value N/E**	

PERSONALIZED ORNAMENTS

	Price Paid	Value of My Collection
1.		
2.		
3.		
4.		
5.		
6.		
7.		

GENERAL KEEPSAKE

8.		
9.		
10.		
11.		
12.		
13.		
14.		
15.		
16.		

PENCIL TOTALS

1992

Of note in the 1992 collection was the debut of the "unofficial series" of handcrafted Coca-Cola® Santa ornaments in the Keepsake and Miniature lines. For 1992, there were 126 Keepsake ornaments, 21 Magic ornaments and 48 Miniature ornaments. See the collectible series section for more 1992 ornaments.

(8) Across The Miles *Acrylic* • RHOD 675QX3044 • **Value $14**	**(9)** Anniversary Year Photoholder *Chrome/Brass* • UNRU 975QX4851 • **Value $28**	**(10)** Baby's First Christmas *Handcrafted* • FRAN 775QX4644 • **Value $40**
(11) Baby's First Christmas *Porcelain* • ANDR 1875QX4581 • **Value $33**	**(12)** Baby's First Christmas – Baby Boy *Satin* • VOTR 475QX2191 • **Value $19**	**(13)** Baby's First Christmas – Baby Girl *Satin* • VOTR 475QX2204 • **Value $19**
(14) Baby's First Christmas Photoholder *Fabric* • VOTR 775QX4641 • **Value $26**	**(15)** Baby's Second Christmas *Handcrafted* • FRAN 675QX4651 • **Value $23**	**(16)** Bear Bell Champ *Handcrafted/Brass* • SEAL 775QX5071 • **Value $28**

(1) Brother	(2) Cheerful Santa	(3) A Child's Christmas	(4) Child's Fifth Christmas
Handcrafted • CROW	Handcrafted • UNRU	Handcrafted • FRAN	Handcrafted • RHOD
675QX4684 • Value $16	975QX5154 • Value $32	975QX4574 • Value $19	675QX4664 • Value $20

(5) Child's Fourth Christmas	(6) Child's Third Christmas	(7) Cool Fliers (set/2)	(8) Dad
Handcrafted • FRAN	Handcrafted • FRAN	Handcrafted • JLEE	Handcrafted • SIED
675QX4661 • Value $23	675QX4654 • Value $21	1075QX5474 • Value $26	775QX4674 • Value $22

1992

(9) Dad-to-Be	(10) Daughter	(11) Deck the Hogs
Handcrafted • JLEE	Handcrafted • FRAN	Handcrafted • FRAN
675QX4611 • Value $18	675QX5031 • Value $27	875QX5204 • Value $25

GENERAL KEEPSAKE

	Price Paid	Value of My Collection
1.		
2.		
3.		
4.		
5.		
6.		
7.		
8.		
9.		
10.		
11.		
12.		
13.		
14.		
15.		
16.		
17.		
18.		
19.		
20.		
PENCIL TOTALS		

(12) Dickens Caroler Bell – Lord Chadwick	(13) Down-Under Holiday	(14) Egg Nog Nest
Porcelain • CHAD	Handcrafted • CROW	Handcrafted • N/A
2175QX4554 • Value $42	775QX5144 • Value $21	775QX5121 • Value $18

(15) Elfin Marionette	(16) Elvis	(17) Eric the Baker
Handcrafted • CHAD	Brass-Plated • RHOD/LYLE	Handcrafted • SICK
1175QX5931 • Value $24	1475QX5624 • Value $26	875QX5244 • Value $22

(18) Feliz Navidad	(19) For My Grandma Photoholder	(20) For The One I Love
Handcrafted • ANDR	Fabric • N/A	Porcelain • LYLE
675QX5181 • Value $23	775QX5184 • Value $17	975QX4844 • Value $24

1

Franz the Artist
Handcrafted • SICK
875QX5261 • **Value $27**

2

Frieda the Animals' Friend
Handcrafted • SICK
875QX5264 • **Value $25**

3

• A • Friendly Christmas Greeting 1992

Friendly Greetings
Handcrafted • CHAD
775QX5041 • **Value $17**

4

Friendship Line
Handcrafted • SEAL
975QX5034 • **Value $30**

5

From Our Home to Yours
Glass • VOTR
475QX2131 • **Value $15**

6

Fun on a Big Scale
Handcrafted • CROW
1075QX5134 • **Value $25**

7

GARFIELD
Handcrafted • PALM
775QX5374 • **Value $19**

8

Genius at Work
Handcrafted • CROW
1075QX5371 • **Value $22**

9

Godchild 1992

Godchild
Handcrafted • UNRU
675QX5941 • **Value $21**

10

Golf's a Ball 1992

Golf's a Ball
Handcrafted • SCHU
675QX5984 • **Value $29**

11

Gone Wishin'
Handcrafted • DLEE
875QX5171 • **Value $19**

12

Granddaughter

Granddaughter
Handcrafted • SEAL
675QX5604 • **Value $22**

13

Granddaughter's First Christmas
Handcrafted • SIED
675QX4634 • **Value $19**

14

Grandmother
Glass • N/A
475QX2011 • **Value $19**

15

Grandparents have a special way of brightening up the holiday! CHRISTMAS 1992

Grandparents
Glass • N/A
475QX2004 • **Value $17**

16

Grandson

Grandson
Handcrafted • SEAL
675QX5611 • **Value $19**

17

Grandson's First Christmas
Handcrafted • SIED
675QX4621 • **Value $19**

18

Green Thumb Santa
Handcrafted • PALM
775QX5101 • **Value $18**

19

Hello-Ho-Ho
Handcrafted • CROW
975QX5141 • **Value $25**

20

Holiday Memo
Handcrafted • RGRS
775QX5044 • **Value $18**

GENERAL KEEPSAKE

	Price Paid	Value of My Collection
1.		
2.		
3.		
4.		
5.		
6.		
7.		
8.		
9.		
10.		
11.		
12.		
13.		
14.		
15.		
16.		
17.		
18.		
19.		
20.		
PENCIL TOTALS		

VALUE GUIDE — HALLMARK KEEPSAKE ORNAMENTS

(1) **Holiday Teatime (set/2)** *Handcrafted* • RGRS 1475QX5431 • **Value $32**	**(2)** **Holiday Wishes** *Handcrafted* • PIKE 775QX5131 • **Value $17**	**(3)** **Honest George** *Handcrafted* • JLEE 775QX5064 • **Value $17**	**(4)** **Jesus Loves Me** *Cameo* • ANDR 775QX3024 • **Value $18**
(5) **Love to Skate** *Handcrafted* • RGRS 875QX4841 • **Value $22**	**(6)** **Loving Shepherd** *Handcrafted/Brass* • ANDR 775QX5151 • **Value $19**	**(7)** **Ludwig the Musician** *Handcrafted* • SICK 875QX5281 • **Value $22**	**(8)** **Max the Tailor** *Handcrafted* • SICK 875QX5251 • **Value $23**

1992

(9) **Memories to Cherish Photoholder** *Porcelain* • ANDR 1075QX5161 • **Value $23**	**(10)** **Merry "Swiss" Mouse** *Handcrafted* • SEAL 775QX5114 • **Value $16**	**(11)** **Mom** *Handcrafted* • RGRS 775QX5164 • **Value $20**
(12) **Mom and Dad** *Handcrafted* • SIED 975QX4671 • **Value $38**	**(13)** **Mom-to-Be** *Handcrafted* • JLEE 675QX4614 • **Value $18**	**(14)** **Mother Goose** *Handcrafted* • CROW 1375QX4984 • **Value $32**
(15) **New Home** *Handcrafted* • PIKE 875QX5191 • **Value $18**	**(16)** **Norman Rockwell Art** *Glass* • LYLE 500QX2224 • **Value $24**	**(17)** **North Pole Fire Fighter** *Handcrafted/Brass* • SEAL 975QX5104 • **Value $22**
(18) **Otto the Carpenter** *Handcrafted* • SICK 875QX5254 • **Value $23**	**(19)** **Our First Christmas Together** *Acrylic* • VOTR 675QX3011 • **Value $19**	**(20)** **Our First Christmas Together** *Handcrafted* • JLEE 975QX5061 • **Value $20**

GENERAL KEEPSAKE

	Price Paid	Value of My Collection
1.		
2.		
3.		
4.		
5.		
6.		
7.		
8.		
9.		
10.		
11.		
12.		
13.		
14.		
15.		
16.		
17.		
18.		
19.		
20.		
PENCIL TOTALS		

Value Guide — Hallmark Keepsake Ornaments

(1) Our First Christmas Together Photoholder
Handcrafted • SEAL
875QX4694 • **Value $25**

(2) Owl
Handcrafted • SIED
975QX5614 • **Value $28**

(3) Partridge IN a Pear Tree
Handcrafted • SIED
875QX5234 • **Value $21**

(4) PEANUTS®
Glass • N/A
500QX2244 • **Value $28**

(5) Please Pause Here
Handcrafted • DLEE
1475QX5291 • **Value $35**

(6) Polar Post
Handcrafted • SEAL
875QX4914 • **Value $22**

(7) Rapid Delivery
Handcrafted • PALM
875QX5094 • **Value $23**

(8) A Santa-Full!
Handcrafted • FRAN
975QX5991 • **Value $42**

(9) Santa Maria
Handcrafted • CROW
1275QX5074 • **Value $24**

(10) Santa's Hook Shot (set/2)
Handcrafted • SEAL
1275QX5434 • **Value $30**

(11) Santa's Roundup
Handcrafted • JLEE
875QX5084 • **Value $27**

(12) Secret Pal
Handcrafted • RGRS
775QX5424 • **Value $15**

(13) Silver Star Train Set (set/3)
Die-Cast Metal • SICK
2800QX5324 • **Value $58**

(14) Sister
Handcrafted • CROW
675QX4681 • **Value $16**

(15) Skiing 'Round
Handcrafted • JLEE
875QX5214 • **Value $20**

(16) Sky Line Caboose
Die-Cast Metal • SICK
975QX5321 • **Value $27**

(17) Sky Line Coal Car
Die-Cast Metal • SICK
975QX5401 • **Value $22**

(18) Sky Line Locomotive
Die-Cast Metal • SICK
975QX5311 • **Value $45**

(19) Sky Line Stock Car
Die-Cast Metal • SICK
975QX5314 • **Value $22**

(20) SNOOPY® and WOODSTOCK
Handcrafted • RGRS
875QX5954 • **Value $39**

General Keepsake

	Price Paid	Value of My Collection
1.		
2.		
3.		
4.		
5.		
6.		
7.		
8.		
9.		
10.		
11.		
12.		
13.		
14.		
15.		
16.		
17.		
18.		
19.		
20.		
PENCIL TOTALS		

1. Son
Handcrafted • FRAN
675QX5024 • **Value $25**

2. Special Cat Photoholder
Handcrafted • CHAD
775QX5414 • **Value $19**

3. Special Dog Photoholder
Handcrafted • CHAD
775QX5421 • **Value $27**

4. Spirit of Christmas Stress
Handcrafted • CHAD
875QX5231 • **Value $23**

5. Stocked With Joy
Pressed Tin • SICK
775QX5934 • **Value $22**

6. Tasty Christmas
Handcrafted • FRAN
975QX5994 • **Value $26**

7. Teacher
Glass • N/A
475QX2264 • **Value $17**

8. Toboggan Tail
Handcrafted • ANDR
775QX5459 • **Value $19**

9. Tread Bear
Handcrafted • SEAL
875QX5091 • **Value $25**

10. Turtle Dreams
Handcrafted • JLEE
875QX4991 • **Value $26**

11. Uncle Art's Ice Cream
Handcrafted • SIED
875QX5001 • **Value $27**

12. V.P. of Important Stuff
Handcrafted • SIED
675QX5051 • **Value $16**

13. World-Class Teacher
Handcrafted • SIED
775QX5054 • **Value $19**

14. Baby's First Christmas
Handcrafted • CROW
2200QLX7281 • **Value $90**

15. Christmas Parade
Handcrafted • SICK
3000QLX7271 • **Value $64**

16. Continental Express
Handcrafted • SICK
3200QLX7264 • **Value $75**

17. The Dancing Nutcracker
Handcrafted • VOTR
3000QLX7261 • **Value $58**

18. Enchanted Clock
Handcrafted • CROW
3000QLX7274 • **Value $62**

19. Feathered Friends
Handcrafted • SICK
1400QLX7091 • **Value $32**

20. Good Sledding Ahead
Handcrafted • PALM
2800QLX7244 • **Value $57**

1992

GENERAL KEEPSAKE

	Price Paid	Value of My Collection
1.		
2.		
3.		
4.		
5.		
6.		
7.		
8.		
9.		
10.		
11.		
12.		
13.		

GENERAL MAGIC

14.		
15.		
16.		
17.		
18.		
19.		
20.		
PENCIL TOTALS		

VALUE GUIDE — HALLMARK KEEPSAKE ORNAMENTS

(1) Lighting the Way *Handcrafted* • ANDR 1800QLX7231 • **Value $48**	**(2)** Look! It's Santa *Handcrafted* • DLEE 1400QLX7094 • **Value $45**	**(3)** Nut Sweet Nut *Handcrafted* • CROW 1000QLX7081 • **Value $24**	**(4)** Our First Christmas Together *Panorama Ball* • CHAD 2000QLX7221 • **Value $44**
(5) Santa Special (re-issued from 1991) *Handcrafted* • SEAL 4000QLX7167 • **Value $75**	**(6)** Santa Sub *Handcrafted* • CROW 1800QLX7321 • **Value $40**	**(7)** Santa's Answering Machine *Handcrafted* • JLEE 2200QLX7241 • **Value $42**	**(8)** Shuttlecraft Galileo™ From the Starship Enterprise™ *Handcrafted* • RHOD 2400QLX7331 • **Value $48**

GENERAL MAGIC

	Price Paid	Value of My Collection
1.		
2.		
3.		
4.		
5.		
6.		
7.		
8.		
9.		
10.		
11.		

GENERAL MINIATURE

12.		
13.		
14.		
15.		
16.		
17.		
18.		
19.		
20.		

PENCIL TOTALS

(9) Under Construction *Handcrafted* • PALM 1800QLX7324 • **Value $42**	**(10)** Watch Owls *Porcelain* • FRAN 1200QLX7084 • **Value $30**	**(11)** Yuletide Rider *Handcrafted* • SEAL 2800QLX7314 • **Value $58**
(12) A+ Teacher *Handcrafted* • UNRU 375QXM5511 • **Value $9**	**(13)** Angelic Harpist *Handcrafted* • LYLE 450QXM5524 • **Value $16**	**(14)** Baby's First Christmas *Handcrafted/Brass* • LYLE 450QXM5494 • **Value $21**
(15) Black-Capped Chickadee *Handcrafted* • FRAN 300QXM5484 • **Value $17**	**(16)** Bright Stringers *Handcrafted* • SEAL 375QXM5841 • **Value $17**	**(17)** Buck-A-Roo *Handcrafted* • CROW 450QXM5814 • **Value $16**
(18) Christmas Bonus *Handcrafted* • PALM 300QXM5811 • **Value $9**	**(19)** Christmas Copter *Handcrafted* • FRAN 575QXM5844 • **Value $15**	**(20)** Coca-Cola® Santa *Handcrafted* • UNRU 575QXM5884 • **Value $18**

1	2	3	4
Cool Uncle Sam	**Cozy Kayak**	**Fast Finish**	**Feeding Time**
Handcrafted • JLEE	*Handcrafted* • JLEE	*Handcrafted* • RHOD	*Handcrafted* • CROW
300QXM5561 • **Value $16**	375QXM5551 • **Value $14**	375QXM5301 • **Value $13**	575QXM5481 • **Value $16**

5	6	7	8
Friendly Tin Soldier	**Friends Are Tops**	**Gerbil Inc.**	**Going Places**
Pressed Tin • SICK	*Handcrafted* • CROW	*Handcrafted* • SIED	*Handcrafted* • ANDR
450QXM5874 • **Value $18**	450QXM5521 • **Value $12**	375QXM5924 • **Value $12**	375QXM5871 • **Value $11**

9	10	11	GENERAL MINIATURE
Grandchild's First Christmas	**Grandma**	**Harmony Trio (set/3)**	
Handcrafted • FRAN	*Handcrafted* • UNRU	*Handcrafted* • VOTR	
575QXM5501 • **Value $14**	450QXM5514 • **Value $15**	1175QXM5471 • **Value $24**	

	Price Paid	Value of My Collection
1.		
2.		
3.		
4.		
5.		
6.		
7.		
8.		
9.		
10.		
11.		
12.		
13.		
14.		
15.		
16.		
17.		
18.		
19.		
20.		
PENCIL TOTALS		

12	13	14
Hickory, Dickory, Dock	**Holiday Holly**	**Holiday Splash**
Handcrafted • CHAD	*Gold-Plated* • N/A	*Handcrafted* • FRAN
375QXM5861 • **Value $14**	975QXM5364 • **Value $17**	575QXM5834 • **Value $14**

15	16	17
Hoop It Up	**Inside Story**	**Little Town of Bethlehem**
Handcrafted • CROW	*Handcrafted* • SEAL	*Handcrafted* • SICK
450QXM5831 • **Value $13**	725QXM5881 • **Value $22**	300QXM5864 • **Value $23**

18	19	20
Minted for Santa	**Mom**	**Perfect Balance**
Copper • UNRU	*Handcrafted* • ANDR	*Handcrafted* • RGRS
375QXM5854 • **Value $14**	450QXM5504 • **Value $16**	300QXM5571 • **Value $12**

1992

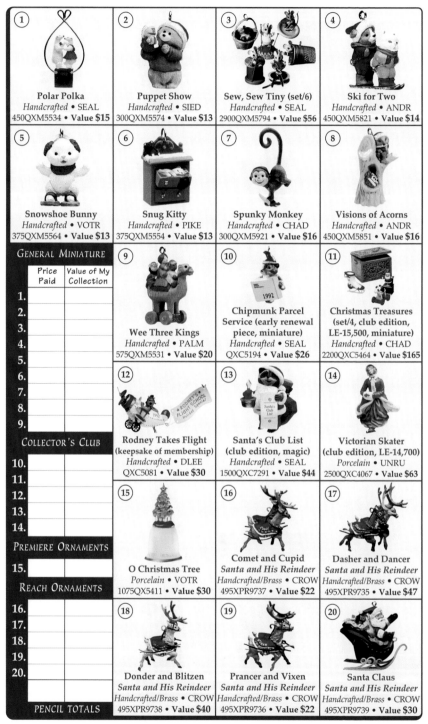

(1) **Polar Polka** *Handcrafted* • SEAL 450QXM5534 • **Value $15**	**(2)** **Puppet Show** *Handcrafted* • SIED 300QXM5574 • **Value $13**	**(3)** **Sew, Sew Tiny (set/6)** *Handcrafted* • SEAL 2900QXM5794 • **Value $56**	**(4)** **Ski for Two** *Handcrafted* • ANDR 450QXM5821 • **Value $14**

(5) **Snowshoe Bunny** *Handcrafted* • VOTR 375QXM5564 • **Value $13**

(6) **Snug Kitty** *Handcrafted* • PIKE 375QXM5554 • **Value $13**

(7) **Spunky Monkey** *Handcrafted* • CHAD 300QXM5921 • **Value $16**

(8) **Visions of Acorns** *Handcrafted* • ANDR 450QXM5851 • **Value $16**

GENERAL MINIATURE

	Price Paid	Value of My Collection
1.		
2.		
3.		
4.		
5.		
6.		
7.		
8.		
9.		

(9) **Wee Three Kings** *Handcrafted* • PALM 575QXM5531 • **Value $20**

(10) **Chipmunk Parcel Service (early renewal piece, miniature)** *Handcrafted* • SEAL QXC5194 • **Value $26**

(11) **Christmas Treasures (set/4, club edition, LE-15,500, miniature)** *Handcrafted* • CHAD 2200QXC5464 • **Value $165**

(12) **Rodney Takes Flight (keepsake of membership)** *Handcrafted* • DLEE QXC5081 • **Value $30**

(13) **Santa's Club List (club edition, magic)** *Handcrafted* • SEAL 1500QXC7291 • **Value $44**

(14) **Victorian Skater (club edition, LE-14,700)** *Porcelain* • UNRU 2500QXC4067 • **Value $63**

COLLECTOR'S CLUB

10.
11.
12.
13.
14.

PREMIERE ORNAMENTS

15.

REACH ORNAMENTS

(15) **O Christmas Tree** *Porcelain* • VOTR 1075QX5411 • **Value $30**

(16) **Comet and Cupid** *Santa and His Reindeer* *Handcrafted/Brass* • CROW 495XPR9737 • **Value $22**

(17) **Dasher and Dancer** *Santa and His Reindeer* *Handcrafted/Brass* • CROW 495XPR9735 • **Value $47**

16.
17.
18.
19.
20.

(18) **Donder and Blitzen** *Santa and His Reindeer* *Handcrafted/Brass* • CROW 495XPR9738 • **Value $40**

(19) **Prancer and Vixen** *Santa and His Reindeer* *Handcrafted/Brass* • CROW 495XPR9736 • **Value $22**

(20) **Santa Claus** *Santa and His Reindeer* *Handcrafted/Brass* • CROW 495XPR9739 • **Value $30**

PENCIL TOTALS

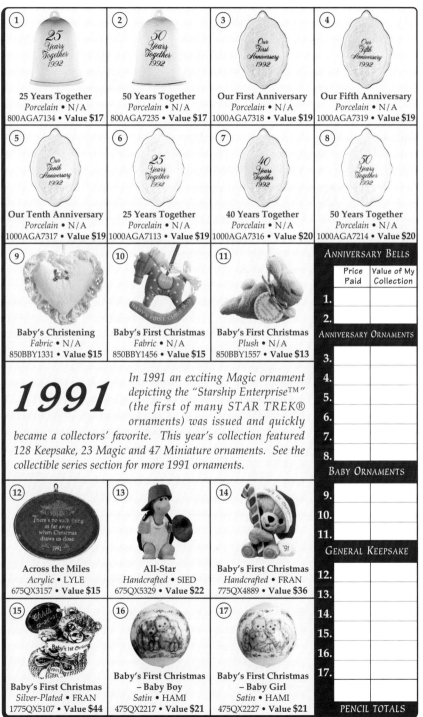

1 25 Years Together 1992
2 50 Years Together 1992
3 Our First Anniversary 1992
4 Our Fifth Anniversary 1992

25 Years Together	50 Years Together	Our First Anniversary	Our Fifth Anniversary
Porcelain • N/A	Porcelain • N/A	Porcelain • N/A	Porcelain • N/A
800AGA7134 • **Value $17**	800AGA7235 • **Value $17**	1000AGA7318 • **Value $19**	1000AGA7319 • **Value $19**

5 Our Tenth Anniversary 1992
6 25 Years Together 1992
7 40 Years Together 1992
8 50 Years Together 1992

Our Tenth Anniversary	25 Years Together	40 Years Together	50 Years Together
Porcelain • N/A	Porcelain • N/A	Porcelain • N/A	Porcelain • N/A
1000AGA7317 • **Value $19**	1000AGA7113 • **Value $19**	1000AGA7316 • **Value $20**	1000AGA7214 • **Value $20**

9
10
11

Baby's Christening	Baby's First Christmas	Baby's First Christmas
Fabric • N/A	Fabric • N/A	Plush • N/A
850BBY1331 • **Value $15**	850BBY1456 • **Value $15**	850BBY1557 • **Value $13**

1991

In 1991 an exciting Magic ornament depicting the "Starship Enterprise™" (the first of many STAR TREK® ornaments) was issued and quickly became a collectors' favorite. This year's collection featured 128 Keepsake, 23 Magic and 47 Miniature ornaments. See the collectible series section for more 1991 ornaments.

12
13
14

Across the Miles	All-Star	Baby's First Christmas
Acrylic • LYLE	Handcrafted • SIED	Handcrafted • FRAN
675QX3157 • **Value $15**	675QX5329 • **Value $22**	775QX4889 • **Value $36**

15
16
17

Baby's First Christmas	Baby's First Christmas – Baby Boy	Baby's First Christmas – Baby Girl
Silver-Plated • FRAN	Satin • HAMI	Satin • HAMI
1775QX5107 • **Value $44**	475QX2217 • **Value $21**	475QX2227 • **Value $21**

ANNIVERSARY BELLS

	Price Paid	Value of My Collection
1.		
2.		

ANNIVERSARY ORNAMENTS

3.		
4.		
5.		
6.		
7.		
8.		

BABY ORNAMENTS

9.		
10.		
11.		

GENERAL KEEPSAKE

12.		
13.		
14.		
15.		
16.		
17.		

PENCIL TOTALS

1991

(1) Baby's First Christmas Photoholder
Fabric • VOTR
775QX4869 • **Value $30**

(2) Baby's Second Christmas
Handcrafted • FRAN
675QX4897 • **Value $33**

(3) Basket Bell Players
Handcrafted/Wicker • SEAL
775QX5377 • **Value $27**

(4) The Big Cheese
Handcrafted • SIED
675QX5327 • **Value $20**

(5) Bob Cratchit
Porcelain • UNRU
1375QX4997 • **Value $38**

(6) Brother
Handcrafted • SIED
675QX5479 • **Value $21**

(7) A Child's Christmas
Handcrafted • FRAN
975QX4887 • **Value $17**

(8) Child's Fifth Christmas
Handcrafted • RHOD
675QX4909 • **Value $19**

(9) Child's Fourth Christmas
Handcrafted • FRAN
675QX4907 • **Value $20**

(10) Child's Third Christmas
Handcrafted • FRAN
675QX4899 • **Value $30**

(11) Chilly Chap
Handcrafted • DLEE
675QX5339 • **Value $18**

(12) Christmas Welcome
Handcrafted • SICK
975QX5299 • **Value $24**

(13) Christopher Robin
Handcrafted • SIED
975QX5579 • **Value $40**

(14) Cuddly Lamb
Handcrafted • RGRS
675QX5199 • **Value $22**

(15) Dad
Handcrafted • JLEE
775QX5127 • **Value $19**

(16) Dad-to-Be
Handcrafted • JLEE
575QX4879 • **Value $17**

(17) Daughter
Handcrafted • SIED
575QX5477 • **Value $42**

(18) Dickens Caroler Bell – Mrs. Beaumont
Porcelain • CHAD
2175QX5039 • **Value $42**

(19) Dinoclaus
Handcrafted • CHAD
775QX5277 • **Value $24**

(20) Ebenezer Scrooge
Porcelain • UNRU
1375QX4989 • **Value $48**

	Price Paid	Value of My Collection
GENERAL KEEPSAKE		
1.		
2.		
3.		
4.		
5.		
6.		
7.		
8.		
9.		
10.		
11.		
12.		
13.		
14.		
15.		
16.		
17.		
18.		
19.		
20.		
PENCIL TOTALS		

1.
Evergreen Inn
Handcrafted • SEAL
875QX5389 • **Value $18**

2.
Extra-Special Friends
Glass • N/A
475QX2279 • **Value $16**

3.
Fanfare Bear
Handcrafted • SEAL
875QX5337 • **Value $20**

4.
Feliz Navidad
Handcrafted • JLEE
675QX5279 • **Value $27**

5.
Fiddlin' Around
Handcrafted • VOTR
775QX4387 • **Value $19**

6.
Fifty Years Together
Photoholder
Handcrafted/Brass • VOTR
875QX4947 • **Value $19**

7.
First Christmas
Together
Acrylic • PIKE
675QX3139 • **Value $25**

8.
First Christmas
Together
Glass • N/A
475QX2229 • **Value $21**

9.
First Christmas
Together
Handcrafted • SICK
875QX4919 • **Value $28**

10.
First Christmas
Together Photoholder
Handcrafted/Brass • VOTR
875QX4917 • **Value $28**

11.
Five Years Together
Faceted Glass • N/A
775QX4927 • **Value $18**

12.
Flag of Liberty
Handcrafted • DLEE
675QX5249 • **Value $19**

13.
Folk Art Reindeer
Wood/Brass • VOTR
875QX5359 • **Value $20**

14.
Forty Years Together
Faceted Glass • N/A
775QX4939 • **Value $18**

15.
Friends Are Fun
Handcrafted • CROW
975QX5289 • **Value $24**

16.
From Our Home
to Yours
Glass • VOTR
475QX2287 • **Value $23**

17.
GARFIELD®
Handcrafted • RHOD
775QX5177 • **Value $32**

18.
Gift of Joy
Brass/Chrome/Copper • MCGE
875QX5319 • **Value $25**

19.
Glee Club Bears
Handcrafted • SEAL
875QX4969 • **Value $22**

20.
Godchild
Handcrafted • BISH
675QX5489 • **Value $22**

GENERAL KEEPSAKE

	Price Paid	Value of My Collection
1.		
2.		
3.		
4.		
5.		
6.		
7.		
8.		
9.		
10.		
11.		
12.		
13.		
14.		
15.		
16.		
17.		
18.		
19.		
20.		
PENCIL TOTALS		

1991

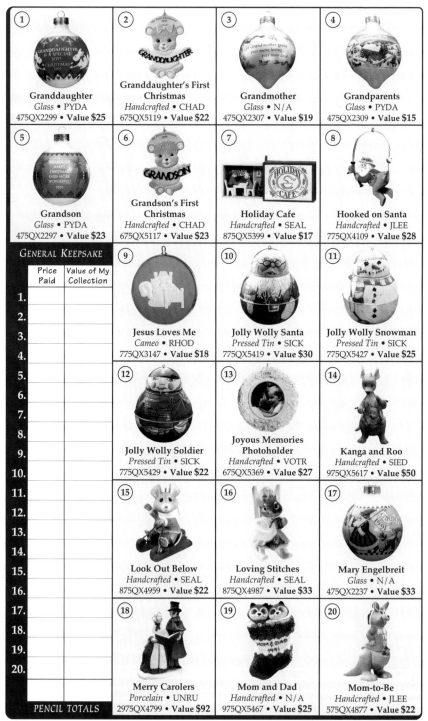

1

Granddaughter
Glass • PYDA
475QX2299 • **Value $25**

2

Granddaughter's First Christmas
Handcrafted • CHAD
675QX5119 • **Value $22**

3

Grandmother
Glass • N/A
475QX2307 • **Value $19**

4

Grandparents
Glass • PYDA
475QX2309 • **Value $15**

5

Grandson
Glass • PYDA
475QX2297 • **Value $23**

6

Grandson's First Christmas
Handcrafted • CHAD
675QX5117 • **Value $23**

7

Holiday Cafe
Handcrafted • SEAL
875QX5399 • **Value $17**

8

Hooked on Santa
Handcrafted • JLEE
775QX4109 • **Value $28**

GENERAL KEEPSAKE

	Price Paid	Value of My Collection
1.		
2.		
3.		
4.		
5.		
6.		
7.		
8.		
9.		
10.		
11.		
12.		
13.		
14.		
15.		
16.		
17.		
18.		
19.		
20.		
PENCIL TOTALS		

9

Jesus Loves Me
Cameo • RHOD
775QX3147 • **Value $18**

10

Jolly Wolly Santa
Pressed Tin • SICK
775QX5419 • **Value $30**

11

Jolly Wolly Snowman
Pressed Tin • SICK
775QX5427 • **Value $25**

12

Jolly Wolly Soldier
Pressed Tin • SICK
775QX5429 • **Value $22**

13

Joyous Memories Photoholder
Handcrafted • VOTR
675QX5369 • **Value $27**

14

Kanga and Roo
Handcrafted • SIED
975QX5617 • **Value $50**

15

Look Out Below
Handcrafted • SEAL
875QX4959 • **Value $22**

16

Loving Stitches
Handcrafted • SEAL
875QX4987 • **Value $33**

17

Mary Engelbreit
Glass • N/A
475QX2237 • **Value $33**

18

Merry Carolers
Porcelain • UNRU
2975QX4799 • **Value $92**

19

Mom and Dad
Handcrafted • N/A
975QX5467 • **Value $25**

20

Mom-to-Be
Handcrafted • JLEE
575QX4877 • **Value $22**

(1) **Mother** *Porcelain/Tin* • N/A 975QX5457 • **Value $35**	**(2)** **Mrs. Cratchit** *Porcelain* • UNRU 1375QX4999 • **Value $34**	**(3)** **New Home** *Handcrafted* • BISH 675QX5449 • **Value $32**	**(4)** **Night Before Christmas** *Handcrafted* • SICK 975QX5307 • **Value $24**
(5) **Noah's Ark** *Handcrafted* • CROW 1375QX4867 • **Value $50**	**(6)** **Norman Rockwell Art** *Glass* • LYLE 500QX2259 • **Value $30**	**(7)** **Notes of Cheer** *Handcrafted* • SIED 575QX5357 • **Value $14**	**(8)** **Nutshell Nativity** *Handcrafted* • RGRS 675QX5176 • **Value $26**

1991

General Keepsake

	Price Paid	Value of My Collection
(9) **Nutty Squirrel** *Handcrafted* • PIKE 575QX4833 • **Value $15**	**(10)** **Old-Fashioned Sled** *Handcrafted* • SICK 875QX4317 • **Value $21**	**(11)** **On a Roll** *Handcrafted* • CROW 675QX5347 • **Value $21**
1.		
2.		
3.		
4.		

(12) **Partridge in a Pear Tree** *Handcrafted* • SICK 975QX5297 • **Value $19**	**(13)** **PEANUTS®** *Glass* • N/A 500QX2257 • **Value $29**	**(14)** **Piglet and Eeyore** *Handcrafted* • SIED 975QX5577 • **Value $57**

5.		
6.		
7.		
8.		
9.		
10.		

(15) **Plum Delightful** *Handcrafted* • SEAL 875QX4977 • **Value $20**	**(16)** **Polar Circus Wagon** *Handcrafted* • SICK 1375QX4399 • **Value $28**	**(17)** **Polar Classic** *Handcrafted* • SIED 675QX5287 • **Value $22**

11.		
12.		
13.		
14.		
15.		
16.		

(18) **Rabbit** *Handcrafted* • SIED 975QX5607 • **Value $35**	**(19)** **Santa Sailor** *Handcrafted/Metal* • SEAL 975QX4389 • **Value $26**	**(20)** **Santa's Studio** *Handcrafted* • SEAL 875QX5397 • **Value $19**

17.		
18.		
19.		
20.		
PENCIL TOTALS		

(1) **Sister** *Handcrafted* • LYLE 675QX5487 • **Value $20**	**(2)** **Ski Lift Bunny** *Handcrafted* • JLEE 675QX5447 • **Value $21**	**(3)** **SNOOPY® and WOODSTOCK** *Handcrafted* • RHOD 675QX5197 • **Value $36**	**(4)** **Snow Twins** *Handcrafted* • SEAL 875QX4979 • **Value $22**

(5) **Snowy Owl** *Handcrafted* • SICK 775QX5269 • **Value $20**	**(6)** **Son** *Handcrafted* • SIED 575QX5469 • **Value $20**	**(7)** **Sweet Talk** *Handcrafted* • UNRU 875QX5367 • **Value $25**	**(8)** **Sweetheart** *Porcelain* • N/A 975QX4957 • **Value $27**

GENERAL KEEPSAKE

	Price Paid	Value of My Collection
1.		
2.		
3.		
4.		
5.		
6.		
7.		
8.		
9.		
10.		
11.		
12.		
13.		
14.		
15.		
16.		
17.		
18.		
19.		

GENERAL MAGIC

20.		

PENCIL TOTALS

(9) **Teacher** *Glass* • RGRS 475QX2289 • **Value $13**	**(10)** **Ten Years Together** *Faceted Glass* • N/A 775QX4929 • **Value $19**	**(11)** **Terrific Teacher** *Handcrafted* • SICK 675QX5309 • **Value $18**
(12) **Tigger** *Handcrafted* • SIED 975QX5609 • **Value $125**	**(13)** **Tiny Tim** *Porcelain* • UNRU 1075QX5037 • **Value $42**	**(14)** **Tramp and Laddie** *Handcrafted* • FRAN 775QX4397 • **Value $44**
(15) **Twenty-Five Years Together Photoholder** *Handcrafted/Chrome* • VOTR 875QX4937 • **Value $17**	**(16)** **Under the Mistletoe** *Handcrafted* • PIKE 875QX4949 • **Value $21**	**(17)** **Up 'N' Down Journey** *Handcrafted* • CROW 975QX5047 • **Value $29**
(18) **Winnie-the-Pooh** *Handcrafted* • SIED 975QX5569 • **Value $58**	**(19)** **Yule Logger** *Handcrafted* • SEAL 875QX4967 • **Value $25**	**(20)** **Arctic Dome** *Handcrafted* • CROW 2500QLX7117 • **Value $58**

Value Guide — Hallmark Keepsake Ornaments

(1) Baby's First Christmas
Handcrafted • SEAL
3000QLX7247 • **Value $95**

(2) Bringing Home the Tree
Handcrafted • UNRU
2800QLX7249 • **Value $65**

(3) Elfin Engineer
Handcrafted • CHAD
1000QLX7209 • **Value $26**

(4) Father Christmas
Handcrafted • UNRU
1400QLX7147 • **Value $40**

(5) Festive Brass Church
Brass • MCGE
1400QLX7179 • **Value $34**

(6) First Christmas Together
Handcrafted • SICK
2500QLX7137 • **Value $57**

(7) Friendship Tree
Handcrafted • DUTK
1000QLX7169 • **Value $27**

(8) Holiday Glow
Panorama Ball • PIKE
1400QLX7177 • **Value $32**

(9) It's a Wonderful Life
Handcrafted • DLEE
2000QLX7237 • **Value $75**

(10) Jingle Bears
Handcrafted • JLEE
2500QLX7323 • **Value $55**

(11) Kringle's Bumper Cars
Handcrafted • SICK
2500QLX7119 • **Value $58**

(12) Mole Family Home
Handcrafted • JLEE
2000QLX7149 • **Value $46**

(13) Salvation Army Band
Handcrafted • UNRU
3000QLX7273 • **Value $75**

(14) Santa Special (re-issued in 1992)
Handcrafted • SEAL
4000QLX7167 • **Value $75**

(15) Santa's Hot Line
Handcrafted • CROW
1800QLX7159 • **Value $42**

(16) Ski Trip
Handcrafted • SEAL
2800QLX7266 • **Value $58**

(17) Sparkling Angel
Handcrafted • CHAD
1800QLX7157 • **Value $38**

(18) Starship Enterprise™
Handcrafted • NORT
2000QLX7199 • **Value $390**

(19) Toyland Tower
Handcrafted • CROW
2000QLX7129 • **Value $43**

(20) All Aboard
Handcrafted • CHAD
450QXM5869 • **Value $18**

1991

	Price Paid	Value of My Collection
	General Magic	
1.		
2.		
3.		
4.		
5.		
6.		
7.		
8.		
9.		
10.		
11.		
12.		
13.		
14.		
15.		
16.		
17.		
18.		
19.		
	General Miniature	
20.		
	Pencil Totals	

(1)	**(2)**	**(3)**	**(4)**
Baby's First Christmas *Handcrafted* • FRAN 600QXM5799 • **Value $22**	**Brass Bells** *Brass* • ANDR 300QXM5977 • **Value $10**	**Brass Church** *Brass* • N/A 300QXM5979 • **Value $10**	**Brass Soldier** *Brass* • N/A 300QXM5987 • **Value $10**
(5)	**(6)**	**(7)**	**(8)**
Bright Boxers *Handcrafted* • RHOD 450QXM5877 • **Value $16**	**Busy Bear** *Wood* • RHOD 450QXM5939 • **Value $11**	**Cardinal Cameo** *Handcrafted* • LYLE 600QXM5957 • **Value $18**	**Caring Shepherd** *Porcelain* • FRAN 600QXM5949 • **Value $18**

GENERAL MINIATURE

	Price Paid	Value of My Collection
1.		
2.		
3.		
4.		
5.		
6.		
7.		
8.		
9.		
10.		
11.		
12.		
13.		
14.		
15.		
16.		
17.		
18.		
19.		
20.		
PENCIL TOTALS		

(9)	**(10)**	**(11)**
Cool 'n Sweet *Porcelain* • PIKE 450QXM5867 • **Value $22**	**Country Sleigh** *Enamel* • VOTR 450QXM5999 • **Value $16**	**Courier Turtle** *Handcrafted* • PIKE 450QXM5857 • **Value $14**
(12)	**(13)**	**(14)**
Fancy Wreath *Handcrafted* • LYLE 450QXM5917 • **Value $13**	**Feliz Navidad** *Handcrafted/Straw* • RGRS 600QXM5887 • **Value $18**	**First Christmas Together** *Handcrafted/Brass* • UNRU 600QXM5819 • **Value $16**
(15)	**(16)**	**(17)**
Fly By *Handcrafted* • CROW 450QXM5859 • **Value $17**	**Friendly Fawn** *Handcrafted* • JLEE 600QXM5947 • **Value $17**	**Grandchild's First Christmas** *Porcelain* • RGRS 450QXM5697 • **Value $14**
(18)	**(19)**	**(20)**
Heavenly Minstrel *Handcrafted* • DLEE 975QXM5687 • **Value $25**	**Holiday Snowflake** *Acrylic* • RHOD 300QXM5997 • **Value $14**	**Key to Love** *Handcrafted* • CROW 450QXM5689 • **Value $17**

1. Kitty in a Mitty
Handcrafted • ANDR
450QXM5879 • **Value $12**

2. Li'l Popper
Handcrafted • SICK
450QXM5897 • **Value $21**

3. Love Is Born
Porcelain • VOTR
600QXM5959 • **Value $20**

4. Lulu & Family
Handcrafted • RGRS
600QXM5677 • **Value $22**

5. Mom
Handcrafted • SIED
600QXM5699 • **Value $17**

6. N. Pole Buddy
Handcrafted • PALM
450QXM5927 • **Value $18**

7. Noel
Acrylic • N/A
300QXM5989 • **Value $13**

8. Ring-A-Ding Elf
Handcrafted/Brass • CHAD
850QXM5669 • **Value $21**

1991

9. Seaside Otter
Handcrafted • SIED
450QXM5909 • **Value $14**

10. Silvery Santa
Silver-Plated • JLEE
975QXM5679 • **Value $23**

11. Special Friends
Handcrafted/Wicker • JLEE
850QXM5797 • **Value $21**

12. Tiny Tea Party Set (set/6)
Handcrafted/Porcelain • SEAL
2900QXM5827 • **Value $165**

13. Top Hatter
Handcrafted • SEAL
600QXM5889 • **Value $18**

14. Treeland Trio
Handcrafted • CHAD
850QXM5899 • **Value $18**

15. Upbeat Bear
Handcrafted/Metal • FRAN
600QXM5907 • **Value $17**

16. Vision of Santa
Handcrafted • CHAD
450QXM5937 • **Value $14**

17. Wee Toymaker
Handcrafted • BISH
850QXM5967 • **Value $17**

18. Beary Artistic (club edition, magic)
Handcrafted/Acrylic • SIED
1000QXC7259 • **Value $38**

19. Five Years Together (charter member gift)
Acrylic • N/A
QXC3159 • **Value $55**

20. Galloping Into Christmas (club edition, LE-28,400)
Pressed Tin • SICK
1975QXC4779 • **Value $120**

GENERAL MINIATURE

	Price Paid	Value of My Collection
1.		
2.		
3.		
4.		
5.		
6.		
7.		
8.		
9.		
10.		
11.		
12.		
13.		
14.		
15.		
16.		
17.		

COLLECTOR'S CLUB

18.		
19.		
20.		
PENCIL TOTALS		

(1) Hidden Treasure & Li'l Keeper (set/2, keepsake of membership)
Handcrafted • CROW
QXC4769 • **Value $45**

(2) Secrets for Santa (club edition, LE-28,700)
Handcrafted • RGRS
2375QXC4797 • **Value $55**

(3) Santa's Premiere
Porcelain • N/A
1075QX5237 • **Value $38**

(4) Caboose
Claus & Co. R.R.
Handcrafted • PALM
($3.95)411XPR9733 • **Value $17**

(5) Claus & Co. R.R. Trestle Display Stand
Claus & Co. R.R.
Handcrafted • PALM
($2.95)411XPR9734 • **Value $12**

(6) Gift Car
Claus & Co. R.R.
Handcrafted • PALM
($3.95)411XPR9731 • **Value $15**

(7) Locomotive
Claus & Co. R.R.
Handcrafted • PALM
($3.95)411XPR9730 • **Value $35**

(8) Passenger Car
Claus & Co. R.R.
Handcrafted • PALM
($3.95)411XPR9732 • **Value $15**

(9) Baby's Christening 1991
Porcelain • JLEE
1000BBY1317 • **Value $18**

(10) Baby's First Christmas 1991
Porcelain • JLEE
1000BBY1416 • **Value $18**

(11) Baby's First Christmas 1991
Porcelain • RGRS
1000BBY1514 • **Value $18**

(12) Kansas City Santa
Silver-Plated • N/A
(N/C) No stock # • **Value $925**

1990

The 1990 collection included an adorable group of six "polar penguins" as well as the first of four porcelain ornaments in the "Dickens Caroler Bell" collection. In all, there were 128 Keepsake ornaments, 21 Magic ornaments and a whopping 54 Miniature ornaments in the 1990 line. See the collectible series section for more 1990 ornaments.

(13) Across the Miles
Acrylic • VOTR
675QX3173 • **Value $16**

(14) Angel Kitty
Handcrafted • PYDA
875QX4746 • **Value $26**

(15) Baby Unicorn
Porcelain • RGRS
975QX5486 • **Value $24**

COLLECTOR'S CLUB	Price Paid	Value of My Collection
1.		
2.		
PREMIERE ORNAMENTS		
3.		
REACH ORNAMENTS		
4.		
5.		
6.		
7.		
8.		
BABY CELEBRATIONS		
9.		
10.		
11.		
CONVENTION ORNAMENTS		
12.		
GENERAL KEEPSAKE		
13.		
14.		
15.		
PENCIL TOTALS		

1
Baby's First Christmas
Acrylic • RGRS
675QX3036 • **Value $22**

2
Baby's First Christmas
Handcrafted • FRAN
775QX4856 • **Value $39**

3
Baby's First Christmas
Handcrafted • FRAN
975QX4853 • **Value $24**

4
Baby's First Christmas
– Baby Boy
Satin • N/A
475QX2063 • **Value $24**

5
Baby's First Christmas
– Baby Girl
Satin • N/A
475QX2066 • **Value $24**

6
Baby's First Christmas
Photoholder
Fabric • N/A
775QX4843 • **Value $28**

7
Baby's Second
Christmas
Handcrafted • FRAN
675QX4863 • **Value $37**

8
Bearback Rider
Handcrafted • CROW
975QX5483 • **Value $30**

9
Beary Good Deal
Handcrafted • SIED
675QX4733 • **Value $16**

10
Billboard Bunny
Handcrafted • JLEE
775QX5196 • **Value $22**

11
Born to Dance
Handcrafted • PIKE
775QX5043 • **Value $23**

12
Brother
Handcrafted • SIED
575QX4493 • **Value $14**

13
Child Care Giver
Acrylic • N/A
675QX3166 • **Value $13**

14
Child's Fifth Christmas
Handcrafted • RHOD
675QX4876 • **Value $20**

15
Child's Fourth
Christmas
Handcrafted • FRAN
675QX4873 • **Value $20**

16
Child's Third Christmas
Handcrafted • FRAN
675QX4866 • **Value $23**

17
Chiming In
Handcrafted/Brass • PIKE
975QX4366 • **Value $24**

18
Christmas Croc
Handcrafted • PYDA
775QX4373 • **Value $24**

19
Christmas Partridge
Dimensional Brass • SICK
775QX5246 • **Value $22**

20
Claus Construction
(re-issued from 1989)
Handcrafted • SEAL
775QX4885 • **Value $35**

	Price Paid	Value of My Collection
GENERAL KEEPSAKE		
1.		
2.		
3.		
4.		
5.		
6.		
7.		
8.		
9.		
10.		
11.		
12.		
13.		
14.		
15.		
16.		
17.		
18.		
19.		
20.		
PENCIL TOTALS		

1990

(1) Copy of Cheer
Handcrafted • SIED
775QX4486 • **Value $18**

(2) Country Angel (cancelled after limited production)
Handcrafted • N/A
675QX5046 • **Value $190**

(3) Coyote Carols
Handcrafted • JLEE
875QX4993 • **Value $27**

(4) Cozy Goose
Handcrafted • PIKE
575QX4966 • **Value $15**

(5) Dad
Handcrafted • JLEE
675QX4533 • **Value $18**

(6) Dad-to-Be
Handcrafted • SIED
575QX4913 • **Value $22**

(7) Daughter
Handcrafted • SIED
575QX4496 • **Value $23**

(8) Dickens Caroler Bell – Mr. Ashbourne
Porcelain • CHAD
2175QX5056 • **Value $49**

(9) Donder's Diner
Handcrafted • DLEE
1375QX4823 • **Value $21**

(10) Feliz Navidad
Handcrafted • N/A
675QX5173 • **Value $28**

(11) Fifty Years Together
Faceted Glass • PATT
975QX4906 • **Value $20**

(12) First Christmas Together
Acrylic • VOTR
675QX3146 • **Value $27**

(13) First Christmas Together
Glass • VOTR
475QX2136 • **Value $25**

(14) First Christmas Together
Handcrafted • PYDA
975QX4883 • **Value $28**

(15) First Christmas Together – Photoholder
Fabric • VOTR
775QX4886 • **Value $20**

(16) Five Years Together
Glass • VOTR
475QX2103 • **Value $18**

(17) Forty Years Together
Faceted Glass • PATT
975QX4903 • **Value $19**

(18) Friendship Kitten
Handcrafted • RHOD
675QX4143 • **Value $25**

(19) From Our Home to Yours
Glass • N/A
475QX2166 • **Value $21**

(20) GARFIELD®
Glass • N/A
475QX2303 • **Value $25**

General Keepsake

	Price Paid	Value of My Collection
1.		
2.		
3.		
4.		
5.		
6.		
7.		
8.		
9.		
10.		
11.		
12.		
13.		
14.		
15.		
16.		
17.		
18.		
19.		
20.		
PENCIL TOTALS		

1990

(1)	**(2)**	**(3)**	**(4)**
Gentle Dreamers	**Gingerbread Elf**	**Godchild**	**Golf's My Bag**
Handcrafted • FRAN	*Handcrafted* • N/A	*Acrylic* • FRAN	*Handcrafted* • JLEE
875QX4756 • **Value $33**	575QX5033 • **Value $21**	675QX3176 • **Value $18**	775QX4963 • **Value $30**

(5)	**(6)**	**(7)**	**(8)**
Goose Cart	**Granddaughter**	**Granddaughter's First Christmas**	**Grandmother**
Handcrafted • N/A	*Glass* • LYLE	*Acrylic* • FRAN	*Glass* • VOTR
775QX5236 • **Value $16**	475QX2286 • **Value $24**	675QX3106 • **Value $21**	475QX2236 • **Value $19**

(9)	**(10)**	**(11)**
Grandparents	**Grandson**	**Grandson's First Christmas**
Glass • N/A	*Glass* • VOTR	*Acrylic* • FRAN
475QX2253 • **Value $18**	475QX2293 • **Value $20**	675QX3063 • **Value $21**

(12)	**(13)**	**(14)**
Hang in There	**Happy Voices**	**Happy Woodcutter**
Handcrafted • SEAL	*Wood* • VOTR	*Handcrafted* • JLEE
675QX4713 • **Value $24**	675QX4645 • **Value $16**	975QX4763 • **Value $23**

(15)	**(16)**	**(17)**
Holiday Cardinals	**Home for the Owlidays**	**Hot Dogger**
Dimensional Brass • LYLE	*Handcrafted* • N/A	*Handcrafted* • CROW
775QX5243 • **Value $24**	675QX5183 • **Value $17**	775QX4976 • **Value $18**

(18)	**(19)**	**(20)**
Jesus Loves Me	**Jolly Dolphin**	**Joy is in the Air**
Acrylic • PATT	*Handcrafted* • RGRS	*Handcrafted* • CROW
675QX3156 • **Value $16**	675QX4683 • **Value $32**	775QX5503 • **Value $27**

General Keepsake

	Price Paid	Value of My Collection
1.		
2.		
3.		
4.		
5.		
6.		
7.		
8.		
9.		
10.		
11.		
12.		
13.		
14.		
15.		
16.		
17.		
18.		
19.		
20.		
PENCIL TOTALS		

(1) **King Klaus** *Handcrafted* • SEAL 775QX4106 • **Value $20**	(2) **Kitty's Best Pal** *Handcrafted* • FRAN 675QX4716 • **Value $24**	(3) **Little Drummer Boy** *Handcrafted* • UNRU 775QX5233 • **Value $21**	(4) **Long Winter's Nap** *Handcrafted* • RGRS 675QX4703 • **Value $26**
(5) **Loveable Dears** *Handcrafted* • UNRU 875QX5476 • **Value $21**	(6) **Meow Mart** *Handcrafted* • PIKE 775QX4446 • **Value $29**	(7) **Mom and Dad** *Handcrafted* • CHAD 875QX4593 • **Value $27**	(8) **Mom-to-Be** *Handcrafted* • SIED 575QX4916 • **Value $32**

GENERAL KEEPSAKE		

	Price Paid	Value of My Collection			
1.			(9) **Mooy Christmas** *Handcrafted* • N/A 675QX4933 • **Value $32**	(10) **Mother** *Ceramic/Bisque* • VOTR 875QX4536 • **Value $24**	(11) **Mouseboat** *Handcrafted* • SEAL 775QX4753 • **Value $18**
2.					
3.					
4.					
5.			(12) **New Home** *Handcrafted* • PYDA 675QX4343 • **Value $27**	(13) **Norman Rockwell Art** *Glass* • LYLE 475QX2296 • **Value $26**	(14) **Nutshell Chat** *Handcrafted* • N/A 675QX5193 • **Value $26**
6.					
7.					
8.					
9.					
10.					
11.			(15) **Nutshell Holiday** **(re-issued from 1989)** *Handcrafted* • RGRS 575QX4652 • **Value $26**	(16) **Peaceful Kingdom** *Glass* • N/A 475QX2106 • **Value $23**	(17) **PEANUTS®** *Glass* • N/A 475QX2233 • **Value $28**
12.					
13.					
14.					
15.					
16.					
17.			(18) **Pepperoni Mouse** *Handcrafted* • SIED 675QX4973 • **Value $20**	(19) **Perfect Catch** *Handcrafted* • SIED 775QX4693 • **Value $21**	(20) **Polar Jogger** *Handcrafted* • SIED 575QX4666 • **Value $19**
18.					
19.					
20.					
PENCIL TOTALS					

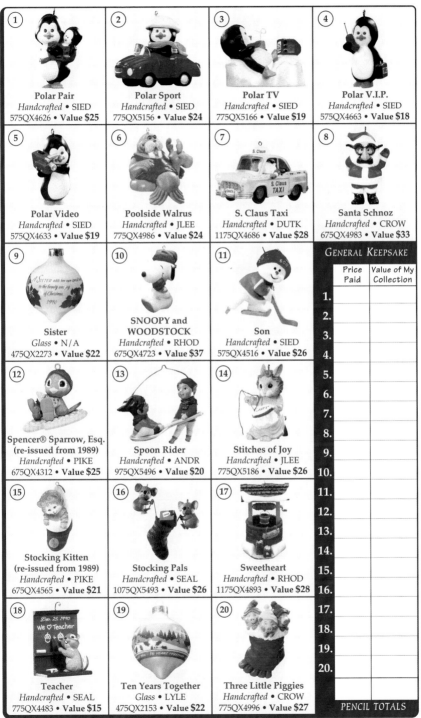

1 Polar Pair
Handcrafted • SIED
575QX4626 • **Value $25**

2 Polar Sport
Handcrafted • SIED
775QX5156 • **Value $24**

3 Polar TV
Handcrafted • SIED
775QX5166 • **Value $19**

4 Polar V.I.P.
Handcrafted • SIED
575QX4663 • **Value $18**

5 Polar Video
Handcrafted • SIED
575QX4633 • **Value $19**

6 Poolside Walrus
Handcrafted • JLEE
775QX4986 • **Value $24**

7 S. Claus Taxi
Handcrafted • DUTK
1175QX4686 • **Value $28**

8 Santa Schnoz
Handcrafted • CROW
675QX4983 • **Value $33**

9 Sister
Glass • N/A
475QX2273 • **Value $22**

10 SNOOPY and WOODSTOCK
Handcrafted • RHOD
675QX4723 • **Value $37**

11 Son
Handcrafted • SIED
575QX4516 • **Value $26**

12 Spencer® Sparrow, Esq.
(re-issued from 1989)
Handcrafted • PIKE
675QX4312 • **Value $25**

13 Spoon Rider
Handcrafted • ANDR
975QX5496 • **Value $20**

14 Stitches of Joy
Handcrafted • JLEE
775QX5186 • **Value $26**

15 Stocking Kitten
(re-issued from 1989)
Handcrafted • PIKE
675QX4565 • **Value $21**

16 Stocking Pals
Handcrafted • SEAL
1075QX5493 • **Value $26**

17 Sweetheart
Handcrafted • RHOD
1175QX4893 • **Value $28**

18 Teacher
Handcrafted • SEAL
775QX4483 • **Value $15**

19 Ten Years Together
Glass • LYLE
475QX2153 • **Value $22**

20 Three Little Piggies
Handcrafted • CROW
775QX4996 • **Value $27**

1990

GENERAL KEEPSAKE

	Price Paid	Value of My Collection
1.		
2.		
3.		
4.		
5.		
6.		
7.		
8.		
9.		
10.		
11.		
12.		
13.		
14.		
15.		
16.		
17.		
18.		
19.		
20.		
PENCIL TOTALS		

1	2	3	4
Time for Love *Glass* • LYLE 475QX2133 • **Value $25**	**Twenty-Five Years Together** *Faceted Glass* • PATT 975QX4896 • **Value $20**	**Two Peas in a Pod** *Handcrafted* • ANDR 475QX4926 • **Value $36**	**Welcome, Santa** *Handcrafted* • CROW 1175QX4773 • **Value $26**

5	6	7	8
Baby's First Christmas *Handcrafted* • PALM 2800QLX7246 • **Value $60**	**Beary Short Nap** *Handcrafted* • SIED 1000QLX7326 • **Value $30**	**Blessings of Love** *Panorama Ball* • N/A 1400QLX7363 • **Value $52**	**Children's Express** *Handcrafted* • SICK 2800QLX7243 • **Value $77**

9	10	11
Christmas Memories *Handcrafted* • UNRU 2500QLX7276 • **Value $54**	**Deer Crossing** *Handcrafted* • SIED 1800QLX7213 • **Value $48**	**Elf of the Year** *Handcrafted* • ANDR 1000QLX7356 • **Value $24**

12	13	14
Elfin Whittler *Handcrafted* • CROW 2000QLX7265 • **Value $50**	**First Christmas Together** *Handcrafted* • DLEE 1800QLX7255 • **Value $46**	**Holiday Flash** *Handcrafted* • CHAD 1800QLX7333 • **Value $37**

15	16	17
Hop 'N Pop Popper *Handcrafted* • SIED 2000QLX7353 • **Value $95**	**Letter to Santa** *Handcrafted* • RGRS 1400QLX7226 • **Value $35**	**Mrs. Santa's Kitchen** *Handcrafted* • RHOD 2500QLX7263 • **Value $72**

18	19	20
Partridges in a Pear *Dimensional Brass* • LYLE 1400QLX7212 • **Value $34**	**Santa's Ho-Ho-Hoedown** *Handcrafted* • CROW 2500QLX7256 • **Value $88**	**Song and Dance** *Handcrafted* • RGRS 2000QLX7253 • **Value $92**

General Keepsake

	Price Paid	Value of My Collection
1.		
2.		
3.		
4.		

General Magic

5.		
6.		
7.		
8.		
9.		
10.		
11.		
12.		
13.		
14.		
15.		
16.		
17.		
18.		
19.		
20.		
PENCIL TOTALS		

Value Guide — Hallmark Keepsake Ornaments

1. Starlight Angel
Handcrafted • RGRS
1400QLX7306 • **Value $38**

2. Starship Christmas
Handcrafted • SIED
1800QLX7336 • **Value $50**

3. Acorn Squirrel
(re-issued from 1989)
Handcrafted • PIKE
450QXM5682 • **Value $12**

4. Acorn Wreath
Handcrafted • CROW
600QXM5686 • **Value $13**

5. Air Santa
Handcrafted • N/A
450QXM5656 • **Value $15**

6. Baby's First Christmas
Handcrafted • FRAN
850QXM5703 • **Value $17**

7. Basket Buddy
Handcrafted/Wicker • RGRS
600QXM5696 • **Value $13**

8. Bear Hug
Handcrafted • PALM
600QXM5633 • **Value $14**

9. Brass Bouquet
Brass • LYLE
600QXM5776 • **Value $7**

10. Brass Horn
Brass • N/A
300QXM5793 • **Value $8**

11. Brass Peace
Brass • N/A
300QXM5796 • **Value $8**

12. Brass Santa
Brass • PATT
300QXM5786 • **Value $9**

13. Brass Year
Brass • N/A
300QXM5833 • **Value $8**

14. Busy Carver
Handcrafted • CROW
450QXM5673 • **Value $10**

15. Christmas Dove
Handcrafted • SIED
450QXM5636 • **Value $16**

16. Cloisonné Poinsettia
Cloisonné • VOTR
1050QXM5533 • **Value $22**

17. Country Heart
Handcrafted • RGRS
450QXM5693 • **Value $10**

18. Cozy Skater
(re-issued from 1989)
Handcrafted • LYLE
450QXM5735 • **Value $13**

19. First Christmas
Together
Porcelain • ANDR
600QXM5536 • **Value $13**

20. Going Sledding
Handcrafted • JLEE
450QXM5683 • **Value $17**

General Magic	Price Paid	Value of My Collection
1.		
2.		

General Miniature		
3.		
4.		
5.		
6.		
7.		
8.		
9.		
10.		
11.		
12.		
13.		
14.		
15.		
16.		
17.		
18.		
19.		
20.		
PENCIL TOTALS		

1990

VALUE GUIDE — HALLMARK KEEPSAKE ORNAMENTS

(1) Grandchild's First Christmas
Handcrafted • SIED
600QXM5723 • **Value $12**

(2) Happy Bluebird
(re-issued from 1989)
Handcrafted • RGRS
450QXM5662 • **Value $16**

(3) Holiday Cardinal
Acrylic • FRAN
300QXM5526 • **Value $12**

(4) Lion and Lamb
Wood • SICK
450QXM5676 • **Value $11**

(5) Little Soldier
(re-issued from 1989)
Handcrafted • SICK
450QXM5675 • **Value $11**

(6) Loving Hearts
Acrylic • N/A
300QXM5523 • **Value $12**

(7) Madonna and Child
Handcrafted • RGRS
600QXM5643 • **Value $13**

(8) Mother
Cameo • LYLE
450QXM5716 • **Value $17**

(9) Nativity
Handcrafted • UNRU
450QXM5706 • **Value $21**

(10) Old-World Santa
(re-issued from 1989)
Handcrafted • SIED
300QXM5695 • **Value $10**

(11) Panda's Surprise
Handcrafted • FRAN
450QXM5616 • **Value $13**

(12) Perfect Fit
Handcrafted • CHAD
450QXM5516 • **Value $14**

(13) Puppy Love
Handcrafted • PALM
600QXM5666 • **Value $14**

(14) Roly-Poly Pig
(re-issued from 1989)
Handcrafted • PIKE
300QXM5712 • **Value $19**

(15) Ruby Reindeer
Glass • PATT
600QXM5816 • **Value $13**

(16) Santa's Journey
Handcrafted • SICK
850QXM5826 • **Value $22**

(17) Santa's Streetcar
Handcrafted • DLEE
850QXM5766 • **Value $19**

(18) Snow Angel
Handcrafted • JLEE
600QXM5773 • **Value $14**

(19) Special Friends
Handcrafted • PIKE
600QXM5726 • **Value $15**

(20) Stamp Collector
Handcrafted • CROW
450QXM5623 • **Value $11**

GENERAL MINIATURE

	Price Paid	Value of My Collection
1.		
2.		
3.		
4.		
5.		
6.		
7.		
8.		
9.		
10.		
11.		
12.		
13.		
14.		
15.		
16.		
17.		
18.		
19.		
20.		
PENCIL TOTALS		

1 Stocking Pal
(re-issued from 1989)
Handcrafted • JLEE
450QXM5672 • **Value $11**

2 Stringing Along
Handcrafted • SEAL
850QXM5606 • **Value $17**

3 Sweet Slumber
Handcrafted • SIED
450QXM5663 • **Value $11**

4 Teacher
Handcrafted • PIKE
450QXM5653 • **Value $10**

5 Type of Joy
Handcrafted • CHAD
450QXM5646 • **Value $11**

6 Warm Memories
Handcrafted • SEAL
450QXM5713 • **Value $10**

7 Wee Nutcracker
Handcrafted • SIED
850QXM5843 • **Value $16**

8 Armful of Joy
(members only ornament)
Handcrafted • FRAN
975QXC4453 • **Value $45**

1990

9 Christmas Limited
(club edition, LE-38,700)
Die-Cast Metal • SICK
1975QXC4766 • **Value $110**

10 Club Hollow
(keepsake of membership)
Handcrafted • CROW
QXC4456 • **Value $38**

11 Crown Prince
(keepsake of
membership, miniature)
Handcrafted • RGRS
QXC5603 • **Value $36**

12 Dove of Peace
(club edition, LE-25,400)
Porcelain/Brass • SICK
2475QXC4476 • **Value $77**

13 Sugar Plum Fairy
(club edition, LE-25,400)
Porcelain • ANDR
2775QXC4473 • **Value $60**

14 Little Bear (miniature)
Handcrafted • SIED
($2.95)620XPR9723 • **Value $10**

15 Little Frosty (miniature)
Handcrafted • SIED
($2.95)620XPR9720 • **Value $10**

16 Little Husky (miniature)
Handcrafted • SEAL
($2.95)620XPR9722 • **Value $11**

17 Little Seal (miniature)
Handcrafted • JLEE
($2.95)620XPR9721 • **Value $10**

18 Memory Wreath
(miniature)
Handcrafted • DLEE
($2.95)620XPR9724 • **Value $10**

19 Baby's Christening 1990
Porcelain • JLEE
1000BBY1326 • **Value $28**

20 Baby's First
Christmas 1990
Handcrafted • JLEE
1000BBY1454 • **Value $28**

General Miniature	Price Paid	Value of My Collection
1.		
2.		
3.		
4.		
5.		
6.		
7.		
Collector's Club		
8.		
9.		
10.		
11.		
12.		
13.		
Reach Ornaments		
14.		
15.		
16.		
17.		
18.		
Baby Celebrations		
19.		
20.		
Pencil Totals		

1

Baby's First
Christmas 1990
Porcelain • RGRS
1000BBY1554 • **Value $28**

1989

In 1989 Hallmark debuted a popular collection of dated teddy bear ornaments celebrating a child's first five Christmases. In the 1989 collection, there were 123 Keepsake ornaments, 19 Magic ornaments and 41 Miniature ornaments. See the collectibles series section for more 1989 ornaments.

2

Baby Partridge
Handcrafted • FRAN
675QX4525 • **Value $16**

3

Baby's First Christmas
Acrylic • FRAN
675QX3815 • **Value $20**

4

Baby's First Christmas
Handcrafted • CHAD
725QX4492 • **Value $90**

5

Baby's First Christmas
– Baby Boy
Satin • VOTR
475QX2725 • **Value $21**

Baby Celebrations

	Price Paid	Value of My Collection
1.		

General Keepsake

2.		
3.		
4.		
5.		
6.		
7.		
8.		
9.		
10.		
11.		
12.		
13.		
14.		
15.		
16.		
17.		

PENCIL TOTALS

6

Baby's First Christmas
– Baby Girl
Satin • VOTR
475QX2722 • **Value $21**

7

Baby's First Christmas
Photoholder
Handcrafted • VOTR
625QX4682 • **Value $50**

8

Baby's Second
Christmas
Handcrafted • FRAN
675QX4495 • **Value $30**

9

Balancing Elf
Handcrafted • CHAD
675QX4895 • **Value $23**

10

Bear-i-Tone
Handcrafted • SIED
475QX4542 • **Value $20**

11

Brother
Handcrafted • LYLE
725QX4452 • **Value $20**

12

Cactus Cowboy
Handcrafted • DUTK
675QX4112 • **Value $45**

13

Camera Claus
Handcrafted • SIED
575QX5465 • **Value $22**

14

Carousel Zebra
Handcrafted • SICK
925QX4515 • **Value $22**

15

Cherry Jubilee
Handcrafted • SICK
500QX4532 • **Value $27**

16

Child's Fifth Christmas
Handcrafted • RHOD
675QX5435 • **Value $20**

17

Child's Fourth
Christmas
Handcrafted • FRAN
675QX5432 • **Value $20**

1
Child's Third Christmas
Handcrafted • FRAN
675QX4695 • **Value $22**

2
Claus Construction
(re-issued in 1990)
Handcrafted • SEAL
775QX4885 • **Value $35**

3
Cool Swing
Handcrafted • CROW
625QX4875 • **Value $35**

4
Country Cat
Handcrafted • PYDA
625QX4672 • **Value $20**

5
Cranberry Bunny
Handcrafted • RGRS
575QX4262 • **Value $18**

6
Dad
Handcrafted • N/A
725QX4412 • **Value $16**

7
Daughter
Handcrafted • SICK
625QX4432 • **Value $20**

8
Deer Disguise
Handcrafted • SIED
575QX4265 • **Value $23**

1989

9
Feliz Navidad
Handcrafted • PYDA
675QX4392 • **Value $28**

10
Festive Angel
Dimensional Brass • N/A
675QX4635 • **Value $26**

11
Festive Year
Acrylic • VOTR
775QX3842 • **Value $23**

12
Fifty Years Together
Photoholder
Porcelain • RGRS
875QX4862 • **Value $17**

13
The First Christmas
Cameo • N/A
775QX5475 • **Value $19**

14
First Christmas
Together
Acrylic • RHOD
675QX3832 • **Value $24**

15
First Christmas
Together
Glass • N/A
475QX2732 • **Value $24**

16
First Christmas
Together
Handcrafted • RGRS
975QX4852 • **Value $24**

17
Five Years Together
Glass • N/A
475QX2735 • **Value $19**

18
Forty Years Together
Photoholder
Porcelain • RGRS
875QX5452 • **Value $17**

19
Friendship Time
Handcrafted • N/A
975QX4132 • **Value $34**

20
From Our
Home to Yours
Acrylic • N/A
625QX3845 • **Value $20**

	Price Paid	Value of My Collection
GENERAL KEEPSAKE		
1.		
2.		
3.		
4.		
5.		
6.		
7.		
8.		
9.		
10.		
11.		
12.		
13.		
14.		
15.		
16.		
17.		
18.		
19.		
20.		
PENCIL TOTALS		

(1) Gentle Fawn	(2) George Washington Bicentennial	(3) Godchild	(4) Goin' South
Handcrafted • RGRS	*Acrylic* • N/A	*Acrylic* • FRAN	*Handcrafted* • CROW
775QX5485 • **Value $22**	625QX3862 • **Value $19**	625QX3112 • **Value $16**	425QX4105 • **Value $24**

(5) Gone Fishing (re-issued from 1988)	(6) Graceful Swan	(7) Granddaughter	(8) Granddaughter's First Christmas
Handcrafted • SIED	*Dimensional Brass* • N/A	*Glass* • N/A	*Acrylic* • FRAN
575QX4794 • **Value $23**	675QX4642 • **Value $21**	475QX2782 • **Value $25**	675QX3822 • **Value $22**

General Keepsake

	Price Paid	Value of My Collection
1.		
2.		
3.		
4.		
5.		
6.		
7.		
8.		
9.		
10.		
11.		
12.		
13.		
14.		
15.		
16.		
17.		
18.		
19.		
20.		
PENCIL TOTALS		

(9) Grandmother	(10) Grandparents	(11) Grandson
Glass • LYLE	*Glass* • LYLE	*Glass* • N/A
475QX2775 • **Value $18**	475QX2772 • **Value $18**	475QX2785 • **Value $22**

(12) Grandson's First Christmas	(13) Gratitude	(14) Gym Dandy
Acrylic • FRAN	*Acrylic* • VOTR	*Handcrafted* • SIED
675QX3825 • **Value $18**	675QX3852 • **Value $14**	575QX4185 • **Value $20**

(15) Hang in There	(16) Here's the Pitch	(17) Hoppy Holidays
Handcrafted • CROW	*Handcrafted* • SIED	*Handcrafted* • SIED
525QX4305 • **Value $35**	575QX5455 • **Value $22**	775QX4692 • **Value $24**

(18) Horse Weathervane	(19) Joyful Trio	(20) A KISS™ From Santa (re-issued from 1988)
Handcrafted • SICK	*Handcrafted* • FRAN	*Handcrafted* • UNRU
575QX4632 • **Value $18**	975QX4372 • **Value $16**	450QX4821 • **Value $30**

(1) **Kristy Claus** *Handcrafted* • SIED 575QX4245 • **Value $15**	**(2)** **Language of Love** *Acrylic* • N/A 625QX3835 • **Value $25**	**(3)** **Let's Play** *Handcrafted* • CROW 725QX4882 • **Value $28**	**(4)** **Mail Call** *Handcrafted* • SEAL 875QX4522 • **Value $21**
(5) **Merry-Go-Round Unicorn** *Porcelain* • RGRS 1075QX4472 • **Value $23**	**(6)** **Mom and Dad** *Handcrafted* • PIKE 975QX4425 • **Value $22**	**(7)** **Mother** *Porcelain* • N/A 975QX4405 • **Value $30**	**(8)** **New Home** *Glass* • VOTR 475QX2755 • **Value $21**

1989

			GENERAL KEEPSAKE	
(9) **Norman Rockwell** *Glass* • LYLE 475QX2762 • **Value $22**	**(10)** **North Pole Jogger** *Handcrafted* • SIED 575QX5462 • **Value $22**	**(11)** **Nostalgic Lamb** *Handcrafted* • PYDA 675QX4665 • **Value $15**		Price Paid	Value of My Collection

(12) **Nutshell Dreams** *Handcrafted* • CHAD 575QX4655 • **Value $23**	**(13)** **Nutshell Holiday** (re-issued in 1990) *Handcrafted* • RGRS 575QX4652 • **Value $26**	**(14)** **Nutshell Workshop** *Handcrafted* • CHAD 575QX4872 • **Value $24**

(15) **Old-World Gnome** *Handcrafted* • N/A 775QX4345 • **Value $25**	**(16)** **On the Links** *Handcrafted* • SIED 575QX4192 • **Value $24**	**(17)** **OREO® Chocolate Sandwich Cookies** (re-issued from 1988) *Handcrafted* • UNRU 400QX4814 • **Value $22**

(18) **The Ornament Express (set/3)** *Handcrafted* • SICK 2200QX5805 • **Value $44**	**(19)** **Owliday Greetings** *Handcrafted* • PIKE 400QX4365 • **Value $21**	**(20)** **Paddington™ Bear** *Handcrafted* • FRAN 575QX4292 • **Value $23**

GENERAL KEEPSAKE

	Price Paid	Value of My Collection
1.		
2.		
3.		
4.		
5.		
6.		
7.		
8.		
9.		
10.		
11.		
12.		
13.		
14.		
15.		
16.		
17.		
18.		
19.		
20.		
PENCIL TOTALS		

①

Party Line
(re-issued from 1988)
Handcrafted • PIKE
875QX4761 • **Value $30**

②

PEANUTS® – A Charlie Brown Christmas
Glass • N/A
475QX2765 • **Value $44**

③

Peek-a-Boo Kitties
(re-issued from 1988)
Handcrafted • CROW
750QX4871 • **Value $24**

④

Peppermint Clown
Porcelain • DUTK
2475QX4505 • **Value $45**

⑤

Playful Angel
Handcrafted • DLEE
675QX4535 • **Value $24**

⑥

Polar Bowler
(re-issued from 1988)
Handcrafted • SIED
575QX4784 • **Value $19**

⑦

Rodney Reindeer
Handcrafted • SIED
675QX4072 • **Value $17**

⑧

Rooster Weathervane
Handcrafted • SICK
575QX4675 • **Value $18**

General Keepsake

	Price Paid	Value of My Collection
1.		
2.		
3.		
4.		
5.		
6.		
7.		
8.		
9.		
10.		
11.		
12.		
13.		
14.		
15.		
16.		
17.		
18.		
19.		
20.		
PENCIL TOTALS		

⑨

Sea Santa
Handcrafted • SIED
575QX4152 • **Value $29**

⑩

Sister
Glass • N/A
475QX2792 • **Value $20**

⑪

SNOOPY and WOODSTOCK
Handcrafted • RHOD
675QX4332 • **Value $37**

⑫

Snowplow Santa
Handcrafted • SIED
575QX4205 • **Value $23**

⑬

Son
Handcrafted • SICK
625QX4445 • **Value $21**

⑭

Sparkling Snowflake
Brass • LYLE
775QX5472 • **Value $23**

⑮

Special Delivery
Handcrafted • RGRS
525QX4325 • **Value $24**

⑯

Spencer® Sparrow, Esq.
(re-issued in 1990)
Handcrafted • PIKE
675QX4312 • **Value $25**

⑰

Stocking Kitten
(re-issued in 1990)
Handcrafted • PIKE
675QX4565 • **Value $21**

⑱

Sweet Memories Photoholder
Handcrafted • N/A
675QX4385 • **Value $23**

⑲

Sweetheart
Handcrafted • SICK
975QX4865 • **Value $34**

⑳

Teacher
Handcrafted • SIED
575QX4125 • **Value $23**

① Teeny Taster
(re-issued from 1988)
Handcrafted • SEAL
475QX4181 • **Value $30**

② Ten Years Together
Glass • LYLE
475QX2742 • **Value $26**

③ TV Break
Handcrafted • DLEE
625QX4092 • **Value $19**

④ Twenty-Five Years Together Photoholder
Porcelain • RGRS
875QX4855 • **Value $17**

⑤ Wiggly Snowman
Handcrafted • RHOD
675QX4892 • **Value $26**

⑥ World of Love
Glass • N/A
475QX2745 • **Value $34**

⑦ Angel Melody
Acrylic • VOTR
950QLX7202 • **Value $23**

⑧ The Animals Speak
Panorama Ball • FRAN
1350QLX7232 • **Value $112**

1989

⑨ Baby's First Christmas
Handcrafted • SEAL
3000QLX7272 • **Value $62**

⑩ Backstage Bear
Handcrafted • SIED
1350QLX7215 • **Value $37**

⑪ Busy Beaver
Handcrafted • DLEE
1750QLX7245 • **Value $47**

⑫ First Christmas Together
Handcrafted • DLEE
1750QLX7342 • **Value $44**

⑬ Holiday Bell
Lead Crystal • N/A
1750QLX7222 • **Value $34**

⑭ Joyous Carolers
Handcrafted • UNRU
3000QLX7295 • **Value $72**

⑮ Kringle's Toy Shop
(re-issued from 1988)
Handcrafted • SEAL
2450QLX7017 • **Value $50**

⑯ Loving Spoonful
Handcrafted • SIED
1950QLX7262 • **Value $40**

⑰ Metro Express
Handcrafted • SICK
2800QLX7275 • **Value $83**

⑱ Moonlit Nap
(re-issued from 1988)
Handcrafted • CHAD
875QLX7134 • **Value $27**

⑲ Rudolph the Red-Nosed Reindeer®
Handcrafted • CHAD
1950QLX7252 • **Value $60**

⑳ Spirit of St. Nick
Handcrafted • SEAL
2450QLX7285 • **Value $65**

GENERAL KEEPSAKE

	Price Paid	Value of My Collection
1.		
2.		
3.		
4.		
5.		
6.		

GENERAL MAGIC

7.		
8.		
9.		
10.		
11.		
12.		
13.		
14.		
15.		
16.		
17.		
18.		
19.		
20.		
PENCIL TOTALS		

(1) Tiny Tinker
Handcrafted • CROW
1950QLX7174 • **Value $55**

(2) Unicorn Fantasy
Handcrafted • RHOD
950QLX7235 • **Value $23**

(3) Acorn Squirrel
(re-issued in 1990)
Handcrafted • PIKE
450QXM5682 • **Value $12**

(4) Baby's First Christmas
Handcrafted • PIKE
600QXM5732 • **Value $14**

(5) Brass Partridge
Brass • LYLE
300QXM5725 • **Value $13**

(6) Brass Snowflake
Dimensional Brass • LYLE
450QXM5702 • **Value $14**

(7) Bunny Hug
Acrylic • VOTR
300QXM5775 • **Value $11**

(8) Country Wreath
(re-issued from 1988)
Handcrafted • RGRS
450QXM5731 • **Value $12**

(9) Cozy Skater
(re-issued in 1990)
Handcrafted • LYLE
450QXM5735 • **Value $13**

(10) First Christmas Together
Ceramic • VOTR
850QXM5642 • **Value $11**

(11) Folk Art Bunny
Handcrafted • PATT
450QXM5692 • **Value $11**

(12) Happy Bluebird
(re-issued in 1990)
Handcrafted • RGRS
450QXM5662 • **Value $16**

(13) Holiday Deer
Acrylic • VOTR
300QXM5772 • **Value $12**

(14) Holy Family
(re-issued from 1988)
Handcrafted • UNRU
850QXM5611 • **Value $16**

(15) Kitty Cart
Wood • PATT
300QXM5722 • **Value $10**

(16) Little Soldier
(re-issued in 1990)
Handcrafted • SICK
450QXM5675 • **Value $11**

(17) Little Star Bringer
Handcrafted • LYLE
600QXM5622 • **Value $20**

(18) Load of Cheer
Handcrafted • RHOD
600QXM5745 • **Value $19**

(19) Lovebirds
Handcrafted/Brass • PIKE
600QXM5635 • **Value $14**

(20) Merry Seal
Porcelain • FRAN
600QXM5755 • **Value $15**

General Magic

	Price Paid	Value of My Collection
1.		
2.		

General Miniature

	Price Paid	Value of My Collection
3.		
4.		
5.		
6.		
7.		
8.		
9.		
10.		
11.		
12.		
13.		
14.		
15.		
16.		
17.		
18.		
19.		
20.		
PENCIL TOTALS		

VALUE GUIDE — HALLMARK KEEPSAKE ORNAMENTS

(1) Mother *Cameo* • N/A 600QXM5645 • **Value $13**	**(2) Old-World Santa** (re-issued in 1990) *Handcrafted* • SIED 300QXM5695 • **Value $10**	**(3) Pinecone Basket** *Handcrafted* • RHOD 450QXM5734 • **Value $9**	**(4) Puppy Cart** *Wood* • SICK 300QXM5715 • **Value $9**
(5) Rejoice *Acrylic* • VOTR 300QXM5782 • **Value $9**	**(6) Roly-Poly Pig** (re-issued in 1990) *Handcrafted* • PIKE 300QXM5712 • **Value $19**	**(7) Roly-Poly Ram** *Handcrafted* • N/A 300QXM5705 • **Value $14**	**(8) Santa's Magic Ride** *Handcrafted* • RGRS 850QXM5632 • **Value $19**

			GENERAL MINIATURE		
(9) Santa's Roadster *Handcrafted* • CROW 600QXM5665 • **Value $20**	**(10) Scrimshaw Reindeer** *Handcrafted* • VOTR 450QXM5685 • **Value $11**	**(11) Sharing a Ride** *Handcrafted* • DUTK 850QXM5765 • **Value $17**		Price Paid	Value of My Collection
			1.		
			2.		
			3.		
(12) Slow Motion *Handcrafted* • SIED 600QXM5752 • **Value $16**	**(13) Special Friend** *Handcrafted/Willow* • N/A 450QXM5652 • **Value $13**	**(14) Starlit Mouse** *Handcrafted* • RHOD 450QXM5655 • **Value $17**	4.		
			5.		
			6.		
			7.		
			8.		
			9.		
			10.		
(15) Stocking Pal (re-issued in 1990) *Handcrafted* • JLEE 450QXM5672 • **Value $11**	**(16) Strollin' Snowman** *Porcelain* • SIED 450QXM5742 • **Value $17**	**(17) Three Little Kitties** (re-issued from 1988) *Handcrafted/Willow* • PIKE 600QXM5694 • **Value $18**	11.		
			12.		
			13.		
			14.		
			15.		
			16.		
			17.		
(18) Christmas is Peaceful (club edition, LE-49,900) *Bone China* • SEAL 1850QXC4512 • **Value $45**	**(19) Collect a Dream** (club edition) *Handcrafted* • PIKE 900QXC4285 • **Value $67**	**(20) Noelle** (club edition, LE-49,900) *Porcelain* • UNRU 1975QXC4483 • **Value $58**	COLLECTOR'S CLUB		
			18.		
			19.		
			20.		
			PENCIL TOTALS		

(1) Sitting Purrty
(keepsake of membership, miniature)
Handcrafted • DUTK
QXC5812 • **Value $46**

(2) Visit From Santa
(keepsake of membership)
Handcrafted • CROW
QXC5802 • **Value $53**

(3) Carousel Display Stand
Handcrafted/Brass • N/A
($1.00)629XPR9723 • **Value $10**

(4) Ginger
Handcrafted/Brass • JLEE
($3.95)629XPR9721 • **Value $20**

(5) Holly
Handcrafted/Brass • JLEE
($3.95)629XPR9722 • **Value $20**

(6) Snow
Handcrafted/Brass • JLEE
($3.95)629XPR9719 • **Value $35**

(7) Star
Handcrafted/Brass • JLEE
($3.95)629XPR9720 • **Value $20**

(8) Baby's Christening Keepsake
Acrylic • N/A
700BBY1325 • **Value $30**

(9) Baby's First Birthday
Acrylic • N/A
550BBY1729 • **Value $32**

(10) Baby's First Christmas – Baby Boy
(same as #475QX2725)
Satin • VOTR
475BBY1453 • **Value $15**

(11) Baby's First Christmas – Baby Girl
(same as #475QX2722)
Satin • VOTR
475BBY1553 • **Value $15**

1988

1988 was the year Hallmark introduced Miniature ornaments to the collection. In its debut year, the Miniature line featured 27 ornaments, while the Keepsake line had 118 and Magic had 20. See the collectible series section for more 1988 ornaments.

(12) Americana Drum
Tin • SICK
775QX4881 • **Value $33**

(13) Arctic Tenor
Handcrafted • SIED
400QX4721 • **Value $18**

(14) Baby Redbird
Handcrafted • CHAD
500QX4101 • **Value $21**

(15) Baby's First Christmas
Acrylic • PIKE
600QX3721 • **Value $22**

(16) Baby's First Christmas
Handcrafted • CROW
975QX4701 • **Value $40**

(17) Baby's First Christmas – Baby Boy
Satin • N/A
475QX2721 • **Value $25**

	Price Paid	Value of My Collection
COLLECTOR'S CLUB		
1.		
2.		
REACH ORNAMENTS		
3.		
4.		
5.		
6.		
7.		
BABY CELEBRATIONS		
8.		
9.		
10.		
11.		
GENERAL KEEPSAKE		
12.		
13.		
14.		
15.		
16.		
17.		
PENCIL TOTALS		

1
Baby's First Christmas
– Baby Girl
Satin • N/A
475QX2724 • **Value $25**

2
Baby's First Christmas
Photoholder
Fabric • N/A
750QX4704 • **Value $29**

3
Baby's Second
Christmas
Handcrafted • PIKE
600QX4711 • **Value $35**

4
Babysitter
Glass • SICK
475QX2791 • **Value $12**

5
Child's Third Christmas
Handcrafted • CHAD
600QX4714 • **Value $28**

6
Christmas Cardinal
Handcrafted • RGRS
475QX4941 • **Value $21**

7
Christmas Cuckoo
Handcrafted • CROW
800QX4801 • **Value $32**

8
Christmas Memories
Photoholder
Acrylic • PATT
650QX3724 • **Value $24**

1988

9
Cool Juggler
Handcrafted • CROW
650QX4874 • **Value $23**

10
Cymbals of Christmas
Handcrafted/Acrylic • DLEE
550QX4111 • **Value $29**

11
Dad
Handcrafted • SIED
700QX4141 • **Value $26**

12
Daughter
Handcrafted • PATT
575QX4151 • **Value $58**

13
Feliz Navidad
Handcrafted • UNRU
675QX4161 • **Value $34**

14
Fifty Years Together
Acrylic • N/A
675QX3741 • **Value $19**

15
Filled With Fudge
Handcrafted • SEAL
475QX4191 • **Value $32**

16
First Christmas
Together
Acrylic • VOTR
675QX3731 • **Value $25**

17
First Christmas
Together
Glass • N/A
475QX2741 • **Value $25**

18
First Christmas
Together
Handcrafted • PIKE
900QX4894 • **Value $32**

19
Five Years Together
Glass • MCGE
475QX2744 • **Value $20**

20
From Our
Home to Yours
Glass • PATT
475QX2794 • **Value $18**

General Keepsake		
	Price Paid	Value of My Collection
1.		
2.		
3.		
4.		
5.		
6.		
7.		
8.		
9.		
10.		
11.		
12.		
13.		
14.		
15.		
16.		
17.		
18.		
19.		
20.		
PENCIL TOTALS		

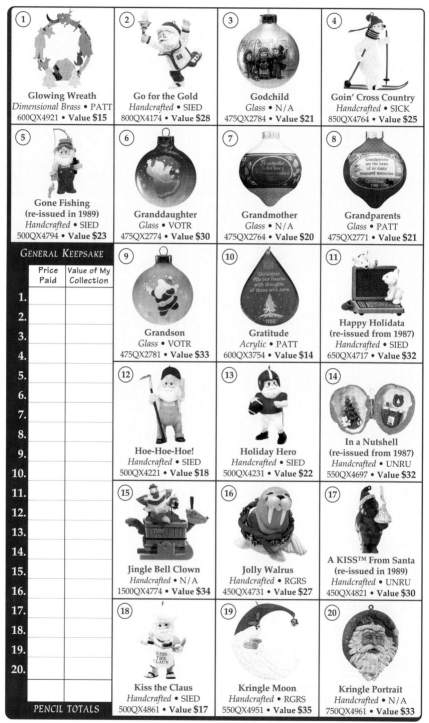

(1) Glowing Wreath
Dimensional Brass • PATT
600QX4921 • **Value $15**

(2) Go for the Gold
Handcrafted • SIED
800QX4174 • **Value $28**

(3) Godchild
Glass • N/A
475QX2784 • **Value $21**

(4) Goin' Cross Country
Handcrafted • SICK
850QX4764 • **Value $25**

(5) Gone Fishing
(re-issued in 1989)
Handcrafted • SIED
500QX4794 • **Value $23**

(6) Granddaughter
Glass • VOTR
475QX2774 • **Value $30**

(7) Grandmother
Glass • N/A
475QX2764 • **Value $20**

(8) Grandparents
Glass • PATT
475QX2771 • **Value $21**

(9) Grandson
Glass • VOTR
475QX2781 • **Value $33**

(10) Gratitude
Acrylic • PATT
600QX3754 • **Value $14**

(11) Happy Holidata
(re-issued from 1987)
Handcrafted • SIED
650QX4717 • **Value $32**

(12) Hoe-Hoe-Hoe!
Handcrafted • SIED
500QX4221 • **Value $18**

(13) Holiday Hero
Handcrafted • SIED
500QX4231 • **Value $22**

(14) In a Nutshell
(re-issued from 1987)
Handcrafted • UNRU
550QX4697 • **Value $32**

(15) Jingle Bell Clown
Handcrafted • N/A
1500QX4774 • **Value $34**

(16) Jolly Walrus
Handcrafted • RGRS
450QX4731 • **Value $27**

(17) A KISS™ From Santa
(re-issued in 1989)
Handcrafted • UNRU
450QX4821 • **Value $30**

(18) Kiss the Claus
Handcrafted • SIED
500QX4861 • **Value $17**

(19) Kringle Moon
Handcrafted • RGRS
550QX4951 • **Value $35**

(20) Kringle Portrait
Handcrafted • N/A
750QX4961 • **Value $33**

GENERAL KEEPSAKE

	Price Paid	Value of My Collection
1.		
2.		
3.		
4.		
5.		
6.		
7.		
8.		
9.		
10.		
11.		
12.		
13.		
14.		
15.		
16.		
17.		
18.		
19.		
20.		
PENCIL TOTALS		

1. Kringle Tree
Handcrafted • N/A
650QX4954 • **Value $40**

2. Little Jack Horner
Handcrafted • SIED
800QX4081 • **Value $26**

3. Love Fills the Heart
Acrylic • VOTR
600QX3744 • **Value $26**

4. Love Grows
Glass • VOTR
475QX2754 • **Value $34**

5. Love Santa
Handcrafted • SIED
500QX4864 • **Value $19**

6. Loving Bear
Handcrafted • RGRS
475QX4934 • **Value $20**

7. Merry-Mint Unicorn
Porcelain • RGRS
850QX4234 • **Value $23**

8. Midnight Snack
Handcrafted • SIED
600QX4104 • **Value $22**

9. Mistletoad
(re-issued from 1987)
Handcrafted • CROW
700QX4687 • **Value $32**

10. Mother
Acrylic • N/A
650QX3751 • **Value $20**

11. Mother and Dad
Porcelain • LYLE
800QX4144 • **Value $21**

12. New Home
Acrylic • VOTR
600QX3761 • **Value $21**

13. Nick the Kick
Handcrafted • SIED
500QX4224 • **Value $25**

14. Night Before Christmas
(re-issued from 1987)
Handcrafted • CROW
650QX4517 • **Value $34**

15. Noah's Ark
Pressed Tin • SICK
850QX4904 • **Value $44**

16. Norman Rockwell: Christmas Scenes
Glass • LYLE
475QX2731 • **Value $27**

17. Old-Fashioned Church
Wood • SICK
400QX4981 • **Value $25**

18. Old-Fashioned Schoolhouse
Wood • SICK
400QX4971 • **Value $25**

19. OREO® Chocolate Sandwich Cookies
(re-issued in 1989)
Handcrafted • UNRU
400QX4814 • **Value $22**

20. "Owliday" Wish
(re-issued from 1987)
Handcrafted • PIKE
650QX4559 • **Value $21**

GENERAL KEEPSAKE

	Price Paid	Value of My Collection
1.		
2.		
3.		
4.		
5.		
6.		
7.		
8.		
9.		
10.		
11.		
12.		
13.		
14.		
15.		
16.		
17.		
18.		
19.		
20.		
PENCIL TOTALS		

1988

(1) **Par for Santa** *Handcrafted* • SIED 500QX4791 • **Value $21**	**(2)** **Party Line** **(re-issued in 1989)** *Handcrafted* • PIKE 875QX4761 • **Value $30**	**(3)** **PEANUTS®** *Glass* • N/A 475QX2801 • **Value $48**	**(4)** **Peek-a-Boo Kitties** **(re-issued in 1989)** *Handcrafted* • CROW 750QX4871 • **Value $24**
(5) **Polar Bowler** **(re-issued in 1989)** *Handcrafted* • SIED 500QX4784 • **Value $19**	**(6)** **Purrfect Snuggle** *Handcrafted* • RGRS 625QX4744 • **Value $29**	**(7)** **Reindoggy** **(re-issued from 1987)** *Handcrafted* • SIED 575QX4527 • **Value $37**	**(8)** **Sailing! Sailing!** *Pressed Tin* • SICK 850QX4911 • **Value $26**

GENERAL KEEPSAKE		
	Price Paid	Value of My Collection
1.		
2.		
3.		
4.		
5.		
6.		
7.		
8.		
9.		
10.		
11.		
12.		
13.		
14.		
15.		
16.		
17.		
18.		
19.		
20.		
PENCIL TOTALS		

(9) **St. Louie Nick** **(re-issued from 1987)** *Handcrafted* • DUTK 775QX4539 • **Value $33**	**(10)** **Santa Flamingo** *Handcrafted* • PYDA 475QX4834 • **Value $37**	**(11)** **Shiny Sleigh** *Dimensional Brass* • PATT 575QX4924 • **Value $18**
(12) **Sister** *Porcelain* • VOTR 800QX4994 • **Value $32**	**(13)** **Slipper Spaniel** *Handcrafted* • CROW 425QX4724 • **Value $20**	**(14)** **SNOOPY® and WOODSTOCK** *Handcrafted* • UNRU 600QX4741 • **Value $46**
(15) **Soft Landing** *Handcrafted* • CHAD 700QX4751 • **Value $25**	**(16)** **Son** *Handcrafted* • PATT 575QX4154 • **Value $40**	**(17)** **Sparkling Tree** *Dimensional Brass* • PATT 600QX4931 • **Value $20**
(18) **Spirit of Christmas** *Glass* • LYLE 475QX2761 • **Value $25**	**(19)** **Squeaky Clean** *Handcrafted* • PIKE 675QX4754 • **Value $23**	**(20)** **Starry Angel** *Handcrafted* • RGRS 475QX4944 • **Value $21**

1988

(1) **Sweet Star** *Handcrafted* • SEAL 500QX4184 • **Value $32**	**(2)** **Sweetheart** *Handcrafted* • UNRU 975QX4901 • **Value $24**	**(3)** **Teacher** *Handcrafted* • PIKE 625QX4171 • **Value $21**	**(4)** **Teeny Taster** **(re-issued in 1989)** *Handcrafted* • SEAL 475QX4181 • **Value $30**
(5) **Ten Years Together** *Glass* • N/A 475QX2751 • **Value $22**	**(6)** **The Town Crier** *Handcrafted* • SEAL 550QX4734 • **Value $22**	**(7)** **Travels with Santa** *Handcrafted* • DLEE 1000QX4771 • **Value $40**	**(8)** **Treetop Dreams** **(re-issued from 1987)** *Handcrafted* • SEAL 675QX4597 • **Value $30**

(9) **Twenty-Five Years Together** *Acrylic* • PATT 675QX3734 • **Value $18**	**(10)** **Uncle Sam Nutcracker** *Handcrafted* • DLEE 700QX4884 • **Value $35**	**(11)** **Very Strawbeary** *Handcrafted* • DUTK 475QX4091 • **Value $23**
(12) **Winter Fun** *Handcrafted* • CHAD 850QX4781 • **Value $23**	**(13)** **The Wonderful Santacycle** *Handcrafted* • SEAL 2250QX4114 • **Value $47**	**(14)** **Year to Remember** *Ceramic* • N/A 700QX4164 • **Value $25**
(15) **Baby's First Christmas** *Handcrafted* • SEAL 2400QLX7184 • **Value $60**	**(16)** **Bearly Reaching** *Handcrafted* • SICK 950QLX7151 • **Value $36**	**(17)** **Christmas Is Magic** *Handcrafted* • CROW 1200QLX7171 • **Value $56**
(18) **Christmas Morning** **(re-issued from 1987)** *Handcrafted* • CROW 2450QLX7013 • **Value $48**	**(19)** **Circling the Globe** *Handcrafted* • CROW 1050QLX7124 • **Value $43**	**(20)** **Country Express** *Handcrafted* • SICK 2450QLX7211 • **Value $70**

GENERAL KEEPSAKE

	Price Paid	Value of My Collection
1.		
2.		
3.		
4.		
5.		
6.		
7.		
8.		
9.		
10.		
11.		
12.		
13.		
14.		

GENERAL MAGIC

15.		
16.		
17.		
18.		
19.		
20.		
PENCIL TOTALS		

VALUE GUIDE — HALLMARK KEEPSAKE ORNAMENTS

(1) Festive Feeder *Handcrafted* • SICK 1150QLX7204 • **Value $48**	**(2)** First Christmas Together *Handcrafted* • SICK 1200QLX7027 • **Value $40**	**(3)** Heavenly Glow *Brass* • PYDA 1175QLX7114 • **Value $26**	**(4)** Kitty Capers *Handcrafted* • PIKE 1300QLX7164 • **Value $44**
(5) Last-Minute Hug *Handcrafted* • UNRU 2200QLX7181 • **Value $47**	**(6)** Moonlit Nap (re-issued in 1989) *Handcrafted* • CHAD 875QLX7134 • **Value $27**	**(7)** Parade of the Toys *Handcrafted* • SICK 2450QLX7194 • **Value $50**	**(8)** Radiant Tree *Brass* • LYLE 1175QLX7121 • **Value $27**

(9) Skater's Waltz *Handcrafted* • UNRU 2450QLX7201 • **Value $56**	**(10)** Song of Christmas *Acrylic* • N/A 850QLX7111 • **Value $28**	**(11)** Tree of Friendship *Acrylic* • N/A 850QLX7104 • **Value $27**
(12) Baby's First Christmas *Handcrafted* • DLEE 600QXM5744 • **Value $12**	**(13)** Brass Angel *Brass* • LYLE 150QXM5671 • **Value $20**	**(14)** Brass Star *Brass* • LYLE 150QXM5664 • **Value $20**
(15) Brass Tree *Brass* • LYLE 150QXM5674 • **Value $20**	**(16)** Candy Cane Elf *Handcrafted* • SIED 300QXM5701 • **Value $19**	**(17)** Country Wreath (re-issued in 1989) *Handcrafted* • RGRS 400QXM5731 • **Value $12**
(18) First Christmas Together *Wood/Straw* • MCGE 400QXM5741 • **Value $13**	**(19)** Folk Art Lamb *Wood* • PATT 275QXM5681 • **Value $23**	**(20)** Folk Art Reindeer *Wood* • PATT 300QXM5684 • **Value $20**

1. Friends Share Joy
Acrylic • PATT
200QXM5764 • **Value $14**

2. Gentle Angel
Acrylic • VOTR
200QXM5771 • **Value $20**

3. Happy Santa
Glass • PATT
450QXM5614 • **Value $22**

4. Holy Family
(re-issued in 1989)
Handcrafted • UNRU
850QXM5611 • **Value $16**

5. Jolly St. Nick
Handcrafted • UNRU
800QXM5721 • **Value $33**

6. Joyous Heart
Wood • MCGE
350QXM5691 • **Value $30**

7. Little Drummer Boy
Handcrafted • SIED
450QXM5784 • **Value $28**

8. Love Is Forever
Acrylic • PATT
200QXM5774 • **Value $16**

1988

9. Mother
Handcrafted • PIKE
300QXM5724 • **Value $13**

10. Skater's Waltz
Handcrafted • UNRU
700QXM5601 • **Value $21**

11. Sneaker Mouse
Handcrafted • N/A
400QXM5711 • **Value $21**

12. Snuggly Skater
Handcrafted • SIED
450QXM5714 • **Value $26**

13. Sweet Dreams
Handcrafted • N/A
700QXM560-4 • **Value $22**

14. Three Little Kitties
(re-issued in 1989)
Handcrafted/Willow • PIKE
600QXM5694 • **Value $18**

15. Angelic Minstrel
(club edition, LE-49,900)
Porcelain • DLEE
2950QX4084 • **Value $52**

16. Christmas is Sharing
(club edition, LE-49,900)
Bone China • SEAL
1750QX4071 • **Value $48**

17. Hold on Tight
(early renewal piece, miniature)
Handcrafted • SIED
QXC5704 • **Value $74**

18. Our Clubhouse
(keepsake of membership)
Handcrafted • SIED
QXC5804 • **Value $45**

19. Seal of Friendship
(gift membership bonus, Merry Miniature)
Handcrafted • VOTR
QXC5104 • **Value $60**

20. Sleighful of Dreams
(club edition)
Handcrafted • SICK
800QXC5801 • **Value $70**

General Miniature	Price Paid	Value of My Collection
1.		
2.		
3.		
4.		
5.		
6.		
7.		
8.		
9.		
10.		
11.		
12.		
13.		
14.		
Collector's Club		
15.		
16.		
17.		
18.		
19.		
20.		
Pencil Totals		

(1)
Kringle's Toy Shop
(re-issued in 1989, magic)
Handcrafted • SEAL
2450QLX7017 • **Value $50**

1987

Among the most sought-after ornaments from 1987 is "Bright Christmas Dreams," which is coveted by collectors of the "CRAYOLA® Crayon" collectible series, although it is not officially a part of that series. Overall, there were 122 Keepsake ornaments and 18 Magic ornaments. See the collectible series section for more 1987 ornaments.

(2)
Baby Locket
Textured Metal • N/A
1500QX4617 • **Value $30**

(3)
Baby's First Christmas
Acrylic • N/A
600QX3729 • **Value $19**

(4)
Baby's First Christmas
Handcrafted • DLEE
975QX4113 • **Value $28**

(5)
Baby's First Christmas
– Baby Boy
Satin • PATT
475QX2749 • **Value $30**

(6)
Baby's First Christmas
– Baby Girl
Satin • PATT
475QX2747 • **Value $27**

(7)
Baby's First Christmas
Photoholder
Fabric • N/A
750QX4619 • **Value $30**

(8)
Baby's Second
Christmas
Handcrafted • DLEE
575QX4607 • **Value $32**

(9)
Babysitter
Glass • PIKE
475QX2797 • **Value $21**

(10)
Beary Special
Handcrafted • SIED
475QX4557 • **Value $28**

(11)
Bright
Christmas Dreams
Handcrafted • SIED
725QX4737 • **Value $92**

(12)
Child's Third Christmas
Handcrafted • CROW
575QX4599 • **Value $27**

(13)
Chocolate Chipmunk
Handcrafted • SEAL
600QX4567 • **Value $54**

(14)
Christmas Cuddle
Handcrafted • N/A
575QX4537 • **Value $34**

(15)
Christmas Fun Puzzle
Handcrafted • DLEE
800QX4679 • **Value $29**

(16)
Christmas is Gentle
(LE-24,700)
Bone China • SEAL
1750QX4449 • **Value $80**

(17)
Christmas Keys
Handcrafted • UNRU
575QX4739 • **Value $33**

OPEN HOUSE ORNAMENTS

	Price Paid	Value of My Collection
1.		
GENERAL KEEPSAKE		
2.		
3.		
4.		
5.		
6.		
7.		
8.		
9.		
10.		
11.		
12.		
13.		
14.		
15.		
16.		
17.		
PENCIL TOTALS		

1. Christmas Time Mime
(LE-24,700)
Porcelain • UNRU
2750QX4429 • **Value $60**

2. The Constitution
Acrylic • PATT
650QX3777 • **Value $27**

3. Country Wreath
Wood/Straw • PYDA
575QX4709 • **Value $29**

4. Currier & Ives:
American Farm Scene
Glass • LYLE
475QX2829 • **Value $30**

5. Dad
Handcrafted • SIED
600QX4629 • **Value $40**

6. Daughter
Handcrafted • SICK
575QX4637 • **Value $27**

7. December Showers
Handcrafted • DLEE
550QX4487 • **Value $36**

8. Doc Holiday
Handcrafted • SEAL
800QX4677 • **Value $45**

9. Dr. Seuss: The
Grinch's Christmas
Glass • N/A
475QX2783 • **Value $98**

10. Favorite Santa
Porcelain • DUTK
2250QX4457 • **Value $48**

11. Fifty Years Together
Porcelain • SEAL
800QX4437 • **Value $27**

12. First Christmas
Together
Acrylic • N/A
650QX3719 • **Value $25**

13. First Christmas
Together
Glass • LYLE
475QX2729 • **Value $24**

14. First Christmas
Together
Handcrafted • N/A
800QX4459 • **Value $38**

15. First Christmas
Together
Handcrafted • DLEE
950QX4467 • **Value $28**

16. First Christmas
Together
Textured Brass • N/A
1500QX4469 • **Value $30**

17. Folk Art Santa
Handcrafted • SICK
525QX4749 • **Value $36**

18. From Our
Home to Yours
Glass • PYDA
475QX2799 • **Value $44**

19. Fudge Forever
Handcrafted • DUTK
500QX4497 • **Value $35**

20. Godchild
Glass • PYDA
475QX2767 • **Value $22**

1987

GENERAL KEEPSAKE

	Price Paid	Value of My Collection
1.		
2.		
3.		
4.		
5.		
6.		
7.		
8.		
9.		
10.		
11.		
12.		
13.		
14.		
15.		
16.		
17.		
18.		
19.		
20.		
PENCIL TOTALS		

Value Guide — Hallmark Keepsake Ornaments

① Goldfinch
Porcelain • SICK
700QX4649 • **Value $82**

② Grandchild's First Christmas
Handcrafted • SEAL
900QX4609 • **Value $25**

③ Granddaughter
Bezeled Satin • VOTR
600QX3747 • **Value $22**

④ Grandmother
Glass • N/A
475QX2779 • **Value $16**

⑤ Grandparents
Glass • PIKE
475QX2777 • **Value $18**

⑥ Grandson
Glass • VOTR
475QX2769 • **Value $28**

⑦ Happy Holidata
(re-issued in 1988)
Handcrafted • SIED
650QX4717 • **Value $32**

⑧ Happy Santa
Handcrafted • CROW
475QX4569 • **Value $30**

GENERAL KEEPSAKE		
	Price Paid	Value of My Collection
1.		
2.		
3.		
4.		
5.		
6.		
7.		
8.		
9.		
10.		
11.		
12.		
13.		
14.		
15.		
16.		
17.		
18.		
19.		
20.		
PENCIL TOTALS		

⑨ Heart in Blossom
Acrylic • VOTR
600QX3727 • **Value $22**

⑩ Heavenly Harmony
Handcrafted • CROW
1500QX4659 • **Value $34**

⑪ Holiday Greetings
Bezeled Foil • N/A
600QX3757 • **Value $13**

⑫ Holiday Hourglass
Handcrafted • UNRU
800QX4707 • **Value $28**

⑬ Hot Dogger
Handcrafted • UNRU
650QX4719 • **Value $28**

⑭ Husband
Cameo • VOTR
700QX3739 • **Value $10**

⑮ I Remember Santa
Glass • LYLE
475QX278-9 • **Value $35**

⑯ Icy Treat
Handcrafted • SIED
450QX4509 • **Value $29**

⑰ In a Nutshell
(re-issued in 1988)
Handcrafted • UNRU
550QX4697 • **Value $32**

⑱ Jack Frosting
Handcrafted • SEAL
700QX4499 • **Value $54**

⑲ Jammie Pies™
Glass • N/A
475QX2839 • **Value $19**

⑳ Jogging Through the Snow
Handcrafted • DUTK
725QX4577 • **Value $38**

1. Jolly Follies
Handcrafted • CROW
850QX4669 • **Value $35**

2. Jolly Hiker
(re-issued from 1986)
Handcrafted • SIED
500QX4832 • **Value $30**

3. Joy Ride
Handcrafted • SEAL
1150QX4407 • **Value $77**

4. Joyous Angels
Handcrafted • SEAL
775QX4657 • **Value $26**

5. Let It Snow
Handcrafted • N/A
650QX4589 • **Value $24**

6. L'il Jingler
(re-issued from 1986)
Handcrafted • SEAL
675QX4193 • **Value $40**

7. Little Whittler
Handcrafted • DUTK
600QX4699 • **Value $33**

8. Love Is Everywhere
Glass • LYLE
475QX2787 • **Value $25**

9. Merry Koala
(re-issued from 1986)
Handcrafted • SICK
500QX4153 • **Value $24**

10. Mistletoad
(re-issued in 1988)
Handcrafted • CROW
700QX4687 • **Value $32**

11. Mother
Acrylic • PIKE
650QX3737 • **Value $17**

12. Mother and Dad
Porcelain • PIKE
700QX4627 • **Value $25**

13. Mouse in the Moon
(re-issued from 1986)
Handcrafted • SEAL
550QX4166 • **Value $23**

14. Nature's Decorations
Glass • VOTR
475QX2739 • **Value $33**

15. New Home
Acrylic • PATT
600QX3767 • **Value $27**

16. Niece
Glass • N/A
475QX2759 • **Value $13**

17. Night Before Christmas
(re-issued in 1988)
Handcrafted • CROW
650QX4517 • **Value $34**

18. Norman Rockwell:
Christmas Scenes
Glass • LYLE
475QX2827 • **Value $27**

19. Nostalgic Rocker
Wood • SICK
650QX4689 • **Value $29**

20. "Owliday" Wish
(re-issued in 1988)
Handcrafted • PIKE
650QX4559 • **Value $21**

1987

GENERAL KEEPSAKE

	Price Paid	Value of My Collection
1.		
2.		
3.		
4.		
5.		
6.		
7.		
8.		
9.		
10.		
11.		
12.		
13.		
14.		
15.		
16.		
17.		
18.		
19.		
20.		
PENCIL TOTALS		

(1)
Paddington™ Bear
Handcrafted • PIKE
550QX4727 • **Value $34**

(2)
PEANUTS®
Glass • N/A
475QX2819 • **Value $35**

(3)
Pretty Kitty
Handcrafted/Glass • CROW
1100QX4489 • **Value $30**

(4)
Promise of Peace
Acrylic • PIKE
650QX3749 • **Value $24**

(5)
Raccoon Biker
Handcrafted • SIED
700QX4587 • **Value $29**

(6)
Reindoggy
(re-issued in 1988)
Handcrafted • SIED
575QX4527 • **Value $37**

(7)
St. Louie Nick
(re-issued in 1988)
Handcrafted • DUTK
775QX4539 • **Value $33**

(8)
Santa at the Bat
Handcrafted • SIED
775QX4579 • **Value $28**

(9)
Seasoned Greetings
Handcrafted • SEAL
625QX4549 • **Value $28**

(10)
Sister
Wood • SICK
600QX4747 • **Value $15**

(11)
Sleepy Santa
Handcrafted • CROW
625QX4507 • **Value $38**

(12)
SNOOPY and
WOODSTOCK
Handcrafted • SIED
725QX4729 • **Value $50**

(13)
Son
Handcrafted • SICK
575QX4639 • **Value $42**

(14)
Special Memories
Photoholder
Fabric • N/A
675QX4647 • **Value $25**

(15)
Spots 'n Stripes
Handcrafted • N/A
550QX4529 • **Value $26**

(16)
Sweetheart
Handcrafted • SICK
1100QX4479 • **Value $30**

(17)
Teacher
Handcrafted • SIED
575QX4667 • **Value $22**

(18)
Ten Years Together
Porcelain • VOTR
700QX4447 • **Value $23**

(19)
Three Men in a Tub
Handcrafted • DLEE
800QX4547 • **Value $27**

(20)
Time for Friends
Glass • VOTR
475QX2807 • **Value $24**

GENERAL KEEPSAKE

	Price Paid	Value of My Collection
1.		
2.		
3.		
4.		
5.		
6.		
7.		
8.		
9.		
10.		
11.		
12.		
13.		
14.		
15.		
16.		
17.		
18.		
19.		
20.		
PENCIL TOTALS		

Value Guide — Hallmark Keepsake Ornaments

1. Treetop Dreams
(re-issued in 1988)
Handcrafted • SEAL
675QX4597 • **Value $30**

2. Treetop Trio
(re-issued from 1986)
Handcrafted • DLEE
1100QX4256 • **Value $32**

3. Twenty-Five
Years Together
Porcelain • N/A
750QX4439 • **Value $25**

4. Walnut Shell Rider
(re-issued from 1986)
Handcrafted • SEAL
600QX4196 • **Value $25**

5. Warmth of Friendship
Acrylic • N/A
600QX3759 • **Value $12**

6. Wee Chimney Sweep
Handcrafted • SEAL
625QX4519 • **Value $27**

7. Word of Love
Porcelain • N/A
800QX4477 • **Value $24**

8. Angelic Messengers
Panorama Ball • UNRU
1875QLX7113 • **Value $58**

9. Baby's First Christmas
Handcrafted • N/A
1350QLX7049 • **Value $36**

10. Bright Noel
Acrylic • VOTR
700QLX7059 • **Value $31**

11. Christmas Morning
(re-issued in 1988)
Handcrafted • CROW
2450QLX7013 • **Value $48**

12. First Christmas
Together
Handcrafted • N/A
1150QLX7087 • **Value $49**

13. Good Cheer Blimp
Handcrafted • SICK
1600QLX7046 • **Value $55**

14. Keep on Glowin'!
(re-issued from 1986)
Handcrafted • CROW
1000QLX7076 • **Value $45**

15. Keeping Cozy
Handcrafted • CROW
1175QLX7047 • **Value $35**

16. Lacy Brass Snowflake
Brass • N/A
1150QLX7097 • **Value $26**

17. Loving Holiday
Handcrafted • SEAL
2200QLX7016 • **Value $53**

18. Memories Are Forever
Photoholder
Handcrafted • SEAL
850QLX7067 • **Value $34**

19. Meowy Christmas!
Handcrafted • PIKE
1000QLX7089 • **Value $59**

20. Season for Friendship
Acrylic • N/A
850QLX7069 • **Value $21**

General Keepsake	Price Paid	Value of My Collection
1.		
2.		
3.		
4.		
5.		
6.		
7.		
General Magic		
8.		
9.		
10.		
11.		
12.		
13.		
14.		
15.		
16.		
17.		
18.		
19.		
20.		
PENCIL TOTALS		

1987

(1) Train Station
Handcrafted • DLEE
1275QLX7039 • **Value $50**

(2) Village Express
(re-issued from 1986)
Handcrafted • SICK
2450QLX7072 • **Value $110**

(3) Carousel Reindeer
(club edition)
Handcrafted • SICK
800QXC5817 • **Value $67**

(4) Wreath of Memories
(keepsake of membership)
Handcrafted • UNRU
QXC5809 • **Value $56**

(5) North Pole Power & Light
Handcrafted • CROW
($2.95)627XPR9333 • **Value $26**

1986

One of the biggest stories among Hallmark collectors in 1986 was the hard-to-find porcelain "Magical Unicorn" ornament which was limited to 24,700 pieces. The 1986 collection featured 120 Keepsake ornaments and 16 Magic ornaments. See the collectible series section for more 1986 ornaments.

GENERAL MAGIC

	Price Paid	Value of My Collection
1.		
2.		

COLLECTOR'S CLUB

3.		
4.		

OPEN HOUSE ORNAMENTS

5.		

GENERAL KEEPSAKE

6.		
7.		
8.		
9.		
10.		
11.		
12.		
13.		
14.		
15.		
16.		
17.		

PENCIL TOTALS

(6) Acorn Inn
Handcrafted • UNRU
850QX4243 • **Value $30**

(7) Baby Locket
Textured Brass • MCGE
1600QX4123 • **Value $29**

(8) Baby's First Christmas
Acrylic • PALM
600QX3803 • **Value $24**

(9) Baby's First Christmas
Handcrafted • SICK
900QX4126 • **Value $40**

(10) Baby's First Christmas
Satin • PATT
550QX2713 • **Value $24**

(11) Baby's First Christmas Photoholder
Fabric • PATT
800QX3792 • **Value $24**

(12) Baby's Second Christmas
Handcrafted • SIED
650QX4133 • **Value $29**

(13) Baby-Sitter
Glass • N/A
475QX2756 • **Value $12**

(14) Beary Smooth Ride
(re-issued from 1985)
Handcrafted • SICK
650QX4805 • **Value $23**

(15) Bluebird
Porcelain • SICK
725QX4283 • **Value $57**

(16) Chatty Penguin
Plush • CROW
575QX4176 • **Value $26**

(17) Child's Third Christmas
Fabric • VOTR
650QX4136 • **Value $24**

1. Christmas Beauty
Lacquer • PATT
600QX3223 • **Value $11**

2. Christmas Guitar
Handcrafted • UNRU
700QX5126 • **Value $23**

3. Cookies for Santa
Handcrafted • MCGE
450QX4146 • **Value $30**

4. Country Sleigh
Handcrafted • SICK
1000QX5113 • **Value $28**

5. Daughter
Handcrafted • SEAL
575QX4306 • **Value $48**

6. Do Not Disturb Bear
(re-issued from 1985)
Handcrafted • SEAL
775QX4812 • **Value $32**

7. Father
Wood • VOTR
650QX4313 • **Value $14**

8. Favorite Tin Drum
Tin • SICK
850QX5143 • **Value $32**

9. Festive Treble Clef
Handcrafted • SIED
875QX5133 • **Value $24**

10. Fifty Years Together
Porcelain • PIKE
1000QX4006 • **Value $18**

11. First Christmas
Together
Acrylic • MCGE
700QX3793 • **Value $17**

12. First Christmas
Together
Glass • N/A
475QX2703 • **Value $20**

13. First Christmas
Together
Handcrafted • SICK
1200QX4096 • **Value $25**

14. First Christmas
Together
Textured Brass • N/A
1600QX4003 • **Value $23**

15. Friends Are Fun
Glass • CROW
475QX2723 • **Value $43**

16. Friendship Greeting
Fabric • N/A
800QX4273 • **Value $15**

17. Friendship's Gift
Acrylic • N/A
600QX3816 • **Value $15**

18. From Our
Home to Yours
Acrylic • N/A
600QX3833 • **Value $16**

19. Glowing
Christmas Tree
Acrylic • PATT
700QX4286 • **Value $16**

20. Godchild
Satin • N/A
475QX2716 • **Value $18**

GENERAL KEEPSAKE

	Price Paid	Value of My Collection
1.		
2.		
3.		
4.		
5.		
6.		
7.		
8.		
9.		
10.		
11.		
12.		
13.		
14.		
15.		
16.		
17.		
18.		
19.		
20.		
PENCIL TOTALS		

1986

Value Guide – Hallmark Keepsake Ornaments

(1) Grandchild's First Christmas
Handcrafted • N/A
1000QX4116 • **Value $16**

(2) Granddaughter
Glass • LYLE
475QX2736 • **Value $24**

(3) Grandmother
Satin • PATT
475QX2743 • **Value $16**

(4) Grandparents
Porcelain • PATT
750QX4323 • **Value $22**

(5) Grandson
Glass • VOTR
475QX2733 • **Value $31**

(6) Gratitude
Satin/Wood • PIKE
600QX4326 • **Value $12**

(7) Happy Christmas to Owl
Handcrafted • UNRU
600QX4183 • **Value $25**

(8) Heathcliff
Handcrafted • SEAL
750QX4363 • **Value $28**

(9) Heavenly Dreamer
Handcrafted • DLEE
575QX4173 • **Value $34**

(10) Heirloom Snowflake
Fabric • PATT
675QX5153 • **Value $21**

(11) Holiday Horn
Porcelain • UNRU
800QX5146 • **Value $34**

(12) Holiday Jingle Bell
Handcrafted • N/A
1600QX4046 • **Value $55**

(13) Husband
Cameo • PIKE
800QX3836 • **Value $13**

(14) Jolly Hiker (re-issued in 1987)
Handcrafted • SIED
500QX4832 • **Value $30**

(15) Jolly St. Nick
Porcelain • UNRU
2250QX4296 • **Value $70**

(16) Joy of Friends
Bezeled Satin • PATT
675QX3823 • **Value $16**

(17) Joyful Carolers
Handcrafted • SICK
975QX5136 • **Value $36**

(18) Katybeth
Porcelain • N/A
700QX4353 • **Value $26**

(19) Kitty Mischief (re-issued from 1985)
Handcrafted • DUTK
500QX4745 • **Value $25**

(20) Li'l Jingler (re-issued in 1987)
Handcrafted • SEAL
675QX4193 • **Value $40**

GENERAL KEEPSAKE

	Price Paid	Value of My Collection
1.		
2.		
3.		
4.		
5.		
6.		
7.		
8.		
9.		
10.		
11.		
12.		
13.		
14.		
15.		
16.		
17.		
18.		
19.		
20.		
PENCIL TOTALS		

VALUE GUIDE – HALLMARK KEEPSAKE ORNAMENTS

1. Little Drummers
Handcrafted • CROW
1250QX5116 • **Value $34**

2. Loving Memories
Handcrafted • SEAL
900QX4093 • **Value $35**

3. The Magi
Glass • PIKE
475QX2726 • **Value $23**

4. Magical Unicorn
(LE-24,700)
Porcelain • UNRU
2750QX4293 • **Value $105**

5. Marionette Angel
(cancelled after limited production)
Handcrafted • N/A
850QX4023 • **Value $400**

6. Mary Emmerling: American Country Collection
Glass • N/A
795QX2752 • **Value $26**

7. Memories to Cherish
Ceramic • VOTR
750QX4276 • **Value $29**

8. Merry Koala
(re-issued in 1987)
Handcrafted • SICK
500QX4153 • **Value $24**

9. Merry Mouse
(re-issued from 1985)
Handcrafted • DUTK
450QX4032 • **Value $32**

10. Mother
Acrylic • N/A
700QX3826 • **Value $20**

11. Mother and Dad
Porcelain • PYDA
750QX4316 • **Value $21**

12. Mouse in the Moon
(re-issued in 1987)
Handcrafted • SEAL
550QX4166 • **Value $23**

13. Nephew
Bezeled Lacquer • N/A
625QX3813 • **Value $14**

14. New Home
Glass • CROW
475QX2746 • **Value $52**

15. Niece
Fabric/Wood • N/A
600QX4266 • **Value $12**

16. Norman Rockwell
Glass • PIKE
475QX2763 • **Value $30**

17. Nutcracker Santa
Handcrafted • UNRU
1000QX5123 • **Value $50**

18. Open Me First
Handcrafted • N/A
725QX4226 • **Value $34**

19. Paddington™ Bear
Handcrafted • SIED
600QX4356 • **Value $42**

20. PEANUTS®
Glass • N/A
475QX2766 • **Value $43**

GENERAL KEEPSAKE

	Price Paid	Value of My Collection
1.		
2.		
3.		
4.		
5.		
6.		
7.		
8.		
9.		
10.		
11.		
12.		
13.		
14.		
15.		
16.		
17.		
18.		
19.		
20.		
PENCIL TOTALS		

1986

1 **Playful Possum**
Handcrafted/Glass • CROW
1100QX4253 • **Value $31**

2 **Popcorn Mouse**
Handcrafted • SICK
675QX4213 • **Value $50**

3 **Puppy's Best Friend**
Handcrafted • UNRU
650QX4203 • **Value $27**

4 **Rah Rah Rabbit**
Handcrafted • CROW
700QX4216 • **Value $36**

5 **Remembering Christmas**
Porcelain • N/A
875QX5106 • **Value $29**

6 **Santa's Hot Tub**
Handcrafted • SEAL
1200QX4263 • **Value $57**

7 **Season of the Heart**
Glass • PATT
475QX2706 • **Value $18**

8 **Shirt Tales™ Parade**
Glass • N/A
475QX2773 • **Value $17**

9 **Sister**
Bezeled Satin • VOTR
675QX3806 • **Value $15**

10 **Skateboard Raccoon**
(re-issued from 1985)
Handcrafted • DUTK
650QX4732 • **Value $38**

11 **Ski Tripper**
Handcrafted • SIED
675QX4206 • **Value $22**

12 **SNOOPY® and WOODSTOCK**
Handcrafted • SIED
800QX4346 • **Value $53**

13 **Snow Buddies**
Handcrafted • DUTK
800QX4236 • **Value $38**

14 **Snow-Pitching Snowman**
(re-issued from 1985)
Handcrafted • DLEE
450QX4702 • **Value $22**

15 **Soccer Beaver**
(re-issued from 1985)
Handcrafted • DUTK
650QX4775 • **Value $27**

16 **Son**
Handcrafted • SEAL
575QX4303 • **Value $36**

17 **Special Delivery**
Handcrafted • SIED
500QX4156 • **Value $28**

18 **Star Brighteners**
Acrylic • VOTR
600QX3226 • **Value $19**

19 **The Statue of Liberty**
Acrylic • PYDA
600QX3843 • **Value $27**

20 **Sweetheart**
Handcrafted • SEAL
1100QX4086 • **Value $72**

General Keepsake	Price Paid	Value of My Collection
1.		
2.		
3.		
4.		
5.		
6.		
7.		
8.		
9.		
10.		
11.		
12.		
13.		
14.		
15.		
16.		
17.		
18.		
19.		
20.		
PENCIL TOTALS		

(1) Teacher
Glass • N/A
475QX2753 • **Value $12**

(2) Ten Years Together
Porcelain • N/A
750QX4013 • **Value $20**

(3) Timeless Love
Acrylic • VOTR
600QX3796 • **Value $32**

(4) Tipping the Scales
Handcrafted • DUTK
675QX4186 • **Value $26**

(5) Touchdown Santa
Handcrafted • DUTK
800QX4233 • **Value $45**

(6) Treetop Trio
(re-issued in 1987)
Handcrafted • DLEE
1100QX4256 • **Value $32**

(7) Twenty-Five Years Together
Porcelain • VOTR
800QX4103 • **Value $22**

(8) Walnut Shell Rider
(re-issued in 1987)
Handcrafted • SEAL
600QX4196 • **Value $25**

(9) Welcome, Christmas
Handcrafted • CROW
825QX5103 • **Value $30**

(10) Wynken, Blynken and Nod
Handcrafted • DLEE
975QX4246 • **Value $45**

(11) Baby's First Christmas
Panorama Ball • CROW
1950QLX7103 • **Value $48**

(12) Christmas Sleigh Ride
Handcrafted • SEAL
2450QLX7012 • **Value $130**

(13) First Christmas Together
Handcrafted • SEAL
1400QLX7073 • **Value $43**

(14) General Store
Handcrafted • DLEE
1575QLX7053 • **Value $60**

(15) Gentle Blessings
Panorama Ball • SICK
1500QLX7083 • **Value $165**

(16) Keep on Glowin'!
(re-issued in 1987)
Handcrafted • CROW
1000QLX7076 • **Value $45**

(17) Merry Christmas Bell
Acrylic • VOTR
850QLX7093 • **Value $24**

(18) Mr. and Mrs. Santa
(re-issued from 1985)
Handcrafted • N/A
1450QLX7052 • **Value $82**

(19) Santa's On His Way
Panorama Ball • UNRU
1500QLX7115 • **Value $70**

(20) Santa's Snack
Handcrafted • CROW
1000QLX7066 • **Value $58**

1986

GENERAL KEEPSAKE

	Price Paid	Value of My Collection
1.		
2.		
3.		
4.		
5.		
6.		
7.		
8.		
9.		
10.		

GENERAL MAGIC

11.		
12.		
13.		
14.		
15.		
16.		
17.		
18.		
19.		
20.		
PENCIL TOTALS		

① Sharing Friendship
Acrylic • VOTR
850QLX7063 • **Value $24**

② Sugarplum Cottage
(re-issued from 1984)
Handcrafted • N/A
1100QLX7011 • **Value $38**

③ Village Express
(re-issued in 1987)
Handcrafted • SICK
2450QLX7072 • **Value $110**

④ On the Right Track
Porcelain • DUTK
1500QSP4201 • **Value $48**

⑤ Coca-Cola® Santa
Glass • N/A
475QXO2796 • **Value $23**

⑥ Old-Fashioned Santa
Handcrafted • SICK
1275QXO4403 • **Value $60**

⑦ Santa and His Reindeer
Handcrafted • N/A
975QXO4406 • **Value $37**

⑧ Santa's Panda Pal
Handcrafted • N/A
500QXO4413 • **Value $29**

1985

Some of the most popular pieces in 1985 were based on favorite themes such as Santa Claus, SNOOPY® and Norman Rockwell's art. For 1985, there were 114 Keepsake ornament designs and 14 Magic ornaments. See the collectible series section for more 1985 ornaments.

	Price Paid	Value of My Collection
General Magic		
1.		
2.		
3.		
Gold Crown Ornaments		
4.		
Open House Ornaments		
5.		
6.		
7.		
8.		
General Keepsake		
9.		
10.		
11.		
12.		
13.		
14.		
15.		
16.		
17.		
Pencil Totals		

⑨ Baby Locket
Textured Brass • MCGE
1600QX4012 • **Value $25**

⑩ Baby's First Christmas
Acrylic • N/A
575QX3702 • **Value $19**

⑪ Baby's First Christmas
Embroidered Fabric • N/A
700QX4782 • **Value $17**

⑫ Baby's First Christmas
Fabric • N/A
1600QX4995 • **Value $43**

⑬ Baby's First Christmas
Handcrafted • DLEE
1500QX4992 • **Value $58**

⑭ Baby's First Christmas
Satin • VOTR
500QX2602 • **Value $24**

⑮ Baby's Second Christmas
Handcrafted • N/A
600QX4785 • **Value $38**

⑯ Babysitter
Glass • PYDA
475QX2642 • **Value $13**

⑰ Baker Elf
Handcrafted • SEAL
575QX4912 • **Value $33**

1.
Beary Smooth Ride
(re-issued in 1986)
Handcrafted • SICK
650QX4805 • **Value $23**

2.
Betsey Clark
Porcelain • N/A
850QX5085 • **Value $33**

3.
Bottlecap Fun Bunnies
Handcrafted • SIED
775QX4815 • **Value $36**

4.
Candle Cameo
Bezeled Cameo • PIKE
675QX3742 • **Value $15**

5.
Candy Apple Mouse
Handcrafted • SICK
650QX4705 • **Value $66**

6.
Charming Angel
Fabric • PYDA
975QX5125 • **Value $26**

7.
Children in the Shoe
Handcrafted • SEAL
950QX4905 • **Value $52**

8.
Child's Third Christmas
Handcrafted • SEAL
600QX4755 • **Value $30**

9.
Christmas Treats
Bezeled Glass • N/A
550QX5075 • **Value $18**

10.
Country Goose
Wood • PYDA
775QX5185 • **Value $16**

11.
Dapper Penguin
Handcrafted • SEAL
500QX4772 • **Value $32**

12.
Daughter
Wood • N/A
550QX5032 • **Value $20**

13.
A DISNEY Christmas
Glass • N/A
475QX2712 • **Value $35**

14.
Do Not Disturb Bear
(re-issued in 1986)
Handcrafted • SEAL
775QX4812 • **Value $32**

15.
Doggy in a Stocking
Handcrafted • N/A
550QX4742 • **Value $42**

16.
Engineering Mouse
Handcrafted • SIED
550QX4735 • **Value $28**

17.
Father
Wood • VOTR
650QX3762 • **Value $12**

18.
First Christmas
Together
Acrylic • N/A
675QX3705 • **Value $20**

19.
First Christmas
Together
Brass • SEAL
1675QX4005 • **Value $26**

20.
First Christmas
Together
Fabric/Wood • N/A
800QX5072 • **Value $15**

General Keepsake

	Price Paid	Value of My Collection
1.		
2.		
3.		
4.		
5.		
6.		
7.		
8.		
9.		
10.		
11.		
12.		
13.		
14.		
15.		
16.		
17.		
18.		
19.		
20.		
PENCIL TOTALS		

1985

VALUE GUIDE — HALLMARK KEEPSAKE ORNAMENTS

1 First Christmas Together
Glass • N/A
475QX2612 • **Value $20**

2 First Christmas Together
Porcelain • SICK
1300QX4935 • **Value $25**

3 FRAGGLE ROCK™ Holiday
Glass • N/A
475QX2655 • **Value $29**

4 Friendship
Bezeled Satin • PYDA
675QX3785 • **Value $18**

5 Friendship
Embroidered Satin • PATT
775QX5062 • **Value $16**

6 From Our House to Yours
Needlepoint Fabric • PATT
775QX5202 • **Value $13**

7 Godchild
Bezeled Satin • MCGE
675QX3802 • **Value $14**

8 Good Friends
Glass • N/A
475QX2652 • **Value $31**

9 Grandchild's First Christmas
Handcrafted • N/A
1100QX4955 • **Value $23**

10 Grandchild's First Christmas
Satin • VOTR
500QX2605 • **Value $15**

11 Granddaughter
Glass • N/A
475QX2635 • **Value $28**

12 Grandmother
Glass • PATT
475QX2625 • **Value $18**

13 Grandparents
Bezeled Lacquer • PIKE
700QX3805 • **Value $14**

14 Grandson
Glass • VOTR
475QX2622 • **Value $28**

15 Heart Full of Love
Bezeled Satin • N/A
675QX3782 • **Value $21**

16 Heavenly Trumpeter (LE-24,700)
Porcelain • DLEE
2750QX4052 • **Value $105**

17 Holiday Heart
Porcelain • N/A
800QX4982 • **Value $26**

18 Hugga Bunch™
Glass • N/A
500QX2715 • **Value $29**

19 Ice Skating Owl
Handcrafted • SIED
500QX4765 • **Value $23**

20 Keepsake Basket
Fabric • PIKE
1500QX5145 • **Value $22**

GENERAL KEEPSAKE	Price Paid	Value of My Collection
1.		
2.		
3.		
4.		
5.		
6.		
7.		
8.		
9.		
10.		
11.		
12.		
13.		
14.		
15.		
16.		
17.		
18.		
19.		
20.		
PENCIL TOTALS		

① Kit the Shepherd *Handcrafted* • SIED 575QX4845 • **Value $26**	② Kitty Mischief (re-issued in 1986) *Handcrafted* • DUTK 500QX4745 • **Value $25**	③ Lacy Heart *Fabric* • N/A 875QX5112 • **Value $26**	④ Lamb in Legwarmers *Handcrafted* • N/A 700QX4802 • **Value $24**
⑤ Love at Christmas *Acrylic* • MCGE 575QX3715 • **Value $40**	⑥ Merry Mouse (re-issued in 1986) *Handcrafted* • DUTK 450QX4032 • **Value $32**	⑦ Merry Shirt Tales™ *Glass* • N/A 475QX2672 • **Value $22**	⑧ Mother *Acrylic* • PIKE 675QX3722 • **Value $14**

1985

⑨ Mother and Dad *Porcelain* • VOTR 775QX5092 • **Value $22**	⑩ Mouse Wagon *Handcrafted* • N/A 575QX4762 • **Value $63**	⑪ Muffin the Angel *Handcrafted* • SIED 575QX4835 • **Value $27**

GENERAL KEEPSAKE

	Price Paid	Value of My Collection
1.		
2.		
3.		
4.		
5.		
6.		
7.		
8.		
9.		
10.		
11.		
12.		
13.		
14.		
15.		
16.		
17.		
18.		
19.		
20.		
PENCIL TOTALS		

⑫ Nativity Scene *Glass* • N/A 475QX2645 • **Value $34**	⑬ New Home *Glass* • PYDA 475QX2695 • **Value $29**	⑭ Niece *Acrylic* • N/A 575QX5205 • **Value $12**
⑮ Night Before Christmas *Panorama Ball* • SEAL 1300QX4494 • **Value $43**	⑯ Norman Rockwell *Glass* • MCGE 475QX2662 • **Value $43**	⑰ Nostalgic Sled (re-issued from 1984) *Handcrafted* • SICK 600QX4424 • **Value $28**
⑱ Old-Fashioned Doll *Fabric/Porcelain* • N/A 1450QX5195 • **Value $39**	⑲ Old-Fashioned Wreath *Brass/Acrylic* • N/A 750QX3735 • **Value $24**	⑳ Peaceful Kingdom *Acrylic* • PIKE 575QX3732 • **Value $30**

①	②	③	④
PEANUTS®	**Porcelain Bird**	**Rainbow Brite™ and Friends**	**Rocking Horse Memories**
Glass • N/A	*Porcelain* • SICK	*Glass* • N/A	*Fabric/Wood* • VOTR
475QX2665 • **Value $35**	650QX4795 • **Value $33**	475QX2682 • **Value $24**	1000QX5182 • **Value $17**

⑤	⑥	⑦	⑧
Roller Skating Rabbit (re-issued from 1984)	**Santa Pipe**	**Santa's Ski Trip**	**Sewn Photoholder**
Handcrafted • SEAL	*Handcrafted* • DUTK	*Handcrafted* • SEAL	*Embroidered Fabric* • PIKE
500QX4571 • **Value $32**	950QX4942 • **Value $26**	1200QX4962 • **Value $62**	700QX3795 • **Value $34**

GENERAL KEEPSAKE

	Price Paid	Value of My Collection
1.		
2.		
3.		
4.		
5.		
6.		
7.		
8.		
9.		
10.		
11.		
12.		
13.		
14.		
15.		
16.		
17.		
18.		
19.		
20.		
PENCIL TOTALS		

⑨	⑩	⑪
Sheep at Christmas	**Sister**	**Skateboard Raccoon** (re-issued in 1986)
Handcrafted • SICK	*Porcelain* • PATT	*Handcrafted* • DUTK
825QX5175 • **Value $27**	725QX5065 • **Value $23**	650QX4732 • **Value $38**

⑫	⑬	⑭
SNOOPY® and WOODSTOCK	**Snowflake**	**Snow-Pitching Snowman** (re-issued in 1986)
Handcrafted • SIED	*Fabric* • PATT	*Handcrafted* • DLEE
750QX4915 • **Value $82**	650QX5105 • **Value $21**	450QX4702 • **Value $22**

⑮	⑯	⑰
Snowy Seal (re-issued from 1984)	**Soccer Beaver** (re-issued in 1986)	**Son**
Handcrafted • SEAL	*Handcrafted* • DUTK	*Handcrafted* • SIED
400QX4501 • **Value $20**	650QX4775 • **Value $27**	550QX5025 • **Value $46**

⑱	⑲	⑳
Special Friends	**The Spirit of Santa Claus**	**Stardust Angel**
Arylic • PALM	*Handcrafted* • DLEE	*Handcrafted* • DLEE
575QX3725 • **Value $11**	2250QX4985 • **Value $105**	575QX4752 • **Value $38**

1985

(1) Sun and Fun Santa *Handcrafted* • SIED 775QX4922 • **Value $40**	**(2)** Swinging Angel Bell *Handcrafted/Glass* • SIED 1100QX4925 • **Value $35**	**(3)** Teacher *Handcrafted* • N/A 600QX5052 • **Value $20**	**(4)** Three Kittens in a Mitten (re-issued from 1984) *Handcrafted* • DLEE 800QX4311 • **Value $52**

| **(5)** Trumpet Panda
Handcrafted • SEAL
450QX4712 • **Value $26** | **(6)** Twenty-Five
Years Together
Porcelain • N/A
800QX5005 • **Value $17** | **(7)** Victorian Lady
Porcelain/Fabric • N/A
950QX5132 • **Value $25** | **(8)** Whirligig Santa
Wood • N/A
1250QX5192 • **Value $26** |

| **(9)** With Appreciation
Acrylic • N/A
675QX3752 • **Value $12** | **(10)** All Are Precious
(re-issued from 1984)
Acrylic • N/A
800QLX7044 • **Value $25** | **(11)** Baby's First Christmas
Handcrafted • SEAL
1650QLX7005 • **Value $42** |

General Keepsake

	Price Paid	Value of My Collection
1.		
2.		
3.		
4.		
5.		
6.		
7.		
8.		
9.		

| **(12)** Christmas Eve Visit
Etched Brass • N/A
1200QLX7105 • **Value $32** | **(13)** Katybeth
Acrylic • N/A
1075QLX7102 • **Value $42** | **(14)** Little Red Schoolhouse
Handcrafted • DLEE
1575QLX7112 • **Value $85** |

General Magic

10.		
11.		
12.		
13.		
14.		
15.		
16.		
17.		
18.		
19.		
20.		

| **(15)** Love Wreath
Acrylic • VOTR
850QLX7025 • **Value $28** | **(16)** Mr. and Mrs. Santa
(re-issued in 1986)
Handcrafted • N/A
1450QLX7052 • **Value $82** | **(17)** Nativity
(re-issued from 1984)
Panorama Ball • SEAL
1200QLX7001 • **Value $32** |

| **(18)** Santa's Workshop
(re-issued from 1984)
Panorama Ball • N/A
1300QLX7004 • **Value $64** | **(19)** Season of Beauty
Classic Shape • LYLE
800QLX7122 • **Value $27** | **(20)** Sugarplum Cottage
(re-issued from 1984)
Handcrafted • N/A
1100QLX7011 • **Value $38** |

PENCIL TOTALS

① Swiss Cheese Lane
Handcrafted • N/A
1300QLX7065 • **Value $47**

② Village Church (re-issued from 1984)
Handcrafted • DLEE
1500QLX7021 • **Value $48**

③ Santa Claus
Lacquer • N/A
675QX3005 • **Value $12**

④ Santa's Village
Lacquer • N/A
675QX3002 • **Value $12**

1984

1984 was a landmark year for Hallmark ornaments with the debut of lighted Magic ornaments (then called "Lighted Ornaments"). In later years, these ornaments would also incorporate motion and sound. There were 10 Magic ornaments issued in 1984, as well as 110 Keepsake designs. See the collectible series section for more 1984 ornaments.

⑤ Alpine Elf
Handcrafted • SEAL
600QX4521 • **Value $38**

	Price Paid	Value of My Collection
GENERAL MAGIC		
1.		
2.		
SANTA CLAUS – THE MOVIE		
3.		
4.		
GENERAL KEEPSAKE		
5.		
6.		
7.		
8.		
9.		
10.		
11.		
12.		
13.		
14.		
15.		
16.		
17.		
PENCIL TOTALS		

⑥ Amanda
Fabric/Porcelain • N/A
900QX4321 • **Value $33**

⑦ Baby's First Christmas
Acrylic • N/A
600QX3401 • **Value $39**

⑧ Baby's First Christmas
Classic Shape • DLEE
1600QX9041 • **Value $48**

⑨ Baby's First Christmas
Handcrafted • N/A
1400QX4381 • **Value $48**

⑩ Baby's First Christmas – Boy
Satin • N/A
450QX2404 • **Value $30**

⑪ Baby's First Christmas – Girl
Satin • N/A
450QX2401 • **Value $29**

⑫ Baby's First Christmas – Photoholder
Fabric • N/A
700QX3001 • **Value $20**

⑬ Baby's Second Christmas
Satin • N/A
450QX2411 • **Value $38**

⑭ Baby-sitter
Glass • N/A
450QX2531 • **Value $15**

⑮ Bell Ringer Squirrel
Handcrafted/Glass • SEAL
1000QX4431 • **Value $39**

⑯ Betsey Clark Angel
Porcelain • N/A
900QX4624 • **Value $36**

⑰ Chickadee
Porcelain • SICK
600QX4514 • **Value $42**

Value Guide – Hallmark Keepsake Ornaments

(1) Child's Third Christmas
Satin • N/A
450QX2611 • **Value $25**

(2) Christmas Memories Photoholder
Fabric • N/A
650QX3004 • **Value $27**

(3) Christmas Owl
Handcrafted/Acrylic • SEAL
600QX4441 • **Value $32**

(4) A Christmas Prayer
Satin • N/A
450QX2461 • **Value $24**

(5) Classical Angel (LE-24,700)
Porcelain • DLEE
2750QX4591 • **Value $100**

(6) Cuckoo Clock
Handcrafted • DLEE
1000QX4551 • **Value $52**

(7) Currier & Ives
Glass • N/A
450QX2501 • **Value $26**

(8) Daughter
Glass • N/A
450QX2444 • **Value $37**

(9) DISNEY
Glass • N/A
450QX2504 • **Value $42**

(10) Embroidered Heart (re-issued from 1983)
Fabric • N/A
650QX4217 • **Value $26**

(11) Embroidered Stocking (re-issued from 1983)
Fabric • SICK
650QX4796 • **Value $23**

(12) Father
Acrylic • N/A
600QX2571 • **Value $19**

(13) First Christmas Together
Acrylic • N/A
600QX3421 • **Value $22**

(14) First Christmas Together
Brushed Brass • SEAL
1500QX4364 • **Value $36**

(15) First Christmas Together
Cameo • MCGE
750QX3404 • **Value $24**

(16) First Christmas Together
Classic Shape • MCGE
1600QX9044 • **Value $40**

(17) First Christmas Together
Glass • N/A
450QX2451 • **Value $28**

(18) Flights of Fantasy
Glass • N/A
450QX2564 • **Value $23**

(19) Fortune Cookie Elf
Handcrafted • SICK
450QX4524 • **Value $42**

(20) Friendship
Glass • N/A
450QX2481 • **Value $22**

General Keepsake

	Price Paid	Value of My Collection
1.		
2.		
3.		
4.		
5.		
6.		
7.		
8.		
9.		
10.		
11.		
12.		
13.		
14.		
15.		
16.		
17.		
18.		
19.		
20.		
PENCIL TOTALS		

1984

Value Guide — Hallmark Keepsake Ornaments

(1) Frisbee® Puppy *Handcrafted* • N/A 500QX4444 • **Value $56**	**(2)** From Our Home to Yours *Glass* • N/A 450QX2484 • **Value $48**	**(3)** The Fun of Friendship *Acrylic* • N/A 600QX3431 • **Value $36**	**(4)** A Gift of Friendship *Glass* • N/A 450QX2604 • **Value $24**
(5) Gift of Music *Handcrafted* • SEAL 1500QX4511 • **Value $100**	**(6)** Godchild *Glass* • N/A 450QX2421 • **Value $19**	**(7)** Grandchild's First Christmas *Handcrafted* • N/A 1100QX4601 • **Value $26**	**(8)** Grandchild's First Christmas *Satin* • N/A 450QX2574 • **Value $18**

GENERAL KEEPSAKE

	Price Paid	Value of My Collection
1.		
2.		
3.		
4.		
5.		
6.		
7.		
8.		
9.		
10.		
11.		
12.		
13.		
14.		
15.		
16.		
17.		
18.		
19.		
20.		
PENCIL TOTALS		

(9) Granddaughter *Glass* • N/A 450QX2431 • **Value $26**	**(10)** Grandmother *Glass* • N/A 450QX2441 • **Value $19**	**(11)** Grandparents *Glass* • N/A 450QX2561 • **Value $18**
(12) Grandson *Glass* • N/A 450QX2424 • **Value $27**	**(13)** Gratitude *Acrylic* • N/A 600QX3444 • **Value $14**	**(14)** Heartful of Love *Bone China* • N/A 1000QX4434 • **Value $46**
(15) Holiday Friendship *Panorama Ball* • N/A 1300QX4451 • **Value $32**	**(16)** Holiday Jester *Handcrafted* • SICK 1100QX4374 • **Value $35**	**(17)** Holiday Starburst *Glass* • N/A 500QX2534 • **Value $22**
(18) Katybeth *Porcelain* • N/A 900QX4631 • **Value $30**	**(19)** Kit *Handcrafted* • N/A 550QX4534 • **Value $30**	**(20)** Love *Glass* • N/A 450QX2554 • **Value $27**

(1) Love . . . the Spirit of Christmas *Glass* • N/A 450QX2474 • **Value $42**	**(2)** Madonna and Child *Acrylic* • PALM 600QX3441 • **Value $48**
(3) Marathon Santa *Handcrafted* • SEAL 800QX4564 • **Value $42**	**(4)** The Miracle of Love *Acrylic* • N/A 600QX3424 • **Value $34**

(5) Mother *Acrylic* • N/A 600QX3434 • **Value $18**	**(6)** Mother and Dad *Bone China* • N/A 650QX2581 • **Value $28**
(7) Mountain Climbing Santa (re-issued from 1983) *Handcrafted* • SEAL 650QX4077 • **Value $38**	**(8)** Muffin *Handcrafted* • DLEE 550QX4421 • **Value $32**

1984

(9) The MUPPETS™ *Glass* • N/A 450QX2514 • **Value $37**	**(10)** Musical Angel *Handcrafted* • DLEE 550QX4344 • **Value $74**	**(11)** Napping Mouse *Handcrafted* • N/A 550QX4351 • **Value $52**

GENERAL KEEPSAKE

	Price Paid	Value of My Collection
1.		
2.		
3.		
4.		
5.		
6.		
7.		
8.		
9.		
10.		
11.		
12.		
13.		
14.		
15.		
16.		
17.		
18.		
19.		
20.		
PENCIL TOTALS		

(12) Needlepoint Wreath *Fabric* • PIKE 650QX4594 • **Value $15**	**(13)** New Home *Glass* • N/A 450QX2454 • **Value $72**	**(14)** Norman Rockwell *Glass* • MCGE 450QX2511 • **Value $32**

(15) Nostalgic Sled (re-issued in 1985) *Handcrafted* • SICK 600QX4424 • **Value $28**	**(16)** Old Fashioned Rocking Horse *Acrylic/Brass* • N/A 750QX3464 • **Value $22**	**(17)** Peace on Earth *Cameo* • N/A 750QX3414 • **Value $30**

(18) PEANUTS® *Satin* • N/A 450QX2521 • **Value $38**	**(19)** Peppermint 1984 *Handcrafted* • DLEE 450QX4561 • **Value $54**	**(20)** Polar Bear Drummer *Handcrafted* • SEAL 450QX4301 • **Value $29**

(1) Raccoon's Christmas *Handcrafted* • SEAL 900QX4474 • **Value $55**	**(2)** Reindeer Racetrack *Glass* • N/A 450QX2544 • **Value $26**	**(3)** Roller Skating Rabbit (re-issued in 1985) *Handcrafted* • SEAL 500QX4571 • **Value $32**	**(4)** Santa *Fabric* • N/A 750QX4584 • **Value $21**

| **(5)** Santa Mouse *Handcrafted* • SIED 450QX4334 • **Value $52** | **(6)** Santa Star *Handcrafted* • N/A 550QX4504 • **Value $39** | **(7)** Santa Sulky Driver *Etched Brass* • N/A 900QX4361 • **Value $35** | **(8)** A Savior is Born *Glass* • N/A 450QX2541 • **Value $33** |

General Keepsake

	Price Paid	Value of My Collection
1.		
2.		
3.		
4.		
5.		
6.		
7.		
8.		
9.		
10.		
11.		
12.		
13.		
14.		
15.		
16.		
17.		
18.		
19.		
20.		
PENCIL TOTALS		

(9) Shirt Tales™ *Satin* • N/A 450QX2524 • **Value $21**

(10) Sister *Bone China* • N/A 650QX2594 • **Value $30**

(11) SNOOPY® and WOODSTOCK *Handcrafted* • SEAL 750QX4391 • **Value $94**

(12) Snowmobile Santa *Handcrafted* • N/A 650QX4314 • **Value $35**

(13) Snowshoe Penguin *Handcrafted* • SICK 650QX4531 • **Value $44**

(14) Snowy Seal (re-issued in 1985) *Handcrafted* • SEAL 400QX4501 • **Value $20**

(15) Son *Glass* • N/A 450QX2434 • **Value $32**

(16) Teacher *Glass* • N/A 450QX2491 • **Value $15**

(17) Ten Years Together *Bone China* • N/A 650QX2584 • **Value $16**

(18) Three Kittens in a Mitten (re-issued in 1985) *Handcrafted* • DLEE 800QX4311 • **Value $52**

(19) Twelve Days of Christmas *Handcrafted* • SEAL 1500QX4159 • **Value $115**

(20) Twenty-Five Years Together *Bone China* • N/A 650QX2591 • **Value $22**

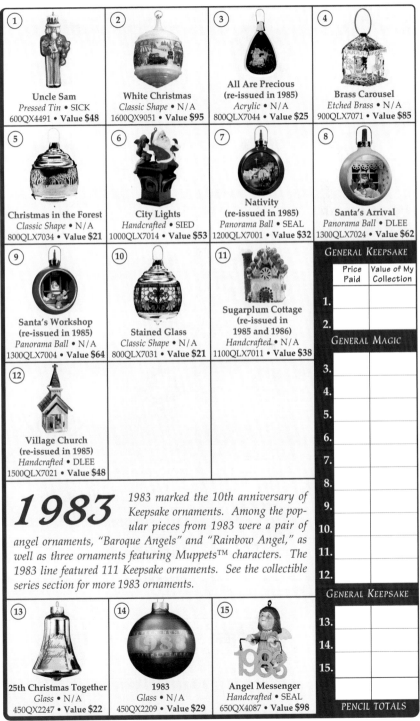

1983

#	Name	Material/Artist	Number • Value
1	**Uncle Sam**	*Pressed Tin* • SICK	600QX4491 • **Value $48**
2	**White Christmas**	*Classic Shape* • N/A	1600QX9051 • **Value $95**
3	**All Are Precious** (re-issued in 1985)	*Acrylic* • N/A	800QLX7044 • **Value $25**
4	**Brass Carousel**	*Etched Brass* • N/A	900QLX7071 • **Value $85**
5	**Christmas in the Forest**	*Classic Shape* • N/A	800QLX7034 • **Value $21**
6	**City Lights**	*Handcrafted* • SIED	1000QLX7014 • **Value $53**
7	**Nativity** (re-issued in 1985)	*Panorama Ball* • SEAL	1200QLX7001 • **Value $32**
8	**Santa's Arrival**	*Panorama Ball* • DLEE	1300QLX7024 • **Value $62**
9	**Santa's Workshop** (re-issued in 1985)	*Panorama Ball* • N/A	1300QLX7004 • **Value $64**
10	**Stained Glass**	*Classic Shape* • N/A	800QLX7031 • **Value $21**
11	**Sugarplum Cottage** (re-issued in 1985 and 1986)	*Handcrafted* • N/A	1100QLX7011 • **Value $38**
12	**Village Church** (re-issued in 1985)	*Handcrafted* • DLEE	1500QLX7021 • **Value $48**

GENERAL KEEPSAKE

	Price Paid	Value of My Collection
1.		
2.		

GENERAL MAGIC

3.		
4.		
5.		
6.		
7.		
8.		
9.		
10.		
11.		
12.		

1983 1983 marked the 10th anniversary of Keepsake ornaments. Among the popular pieces from 1983 were a pair of angel ornaments, "Baroque Angels" and "Rainbow Angel," as well as three ornaments featuring Muppets™ characters. The 1983 line featured 111 Keepsake ornaments. See the collectible series section for more 1983 ornaments.

GENERAL KEEPSAKE

13.		
14.		
15.		

#	Name	Material/Artist	Number • Value
13	**25th Christmas Together**	*Glass* • N/A	450QX2247 • **Value $22**
14	**1983**	*Glass* • N/A	450QX2209 • **Value $29**
15	**Angel Messenger**	*Handcrafted* • SEAL	650QX4087 • **Value $98**

PENCIL TOTALS

(1) **Angels** *Glass* • N/A 500QX2197 • **Value $26**	**(2)** **The Annunciation** *Glass* • N/A 450QX2167 • **Value $30**	**(3)** **Baby's First Christmas** *Acrylic* • N/A 700QX3029 • **Value $23**	**(4)** **Baby's First Christmas** *Cameo* • SICK 750QX3019 • **Value $18**
(5) **Baby's First Christmas** *Handcrafted* • DLEE 1400QX4027 • **Value $38**	**(6)** **Baby's First Christmas – Boy** *Satin* • N/A 450QX2009 • **Value $26**	**(7)** **Baby's First Christmas – Girl** *Satin* • N/A 450QX2007 • **Value $28**	**(8)** **Baby's Second Christmas** *Satin* • N/A 450QX2267 • **Value $35**

GENERAL KEEPSAKE

	Price Paid	Value of My Collection
1.		
2.		
3.		
4.		
5.		
6.		
7.		
8.		
9.		
10.		
11.		
12.		
13.		
14.		
15.		
16.		
17.		
18.		
19.		
20.		
PENCIL TOTALS		

(9) **Baroque Angels** *Handcrafted* • DLEE 1300QX4229 • **Value $125**	**(10)** **Bell Wreath** *Brass* • SICK 650QX4209 • **Value $33**	**(11)** **Betsey Clark** *Handcrafted* • SEAL 650QX4047 • **Value $33**
(12) **Betsey Clark** *Porcelain* • N/A 900QX4401 • **Value $35**	**(13)** **Brass Santa** *Brass* • SEAL 900QX4239 • **Value $25**	**(14)** **Caroling Owl** *Handcrafted* • SEAL 450QX4117 • **Value $41**
(15) **Child's Third Christmas** *Satin Piqué* • N/A 450QX2269 • **Value $27**	**(16)** **Christmas Joy** *Satin* • N/A 450QX2169 • **Value $32**	**(17)** **Christmas Kitten** (re-issued from 1982) *Handcrafted* • N/A 400QX4543 • **Value $38**
(18) **Christmas Koala** *Handcrafted* • SEAL 400QX4199 • **Value $34**	**(19)** **Christmas Stocking** *Acrylic* • N/A 600QX3039 • **Value $42**	**(20)** **Christmas Wonderland** *Glass* • N/A 450QX2219 • **Value $122**

1983

(1) **Currier & Ives** *Glass* • N/A 450QX2159 • **Value $25**	**(2)** **Cycling Santa** **(re-issued from 1982)** *Handcrafted* • N/A 2000QX4355 • **Value $155**
(3) **Daughter** *Glass* • N/A 450QX2037 • **Value $43**	**(4)** **DISNEY** *Glass* • N/A 450QX2129 • **Value $52**

(5) **Embroidered Heart** **(re-issued in 1984)** *Fabric* • N/A 650QX4217 • **Value $26**

(6) **Embroidered Stocking** **(re-issued in 1984)** *Fabric* • SICK 650QX4796 • **Value $23**

(7) **Enameled Christmas Wreath** *Enameled* • N/A 900QX3119 • **Value $15**

(8) **First Christmas Together** *Acrylic* • N/A 600QX3069 • **Value $24**

(9) **First Christmas Together** *Cameo* • N/A 750QX3017 • **Value $23**

(10) **First Christmas Together** *Classic Shape* • N/A 600QX3107 • **Value $37**

(11) **First Christmas Together** *Glass* • SICK 450QX2089 • **Value $29**

(12) **First Christmas Together – Brass Locket** *Brass* • SEAL 1500QX4329 • **Value $35**

(13) **Friendship** *Acrylic* • N/A 600QX3059 • **Value $21**

(14) **Friendship** *Glass* • N/A 450QX2077 • **Value $22**

(15) **Godchild** *Glass* • N/A 450QX2017 • **Value $18**

(16) **Grandchild's First Christmas** *Classic Shape* • N/A 600QX3129 • **Value $24**

(17) **Grandchild's First Christmas** *Handcrafted* • N/A 1400QX4309 • **Value $37**

(18) **Granddaughter** *Glass* • N/A 450QX2027 • **Value $30**

(19) **Grandmother** *Glass* • N/A 450QX2057 • **Value $22**

(20) **Grandparents** *Ceramic* • N/A 650QX4299 • **Value $22**

GENERAL KEEPSAKE		
	Price Paid	Value of My Collection
1.		
2.		
3.		
4.		
5.		
6.		
7.		
8.		
9.		
10.		
11.		
12.		
13.		
14.		
15.		
16.		
17.		
18.		
19.		
20.		
PENCIL TOTALS		

(1) Grandson
Satin • N/A
450QX2019 • **Value $30**

(2) Heart
Acrylic • SICK
400QX3079 • **Value $52**

(3) Here Comes Santa
Glass • N/A
450QX2177 • **Value $42**

(4) Hitchhiking Santa
Handcrafted • SEAL
800QX4247 • **Value $42**

(5) Holiday Puppy
Handcrafted • N/A
350QX4127 • **Value $29**

(6) Jack Frost
Handcrafted • N/A
900QX4079 • **Value $62**

(7) Jolly Santa
Handcrafted • N/A
350QX4259 • **Value $36**

(8) KERMIT the FROG™
(re-issued from 1982)
Handcrafted • DLEE
1100QX4956 • **Value $108**

(9) Love
Acrylic • N/A
600QX3057 • **Value $20**

(10) Love
Classic Shape • N/A
600QX3109 • **Value $37**

(11) Love
Glass • N/A
450QX2079 • **Value $50**

(12) Love
Porcelain • SICK
1300QX4227 • **Value $37**

(13) Love Is a Song
Glass • N/A
450QX2239 • **Value $32**

(14) Madonna and Child
Porcelain • N/A
1200QX4287 • **Value $44**

(15) Mailbox Kitten
Handcrafted • N/A
650QX4157 • **Value $63**

(16) Mary Hamilton
Glass • N/A
450QX2137 • **Value $43**

(17) Memories to Treasure
Acrylic • N/A
700QX3037 • **Value $30**

(18) MISS PIGGY™
Handcrafted • N/A
1300QX4057 • **Value $220**

(19) Mom and Dad
Ceramic • PIKE
650QX4297 • **Value $25**

(20) Mother
Acrylic • N/A
600QX3067 • **Value $21**

GENERAL KEEPSAKE		
	Price Paid	Value of My Collection
1.		
2.		
3.		
4.		
5.		
6.		
7.		
8.		
9.		
10.		
11.		
12.		
13.		
14.		
15.		
16.		
17.		
18.		
19.		
20.		
PENCIL TOTALS		

1.
Mother and Child
Cameo • N/A
750QX3027 • **Value $40**

2.
Mountain Climbing Santa
(re-issued in 1984)
Handcrafted • SEAL
650QX4077 • **Value $38**

3.
Mouse in Bell
Handcrafted/Glass • N/A
1000QX4197 • **Value $64**

4.
Mouse on Cheese
Handcrafted • SICK
650QX4137 • **Value $50**

5.
The MUPPETS™
Satin • N/A
450QX2147 • **Value $50**

6.
New Home
Satin • N/A
450QX2107 • **Value $35**

7.
Norman Rockwell
Glass • N/A
450QX2157 • **Value $55**

8.
An Old Fashioned Christmas
Glass • N/A
450QX2179 • **Value $32**

9.
Old-Fashioned Santa
Handcrafted • SICK
1100QX4099 • **Value $69**

10.
Oriental Butterflies
Glass • N/A
450QX2187 • **Value $32**

11.
PEANUTS®
Satin • N/A
450QX2127 • **Value $37**

12.
Peppermint Penguin
Handcrafted • N/A
650QX4089 • **Value $45**

13.
Porcelain Doll, Diana
Porcelain/Fabric • DLEE
900QX4237 • **Value $33**

14.
Rainbow Angel
Handcrafted • DLEE
550QX4167 • **Value $105**

15.
Santa
Acrylic • N/A
400QX3087 • **Value $35**

16.
Santa's Many Faces
Classic Shape • N/A
600QX3117 • **Value $33**

17.
Santa's on His Way
Handcrafted • N/A
1000QX4269 • **Value $38**

18.
Santa's Workshop
(re-issued from 1982)
Handcrafted • DLEE
1000QX4503 • **Value $85**

19.
Scrimshaw Reindeer
Handcrafted • SEAL
800QX4249 • **Value $35**

20.
Season's Greetings
Glass • N/A
450QX2199 • **Value $25**

1983

GENERAL KEEPSAKE		
	Price Paid	Value of My Collection
1.		
2.		
3.		
4.		
5.		
6.		
7.		
8.		
9.		
10.		
11.		
12.		
13.		
14.		
15.		
16.		
17.		
18.		
19.		
20.		
PENCIL TOTALS		

VALUE GUIDE — HALLMARK KEEPSAKE ORNAMENTS

(1) **SHIRT TALES™** *Glass* • N/A 450QX2149 • **Value $27**	**(2)** **Sister** *Glass* • N/A 450QX2069 • **Value $25**	**(3)** **Skating Rabbit** *Handcrafted* • N/A 800QX4097 • **Value $55**	**(4)** **Ski Lift Santa** *Handcrafted/Brass* • N/A 800QX4187 • **Value $73**
(5) **Skiing Fox** *Handcrafted* • DLEE 800QX4207 • **Value $40**	**(6)** **Sneaker Mouse** *Handcrafted* • SEAL 450QX4009 • **Value $42**	**(7)** **Son** *Satin* • N/A 450QX2029 • **Value $40**	**(8)** **Star of Peace** *Acrylic* • SEAL 600QX3047 • **Value $20**

GENERAL KEEPSAKE

	Price Paid	Value of My Collection
1.		
2.		
3.		
4.		
5.		
6.		
7.		
8.		
9.		
10.		
11.		
12.		
13.		
14.		
15.		

MUSICAL ORNAMENTS

16.		
17.		
18.		
19.		

PENCIL TOTALS

(9) **Teacher** *Acrylic* • N/A 600QX3049 • **Value $15**	**(10)** **Teacher** *Glass* • N/A 450QX2249 • **Value $16**	**(11)** **Tenth Christmas Together** *Ceramic* • N/A 650QX4307 • **Value $27**
(12) **Time for Sharing** *Acrylic* • N/A 600QX3077 • **Value $38**	**(13)** **Tin Rocking Horse** *Pressed Tin* • SICK 650QX4149 • **Value $53**	**(14)** **Unicorn** *Porcelain* • N/A 1000QX4267 • **Value $66**
(15) **The Wise Men** *Glass* • N/A 450QX2207 • **Value $55**	**(16)** **Baby's First Christmas** *Classic Shape* • N/A 1600QMB9039 • **Value $87**	**(17)** **Friendship** *Classic Shape* • N/A 1600QMB9047 • **Value $115**
(18) **Nativity** *Classic Shape* • N/A 1600QMB9049 • **Value $125**	**(19)** **Twelve Days of Christmas** *Handcrafted* • SEAL 1500QMB4159 • **Value $100**	

1982

The 1982 collection was highlighted by the always-popular creations of Hallmark artist, Donna Lee. Among her sought-after 1982 designs were "Baroque Angel," "Pinecone Home" and "Raccoon Surprises." Overall, there were 104 Keepsake ornaments issued in 1982. See the collectible series section for more 1982 ornaments.

(1) 25th Christmas Together
Glass • N/A
450QX2116 • **Value $21**

(2) 50th Christmas Together
Glass • N/A
450QX2123 • **Value $21**

(3) Angel
Acrylic • N/A
550QX3096 • **Value $34**

(4) Angel Chimes
Chrome-Plated Brass • N/A
550QX5026 • **Value $37**

(5) Arctic Penguin
Acrylic • N/A
400QX3003 • **Value $22**

(6) Baby's First Christmas
Acrylic • SEAL
550QX3023 • **Value $38**

(7) Baby's First Christmas
Handcrafted • SEAL
1300QX4553 • **Value $48**

(8) Baby's First Christmas – Boy
Satin • N/A
450QX2163 • **Value $26**

(9) Baby's First Christmas – Girl
Satin • N/A
450QX2073 • **Value $26**

(10) Baby's First Christmas – Photoholder
Acrylic • N/A
650QX3126 • **Value $28**

(11) Baroque Angel
Handcrafted/Brass • DLEE
1500QX4566 • **Value $170**

(12) Bell Chimes
Chrome-Plated Brass • SICK
550QX4943 • **Value $29**

(13) Betsey Clark
Cameo • N/A
850QX3056 • **Value $28**

(14) Brass Bell
Brass • DLEE
1200QX4606 • **Value $28**

(15) Christmas Angel
Glass • N/A
450QX2206 • **Value $27**

(16) Christmas Fantasy (re-issued from 1981)
Handcrafted/Brass • N/A
1300QX1554 • **Value $85**

(17) Christmas Kitten (re-issued in 1983)
Handcrafted • N/A
400QX4543 • **Value $38**

GENERAL KEEPSAKE

	Price Paid	Value of My Collection
1.		
2.		
3.		
4.		
5.		
6.		
7.		
8.		
9.		
10.		
11.		
12.		
13.		
14.		
15.		
16.		
17.		
PENCIL TOTALS		

1982

(1) Christmas Magic *Acrylic* • N/A 550QX3113 • **Value $30**	**(2)** Christmas Memories – Photoholder *Acrylic* • SICK 650QX3116 • **Value $24**

(3) Christmas Owl
(re-issued from 1980)
Handcrafted • N/A
400QX1314 • **Value $48**

(4) Christmas Sleigh
Acrylic • N/A
550QX3093 • **Value $72**

(5) Cloisonné Angel
Cloisonné • N/A
1200QX1454 • **Value $95**

(6) Cookie Mouse
Handcrafted • SICK
450QX4546 • **Value $60**

(7) Cowboy Snowman
Handcrafted • N/A
800QX4806 • **Value $56**

(8) Currier & Ives
Glass • N/A
450QX2013 • **Value $23**

(9) Cycling Santa
(re-issued in 1983)
Handcrafted • N/A
2000QX4355 • **Value $155**

(10) Daughter
Satin • N/A
450QX2046 • **Value $33**

(11) DISNEY
Satin • N/A
450QX2173 • **Value $34**

(12) THE DIVINE
MISS PIGGY™
(re-issued from 1981)
Handcrafted • FRAN
1200QX4255 • **Value $92**

(13) Dove Love
Acrylic • SICK
450QX4623 • **Value $49**

(14) Elfin Artist
Handcrafted • SICK
900QX4573 • **Value $50**

(15) Embroidered Tree
Fabric • N/A
650QX4946 • **Value $38**

(16) Father
Satin • SICK
450QX2056 • **Value $21**

(17) First Christmas
Together
Acrylic • SEAL
550QX3026 • **Value $20**

(18) First Christmas
Together
Cameo • N/A
850QX3066 • **Value $45**

(19) First Christmas
Together
Glass • N/A
450QX2113 • **Value $36**

(20) First Christmas
Together – Locket
Brass • SEAL
1500QX4563 • **Value $26**

GENERAL KEEPSAKE

	Price Paid	Value of My Collection
1.		
2.		
3.		
4.		
5.		
6.		
7.		
8.		
9.		
10.		
11.		
12.		
13.		
14.		
15.		
16.		
17.		
18.		
19.		
20.		
PENCIL TOTALS		

(1) **Friendship** *Acrylic* • N/A 550QX3046 • **Value $24**	**(2)** **Friendship** *Satin* • N/A 450QX2086 • **Value $21**	**(3)** **Godchild** *Glass* • N/A 450QX2226 • **Value $23**	**(4)** **Granddaughter** *Glass* • N/A 450QX2243 • **Value $26**
(5) **Grandfather** *Satin* • N/A 450QX2076 • **Value $20**	**(6)** **Grandmother** *Satin* • N/A 450QX2003 • **Value $19**	**(7)** **Grandparents** *Glass* • N/A 450QX2146 • **Value $18**	**(8)** **Grandson** *Satin* • N/A 450QX2246 • **Value $27**

1982

(9) **Ice Sculptor** **(re-issued from 1981)** *Handcrafted* • DLEE 800QX4322 • **Value $96**	**(10)** **Jingling Teddy** *Brass* • SEAL 400QX4776 • **Value $40**	**(11)** **Joan Walsh Anglund** *Satin* • N/A 450QX2193 • **Value $22**	**GENERAL KEEPSAKE**

			Price Paid	Value of My Collection
(12) **Jogging Santa** *Handcrafted* • N/A 800QX4576 • **Value $48**	**(13)** **Jolly Christmas Tree** *Handcrafted* • N/A 650QX4653 • **Value $83**	**(14)** **KERMIT the FROG™** **(re-issued in 1983)** *Handcrafted* • DLEE 1100QX4956 • **Value $108**	1. 2. 3. 4. 5. 6. 7. 8. 9. 10.	
(15) **Love** *Acrylic* • N/A 550QX3043 • **Value $30**	**(16)** **Love** *Satin* • N/A 450QX2096 • **Value $18**	**(17)** **Mary Hamilton** *Satin* • N/A 450QX2176 • **Value $26**	11. 12. 13. 14. 15. 16.	
(18) **Merry Christmas** *Glass* • N/A 450QX2256 • **Value $23**	**(19)** **Merry Moose** *Handcrafted* • N/A 550QX4155 • **Value $58**	**(20)** **MISS PIGGY™ and KERMIT™** *Satin* • N/A 450QX2183 • **Value $42**	17. 18. 19. 20.	
			PENCIL TOTALS	

(1) **Moments of Love** *Satin* • N/A 450QX2093 • **Value $19**	**(2)** **Mother** *Glass* • N/A 450QX2053 • **Value $20**	**(3)** **Mother and Dad** *Glass* • N/A 450QX2223 • **Value $17**	**(4)** **MUPPETS™ Party** *Satin* • N/A 450QX2186 • **Value $42**
(5) **Musical Angel** *Handcrafted* • DLEE 550QX4596 • **Value $130**	**(6)** **Nativity** *Acrylic* • N/A 450QX3083 • **Value $48**	**(7)** **New Home** *Satin* • N/A 450QX2126 • **Value $23**	**(8)** **Norman Rockwell** *Satin* • N/A 450QX2023 • **Value $28**

GENERAL KEEPSAKE

	Price Paid	Value of My Collection
1.		
2.		
3.		
4.		
5.		
6.		
7.		
8.		
9.		
10.		
11.		
12.		
13.		
14.		
15.		
16.		
17.		
18.		
19.		
20.		
PENCIL TOTALS		

(9) **Old Fashioned Christmas** *Glass* • N/A 450QX2276 • **Value $45**	**(10)** **Old World Angels** *Glass* • N/A 450QX2263 • **Value $26**	**(11)** **Patterns of Christmas** *Glass* • N/A 450QX2266 • **Value $22**
(12) **PEANUTS®** *Satin* • N/A 450QX2006 • **Value $38**	**(13)** **Peeking Elf** *Handcrafted* • N/A 650QX4195 • **Value $36**	**(14)** **Perky Penguin** **(re-issued from 1981)** *Handcrafted* • N/A 400QX4095 • **Value $58**
(15) **Pinecone Home** *Handcrafted* • DLEE 800QX4613 • **Value $170**	**(16)** **Raccoon Surprises** *Handcrafted* • DLEE 900QX4793 • **Value $155**	**(17)** **Santa** *Glass* • BLAC 450QX2216 • **Value $22**
(18) **Santa and Reindeer** *Handcrafted/Brass* • SICK 900QX4676 • **Value $52**	**(19)** **Santa Bell** *Porcelain* • N/A 1500QX1487 • **Value $60**	**(20)** **Santa's Flight** *Acrylic* • N/A 450QX3086 • **Value $45**

1
Santa's Sleigh
Brass • SEAL
900QX4786 • **Value $32**

2
Santa's Workshop
(re-issued in 1983)
Handcrafted • DLEE
1000QX4503 • **Value $85**

3
Season for Caring
Satin • N/A
450QX2213 • **Value $24**

4
Sister
Glass • N/A
450QX2083 • **Value $30**

5
Snowy Seal
Acrylic • N/A
400QX3006 • **Value $22**

6
Son
Satin • N/A
450QX2043 • **Value $30**

7
The Spirit of Christmas
Handcrafted • SICK
1000QX4526 • **Value $132**

8
Stained Glass
Glass • N/A
450QX2283 • **Value $24**

9
Teacher
Acrylic • SICK
650QX3123 • **Value $18**

10
Teacher
Glass • N/A
450QX2143 • **Value $14**

11
Teacher – Apple
Acrylic • SEAL
550QX3016 • **Value $15**

12
Three Kings
Cameo • BLAC
850QX3073 • **Value $26**

13
Tin Soldier
Pressed Tin • SICK
650QX4836 • **Value $48**

14
Tree Chimes
Stamped Brass • SEAL
550QX4846 • **Value $42**

15
Twelve Days
of Christmas
Glass • N/A
450QX2036 • **Value $28**

16
Dimensional Ornament
Dimensional Brass • N/A
($3.50) No stock # • **Value $42**

17
Baby's First Christmas
Classic Shape • N/A
1600QMB9007 • **Value $85**

18
First Christmas
Together
Classic Shape • N/A
1600QMB9019 • **Value $82**

19
Love
Classic Shape • N/A
1600QMB9009 • **Value $85**

1982

GENERAL KEEPSAKE		
	Price Paid	Value of My Collection
1.		
2.		
3.		
4.		
5.		
6.		
7.		
8.		
9.		
10.		
11.		
12.		
13.		
14.		
15.		
EARLY PROMOTIONAL ORNAMENTS		
16.		
MUSICAL ORNAMENTS		
17.		
18.		
19.		
PENCIL TOTALS		

1981

Santa Claus was well-represented in Hallmark's collection for 1981 with several coveted designs, including the handcrafted ornaments "Sailing Santa" and "Space Santa," as well as the ball ornament "Traditional (Black Santa)." The 1981 line featured 99 Keepsake ornaments. See the collectible series section for more 1981 ornaments.

① 25th Christmas Together
Acrylic • N/A
550QX5042 • **Value $23**

② 25th Christmas Together
Glass • N/A
450QX7075 • **Value $23**

③ 50th Christmas
Glass • N/A
450QX7082 • **Value $18**

④ Angel
Acrylic • N/A
400QX5095 • **Value $65**

⑤ Angel
Acrylic • N/A
450QX5075 • **Value $27**

GENERAL KEEPSAKE

	Price Paid	Value of My Collection
1.		
2.		
3.		
4.		
5.		
6.		
7.		
8.		
9.		
10.		
11.		
12.		
13.		
14.		
15.		
16.		
17.		
PENCIL TOTALS		

⑥ Angel
(re-issued from 1980)
Yarn • N/A
300QX1621 • **Value $11**

⑦ Baby's First Christmas
Acrylic • N/A
550QX5162 • **Value $33**

⑧ Baby's First Christmas
Cameo • N/A
850QX5135 • **Value $20**

⑨ Baby's First Christmas
Handcrafted • N/A
1300QX4402 • **Value $53**

⑩ Baby's First Christmas – Black
Satin • N/A
450QX6022 • **Value $27**

⑪ Baby's First Christmas – Boy
Satin • N/A
450QX6015 • **Value $25**

⑫ Baby's First Christmas – Girl
Satin • N/A
450QX6002 • **Value $25**

⑬ Betsey Clark
Cameo • N/A
850QX5122 • **Value $30**

⑭ Betsey Clark
Handcrafted • FRAN
900QX4235 • **Value $76**

⑮ Calico Kitty
Fabric • N/A
300QX4035 • **Value $20**

⑯ Candyville Express
Handcrafted • N/A
750QX4182 • **Value $105**

⑰ Cardinal Cutie
Fabric • N/A
300QX4002 • **Value $23**

(1) Checking It Twice
(re-issued from 1980)
Handcrafted • BLAC
2250QX1584 • **Value $195**

(2) Christmas 1981 –
Schneeberg
Satin • N/A
450QX8095 • **Value $27**

(3) Christmas Dreams
Handcrafted • DLEE
1200QX4375 • **Value $215**

(4) Christmas Fantasy
(re-issued in 1982)
Handcrafted • N/A
1300QX1554 • **Value $85**

(5) Christmas in the Forest
Glass • N/A
450QX8135 • **Value $140**

(6) Christmas Magic
Satin • N/A
450QX8102 • **Value $27**

(7) Christmas Star
Acrylic • N/A
550QX5015 • **Value $28**

(8) Christmas Teddy
Plush • N/A
550QX4042 • **Value $23**

(9) Clothespin
Drummer Boy
Handcrafted • N/A
450QX4082 • **Value $47**

(10) Daughter
Satin • N/A
450QX6075 • **Value $39**

(11) DISNEY
Satin • N/A
450QX8055 • **Value $32**

(12) THE DIVINE MISS
PIGGY™
(re-issued in 1982)
Handcrafted • FRAN
1200QX4255 • **Value $92**

(13) Dough Angel
(re-issued from 1978)
Handcrafted • DLEE
550QX1396 • **Value $90**

(14) Drummer Boy
Wood • N/A
250QX1481 • **Value $47**

(15) Father
Satin • N/A
450QX6095 • **Value $19**

(16) First Christmas Together
Acrylic • N/A
550QX5055 • **Value $24**

(17) First Christmas Together
Glass • N/A
450QX7062 • **Value $26**

(18) The Friendly Fiddler
Handcrafted • DLEE
800QX4342 • **Value $78**

(19) Friendship
Acrylic • N/A
550QX5035 • **Value $33**

(20) Friendship
Satin • N/A
450QX7042 • **Value $28**

	GENERAL KEEPSAKE	
	Price Paid	Value of My Collection
1.		
2.		
3.		
4.		
5.		
6.		
7.		
8.		
9.		
10.		
11.		
12.		
13.		
14.		
15.		
16.		
17.		
18.		
19.		
20.		
	PENCIL TOTALS	

1981

(1) **The Gift of Love** *Glass* • N/A 450QX7055 • **Value $27**	**(2)** **Gingham Dog** *Fabric* • N/A 300QX4022 • **Value $22**	**(3)** **Godchild** *Satin* • N/A 450QX6035 • **Value $23**	**(4)** **Granddaughter** *Satin* • N/A 450QX6055 • **Value $25**
(5) **Grandfather** *Glass* • N/A 450QX7015 • **Value $22**	**(6)** **Grandmother** *Satin* • N/A 450QX7022 • **Value $22**	**(7)** **Grandparents** *Glass* • N/A 450QX7035 • **Value $20**	**(8)** **Grandson** *Satin* • N/A 450QX6042 • **Value $25**

GENERAL KEEPSAKE

	Price Paid	Value of My Collection
1.		
2.		
3.		
4.		
5.		
6.		
7.		
8.		
9.		
10.		
11.		
12.		
13.		
14.		
15.		
16.		
17.		
18.		
19.		
20.		
PENCIL TOTALS		

(9) **A Heavenly Nap** **(re-issued from 1980)** *Handcrafted* • DLEE 650QX1394 • **Value $48**	**(10)** **Home** *Satin* • N/A 450QX7095 • **Value $21**	**(11)** **Ice Fairy** *Handcrafted* • DLEE 650QX4315 • **Value $110**
(12) **The Ice Sculptor** **(re-issued in 1982)** *Handcrafted* • DLEE 800QX4322 • **Value $96**	**(13)** **Joan Walsh Anglund** *Satin* • N/A 450QX8042 • **Value $26**	**(14)** **Jolly Snowman** *Handcrafted* • N/A 350QX4075 • **Value $59**
(15) **KERMIT the FROG™** *Handcrafted* • FRAN 900QX4242 • **Value $100**	**(16)** **Let Us Adore Him** *Glass* • N/A 450QX8115 • **Value $62**	**(17)** **Love** *Acrylic* • N/A 550QX5022 • **Value $50**
(18) **Love and Joy** **(Porcelain Chimes)** *Porcelain* • N/A 900QX4252 • **Value $98**	**(19)** **Marty Links™** *Satin* • N/A 450QX8082 • **Value $23**	**(20)** **Mary Hamilton** *Glass* • N/A 450QX8062 • **Value $20**

VALUE GUIDE — HALLMARK KEEPSAKE ORNAMENTS

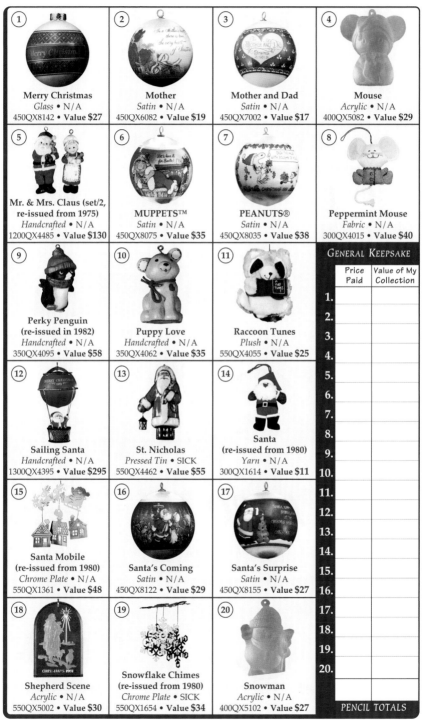

(1) Merry Christmas
Glass • N/A
450QX8142 • **Value $27**

(2) Mother
Satin • N/A
450QX6082 • **Value $19**

(3) Mother and Dad
Satin • N/A
450QX7002 • **Value $17**

(4) Mouse
Acrylic • N/A
400QX5082 • **Value $29**

(5) Mr. & Mrs. Claus (set/2, re-issued from 1975)
Handcrafted • N/A
1200QX4485 • **Value $130**

(6) MUPPETS™
Satin • N/A
450QX8075 • **Value $35**

(7) PEANUTS®
Satin • N/A
450QX8035 • **Value $38**

(8) Peppermint Mouse
Fabric • N/A
300QX4015 • **Value $40**

(9) Perky Penguin (re-issued in 1982)
Handcrafted • N/A
350QX4095 • **Value $58**

(10) Puppy Love
Handcrafted • N/A
350QX4062 • **Value $35**

(11) Raccoon Tunes
Plush • N/A
550QX4055 • **Value $25**

(12) Sailing Santa
Handcrafted • N/A
1300QX4395 • **Value $295**

(13) St. Nicholas
Pressed Tin • SICK
550QX4462 • **Value $55**

(14) Santa (re-issued from 1980)
Yarn • N/A
300QX1614 • **Value $11**

(15) Santa Mobile (re-issued from 1980)
Chrome Plate • N/A
550QX1361 • **Value $48**

(16) Santa's Coming
Satin • N/A
450QX8122 • **Value $29**

(17) Santa's Surprise
Satin • N/A
450QX8155 • **Value $27**

(18) Shepherd Scene
Acrylic • N/A
550QX5002 • **Value $30**

(19) Snowflake Chimes (re-issued from 1980)
Chrome Plate • SICK
550QX1654 • **Value $34**

(20) Snowman
Acrylic • N/A
400QX5102 • **Value $27**

GENERAL KEEPSAKE

	Price Paid	Value of My Collection
1.		
2.		
3.		
4.		
5.		
6.		
7.		
8.		
9.		
10.		
11.		
12.		
13.		
14.		
15.		
16.		
17.		
18.		
19.		
20.		
	PENCIL TOTALS	

1981

1 Snowman
(re-issued from 1980)
Yarn • N/A
300QX1634 • **Value $10**

2 Snowman Chimes
Chrome Plate • N/A
550QX4455 • **Value $32**

3 Soldier
(re-issued from 1980)
Yarn • N/A
300QX1641 • **Value $10**

4 Son
Satin • N/A
450QX6062 • **Value $29**

5 Space Santa
Handcrafted • N/A
650QX4302 • **Value $115**

6 Star Swing
Handcrafted/Brass • SICK
550QX4215 • **Value $37**

7 The Stocking Mouse
Handcrafted • N/A
450QX4122 • **Value $90**

8 Teacher
Satin • N/A
450QX8002 • **Value $14**

9 Topsy-Turvy Tunes
Handcrafted • DLEE
750QX4295 • **Value $75**

10 Traditional (Black Santa)
Satin • N/A
450QX8015 • **Value $95**

11 Tree Photoholder
Acrylic • N/A
550QX5155 • **Value $30**

12 Unicorn
Cameo • N/A
850QX5165 • **Value $25**

13 A Well-Stocked
Stocking
Handcrafted • N/A
900QX1547 • **Value $75**

GENERAL KEEPSAKE

	Price Paid	Value of My Collection
1.		
2.		
3.		
4.		
5.		
6.		
7.		
8.		
9.		
10.		
11.		
12.		
13.		

GENERAL KEEPSAKE

14.		
15.		
16.		

PENCIL TOTALS

1980 Teddy bear lovers have always been able to find great Hallmark bear ornaments and in 1980 Hallmark offered up two special treats in "Caroling Bear" and "Christmas Teddy." In the collection for 1980 there were a total of 85 Keepsake ornaments. See the collectible series section for more 1980 ornaments.

14 25th Christmas Together
Glass • N/A
400QX2061 • **Value $22**

15 Angel
(re-issued in 1981)
Yarn • N/A
300QX1621 • **Value $11**

16 Angel Music
(re-issued from 1979)
Fabric • N/A
200QX3439 • **Value $23**

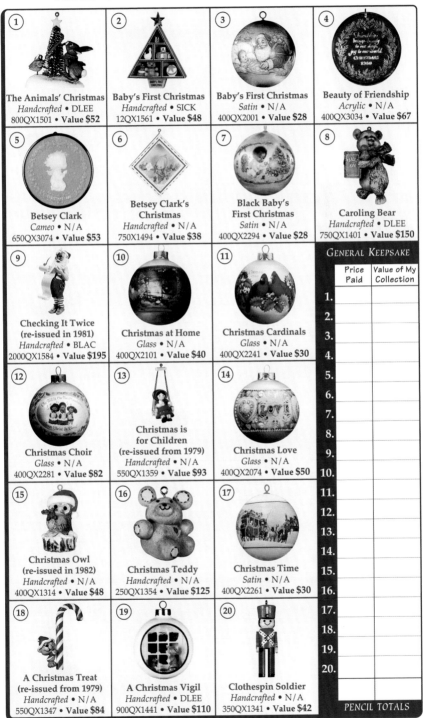

1

The Animals' Christmas
Handcrafted • DLEE
800QX1501 • **Value $52**

2

Baby's First Christmas
Handcrafted • SICK
12QX1561 • **Value $48**

3

Baby's First Christmas
Satin • N/A
400QX2001 • **Value $28**

4

Beauty of Friendship
Acrylic • N/A
400QX3034 • **Value $67**

5

Betsey Clark
Cameo • N/A
650QX3074 • **Value $53**

6

Betsey Clark's Christmas
Handcrafted • N/A
750X1494 • **Value $38**

7

Black Baby's First Christmas
Satin • N/A
400QX2294 • **Value $28**

8

Caroling Bear
Handcrafted • DLEE
750QX1401 • **Value $150**

1980

9

Checking It Twice
(re-issued in 1981)
Handcrafted • BLAC
2000QX1584 • **Value $195**

10

Christmas at Home
Glass • N/A
400QX2101 • **Value $40**

11

Christmas Cardinals
Glass • N/A
400QX2241 • **Value $30**

12

Christmas Choir
Glass • N/A
400QX2281 • **Value $82**

13

Christmas is for Children
(re-issued from 1979)
Handcrafted • N/A
550QX1359 • **Value $93**

14

Christmas Love
Glass • N/A
400QX2074 • **Value $50**

15

Christmas Owl
(re-issued in 1982)
Handcrafted • N/A
400QX1314 • **Value $48**

16

Christmas Teddy
Handcrafted • N/A
250QX1354 • **Value $125**

17

Christmas Time
Satin • N/A
400QX2261 • **Value $30**

18

A Christmas Treat
(re-issued from 1979)
Handcrafted • N/A
550QX1347 • **Value $84**

19

A Christmas Vigil
Handcrafted • DLEE
900QX1441 • **Value $110**

20

Clothespin Soldier
Handcrafted • N/A
350QX1341 • **Value $42**

General Keepsake		
	Price Paid	Value of My Collection
1.		
2.		
3.		
4.		
5.		
6.		
7.		
8.		
9.		
10.		
11.		
12.		
13.		
14.		
15.		
16.		
17.		
18.		
19.		
20.		
PENCIL TOTALS		

Value Guide — Hallmark Keepsake Ornaments

(1) **Dad** *Glass* • N/A 400QX2141 • **Value $18**	**(2)** **Daughter** *Glass* • N/A 400QX2121 • **Value $42**	**(3)** **DISNEY** *Satin* • N/A 400QX2181 • **Value $33**	**(4)** **Dove** *Acrylic* • N/A 400QX3081 • **Value $40**
(5) **Drummer Boy** *Acrylic* • N/A 400QX3094 • **Value $28**	**(6)** **Drummer Boy** *Handcrafted* • DLEE 550QX1474 • **Value $95**	**(7)** **Elfin Antics** *Handcrafted* • N/A 900QX1421 • **Value $220**	**(8)** **First Christmas Together** *Acrylic* • N/A 400QX3054 • **Value $48**

General Keepsake

	Price Paid	Value of My Collection
1.		
2.		
3.		
4.		
5.		
6.		
7.		
8.		
9.		
10.		
11.		
12.		
13.		
14.		
15.		
16.		
17.		
18.		
19.		
20.		
PENCIL TOTALS		

(9) **First Christmas Together** *Glass* • N/A 400QX2054 • **Value $40**	**(10)** **Friendship** *Glass* • N/A 400QX2081 • **Value $22**	**(11)** **Granddaughter** *Satin* • N/A 400QX2021 • **Value $36**
(12) **Grandfather** *Glass* • N/A 400QX2314 • **Value $19**	**(13)** **Grandmother** *Glass* • N/A 400QX2041 • **Value $19**	**(14)** **Grandparents** *Glass* • N/A 400QX2134 • **Value $40**
(15) **Grandson** *Satin* • N/A 400QX2014 • **Value $33**	**(16)** **Happy Christmas** *Satin* • N/A 400QX2221 • **Value $27**	**(17)** **Heavenly Minstrel** *Handcrafted* • DLEE 1500QX1567 • **Value $340**
(18) **A Heavenly Nap** (re-issued in 1981) *Handcrafted* • DLEE 650QX1394 • **Value $48**	**(19)** **Heavenly Sounds** *Handcrafted* • N/A 750QX1521 • **Value $97**	**(20)** **Joan Walsh Anglund** *Satin* • N/A 400QX2174 • **Value $24**

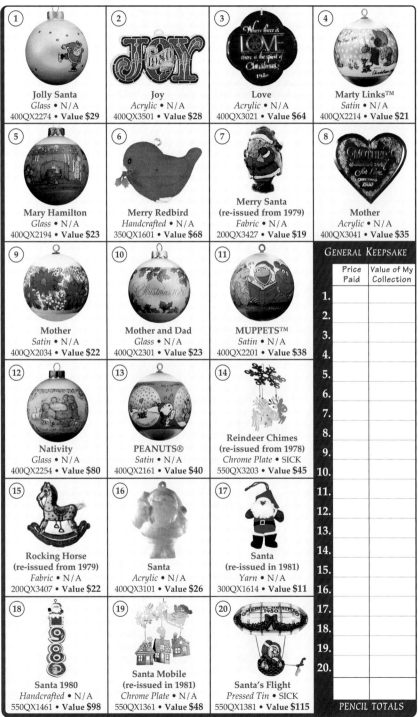

#	Name	Material	SKU • Value
1	**Jolly Santa**	*Glass • N/A*	400QX2274 • **Value $29**
2	**Joy**	*Acrylic • N/A*	400QX3501 • **Value $28**
3	**Love**	*Acrylic • N/A*	400QX3021 • **Value $64**
4	**Marty Links™**	*Satin • N/A*	400QX2214 • **Value $21**
5	**Mary Hamilton**	*Glass • N/A*	400QX2194 • **Value $23**
6	**Merry Redbird**	*Handcrafted • N/A*	350QX1601 • **Value $68**
7	**Merry Santa** (re-issued from 1979)	*Fabric • N/A*	200QX3427 • **Value $19**
8	**Mother**	*Acrylic • N/A*	400QX3041 • **Value $35**
9	**Mother**	*Satin • N/A*	400QX2034 • **Value $22**
10	**Mother and Dad**	*Glass • N/A*	400QX2301 • **Value $23**
11	**MUPPETS™**	*Satin • N/A*	400QX2201 • **Value $38**
12	**Nativity**	*Glass • N/A*	400QX2254 • **Value $80**
13	**PEANUTS®**	*Satin • N/A*	400QX2161 • **Value $40**
14	**Reindeer Chimes** (re-issued from 1978)	*Chrome Plate • SICK*	550QX3203 • **Value $45**
15	**Rocking Horse** (re-issued from 1979)	*Fabric • N/A*	200QX3407 • **Value $22**
16	**Santa**	*Acrylic • N/A*	400QX3101 • **Value $26**
17	**Santa** (re-issued in 1981)	*Yarn • N/A*	300QX1614 • **Value $11**
18	**Santa 1980**	*Handcrafted • N/A*	550QX1461 • **Value $98**
19	**Santa Mobile** (re-issued in 1981)	*Chrome Plate • N/A*	550QX1361 • **Value $48**
20	**Santa's Flight**	*Pressed Tin • SICK*	550QX1381 • **Value $115**

1980

General Keepsake

	Price Paid	Value of My Collection
1.		
2.		
3.		
4.		
5.		
6.		
7.		
8.		
9.		
10.		
11.		
12.		
13.		
14.		
15.		
16.		
17.		
18.		
19.		
20.		
PENCIL TOTALS		

Value Guide — Hallmark Keepsake Ornaments

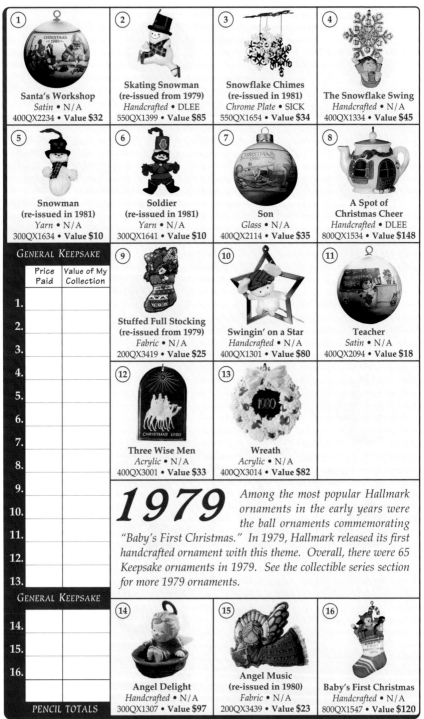

1 — Santa's Workshop
Satin • N/A
400QX2234 • **Value $32**

2 — Skating Snowman
(re-issued from 1979)
Handcrafted • DLEE
550QX1399 • **Value $85**

3 — Snowflake Chimes
(re-issued in 1981)
Chrome Plate • SICK
550QX1654 • **Value $34**

4 — The Snowflake Swing
Handcrafted • N/A
400QX1334 • **Value $45**

5 — Snowman
(re-issued in 1981)
Yarn • N/A
300QX1634 • **Value $10**

6 — Soldier
(re-issued in 1981)
Yarn • N/A
300QX1641 • **Value $10**

7 — Son
Glass • N/A
400QX2114 • **Value $35**

8 — A Spot of Christmas Cheer
Handcrafted • DLEE
800QX1534 • **Value $148**

9 — Stuffed Full Stocking
(re-issued from 1979)
Fabric • N/A
200QX3419 • **Value $25**

10 — Swingin' on a Star
Handcrafted • N/A
400QX1301 • **Value $80**

11 — Teacher
Satin • N/A
400QX2094 • **Value $18**

12 — Three Wise Men
Acrylic • N/A
400QX3001 • **Value $33**

13 — Wreath
Acrylic • N/A
400QX3014 • **Value $82**

1979

Among the most popular Hallmark ornaments in the early years were the ball ornaments commemorating "Baby's First Christmas." In 1979, Hallmark released its first handcrafted ornament with this theme. Overall, there were 65 Keepsake ornaments in 1979. See the collectible series section for more 1979 ornaments.

14 — Angel Delight
Handcrafted • N/A
300QX1307 • **Value $97**

15 — Angel Music
(re-issued in 1980)
Fabric • N/A
200QX3439 • **Value $23**

16 — Baby's First Christmas
Handcrafted • N/A
800QX1547 • **Value $120**

General Keepsake

	Price Paid	Value of My Collection
1.		
2.		
3.		
4.		
5.		
6.		
7.		
8.		
9.		
10.		
11.		
12.		
13.		

General Keepsake

14.		
15.		
16.		
PENCIL TOTALS		

Value Guide — Hallmark Keepsake Ornaments

1 Baby's First Christmas
Satin • N/A
350QX2087 • **Value $32**

2 Behold the Star
Satin • N/A
350QX2559 • **Value $39**

3 Black Angel
Glass • BLAC
350QX2079 • **Value $26**

4 Christmas Angel
Acrylic • N/A
350QX3007 • **Value $132**

5 Christmas Cheer
Acrylic • N/A
350QX3039 • **Value $82**

6 Christmas Chickadees
Glass • N/A
350QX2047 • **Value $34**

7 Christmas Collage
Glass • N/A
350QX2579 • **Value $36**

8 Christmas Eve Surprise
Handcrafted • N/A
650QX1579 • **Value $67**

9 Christmas Heart
Handcrafted • SICK
650QX1407 • **Value $100**

10 Christmas is
for Children
(re-issued in 1980)
Handcrafted • N/A
500QX1359 • **Value $93**

11 Christmas Traditions
Glass • SICK
350QX2539 • **Value $37**

12 A Christmas Treat
(re-issued in 1980)
Handcrafted • N/A
500QX1347 • **Value $84**

13 Christmas Tree
Acrylic • N/A
350QX3027 • **Value $73**

14 The Downhill Run
Handcrafted • DLEE
650QX1459 • **Value $170**

15 The Drummer Boy
Handcrafted • N/A
800QX1439 • **Value $125**

16 Friendship
Glass • N/A
350QX2039 • **Value $25**

17 Granddaughter
Satin • N/A
350QX2119 • **Value $38**

18 Grandmother
Glass • N/A
350QX2527 • **Value $23**

19 Grandson
Satin • N/A
350QX2107 • **Value $34**

20 Green Boy
(re-issued from 1978)
Yarn • N/A
200QX1231 • **Value $28**

1979

General Keepsake

	Price Paid	Value of My Collection
1.		
2.		
3.		
4.		
5.		
6.		
7.		
8.		
9.		
10.		
11.		
12.		
13.		
14.		
15.		
16.		
17.		
18.		
19.		
20.		
PENCIL TOTALS		

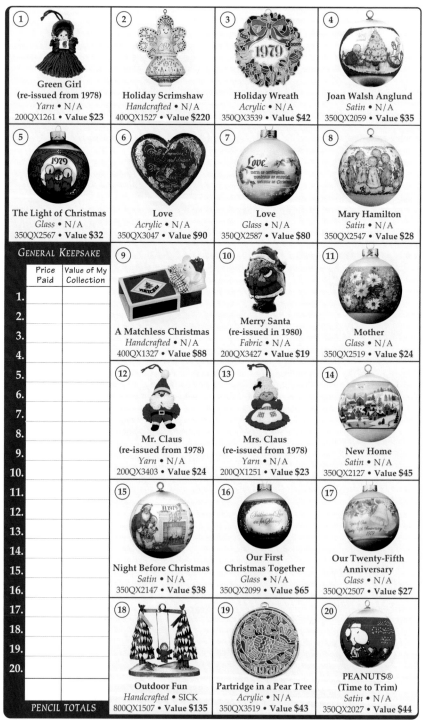

1 — Green Girl
(re-issued from 1978)
Yarn • N/A
200QX1261 • **Value $23**

2 — Holiday Scrimshaw
Handcrafted • N/A
400QX1527 • **Value $220**

3 — Holiday Wreath
Acrylic • N/A
350QX3539 • **Value $42**

4 — Joan Walsh Anglund
Satin • N/A
350QX2059 • **Value $35**

5 — The Light of Christmas
Glass • N/A
350QX2567 • **Value $32**

6 — Love
Acrylic • N/A
350QX3047 • **Value $90**

7 — Love
Glass • N/A
350QX2587 • **Value $80**

8 — Mary Hamilton
Satin • N/A
350QX2547 • **Value $28**

General Keepsake

	Price Paid	Value of My Collection
1.		
2.		
3.		
4.		
5.		
6.		
7.		
8.		
9.		
10.		
11.		
12.		
13.		
14.		
15.		
16.		
17.		
18.		
19.		
20.		
PENCIL TOTALS		

9 — A Matchless Christmas
Handcrafted • N/A
400QX1327 • **Value $88**

10 — Merry Santa
(re-issued in 1980)
Fabric • N/A
200QX3427 • **Value $19**

11 — Mother
Glass • N/A
350QX2519 • **Value $24**

12 — Mr. Claus
(re-issued from 1978)
Yarn • N/A
200QX3403 • **Value $24**

13 — Mrs. Claus
(re-issued from 1978)
Yarn • N/A
200QX1251 • **Value $23**

14 — New Home
Satin • N/A
350QX2127 • **Value $45**

15 — Night Before Christmas
Satin • N/A
350QX2147 • **Value $38**

16 — Our First
Christmas Together
Glass • N/A
350QX2099 • **Value $65**

17 — Our Twenty-Fifth
Anniversary
Glass • N/A
350QX2507 • **Value $27**

18 — Outdoor Fun
Handcrafted • SICK
800QX1507 • **Value $135**

19 — Partridge in a Pear Tree
Acrylic • N/A
350QX3519 • **Value $43**

20 — PEANUTS®
(Time to Trim)
Satin • N/A
350QX2027 • **Value $44**

VALUE GUIDE — HALLMARK KEEPSAKE ORNAMENTS

① Raccoon
(re-issued from 1978)
Handcrafted • DLEE
650QX1423 • **Value $96**

② Ready for Christmas
Handcrafted • DLEE
650QX1339 • **Value $150**

③ Reindeer Chimes
(re-issued from 1978)
Chrome Plate • SICK
450QX3203 • **Value $45**

④ Rocking Horse
(re-issued in 1980)
Fabric • N/A
200QX3407 • **Value $22**

⑤ Santa
(re-issued from 1978)
Handcrafted • N/A
300QX1356 • **Value $68**

⑥ Santa's Here
Handcrafted • SICK
500QX1387 • **Value $70**

⑦ The Skating Snowman
(re-issued in 1980)
Handcrafted • DLEE
500QX1399 • **Value $85**

⑧ Snowflake
Acrylic • N/A
350QX3019 • **Value $42**

⑨ Spencer® Sparrow, Esq.
Satin • N/A
350QX2007 • **Value $44**

⑩ Star Chimes
Chrome Plate • SICK
450QX1379 • **Value $68**

⑪ Star Over Bethlehem
Acrylic • SICK
350QX3527 • **Value $70**

⑫ Stuffed Full Stocking
(re-issued in 1980)
Fabric • N/A
200QX3419 • **Value $25**

⑬ Teacher
Satin • N/A
350QX2139 • **Value $16**

⑭ Winnie-the-Pooh
Satin • N/A
350QX2067 • **Value $47**

⑮ Words of Christmas
Acrylic • N/A
350QX3507 • **Value $75**

	GENERAL KEEPSAKE	
	Price Paid	Value of My Collection
1.		
2.		
3.		
4.		
5.		
6.		
7.		
8.		
9.		
10.		
11.		
12.		
13.		
14.		
15.		
	PENCIL TOTALS	

1979

1978

In the 6th year of Hallmark ornaments several unique handcrafted ornaments proved to be the most popular, including "Angels," "Animal Home," "Calico Mouse," "Red Cardinal" and "Schneeberg Bell." The 1978 collection featured 54 Keepsake ornaments. See the collectible series section for more 1978 ornaments.

(1)

25th Christmas Together
Glass • N/A
350QX2696 • **Value $33**

---

(2)

Angel
Acrylic • N/A
350QX3543 • **Value $47**

(3)

Angel
(re-issued in 1981)
Handcrafted • DLEE
450QX1396 • **Value $90**

(4)

Angels
Handcrafted • N/A
800QX1503 • **Value $370**

(5)

Animal Home
Handcrafted • DLEE
600QX1496 • **Value $180**

GENERAL KEEPSAKE

	Price Paid	Value of My Collection
1.		
2.		
3.		
4.		
5.		
6.		
7.		
8.		
9.		
10.		
11.		
12.		
13.		
14.		
15.		
16.		
17.		
PENCIL TOTALS		

(6)

Baby's First Christmas
Satin • N/A
350QX2003 • **Value $90**

(7)

Calico Mouse
Handcrafted • N/A
450QX1376 • **Value $175**

(8)

Candle
Acrylic • N/A
350QX3576 • **Value $85**

(9)

DISNEY
Satin • N/A
350QX2076 • **Value $112**

(10)

Dove
Acrylic •PALM
350QX3103 • **Value $110**

(11)

Dove
Handcrafted • SICK
450QX1903 • **Value $86**

(12)

Drummer Boy
Glass • N/A
350QX2523 • **Value $42**

(13)

Drummer Boy
Handcrafted • N/A
250QX1363 • **Value $75**

(14)

First Christmas Together
Satin • N/A
350QX2183 • **Value $47**

(15)

For Your New Home
Satin • N/A
350QX2176 • **Value $24**

(16)

Granddaughter
Satin • N/A
350QX2163 • **Value $43**

(17)

Grandmother
Satin • N/A
350QX2676 • **Value $42**

Value Guide — Hallmark Keepsake Ornaments

(1)
Grandson
Satin • N/A
350QX2156 • **Value $45**

(2)
Green Boy
(re-issued in 1979)
Yarn • N/A
200QX1231 • **Value $28**

(3)
Green Girl
(re-issued in 1979)
Yarn • N/A
200QX1261 • **Value $23**

(4)
Hallmark's Antique
Card Collection Design
Satin • N/A
350QX2203 • **Value $45**

(5)
Holly and
Poinsettia Ball
Handcrafted • SICK
600QX1476 • **Value $84**

(6)
Joan Walsh Anglund
Satin • N/A
350QX2216 • **Value $65**

(7)
Joy
Glass • N/A
350QX2543 • **Value $48**

(8)
Joy
Handcrafted • N/A
450QX1383 • **Value $86**

(9)
Locomotive
Acrylic • N/A
350QX3563 • **Value $57**

(10)
Love
Glass • N/A
350QX2683 • **Value $56**

(11)
Merry Christmas
Acrylic • PALM
350QX3556 • **Value $52**

(12)
Merry Christmas (Santa)
Satin • N/A
350QX2023 • **Value $50**

(13)
Mother
Glass • N/A
350QX2663 • **Value $44**

(14)
Mr. Claus
(re-issued in 1979)
Yarn • N/A
200QX3403 • **Value $24**

(15)
Mrs. Claus
(re-issued in 1979)
Yarn • N/A
200QX1251 • **Value $23**

(16)
Nativity
Acrylic • PALM
350QX3096 • **Value $92**

(17)
Nativity
Glass • N/A
350QX2536 • **Value $75**

(18)
Panorama Ball
Handcrafted • N/A
600QX1456 • **Value $140**

(19)
PEANUTS®
Satin • N/A
250QX2036 • **Value $63**

GENERAL KEEPSAKE		
	Price Paid	Value of My Collection
1.		
2.		
3.		
4.		
5.		
6.		
7.		
8.		
9.		
10.		
11.		
12.		
13.		
14.		
15.		
16.		
17.		
18.		
19.		
PENCIL TOTALS		

1978

1. PEANUTS®
Satin • N/A
250QX2043 • **Value $67**

2. PEANUTS®
Satin • N/A
350QX2056 • **Value $70**

3. PEANUTS®
Satin • N/A
350QX2063 • **Value $63**

4. Praying Angel
Handcrafted • DLEE
250QX1343 • **Value $85**

5. The Quail
Glass • N/A
350QX2516 • **Value $38**

6. Red Cardinal
Handcrafted • UNRU
450QX1443 • **Value $172**

7. Reindeer Chimes
(re-issued in 1979 and 1980)
Chrome Plate • SICK
450QX3203 • **Value $45**

8. Rocking Horse
Handcrafted • N/A
600QX1483 • **Value $90**

9. Santa
Acrylic • PALM
350QX3076 • **Value $77**

10. Santa
(re-issued in 1979)
Handcrafted • N/A
250QX1356 • **Value $68**

11. Schneeberg Bell
Handcrafted • N/A
800QX1523 • **Value $185**

12. Skating Raccoon
(re-issued in 1979)
Handcrafted • DLEE
600QX1423 • **Value $96**

13. Snowflake
Acrylic • PALM
350QX3083 • **Value $66**

14. Spencer® Sparrow, Esq.
Satin • N/A
350QX2196 • **Value $48**

15. Yesterday's Toys
Glass • N/A
350QX2503 • **Value $30**

General Keepsake

	Price Paid	Value of My Collection
1.		
2.		
3.		
4.		
5.		
6.		
7.		
8.		
9.		
10.		
11.		
12.		
13.		
14.		
15.		
PENCIL TOTALS		

1977

The 1977 collection was highlighted by a group of handcrafted ornaments designed to have an antique wooden appearance. Called the "Nostalgia Collection," these ornaments were "Angel," "Antique Car," "Nativity," and "Toys." In 1977, there were 53 Keepsake ornaments. See the collectible series section for more 1977 ornaments.

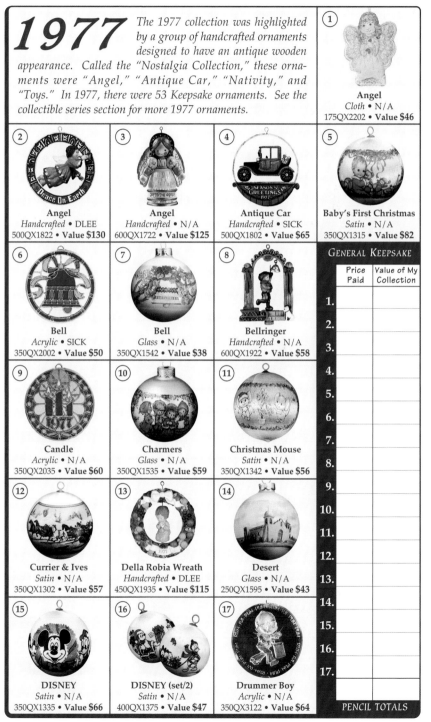

(1)
Angel
Cloth • N/A
175QX2202 • **Value $46**

(2)
Angel
Handcrafted • DLEE
500QX1822 • **Value $130**

(3)
Angel
Handcrafted • N/A
600QX1722 • **Value $125**

(4)
Antique Car
Handcrafted • SICK
500QX1802 • **Value $65**

(5)
Baby's First Christmas
Satin • N/A
350QX1315 • **Value $82**

(6)
Bell
Acrylic • SICK
350QX2002 • **Value $50**

(7)
Bell
Glass • N/A
350QX1542 • **Value $38**

(8)
Bellringer
Handcrafted • N/A
600QX1922 • **Value $58**

(9)
Candle
Acrylic • N/A
350QX2035 • **Value $60**

(10)
Charmers
Glass • N/A
350QX1535 • **Value $59**

(11)
Christmas Mouse
Satin • N/A
350QX1342 • **Value $56**

(12)
Currier & Ives
Satin • N/A
350QX1302 • **Value $57**

(13)
Della Robia Wreath
Handcrafted • DLEE
450QX1935 • **Value $115**

(14)
Desert
Glass • N/A
250QX1595 • **Value $43**

(15)
DISNEY
Satin • N/A
350QX1335 • **Value $66**

(16)
DISNEY (set/2)
Satin • N/A
400QX1375 • **Value $47**

(17)
Drummer Boy
Acrylic • N/A
350QX3122 • **Value $64**

GENERAL KEEPSAKE

	Price Paid	Value of My Collection
1.		
2.		
3.		
4.		
5.		
6.		
7.		
8.		
9.		
10.		
11.		
12.		
13.		
14.		
15.		
16.		
17.		
PENCIL TOTALS		

1977

(1) First Christmas Together
Satin • N/A
350QX1322 • **Value $70**

(2) For Your New Home
Glass • N/A
350QX2635 • **Value $37**

(3) Granddaughter
Satin • N/A
350QX2082 • **Value $38**

(4) Grandma Moses
Glass • N/A
350QX1502 • **Value $62**

(5) Grandmother
Glass • N/A
350QX2602 • **Value $47**

(6) Grandson
Satin • N/A
350QX2095 • **Value $34**

(7) House
Handcrafted • N/A
600QX1702 • **Value $130**

(8) Jack-in-the-Box
Handcrafted • N/A
600QX1715 • **Value $120**

(9) Joy
Acrylic • N/A
350QX2015 • **Value $52**

(10) Joy
Acrylic • N/A
350QX3102 • **Value $47**

(11) Love
Glass • N/A
350QX2622 • **Value $28**

(12) Mandolin
Glass • N/A
350QX1575 • **Value $38**

(13) Mother
Glass • N/A
350QX2615 • **Value $34**

(14) Mountains
Glass • N/A
250QX1582 • **Value $35**

(15) Nativity
Handcrafted • N/A
500QX1815 • **Value $145**

(16) Norman Rockwell
Glass • N/A
350QX1515 • **Value $68**

(17) Ornaments
Glass • N/A
350QX1555 • **Value $40**

(18) Peace on Earth
Acrylic • N/A
350QX3115 • **Value $55**

(19) PEANUTS®
Glass • N/A
250QX1622 • **Value $77**

(20) PEANUTS® (set/2)
Glass • N/A
400QX1635 • **Value $88**

GENERAL KEEPSAKE		
	Price Paid	Value of My Collection
1.		
2.		
3.		
4.		
5.		
6.		
7.		
8.		
9.		
10.		
11.		
12.		
13.		
14.		
15.		
16.		
17.		
18.		
19.		
20.		
PENCIL TOTALS		

Value Guide — Hallmark Keepsake Ornaments

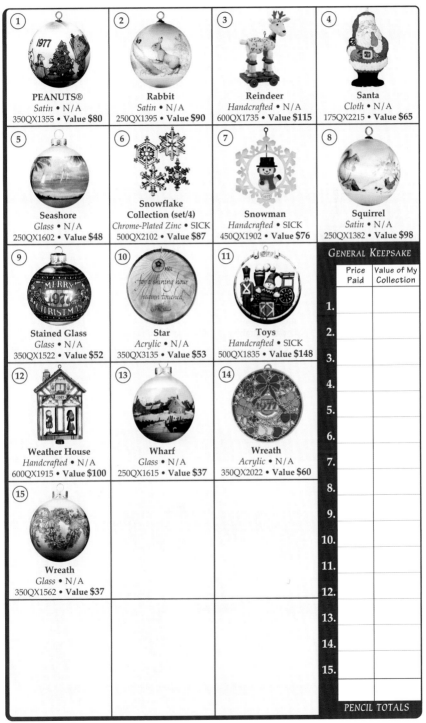

1 PEANUTS®
Satin • N/A
350QX1355 • **Value $80**

2 Rabbit
Satin • N/A
250QX1395 • **Value $90**

3 Reindeer
Handcrafted • N/A
600QX1735 • **Value $115**

4 Santa
Cloth • N/A
175QX2215 • **Value $65**

5 Seashore
Glass • N/A
250QX1602 • **Value $48**

6 Snowflake Collection (set/4)
Chrome-Plated Zinc • SICK
500QX2102 • **Value $87**

7 Snowman
Handcrafted • SICK
450QX1902 • **Value $76**

8 Squirrel
Satin • N/A
250QX1382 • **Value $98**

9 Stained Glass
Glass • N/A
350QX1522 • **Value $52**

10 Star
Acrylic • N/A
350QX3135 • **Value $53**

11 Toys
Handcrafted • SICK
500QX1835 • **Value $148**

12 Weather House
Handcrafted • N/A
600QX1915 • **Value $100**

13 Wharf
Glass • N/A
250QX1615 • **Value $37**

14 Wreath
Acrylic • N/A
350QX2022 • **Value $60**

15 Wreath
Glass • N/A
350QX1562 • **Value $37**

1977

General Keepsake

	Price Paid	Value of My Collection
1.		
2.		
3.		
4.		
5.		
6.		
7.		
8.		
9.		
10.		
11.		
12.		
13.		
14.		
15.		
PENCIL TOTALS		

1977 Collection 253

1976

The 1976 collection of ornaments featured popular themes such as Santa Claus, locomotives, partridges and drummer boys, all in a variety of different handcrafted styles. For the Bicentennial year, Hallmark issued a total of 39 Keepsake ornaments. See the collectible series section for more 1976 ornaments.

(1)
Angel
Handcrafted • N/A
300QX1761 • **Value $170**

(2)
Angel
Handcrafted • SICK
450QX1711 • **Value $170**

(3)
Baby's First Christmas
Satin • N/A
250QX2111 • **Value $150**

(4)
Betsey Clark
Satin • N/A
250QX2101 • **Value $62**

(5)
Betsey Clark (set/3)
Satin • N/A
450QX2181 • **Value $53**

(6)
Bicentennial '76 Commemorative
Satin • N/A
250QX2031 • **Value $58**

(7)
Bicentennial Charmers
Glass • N/A
300QX1981 • **Value $67**

(8)
Cardinals
Glass • N/A
225QX2051 • **Value $60**

(9)
Caroler
(re-issued from 1975)
Yarn • N/A
175QX1261 • **Value $21**

(10)
Charmers (set/2)
Satin • N/A
350QX2151 • **Value $72**

(11)
Chickadees
Glass • N/A
225QX2041 • **Value $60**

(12)
Colonial Children (set/2)
Glass • N/A
400QX2081 • **Value $74**

(13)
Currier & Ives
Glass • N/A
300QX1971 • **Value $47**

(14)
Currier & Ives
Satin • N/A
250QX2091 • **Value $46**

(15)
Drummer Boy
(re-issued from 1975)
Handcrafted • SICK
400QX1301 • **Value $155**

(16)
Drummer Boy
Handcrafted • N/A
500QX1841 • **Value $150**

(17)
Drummer Boy
(re-issued from 1975)
Yarn • N/A
175QX1231 • **Value $25**

General Keepsake

	Price Paid	Value of My Collection
1.		
2.		
3.		
4.		
5.		
6.		
7.		
8.		
9.		
10.		
11.		
12.		
13.		
14.		
15.		
16.		
17.		
PENCIL TOTALS		

1976

(1) Happy the Snowman (set/2) *Satin* • N/A 350QX2161 • **Value $50**	**(2)** Locomotive (re-issued from 1975) *Handcrafted* • SICK 400QX2221 • **Value $190**	**(3)** Marty Links™ (set/2) *Glass* • N/A 400QX2071 • **Value $54**	**(4)** Mrs. Santa (re-issued from 1975) *Yarn* • N/A 175QX1251 • **Value $23**

(5) Norman Rockwell *Glass* • N/A 300QX1961 • **Value $73**

(6) Partridge *Handcrafted* • SICK 450QX1741 • **Value $190**

(7) Partridge *Handcrafted* • N/A 500QX1831 • **Value $115**

(8) Peace on Earth (re-issued from 1975) *Handcrafted* • SICK 400QX2231 • **Value $150**

(9) Raggedy Andy™ (re-issued from 1975) *Yarn* • N/A 175QX1221 • **Value $45**

(10) Raggedy Ann™ *Satin* • N/A 250X2121 • **Value $60**

(11) Raggedy Ann™ (re-issued from 1975) *Yarn* • N/A 175QX1211 • **Value $44**

(12) Reindeer *Handcrafted* • N/A 300QX1781 • **Value $110**

(13) Rocking Horse (re-issued from 1975) *Handcrafted* • SICK 400QX1281 • **Value $170**

(14) Rudolph and Santa *Satin* • N/A 250QX2131 • **Value $90**

(15) Santa *Handcrafted* • N/A 300QX1771 • **Value $210**

(16) Santa *Handcrafted* • SICK 450QX1721 • **Value $110**

(17) Santa *Handcrafted* • N/A 500QX1821 • **Value $168**

(18) Santa (re-issued from 1975) *Yarn* • N/A 175QX1241 • **Value $23**

(19) Shepherd *Handcrafted* • N/A 300QX1751 • **Value $130**

(20) Soldier *Handcrafted* • SICK 450QX1731 • **Value $98**

GENERAL KEEPSAKE		
	Price Paid	Value of My Collection
1.		
2.		
3.		
4.		
5.		
6.		
7.		
8.		
9.		
10.		
11.		
12.		
13.		
14.		
15.		
16.		
17.		
18.		
19.		
20.		
PENCIL TOTALS		

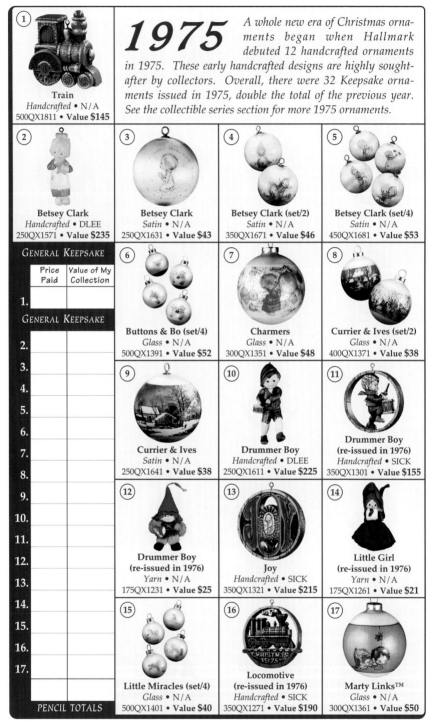

(1)
Train
Handcrafted • N/A
500QX1811 • **Value $145**

1975

A whole new era of Christmas ornaments began when Hallmark debuted 12 handcrafted ornaments in 1975. These early handcrafted designs are highly sought-after by collectors. Overall, there were 32 Keepsake ornaments issued in 1975, double the total of the previous year. See the collectible series section for more 1975 ornaments.

(2)
Betsey Clark
Handcrafted • DLEE
250QX1571 • **Value $235**

(3)
Betsey Clark
Satin • N/A
250QX1631 • **Value $43**

(4)
Betsey Clark (set/2)
Satin • N/A
350QX1671 • **Value $46**

(5)
Betsey Clark (set/4)
Satin • N/A
450QX1681 • **Value $53**

General Keepsake

	Price Paid	Value of My Collection
General Keepsake		
1.		
2.		
3.		
4.		
5.		
6.		
7.		
8.		
9.		
10.		
11.		
12.		
13.		
14.		
15.		
16.		
17.		
PENCIL TOTALS		

(6)
Buttons & Bo (set/4)
Glass • N/A
500QX1391 • **Value $52**

(7)
Charmers
Glass • N/A
300QX1351 • **Value $48**

(8)
Currier & Ives (set/2)
Glass • N/A
400QX1371 • **Value $38**

(9)
Currier & Ives
Satin • N/A
250QX1641 • **Value $38**

(10)
Drummer Boy
Handcrafted • DLEE
250QX1611 • **Value $225**

(11)
Drummer Boy
(re-issued in 1976)
Handcrafted • SICK
350QX1301 • **Value $155**

(12)
Drummer Boy
(re-issued in 1976)
Yarn • N/A
175QX1231 • **Value $25**

(13)
Joy
Handcrafted • SICK
350QX1321 • **Value $215**

(14)
Little Girl
(re-issued in 1976)
Yarn • N/A
175QX1261 • **Value $21**

(15)
Little Miracles (set/4)
Glass • N/A
500QX1401 • **Value $40**

(16)
Locomotive
(re-issued in 1976)
Handcrafted • SICK
350QX1271 • **Value $190**

(17)
Marty Links™
Glass • N/A
300QX1361 • **Value $50**

VALUE GUIDE – HALLMARK KEEPSAKE ORNAMENTS

① **Mrs. Santa**
(re-issued in 1981)
Handcrafted • DLEE
250QX1561 • **Value $220**

② **Mrs. Santa**
(re-issued in 1976)
Yarn • N/A
175QX1251 • **Value $23**

③ **Norman Rockwell**
Glass • N/A
300QX1341 • **Value $65**

④ **Norman Rockwell**
Satin • N/A
250QX1661 • **Value $60**

⑤ **Peace On Earth**
(re-issued in 1976)
Handcrafted • SICK
350QX1311 • **Value $150**

⑥ **Raggedy Andy™**
Handcrafted • DLEE
250QX1601 • **Value $350**

⑦ **Raggedy Andy™**
(re-issued in 1976)
Yarn • N/A
175QX1221 • **Value $45**

⑧ **Raggedy Ann™**
Handcrafted • DLEE
250QX1591 • **Value $305**

⑨ **Raggedy Ann™**
Satin • N/A
250QX1651 • **Value $50**

⑩ **Raggedy Ann™**
(re-issued in 1976)
Yarn • N/A
175QX1211 • **Value $44**

⑪ **Raggedy Ann™ and Raggedy Andy™ (set/2)**
Glass • N/A
400QX1381 • **Value $68**

⑫ **Rocking Horse**
(re-issued in 1976)
Handcrafted • SICK
350QX1281 • **Value $170**

⑬ **Santa**
(re-issued in 1981)
Handcrafted • DLEE
250QX1551 • **Value $220**

⑭ **Santa**
(re-issued in 1976)
Yarn • N/A
175QX1241 • **Value $23**

⑮ **Santa & Sleigh**
Handcrafted • SICK
350QX1291 • **Value $240**

GENERAL KEEPSAKE

	Price Paid	Value of My Collection
1.		
2.		
3.		
4.		
5.		
6.		
7.		
8.		
9.		
10.		
11.		
12.		
13.		
14.		
15.		
PENCIL TOTALS		

1974

In the second year of Keepsake ornaments, the collection featured popular Christmas scenes from Norman Rockwell, Betsey Clark and Currier & Ives. Of the 16 Keepsake designs or sets offered in 1974, 10 were ball ornaments and 6 were made from yarn. See the collectible series section for more 1974 ornaments.

(1)
Angel
Glass • N/A
250QX1101 • **Value $77**

(2)
Angel
Yarn • N/A
150QX1031 • **Value $29**

(3)
Buttons & Bo (set/2)
Glass • N/A
350QX1131 • **Value $50**

(4)
Charmers
Glass • N/A
250QX1091 • **Value $52**

(5)
Currier & Ives (set/2)
Glass • N/A
350QX1121 • **Value $59**

GENERAL KEEPSAKE

	Price Paid	Value of My Collection
1.		
2.		
3.		
4.		
5.		
6.		
7.		
8.		
9.		
10.		
11.		
12.		
13.		
14.		
15.		
PENCIL TOTALS		

(6)
Elf
Yarn • N/A
150QX1011 • **Value $26**

(7)
Little Miracles (set/4)
Glass • N/A
450QX1151 • **Value $60**

(8)
Mrs. Santa
Yarn • N/A
150QX1001 • **Value $24**

(9)
Norman Rockwell
Glass • N/A
250QX1061 • **Value $98**

(10)
Norman Rockwell
Glass • N/A
250QX1111 • **Value $86**

(11)
Raggedy Ann™ and Raggedy Andy™ (set/4)
Glass • N/A
450QX1141 • **Value $88**

(12)
Santa
Yarn • N/A
150QX1051 • **Value $26**

(13)
Snowgoose
Glass • N/A
250QX1071 • **Value $72**

(14)
Snowman
Yarn • N/A
150QX1041 • **Value $24**

(15)
Soldier
Yarn • N/A
150QX1021 • **Value $25**

1973

The very first year of Hallmark Keepsake Ornaments was 1973. This year's debut offering consisted of 6 ball ornaments and 12 yarn ornaments, making a total of 18 Keepsake designs. The first Keepsake series, "Betsey Clark," began this year. See the collectible series section for more 1973 ornaments.

①

Angel
Yarn • N/A
125XHD785 • **Value $28**

②
Betsey Clark
Glass • N/A
250XHD1002 • **Value $93**

③
Blue Girl
Yarn • N/A
125XHD852 • **Value $24**

④
Boy Caroler
Yarn • N/A
125XHD832 • **Value $25**

⑤
Choir Boy
Yarn • N/A
125XHD805 • **Value $26**

⑥
Christmas Is Love
Glass • N/A
250XHD1062 • **Value $76**

⑦
Elf
Yarn • N/A
125XHD792 • **Value $26**

⑧
Elves
Glass • N/A
250XHD1035 • **Value $82**

⑨
Green Girl
Yarn • N/A
125XHD845 • **Value $26**

⑩
Little Girl
Yarn • N/A
125XHD825 • **Value $26**

⑪
Manger Scene
Glass • N/A
250XHD1022 • **Value $88**

⑫
Mr. Santa
Yarn • N/A
125XHD745 • **Value $26**

⑬
Mrs. Santa
Yarn • N/A
125XHD752 • **Value $25**

⑭
Mr. Snowman
Yarn • N/A
125XHD765 • **Value $24**

⑮
Mrs. Snowman
Yarn • N/A
125XHD772 • **Value $24**

⑯
Santa with Elves
Glass • N/A
250XHD1015 • **Value $80**

⑰
Soldier
Yarn • N/A
100XHD812 • **Value $23**

GENERAL KEEPSAKE

	Price Paid	Value of My Collection
1.		
2.		
3.		
4.		
5.		
6.		
7.		
8.		
9.		
10.		
11.		
12.		
13.		
14.		
15.		
16.		
17.		
PENCIL TOTALS		

1973

Spring Ornaments

Twenty-five new pieces joined the Spring ornaments collection in 1999, eight of which are in a series. Three new series make their debut this year ("Easter Egg Surprise," "Fairy Berry Bears" and "Winner's Circle"), while the "Children's Collector BARBIE™ Ornament" series concludes this year.

Collectible Series

1
Apple Blossom Lane
(1st, 1995)
Handcrafted • FRAN
895QEO8207 • **Value $21**

2
Apple Blossom Lane
(2nd, 1996)
Handcrafted • FRAN
895QEO8084 • **Value $17**

3
Apple Blossom Lane
(3rd & final, 1997)
Handcrafted • FRAN
895QEO8662 • **Value $18**

4
Peter Rabbit™
(1st, 1996)
Handcrafted • VOTR
895QEO8071 • **Value $80**

5
Jemima Puddle-duck™
(2nd, 1997)
Handcrafted • VOTR
895QEO8645 • **Value $24**

6
Benjamin Bunny™
Beatrix Potter™
(3rd, 1998)
Handcrafted • VOTR
895QEO8383 • **Value $19**

7 NEW!
Tom Kitten™
(4th, 1999)
Handcrafted • VOTR
895QEO8329 • **Value $8.95**

8
Based on the BARBIE® as
Rapunzel Doll (1st, 1997)
Handcrafted • RGRS
1495QEO8635 • **Value $30**

9
Based on the BARBIE®
as Little Bo Peep Doll
(2nd, 1998)
Handcrafted • RGRS
1495QEO8373 • **Value $23**

10 NEW!
Based on the BARBIE™
as Cinderella Doll
(3rd & final, 1999)
Handcrafted • RGRS
1495QEO8327 • **Value $14.95**

11
"Gathering Sunny
Memories" (1st, 1994)
Porcelain • VOTR
775QEO8233 • **Value $33**

12
"Catching the Breeze"
(2nd, 1995)
Porcelain • VOTR
795QEO8219 • **Value $20**

13
"Keeping a Secret"
(3rd, 1996)
Porcelain • VOTR
795QEO8221 • **Value $17**

14
"Sunny Sunday Best"
(4th & final, 1997)
Porcelain • VOTR
795QEO8675 • **Value $16**

15
Locomotive (1st, 1996)
Handcrafted • CROW
895QEO8074 • **Value $43**

16
Colorful Coal Car
(2nd, 1997)
Handcrafted • CROW
895QEO8652 • **Value $20**

APPLE BLOSSOM LANE	Price Paid	Value of My Collection
1.		
2.		
3.		
BEATRIX POTTER™		
4.		
5.		
6.		
7.		
CHILDREN'S COLLECTOR BARBIE™ ORNAMENT		
8.		
9.		
10.		
COLLECTOR'S PLATE		
11.		
12.		
13.		
14.		
COTTONTAIL EXPRESS		
15.		
16.		
PENCIL TOTALS		

(1) Passenger Car (3rd, 1998) *Handcrafted* • CROW 995QEO8376 • **Value $18**	**(2)** NEW! Flatbed Car (4th, 1999) *Handcrafted* • CROW 995QEO8387 • **Value $9.95**

(3) NEW! Easter Egg Surprise (1st, 1999) *Porcelain* • VOTR 1495QEO8377 • **Value $14.95**

(4) Easter Parade (1st, 1992) *Handcrafted* • CROW 675QEO9301 • **Value $28**

(5) Easter Parade (2nd, 1993) *Handcrafted* • JLEE 675QEO8325 • **Value $21**

(6) Easter Parade (3rd & final, 1994) *Handcrafted* • RHOD 675QEO8136 • **Value $20**

(7) Eggs in Sports (1st, 1992) *Handcrafted* • SIED 675QEO9341 • **Value $33**

(8) Eggs in Sports (2nd, 1993) *Handcrafted* • SIED 675QEO8332 • **Value $21**

(9) Eggs in Sports (3rd & final, 1994) *Handcrafted* • SIED 675QEO8133 • **Value $20**

(10) NEW! Strawberry (1st, 1999) *Handcrafted* • TAGU 995QEO8369 • **Value $9.95**

(11) Garden Club (1st, 1995) *Handcrafted* • SICK 795QEO8209 • **Value $20**

(12) Garden Club (2nd, 1996) *Handcrafted* • PALM 795QEO8091 • **Value $16**

(13) Garden Club (3rd, 1997) *Handcrafted* • BRIC 795QEO8665 • **Value $15**

(14) Garden Club (4th & final, 1998) *Handcrafted* • PIKE 795QEO8426 • **Value $15**

(15) Here Comes Easter (1st, 1994) *Handcrafted* • CROW 775QEO8093 • **Value $36**

(16) Here Comes Easter (2nd, 1995) *Handcrafted* • CROW 795QEO8217 • **Value $20**

	Price Paid	Value of My Collection
COTTONTAIL EXPRESS		
1.		
2.		
EASTER EGG SURPRISE		
3.		
EASTER PARADE		
4.		
5.		
6.		
EGGS IN SPORTS		
7.		
8.		
9.		
FAIRY BERRY BEARS		
10.		
GARDEN CLUB		
11.		
12.		
13.		
14.		
HERE COMES EASTER		
15.		
16.		
PENCIL TOTALS		

SPRING ORNAMENTS

(1) Here Comes Easter (3rd, 1996) *Handcrafted* • CROW 795QEO8094 • **Value $18**	**(2)** Here Comes Easter (4th & final, 1997) *Handcrafted* • CROW 795QEO8682 • **Value $17**	**(3)** Joyful Angels (1st, 1996) *Handcrafted* • LYLE 995QEO8184 • **Value $28**	**(4)** Joyful Angels (2nd, 1997) *Handcrafted* • LYLE 1095QEO8655 • **Value $21**
(5) Joyful Angels (3rd & final, 1998) *Handcrafted* • LYLE 1095QEO8386 • **Value $18**	**(6)** 1935 Steelcraft Streamline Velocipede by Murray® (1st, 1997) *Die-Cast Metal* • RHOD 1295QEO8632 • **Value $25**	**(7)** 1939 Mobo Horse (2nd, 1998) *Die-Cast Metal* • N/A 1295QEO8393 • **Value $21**	**(8)** NEW! 1950 GARTON® Delivery Cycle (3rd, 1999) *Die-Cast Metal* • N/A 1295QEO8367 • **Value $12.95**

HERE COMES EASTER

	Price Paid	Value of My Collection
1.		
2.		

JOYFUL ANGELS

3.		
4.		
5.		

SIDEWALK CRUISERS

6.		
7.		
8.		

SPRINGTIME BARBIE™

9.		
10.		
11.		

SPRINGTIME BONNETS

12.		
13.		
14.		
15.		
16.		

VINTAGE ROADSTER

17.		
18.		

PENCIL TOTALS

(9) Springtime BARBIE™ (1st, 1995) *Handcrafted* • ANDR 1295QEO8069 • **Value $33**	**(10)** Springtime BARBIE™ (2nd, 1996) *Handcrafted* • ANDR 1295QEO8081 • **Value $27**	**(11)** Springtime BARBIE™ (3rd & final, 1997) *Handcrafted* • ANDR 1295QEO8642 • **Value $24**
(12) Springtime Bonnets (1st, 1993) *Handcrafted* • DLEE 775QEO8322 • **Value $30**	**(13)** Springtime Bonnets (2nd, 1994) *Handcrafted* • BISH 775QEO8096 • **Value $26**	**(14)** Springtime Bonnets (3rd, 1995) *Handcrafted* • UNRU 795QEO8227 • **Value $20**
(15) Springtime Bonnets (4th, 1996) *Handcrafted* • PIKE 795QEO8134 • **Value $24**	**(16)** Springtime Bonnets (5th & final, 1997) *Handcrafted* • PIKE 795QEO8672 • **Value $16**	**(17)** 1931 Ford Model A Roadster (1st, 1998) *Die-Cast Metal* • PALM 1495QEO8416 • **Value $27**
(18) NEW! 1932 Chevrolet® Standard Sports Roadster (2nd, 1999) *Die-Cast Metal* • PALM 1495QEO8379 • **Value $14.95**		

1 NEW!
1956 GARTON® Hot Rod Racer (1st, 1999)
Die-Cast Metal • UNRU
1395QEO8479 • **Value $13.95**

1999

2
40th Anniversary Edition BARBIE™ Lunch Box
Pressed Tin • N/A
1295QEO8399 • **Value $12.95**

3
Batter Up! Charlie Brown and Snoopy, PEANUTS® (set/2)
Handcrafted • RHOD
1295QEO8389 • **Value $12.95**

4
Birthday Celebration
Handcrafted • AUBE
895QEO8409 • **Value $8.95**

5
Cross of Faith
Precious Metal • VOTR
1395QEO8467 • **Value $13.95**

6
Easter Egg Nest
Pressed Tin • SICK
795QEO8427 • **Value $7.95**

7
Final Putt, Minnie Mouse
Handcrafted • N/A
1095QEO8349 • **Value $10.95**

8
Friendly Delivery, Mary's Bears
Handcrafted • KLIN
1295QEO8419 • **Value $12.95**

9
Happy Bubble Blower
Handcrafted • TAGU
795QEO8437 • **Value $7.95**

10
Happy Diploma Day!
Handcrafted • N/A
1095QEO8357 • **Value $10.95**

11
Inspirational Angel
Handcrafted • LYLE
1295QEO8347 • **Value $12.95**

12
Mop Top Billy, Madame Alexander® (complements Mop Top Wendy, 1998)
Handcrafted • FRAN
1495QEO8337 • **Value $14.95**

13
Precious Baby, Commemorative
Handcrafted • LYLE
995QEO8417 • **Value $9.95**

14
Spring Chick
Handcrafted • AUBE
2200QEO8469 • **Value $22**

15
Springtime Harvest
Handcrafted • SICK
795QEO8429 • **Value $7.95**

16
The Tale of Peter Rabbit™, Beatrix Potter™ (set/3)
Handcrafted • VOTR
1995QEO8397 • **Value $19.95**

17
Tiggerific Easter Delivery
Handcrafted • N/A
1095QEO8359 • **Value $10.95**

18
Wedding Memories
Porcelain • UNRU
995QEO8407 • **Value $9.95**

WINNER'S CIRCLE

	Price Paid	Value of My Collection
1.		

1999 COLLECTION

2.		
3.		
4.		
5.		
6.		
7.		
8.		
9.		
10.		
11.		
12.		
13.		
14.		
15.		
16.		
17.		
18.		
PENCIL TOTALS		

SPRING ORNAMENTS

1998

1 Bashful Gift (set/2)
Handcrafted • AUBE
1195QEO8446 • **Value $20**

2 Bouquet of Memories
Handcrafted • TAGU
795QEO8456 • **Value $16**

3 Forever Friends
The Andrew
Brownsword Collection
Handcrafted • PIKE
995QEO8423 • **Value $18**

4 The Garden of Piglet
and Pooh (set/2)
Handcrafted • N/A
1295QEO8403 • **Value $21**

5 Going Up? Charlie
Brown – PEANUTS®
Handcrafted • PIKE
995QEO8433 • **Value $18**

6 Happy Diploma Day!
Handcrafted • HADD
795QEO8476 • **Value $16**

7 Midge™ – 35th
Anniversary
Handcrafted • ANDR
1495QEO8413 • **Value $22**

1998 COLLECTION

	Price Paid	Value of My Collection
1.		
2.		
3.		
4.		
5.		
6.		
7.		
8.		
9.		
10.		
11.		
12.		
13.		
14.		
15.		
16.		
17.		

1997 COLLECTION

18.		

PENCIL TOTALS

8 Practice Swing –
Donald Duck
Handcrafted • N/A
1095QEO8396 • **Value $18**

9 Precious Baby
Handcrafted • TAGU
995QEO8463 • **Value $18**

10 Special Friends
Handcrafted • VOTR
1295QEO8523 • **Value $20**

11 STAR WARS™
Pressed Tin • N/A
1295QEO8406 • **Value $24**

12 Sweet Birthday
Handcrafted • KLIN
795QEO8473 • **Value $16**

13 Tigger in the Garden
(Spring Preview)
Handcrafted • N/A
995QEO8436 • **Value $18**

14 Victorian Cross
Pewter • UNRU
895QEO8453 • **Value $18**

15 Wedding Memories
Porcelain • VOTR
995QEO8466 • **Value $19**

16 What's Your Name?
Handcrafted • KLIN
795QEO8443 • **Value $17**

17 Fair Valentine™
BARBIE® Doll
(3rd & final in *Be My
Valentine Collector Series™*)
Vinyl • N/A
5000QHV8743 • **Value N/E**

1997

18 Bumper Crop, Tender
Touches (set/3)
Handcrafted • SEAL
1495QEO8735 • **Value $25**

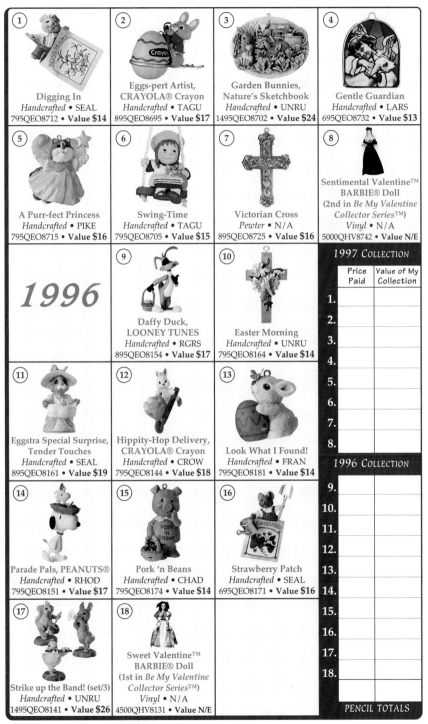

① **Digging In**
Handcrafted • SEAL
795QEO8712 • **Value $14**

② **Eggs-pert Artist,**
CRAYOLA® Crayon
Handcrafted • TAGU
895QEO8695 • **Value $17**

③ **Garden Bunnies,**
Nature's Sketchbook
Handcrafted • UNRU
1495QEO8702 • **Value $24**

④ **Gentle Guardian**
Handcrafted • LARS
695QEO8732 • **Value $13**

⑤ **A Purr-fect Princess**
Handcrafted • PIKE
795QEO8715 • **Value $16**

⑥ **Swing-Time**
Handcrafted • TAGU
795QEO8705 • **Value $15**

⑦ **Victorian Cross**
Pewter • N/A
895QEO8725 • **Value $16**

⑧ **Sentimental Valentine™**
BARBIE® Doll
(2nd in *Be My Valentine Collector Series™*)
Vinyl • N/A
5000QHV8742 • **Value N/E**

1996

⑨ **Daffy Duck,**
LOONEY TUNES
Handcrafted • RGRS
895QEO8154 • **Value $17**

⑩ **Easter Morning**
Handcrafted • UNRU
795QEO8164 • **Value $14**

⑪ **Eggstra Special Surprise,**
Tender Touches
Handcrafted • SEAL
895QEO8161 • **Value $19**

⑫ **Hippity-Hop Delivery,**
CRAYOLA® Crayon
Handcrafted • CROW
795QEO8144 • **Value $18**

⑬ **Look What I Found!**
Handcrafted • FRAN
795QEO8181 • **Value $14**

⑭ **Parade Pals, PEANUTS®**
Handcrafted • RHOD
795QEO8151 • **Value $17**

⑮ **Pork 'n Beans**
Handcrafted • CHAD
795QEO8174 • **Value $14**

⑯ **Strawberry Patch**
Handcrafted • SEAL
695QEO8171 • **Value $16**

⑰ **Strike up the Band! (set/3)**
Handcrafted • UNRU
1495QEO8141 • **Value $26**

⑱ **Sweet Valentine™**
BARBIE® Doll
(1st in *Be My Valentine Collector Series™*)
Vinyl • N/A
4500QHV8131 • **Value N/E**

	1997 COLLECTION	
	Price Paid	Value of My Collection
1.		
2.		
3.		
4.		
5.		
6.		
7.		
8.		
	1996 COLLECTION	
9.		
10.		
11.		
12.		
13.		
14.		
15.		
16.		
17.		
18.		
	PENCIL TOTALS	

SPRING ORNAMENTS

1995

(1) April Shower
Handcrafted • SIED
695QEO8253 • **Value $15**

(2) Baby's First Easter
Handcrafted • PALM
795QEO8237 • **Value $16**

(3) Bugs Bunny,
LOONEY TUNES™
Handcrafted • CHAD
895QEO8279 • **Value $19**

(4) Daughter
Handcrafted • RGRS
595QEO8239 • **Value $14**

(5) Easter Eggspress
Handcrafted • SIED
495QEO8269 • **Value $15**

(6) Elegant Lily
Brass • VOTR
695QEO8267 • **Value $14**

(7) Flowerpot Friends (set/3)
Handcrafted • ANDR
1495QEO8229 • **Value $26**

(8) Ham 'n Eggs
Handcrafted • CHAD
795QEO8277 • **Value $15**

(9) High Hopes,
Tender Touches
Handcrafted • SEAL
895QEO8259 • **Value $21**

(10) PEANUTS®
Handcrafted • RHOD
795QEO8257 • **Value $25**

(11) Picture Perfect,
Crayola® Crayon
Handcrafted • CROW
795QEO8249 • **Value $20**

(12) Son
Handcrafted • RGRS
595QEO8247 • **Value $17**

1994

(13) Baby's First Easter
Handcrafted • FRAN
675QEO8153 • **Value $20**

(14) Colorful Spring
Handcrafted • CROW
775QEO8166 • **Value $30**

(15) Daughter
Handcrafted • ANDR
575QEO8156 • **Value $16**

(16) Divine Duet
Handcrafted • VOTR
675QEO8183 • **Value $18**

(17) Easter Art Show
Handcrafted • VOTR
775QEO8193 • **Value $19**

(18) Joyful Lamb
Handcrafted • UNRU
575QEO8206 • **Value $15**

1995 COLLECTION

	Price Paid	Value of My Collection
1.		
2.		
3.		
4.		
5.		
6.		
7.		
8.		
9.		
10.		
11.		
12.		

1994 COLLECTION

	Price Paid	Value of My Collection
13.		
14.		
15.		
16.		
17.		
18.		
PENCIL TOTALS		

(1) **PEANUTS®** *Handcrafted* • UNRU 775QEO8176 • **Value $38**	**(2)** **Peeping Out** *Handcrafted* • UNRU 675QEO8203 • **Value $17**	**(3)** **Riding a Breeze** *Handcrafted* • PALM 575QEO8213 • **Value $18**	**(4)** **Son** *Handcrafted* • ANDR 575QEO8163 • **Value $17**
(5) **Sunny Bunny Garden (set/3)** *Handcrafted* • SEAL 1500QEO8146 • **Value $32**	**(6)** **Sweet as Sugar** *Handcrafted* • RGRS 875QEO8086 • **Value $20**	**(7)** **Sweet Easter Wishes, Tender Touches** *Handcrafted* • SEAL 875QEO8196 • **Value $26**	**(8)** **Treetop Cottage** *Handcrafted* • SICK 975QEO8186 • **Value $20**

(9) **Yummy Recipe** *Handcrafted* • RGRS 775QEO8143 • **Value $21**	*1993*	**(10)** **Baby's First Easter** *Handcrafted* • PALM 675QEO8345 • **Value $16**
(11) **Backyard Bunny** *Handcrafted* • SICK 675QEO8405 • **Value $17**	**(12)** **Barrow of Giggles** *Handcrafted* • ANDR 875QEO8402 • **Value $21**	**(13)** **Beautiful Memories** *Handcrafted* • UNRU 675QEO8362 • **Value $15**
(14) **Best-dressed Turtle** *Handcrafted* • JLEE 575QEO8392 • **Value $16**	**(15)** **Chicks-on-a-Twirl** *Handcrafted* • LYLE 775QEO8375 • **Value $18**	**(16)** **Daughter** *Handcrafted* • ANDR 575QEO8342 • **Value $17**
(17) **Grandchild** *Handcrafted* • SIED 675QEO8352 • **Value $19**	**(18)** **Li'l Peeper** *Handcrafted* • JLEE 775QEO8312 • **Value $22**	**(19)** **Lop-eared Bunny** *Handcrafted* • SICK 575QEO8315 • **Value $20**

1994 COLLECTION

	Price Paid	Value of My Collection
1.		
2.		
3.		
4.		
5.		
6.		
7.		
8.		
9.		

1993 COLLECTION

10.		
11.		
12.		
13		
14.		
15.		
16.		
17.		
18.		
19.		
PENCIL TOTALS		

SPRING ORNAMENTS

(1) Lovely Lamb
Porcelain • VOTR
975QEO8372 • **Value $23**

(2) Maypole Stroll (set/3)
Handcrafted/Wood
CHAD/FRAN
2800QEO8395 • **Value $52**

(3) Nutty Eggs
Handcrafted • JLEE
675QEO8382 • **Value $16**

(4) Radiant Window
Handcrafted • UNRU
775QEO8365 • **Value $18**

(5) Son
Handcrafted • ANDR
575QEO8335 • **Value $16**

(6) Time for Easter
Handcrafted • CHAD
875QEO8385 • **Value $21**

1992

(7) Baby's First Easter
Handcrafted • FRAN
675QEO9271 • **Value $22**

(8) Belle Bunny
Porcelain • VOTR
975QEO9354 • **Value $20**

(9) Bless You
Handcrafted • FRAN
675QEO9291 • **Value $23**

(10) Cosmic Rabbit
Handcrafted • SIED
775QEO9364 • **Value $20**

(11) CRAYOLA® Bunny
Handcrafted • RGRS
775QEO9304 • **Value $34**

(12) Cultivated Gardener
Handcrafted • SIED
575QEO9351 • **Value $16**

(13) Daughter
Handcrafted • RGRS
575QEO9284 • **Value $20**

(14) Eggspert Painter
Handcrafted • SIED
675QEO9361 • **Value $23**

(15) Everything's Ducky
Handcrafted • PIKE
675QEO9331 • **Value $19**

(16) Grandchild
Handcrafted • CROW
675QEO9274 • **Value $21**

(17) Joy Bearer
Handcrafted • PALM
875QEO9334 • **Value $24**

(18) Promise of Easter
Porcelain • LYLE
875QEO9314 • **Value $18**

(19) Rocking Bunny
Porcelain/Nickel-Plated • VOTR
975QEO9324 • **Value $23**

1993 Collection

	Price Paid	Value of My Collection
1.		
2.		
3.		
4.		
5.		
6.		
7.		

1992 Collection

9.		
8.		
10.		
11.		
12.		
13		
14.		
15.		
16.		
17.		
18.		
19.		
PENCIL TOTALS		

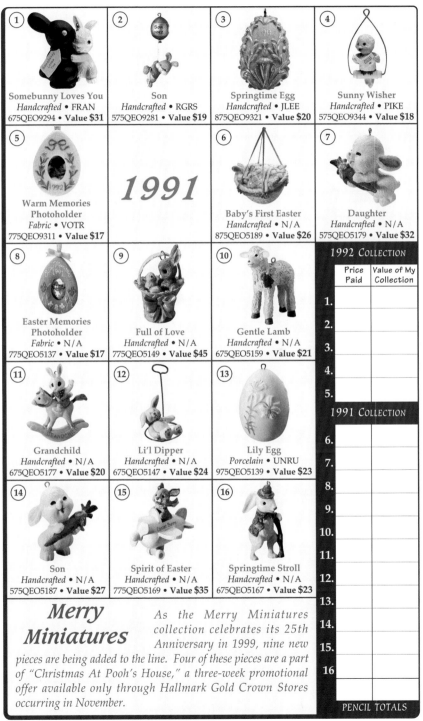

① Somebunny Loves You
Handcrafted • FRAN
675QEO9294 • **Value $31**

② Son
Handcrafted • RGRS
575QEO9281 • **Value $19**

③ Springtime Egg
Handcrafted • JLEE
875QEO9321 • **Value $20**

④ Sunny Wisher
Handcrafted • PIKE
575QEO9344 • **Value $18**

⑤ Warm Memories Photoholder
Fabric • VOTR
775QEO9311 • **Value $17**

1991

⑥ Baby's First Easter
Handcrafted • N/A
875QEO5189 • **Value $26**

⑦ Daughter
Handcrafted • N/A
575QEO5179 • **Value $32**

⑧ Easter Memories Photoholder
Fabric • N/A
775QEO5137 • **Value $17**

⑨ Full of Love
Handcrafted • N/A
775QEO5149 • **Value $45**

⑩ Gentle Lamb
Handcrafted • N/A
675QEO5159 • **Value $21**

⑪ Grandchild
Handcrafted • N/A
675QEO5177 • **Value $20**

⑫ Li'l Dipper
Handcrafted • N/A
675QEO5147 • **Value $24**

⑬ Lily Egg
Porcelain • UNRU
975QEO5139 • **Value $23**

⑭ Son
Handcrafted • N/A
575QEO5187 • **Value $27**

⑮ Spirit of Easter
Handcrafted • N/A
775QEO5169 • **Value $35**

⑯ Springtime Stroll
Handcrafted • N/A
675QEO5167 • **Value $23**

	1992 COLLECTION	
	Price Paid	Value of My Collection
1.		
2.		
3.		
4.		
5.		
	1991 COLLECTION	
6.		
7.		
8.		
9.		
10.		
11.		
12.		
13.		
14.		
15.		
16.		
PENCIL TOTALS		

SPRING ORNAMENTS

Merry Miniatures

As the Merry Miniatures collection celebrates its 25th Anniversary in 1999, nine new pieces are being added to the line. Four of these pieces are a part of "Christmas At Pooh's House," a three-week promotional offer available only through Hallmark Gold Crown Stores occurring in November.

1999

(1) Anniversary Edition (set/2)
Handcrafted • HADD
1295QFM8529 • **Value $12.95**

(2) Bashful Friends Merry Miniatures® (set/3)
Handcrafted • AUBE
1295QSM8459 • **Value $12.95**

(3) Eeyore
Handcrafted • N/A
495QRP8519 • **Value $4.95**

(4) Favorite Friends (set/2)
Handcrafted • KLIN
895QFM8537 • **Value $8.95**

(5) A Kiss For You–HERSHEY'S™ (set/3, 3rd & final, HERSHEY'S™)
Handcrafted • BRIC
1295QFM8497 • **Value $12.95**

(6) Park Avenue Wendy & Alex the Bellhop Madame Alexander® (Premiere, set/2)
Handcrafted • FRAN
1295QFM8499 • **Value $12.95**

(7) Piglet on Base
Handcrafted • N/A
495QRP8507 • **Value $4.95**

1999 Collection

	Price Paid	Value of My Collection
1.		
2.		
3.		
4.		
5.		
6.		
7.		
8.		
9.		

(8) Tigger
Handcrafted • N/A
495QRP8527 • **Value $4.95**

(9) Winnie the Pooh
Handcrafted • N/A
495QRP8509 • **Value $4.95**

1998

(10) Bride and Groom–1996 Madame Alexander® (Premiere)
Handcrafted • FRAN
1295QFM8486 • **Value $21**

(11) Donald's Passenger Car
Handcrafted • N/A
595QRP8513 • **Value $15**

(12) Goofy's Caboose
Handcrafted • N/A
595QRP8516 • **Value $15**

1998 Collection

10.		
11.		
12.		
13.		
14.		
15.		
16.		
17.		

(13) HERSHEY'S™ (Premiere, set/2, 2nd, HERSHEY'S™)
Handcrafted • BRIC
1095QFM8493 • **Value $18**

(14) Mickey's Locomotive
Handcrafted • N/A
595QRP8496 • **Value $15**

(15) Minnie's Luggage Car
Handcrafted • N/A
595QRP8506 • **Value $15**

(16) Pluto's Coal Car
Handcrafted • N/A
595QRP8503 • **Value $15**

(17) Rapunzel (Spring Preview, set/2)
Handcrafted • TAGU
1295QSM8483 • **Value $19**

PENCIL TOTALS

1997

① Apple Harvest – Mary's Bears (set/3)
Handcrafted • HAMI
1295QFM8585 • **Value $19**

② Bashful Visitors (set/3)
Handcrafted • AUBE
1295QFM8582 • **Value $21**

③ Cupid Cameron
Handcrafted • N/A
495QSM8552 • **Value $13**

④ Easter Parade (set/2)
Handcrafted • TAGU
795QSM8562 • **Value $15**

⑤ Getting Ready for Spring (set/3)
Handcrafted • TAGU
1295QSM8575 • **Value $19**

⑥ Happy Birthday Clowns (3rd & final, *Happy Birthday Clowns*)
Handcrafted • N/A
495QSM8565 • **Value $13**

⑦ HERSHEY'S™ (set/2, 1st, *HERSHEY'S*™)
Handcrafted • BRIC
1295QFM8625 • **Value $22**

⑧ Holiday Harmony (set/3)
Handcrafted • TAGU
1295QFM8612 • **Value $19**

⑨ Making a Wish (set/2)
Handcrafted • TAGU
795QFM8592 • **Value $13**

⑩ The Nativity (set/2)
Handcrafted • N/A
795QFM8615 • **Value $14**

⑪ Noah's Friends (set/2)
Handcrafted • ESCH
795QSM8572 • **Value $20**

⑫ Peter Pan (set/5)
Handcrafted • TAGU
1995QSM8605 • **Value $37**

⑬ Santa Cameron
Handcrafted • N/A
495QFM8622 • **Value $16**

⑭ Six Dwarfs (set/3)
Handcrafted • ESCH
1295QFM8685 • **Value $21**

⑮ Snow White and Dancing Dwarf (set/2)
Handcrafted • ESCH
795QFM8535 • **Value $16**

⑯ Snowbear Season (Premiere, set/3)
Handcrafted • ESCH
1295QFM8602 • **Value $20**

⑰ Sule and Sara – PendaKids™ (set/2)
Handcrafted • JOHN
795QSM8545 • **Value $12**

⑱ Tea Time – Mary's Bears (set/3)
Handcrafted • HAMI
1295QSM8542 • **Value $20**

⑲ Three Wee Kings (set/3)
Handcrafted • N/A
1295QFM8692 • **Value $19**

1997 COLLECTION

	Price Paid	Value of My Collection
1.		
2.		
3.		
4.		
5.		
6.		
7.		
8.		
9.		
10.		
11.		
12.		
13.		
14.		
15.		
16.		
17.		
18.		
19.		
PENCIL TOTALS		

MERRY MINIATURES

VALUE GUIDE – MERRY MINIATURES

1996

① Alice in Wonderland (set/5)
Handcrafted • N/A
1995QSM8014 • **Value $35**

② Bashful Mistletoe (Premiere, set/3)
Handcrafted • N/A
1295QFM8319 • **Value $24**

③ Blue-Ribbon Bunny
Handcrafted • N/A
495QSM8064 • **Value $15**

④ Busy Bakers (set/2)
Handcrafted • N/A
795QFM8121 • **Value $14**

⑤ Cowboy Cameron (set/3)
Handcrafted • N/A
1295QFM8041 • **Value $27**

⑥ Easter Egg Hunt
Handcrafted • N/A
495QSM8024 • **Value $15**

⑦ Giving Thanks (set/3)
Handcrafted • N/A
1295QFM8134 • **Value $24**

⑧ Happy Birthday Clowns (set/2, 2nd, *Happy Birthday Clowns*)
Handcrafted • N/A
795QSM8114 • **Value $16**

⑨ Happy Haunting (set/2)
Handcrafted • N/A
1295QFM8124 • **Value $25**

⑩ Lucky Cameron (set/2)
Handcrafted • N/A
795QSM8021 • **Value $16**

⑪ Mr. and Mrs. Claus Bears (set/2)
Handcrafted • N/A
795QFM8044 • **Value $17**

⑫ Noah and Friends (set/5)
Handcrafted • N/A
1995QSM8111 • **Value $38**

⑬ PEANUTS® Pumpkin Patch (set/5)
Handcrafted • N/A
1995QFM8131 • **Value $37**

⑭ Penda Kids (set/2)
Handcrafted • N/A
795QSM8011 • **Value $15**

⑮ Santa's Helpers (set/3)
Handcrafted • N/A
1295QFM8051 • **Value $23**

⑯ The Sewing Club (set/3)
Handcrafted • N/A
1295QFM8061 • **Value $25**

⑰ Sweetheart Cruise (set/3)
Handcrafted • N/A
1295QSM8004 • **Value $22**

1995

⑱ Bashful Boy
Handcrafted • N/A
300QSM8107 • **Value $16**

1996 COLLECTION

	Price Paid	Value of My Collection
1.		
2.		
3.		
4.		
5.		
6.		
7.		
8.		
9.		
10.		
11.		
12.		
13.		
14.		
15.		
16.		
17.		

1995 COLLECTION

	Price Paid	Value of My Collection
18.		
PENCIL TOTALS		

#	Name	Details
1	**Bashful Girl**	*Handcrafted* • N/A 300QSM8109 • **Value $16**
2	**Beauregard**	*Handcrafted* • N/A 300QSM8047 • **Value N/E**
3	**Birthday Bear (1st,** *Happy Birthday Clowns*)	*Handcrafted* • N/A 375QSM8057 • **Value $15**
4	**Bride & Groom**	*Handcrafted* • N/A 375QSM8067 • **Value $15**
5	**Cameron**	*Handcrafted* • N/A 375QSM8009 • **Value $20**
6	**Cameron/Bunny**	*Handcrafted* • N/A 375QSM8029 • **Value $19**
7	**Cameron in Pumpkin Costume**	*Handcrafted* • N/A 375QFM8147 • **Value $18**
8	**Cameron on Sled**	*Handcrafted* • N/A 375QFM8199 • **Value $15**
9	**Cameron Pilgrim**	*Handcrafted* • N/A 375QFM8169 • **Value $16**
10	**Cameron w/Camera**	*Handcrafted* • N/A 375QSM8077 • **Value $16**
11	**Caroling Bear**	*Handcrafted* • N/A 325QFM8307 • **Value $14**
12	**Caroling Bunny**	*Handcrafted* • N/A 325QFM8309 • **Value $14**
13	**Caroling Mouse**	*Handcrafted* • N/A 300QFM8317 • **Value $14**
14	**Chipmunk with Corn**	*Handcrafted* • N/A 375QFM8179 • **Value $11**
15	**Christmas Tree**	*Handcrafted* • N/A 675QFM8197 • **Value $18**
16	**Cinderella**	*Handcrafted* • N/A 400QSM8117 • **Value $35**
17	**Cottage**	*Handcrafted* • N/A 675QSM8027 • **Value $21**
18	**Cute Witch**	*Handcrafted* • N/A 300QFM8157 • **Value $12**
19	**Fairy Godmother**	*Handcrafted* • N/A 400QSM8089 • **Value $21**
20	**Feast Table**	*Handcrafted* • N/A 475QFM8167 • **Value $13**

1995 COLLECTION

	Price Paid	Value of My Collection
1.		
2.		
3.		
4.		
5.		
6.		
7.		
8.		
9.		
10.		
11.		
12.		
13.		
14.		
15.		
16.		
17.		
18.		
19.		
20.		
	PENCIL TOTALS	

MERRY MINIATURES

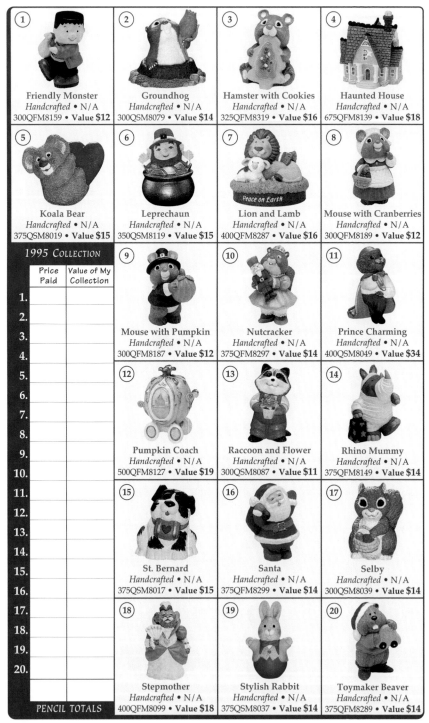

① Friendly Monster
Handcrafted • N/A
300QFM8159 • **Value $12**

② Groundhog
Handcrafted • N/A
300QSM8079 • **Value $14**

③ Hamster with Cookies
Handcrafted • N/A
325QFM8319 • **Value $16**

④ Haunted House
Handcrafted • N/A
675QFM8139 • **Value $18**

⑤ Koala Bear
Handcrafted • N/A
375QSM8019 • **Value $15**

⑥ Leprechaun
Handcrafted • N/A
350QSM8119 • **Value $15**

⑦ Lion and Lamb
Handcrafted • N/A
400QFM8287 • **Value $16**

⑧ Mouse with Cranberries
Handcrafted • N/A
300QFM8189 • **Value $12**

⑨ Mouse with Pumpkin
Handcrafted • N/A
300QFM8187 • **Value $12**

⑩ Nutcracker
Handcrafted • N/A
375QFM8297 • **Value $14**

⑪ Prince Charming
Handcrafted • N/A
400QSM8049 • **Value $34**

⑫ Pumpkin Coach
Handcrafted • N/A
500QFM8127 • **Value $19**

⑬ Raccoon and Flower
Handcrafted • N/A
300QSM8087 • **Value $11**

⑭ Rhino Mummy
Handcrafted • N/A
375QFM8149 • **Value $14**

⑮ St. Bernard
Handcrafted • N/A
375QSM8017 • **Value $15**

⑯ Santa
Handcrafted • N/A
375QFM8299 • **Value $14**

⑰ Selby
Handcrafted • N/A
300QSM8039 • **Value $14**

⑱ Stepmother
Handcrafted • N/A
400QFM8099 • **Value $18**

⑲ Stylish Rabbit
Handcrafted • N/A
375QSM8037 • **Value $14**

⑳ Toymaker Beaver
Handcrafted • N/A
375QFM8289 • **Value $14**

1995 Collection

	Price Paid	Value of My Collection
1.		
2.		
3.		
4.		
5.		
6.		
7.		
8.		
9.		
10.		
11.		
12.		
13.		
14.		
15.		
16.		
17.		
18.		
19.		
20.		
PENCIL TOTALS		

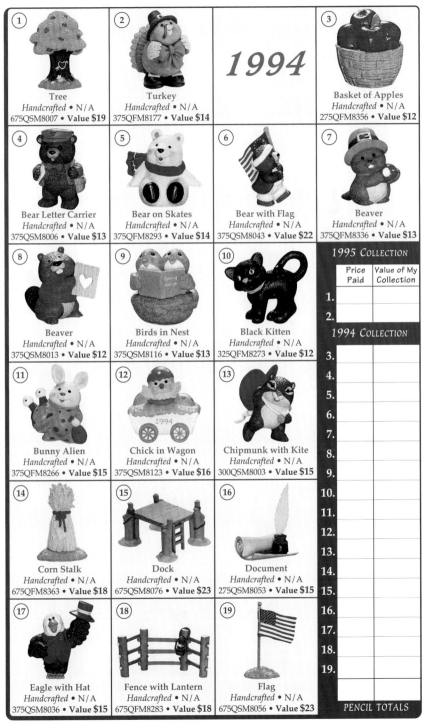

1. Tree
Handcrafted • N/A
675QSM8007 • **Value $19**

2. Turkey
Handcrafted • N/A
375QFM8177 • **Value $14**

1994

3. Basket of Apples
Handcrafted • N/A
275QFM8356 • **Value $12**

4. Bear Letter Carrier
Handcrafted • N/A
375QSM8006 • **Value $13**

5. Bear on Skates
Handcrafted • N/A
375QFM8293 • **Value $14**

6. Bear with Flag
Handcrafted • N/A
375QSM8043 • **Value $22**

7. Beaver
Handcrafted • N/A
375QFM8336 • **Value $13**

8. Beaver
Handcrafted • N/A
375QSM8013 • **Value $12**

9. Birds in Nest
Handcrafted • N/A
375QSM8116 • **Value $13**

10. Black Kitten
Handcrafted • N/A
325QFM8273 • **Value $12**

11. Bunny Alien
Handcrafted • N/A
375QFM8266 • **Value $15**

12. Chick in Wagon
Handcrafted • N/A
375QSM8123 • **Value $16**

13. Chipmunk with Kite
Handcrafted • N/A
300QSM8003 • **Value $15**

14. Corn Stalk
Handcrafted • N/A
675QFM8363 • **Value $18**

15. Dock
Handcrafted • N/A
675QSM8076 • **Value $23**

16. Document
Handcrafted • N/A
275QSM8053 • **Value $15**

17. Eagle with Hat
Handcrafted • N/A
375QSM8036 • **Value $15**

18. Fence with Lantern
Handcrafted • N/A
675QFM8283 • **Value $18**

19. Flag
Handcrafted • N/A
675QSM8056 • **Value $23**

1995 COLLECTION	Price Paid	Value of My Collection
1.		
2.		
1994 COLLECTION		
3.		
4.		
5.		
6.		
7.		
8.		
9.		
10.		
11.		
12.		
13.		
14.		
15.		
16.		
17.		
18.		
19.		
PENCIL TOTALS		

MERRY MINIATURES

(1) Fox on Skates
Handcrafted • N/A
375QFM8303 • **Value $14**

(2) Indian Bunny
Handcrafted • N/A
275QFM8353 • **Value $11**

(3) Indian Chickadee
Handcrafted • N/A
325QFM8346 • **Value $14**

(4) Lamb
Handcrafted • N/A
325QSM8132• **Value $12**

(5) Mailbox
Handcrafted • N/A
675QSM8023 • **Value $18**

(6) Mouse with Flower
Handcrafted • N/A
275QSM8243 • **Value $13**

(7) Mrs. Claus
Handcrafted • N/A
375QFM8286 • **Value $16**

(8) North Pole Sign
Handcrafted • N/A
675QFM8333 • **Value $19**

1994 Collection

	Price Paid	Value of My Collection
1.		
2.		
3.		
4.		
5.		
6.		
7.		
8.		
9.		
10.		
11.		
12.		
13.		
14.		
15.		
16.		
17.		
18.		
19.		
20.		
PENCIL TOTALS		

(9) Owl in Stump
Handcrafted • N/A
275QSM8243 • **Value $13**

(10) Pail of Seashells
Handcrafted • N/A
275QSM8052 • **Value $14**

(11) Penguin
Handcrafted • N/A
275QFM8313 • **Value $18**

(12) Pilgrim Bunny
Handcrafted • N/A
375QFM8343 • **Value $13**

(13) Polar Bears
Handcrafted • N/A
325QFM8323 • **Value $16**

(14) Pumpkin with Hat
Handcrafted • N/A
275QFM8276 • **Value $13**

(15) Rabbit
Handcrafted • N/A
275QSM8066 • **Value $13**

(16) Rabbit
Handcrafted • N/A
325QSM8016 • **Value $12**

(17) Rabbit with Can
Handcrafted • N/A
325QSM8083 • **Value $13**

(18) Rabbit with Croquet
Handcrafted • N/A
375QSM8113 • **Value $11**

(19) Raccoon
Handcrafted • N/A
375QSM8063 • **Value $17**

(20) Sled Dog
Handcrafted • N/A
325QFM8306 • **Value $16**

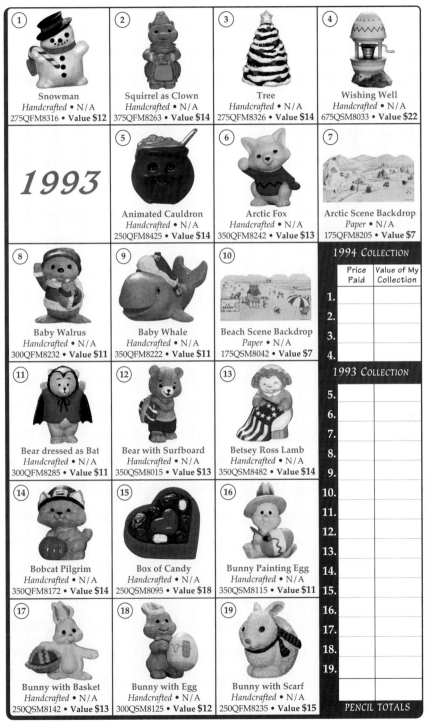

1 Snowman
Handcrafted • N/A
275QFM8316 • **Value $12**

2 Squirrel as Clown
Handcrafted • N/A
375QFM8263 • **Value $14**

3 Tree
Handcrafted • N/A
275QFM8326 • **Value $14**

4 Wishing Well
Handcrafted • N/A
675QSM8033 • **Value $22**

1993

5 Animated Cauldron
Handcrafted • N/A
250QFM8425 • **Value $14**

6 Arctic Fox
Handcrafted • N/A
350QFM8242 • **Value $13**

7 Arctic Scene Backdrop
Paper • N/A
175QFM8205 • **Value $7**

8 Baby Walrus
Handcrafted • N/A
300QFM8232 • **Value $11**

9 Baby Whale
Handcrafted • N/A
350QFM8222 • **Value $11**

10 Beach Scene Backdrop
Paper • N/A
175QSM8042 • **Value $7**

11 Bear dressed as Bat
Handcrafted • N/A
300QFM8285 • **Value $11**

12 Bear with Surfboard
Handcrafted • N/A
350QSM8015 • **Value $13**

13 Betsey Ross Lamb
Handcrafted • N/A
350QSM8482 • **Value $14**

14 Bobcat Pilgrim
Handcrafted • N/A
350QFM8172 • **Value $14**

15 Box of Candy
Handcrafted • N/A
250QSM8095 • **Value $18**

16 Bunny Painting Egg
Handcrafted • N/A
350QSM8115 • **Value $11**

17 Bunny with Basket
Handcrafted • N/A
250QSM8142 • **Value $13**

18 Bunny with Egg
Handcrafted • N/A
300QSM8125 • **Value $12**

19 Bunny with Scarf
Handcrafted • N/A
250QFM8235 • **Value $15**

1994 COLLECTION	Price Paid	Value of My Collection
1.		
2.		
3.		
4.		
1993 COLLECTION		
5.		
6.		
7.		
8.		
9.		
10.		
11.		
12.		
13.		
14.		
15.		
16.		
17.		
18.		
19.		
PENCIL TOTALS		

MERRY MINIATURES

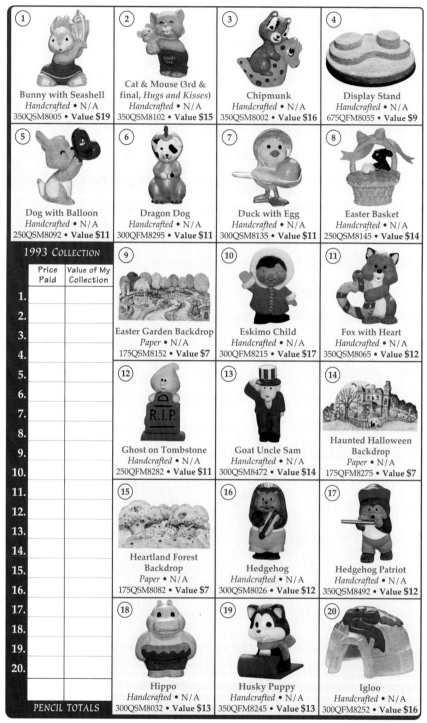

① Bunny with Seashell
Handcrafted • N/A
350QSM8005 • **Value $19**

② Cat & Mouse (3rd & final, *Hugs and Kisses*)
Handcrafted • N/A
350QSM8102 • **Value $15**

③ Chipmunk
Handcrafted • N/A
350QSM8002 • **Value $16**

④ Display Stand
Handcrafted • N/A
675QFM8055 • **Value $9**

⑤ Dog with Balloon
Handcrafted • N/A
250QSM8092 • **Value $11**

⑥ Dragon Dog
Handcrafted • N/A
300QFM8295 • **Value $11**

⑦ Duck with Egg
Handcrafted • N/A
300QSM8135 • **Value $11**

⑧ Easter Basket
Handcrafted • N/A
250QSM8145 • **Value $14**

1993 Collection	Price Paid	Value of My Collection
1.		
2.		
3.		
4.		
5.		
6.		
7.		
8.		
9.		
10.		
11.		
12.		
13.		
14.		
15.		
16.		
17.		
18.		
19.		
20.		
PENCIL TOTALS		

⑨ Easter Garden Backdrop
Paper • N/A
175QSM8152 • **Value $7**

⑩ Eskimo Child
Handcrafted • N/A
300QFM8215 • **Value $17**

⑪ Fox with Heart
Handcrafted • N/A
350QSM8065 • **Value $12**

⑫ Ghost on Tombstone
Handcrafted • N/A
250QFM8282 • **Value $11**

⑬ Goat Uncle Sam
Handcrafted • N/A
300QSM8472 • **Value $14**

⑭ Haunted Halloween Backdrop
Paper • N/A
175QFM8275 • **Value $7**

⑮ Heartland Forest Backdrop
Paper • N/A
175QSM8082 • **Value $7**

⑯ Hedgehog
Handcrafted • N/A
300QSM8026 • **Value $12**

⑰ Hedgehog Patriot
Handcrafted • N/A
350QSM8492 • **Value $12**

⑱ Hippo
Handcrafted • N/A
300QSM8032 • **Value $13**

⑲ Husky Puppy
Handcrafted • N/A
350QFM8245 • **Value $13**

⑳ Igloo
Handcrafted • N/A
300QFM8252 • **Value $16**

1. Indian Bear
Handcrafted • N/A
350QFM8162 • **Value $13**

2. Indian Squirrel
Handcrafted • N/A
300QFM8182 • **Value $14**

3. Indian Turkey
Handcrafted • N/A
350QFM8165 • **Value $14**

4. Lamb
Handcrafted • N/A
350QSM8112 • **Value $12**

5. Liberty Bell
Handcrafted • N/A
250QSM8465 • **Value $14**

6. Liberty Mouse
Handcrafted • N/A
300QSM8475 • **Value $15**

7. Mouse in Sunglasses
Handcrafted • N/A
250QSM8035 • **Value $14**

8. Mouse Witch
Handcrafted • N/A
300QFM8292 • **Value $13**

9. Owl and Pumpkin
Handcrafted • N/A
300QFM8302 • **Value $14**

10. Panda (3rd & final,
Sweet Valentines)
Handcrafted • N/A
350QSM8105 • **Value $15**

11. Patriotic Backdrop
Paper • N/A
175QSM8495 • **Value $8**

12. Penguin in Hat
Handcrafted • N/A
300QFM8212 • **Value $13**

13. Pig in Blanket
Handcrafted • N/A
300QSM8022 • **Value $16**

14. Pilgrim Chipmunk
Handcrafted • N/A
300QFM8185 • **Value $15**

15. Pilgrim Mouse
Handcrafted • N/A
300QFM8175 • **Value $17**

16. Plymouth Rock
Handcrafted • N/A
250QFM8192 • **Value $17**

17. Polar Bear (3rd & final,
Music Makers)
Handcrafted • N/A
350QFM8265 • **Value $17**

18. Prairie Dog
Handcrafted • N/A
350QSM8012 • **Value $16**

19. Princess Cat
Handcrafted • N/A
350QFM8305 • **Value $17**

20. Raccoon with Heart
Handcrafted • N/A
350QSM8062 • **Value $11**

1993 COLLECTION

	Price Paid	Value of My Collection
1.		
2.		
3.		
4.		
5.		
6.		
7.		
8.		
9.		
10.		
11.		
12.		
13.		
14.		
15.		
16.		
17.		
18.		
19.		
20.		
PENCIL TOTALS		

MERRY MINIATURES

(1) Sandcastle
Handcrafted • N/A
300QSM8045 • **Value $15**

(2) Santa Eskimo
Handcrafted • N/A
350QFM8262 • **Value $25**

(3) Seal with Earmuffs
Handcrafted • N/A
250QFM8272 • **Value $12**

(4) Sherlock Duck
Handcrafted • N/A
300QSM8122 • **Value $13**

(5) Skunk with Heart
Handcrafted • N/A
300QSM8072 • **Value $12**

(6) Stump & Can
Handcrafted • N/A
300QSM8075 • **Value $12**

(7) Super Hero Bunny
Handcrafted • N/A
300QFM8422 • **Value $12**

(8) Thanksgiving Feast Backdrop
Paper • N/A
175QFM8195 • **Value $7**

1993 COLLECTION

1992

(9) Baby's 1st Easter
Handcrafted • N/A
350QSM9777 • **Value $14**

(10) Ballet Pig
Handcrafted • N/A
250QSM9759 • **Value $16**

(11) Bear
(2nd, *Sweet Valentines*)
Handcrafted • N/A
350QSM9717 • **Value $22**

(12) Bear With Drum
(2nd, *Music Makers*)
Handcrafted • N/A
350QFM9134 • **Value $18**

(13) Bunny & Carrot
Handcrafted • N/A
250QSM9799 • **Value $15**

1992 COLLECTION

(14) Cat in P.J.'s
Handcrafted • N/A
350QFM9084 • **Value $14**

(15) Chipmunk
Handcrafted • N/A
250QFM9144 • **Value $11**

(16) Clown (3rd & final, *Birthday Clowns*)
Handcrafted • N/A
350QSM9819 • **Value $17**

(17) Clown Mouse
Handcrafted • N/A
250QFM9031 • **Value $14**

(18) Cow
Handcrafted • N/A
300QFM9034 • **Value $15**

(19) Crab
Handcrafted • N/A
300QFM9174 • **Value $11**

	Price Paid	Value of My Collection
1.		
2.		
3.		
4.		
5.		
6.		
7.		
8.		
9.		
10.		
11.		
12.		
13.		
14.		
15.		
16.		
17.		
18.		
19.		
PENCIL TOTALS		

1 Dog
Handcrafted • N/A
300QSM9847 • **Value $17**

2 Dog in P.J.'s
Handcrafted • N/A
350QFM9081 • **Value $14**

3 Ghost with Corn Candy
Handcrafted • N/A
300QFM9014 • **Value $16**

4 Giraffe as Tree
Handcrafted • N/A
300QFM9141 • **Value $14**

5 Goldfish
Handcrafted • N/A
300QFM9181 • **Value $12**

6 Goose in Bonnet
Handcrafted • N/A
300QSM9789 • **Value $15**

7 Grad Dog
Handcrafted • N/A
250QSM9817 • **Value $12**

8 Haunted House
Handcrafted • N/A
350QFM9024 • **Value $14**

9 Hedgehog
Handcrafted • N/A
250QSM9859 • **Value $13**

10 Horse
Handcrafted • N/A
300QFM9051 • **Value $18**

11 Indian Bunnies
Handcrafted • N/A
350QFM9004 • **Value $16**

12 Kitten for Dad
Handcrafted • N/A
350QSM9839 • **Value $15**

13 Kitten for Mom
Handcrafted • N/A
350QSM9837 • **Value $15**

14 Kitten in Bib
Handcrafted • N/A
350QSM9829 • **Value $13**

15 Lamb
Handcrafted • N/A
250QFM9044 • **Value $16**

16 Lamb
Handcrafted • N/A
350QSM9787 • **Value $16**

17 Lion
Handcrafted • N/A
350QSM9719 • **Value $14**

18 Mouse
Handcrafted • N/A
300QSM9769 • **Value $12**

19 Mouse in Car
Handcrafted • N/A
300QFM9114 • **Value $13**

20 Nina Ship
Handcrafted • N/A
350QFM9154 • **Value $13**

1992 Collection

	Price Paid	Value of My Collection
1.		
2.		
3.		
4.		
5.		
6.		
7.		
8.		
9.		
10.		
11.		
12.		
13.		
14.		
15.		
16.		
17.		
18.		
19.		
20.		
PENCIL TOTALS		

MERRY MINIATURES

(1) Octopus
Handcrafted • N/A
300QFM9171 • **Value $12**

(2) Party Dog
Handcrafted • N/A
300QFM9191 • **Value $13**

(3) Penguin in Tux
Handcrafted • N/A
300QSM9757 • **Value $16**

(4) Penguin Skating
Handcrafted • N/A
350QFM9091 • **Value $15**

(5) Pig
Handcrafted • N/A
250QFM9041 • **Value $19**

(6) Pilgrim Beaver
Handcrafted • N/A
300QFM9011 • **Value $14**

(7) Pinta Ship
Handcrafted • N/A
350QFM9161 • **Value $12**

(8) Praying Chipmunk
Handcrafted • N/A
300QSM9797 • **Value $15**

1992 Collection

	Price Paid	Value of My Collection
1.		
2.		
3.		
4.		
5.		
6.		
7.		
8.		
9.		
10.		
11.		
12.		
13.		
14.		
15.		
16.		
17.		
18.		
19.		
20.		
PENCIL TOTALS		

(9) Pumpkin
Handcrafted • N/A
300QFM9021 • **Value $14**

(10) Puppy
Handcrafted • N/A
250QSM9767 • **Value $18**

(11) Rabbit & Squirrel
(2nd, *Hugs and Kisses*)
Handcrafted • N/A
350QSM9827 • **Value $19**

(12) Rabbit Holding Heart Carrot
Handcrafted • N/A
350QFM9201 • **Value $14**

(13) Rabbit On Sled
Handcrafted • N/A
300QFM9151 • **Value $12**

(14) Santa Bee
Handcrafted • N/A
300QFM9061 • **Value $13**

(15) Santa Bell (3rd & final, *Jingle Bell Santa*)
Handcrafted • N/A
350QFM9131 • **Value $19**

(16) Santa Maria Ship
Handcrafted • N/A
350QFM9164 • **Value $13**

(17) Seal
Handcrafted • N/A
300QSM9849 • **Value $13**

(18) Skunk with Butterfly
Handcrafted • N/A
350QFM9184 • **Value $13**

(19) Snow Bunny
Handcrafted • N/A
400QFM9071 • **Value $12**

(20) Squirrel Pal (3rd & final, *Gentle Pals*)
Handcrafted • N/A
350QFM9094 • **Value $21**

(1) Squirrels in Nutshell *Handcrafted* • N/A 350QFM9064 • **Value $14**	**(2)** Sweatshirt Bunny *Handcrafted* • N/A 350QSM9779 • **Value $17**	**(3)** Sweet Angel *Handcrafted* • N/A 300QFM9124 • **Value $17**	**(4)** Teacher Cat *Handcrafted* • N/A 350QFM9074 • **Value $11**
(5) Teddy Bear *Handcrafted* • N/A 250QFM9194 • **Value $15**	**(6)** Thankful Turkey (3rd & final, *Thankful Turkey*) *Handcrafted* • N/A 350QFM9001 • **Value $22**	**(7)** Turtle & Mouse *Handcrafted* • N/A 300QSM9857 • **Value $24**	**(8)** Walrus & Bird *Handcrafted* • N/A 350QFM9054 • **Value $15**

(9) Waving Reindeer *Handcrafted* • N/A 300QFM9121 • **Value $15**	*1991*

(10) 1st Christmas Together *Handcrafted* • N/A 350QFM1799 • **Value $13**

(11) Aerobic Bunny *Handcrafted* • N/A 250QFM1817 • **Value $18**	**(12)** Artist Mouse *Handcrafted* • N/A 250QSM1519 • **Value $17**	**(13)** Baby Bunny *Handcrafted* • N/A 350QSM1619 • **Value $13**
(14) Baby's 1st Christmas *Handcrafted* • N/A 300QFM1797 • **Value $11**	**(15)** Baby's 1st Easter *Handcrafted* • N/A 300QSM1557 • **Value $14**	**(16)** Backpack Chipmunk *Handcrafted* • N/A 250QFM1809 • **Value $18**
(17) Baseball Bear *Handcrafted* • N/A 300QFM1827 • **Value $20**	**(18)** Bear *Handcrafted* • N/A 250QFM1669 • **Value $25**	**(19)** Bear (also avail. in Carousel Set, #2000QSM1667) *Handcrafted* • N/A 300QSM1637 • **Value $13**

1992 COLLECTION

	Price Paid	Value of My Collection
1.		
2.		
3.		
4.		
5.		
6.		
7.		
8.		
9.		

1991 COLLECTION

10.		
11.		
12.		
13.		
14.		
15.		
16.		
17.		
18.		
19.		
PENCIL TOTALS		

MERRY MINIATURES

(1) Bear
(1st, *Sweet Valentines*)
Handcrafted • N/A
350QSM1509 • **Value $24**

(2) Bears Hugging
(1st, *Hugs and Kisses*)
Handcrafted • N/A
350QSM1609 • **Value $26**

(3) Birthday Clown
(2nd, *Birthday Clowns*)
Handcrafted • N/A
350QSM1617 • **Value $20**

(4) Bunny
Handcrafted • N/A
300QFM1719 • **Value $13**

(5) Bunny
Handcrafted • N/A
300QSM1537 • **Value $16**

(6) Bunny Praying
Handcrafted • N/A
250QSM1597 • **Value $17**

(7) Camel
(also avail. in Carousel
Set, #2000QSM1667)
Handcrafted • N/A
300QSM1629 • **Value $13**

(8) Carousel Display
(also avail. in Carousel
Set, #2000QSM1667)
Handcrafted • N/A
500QSM1627 • **Value $17**

(9) Cat Witch
Handcrafted • N/A
300QFM1677 • **Value $16**

(10) Cookie Elf
Handcrafted • N/A
300QFM1769 • **Value $13**

(11) Cookie Reindeer
Handcrafted • N/A
300QFM1777 • **Value $13**

(12) Cookie Santa
Handcrafted • N/A
300QFM1767 • **Value $13**

(13) Daughter Bunny
Handcrafted • N/A
250QSM1587 • **Value $15**

(14) Dog in Cap & Gown
Handcrafted • N/A
250QSM1607 • **Value $14**

(15) Duck
Handcrafted • N/A
300QSM1549 • **Value $19**

(16) Elephant
(also avail. in Carousel
Set, #2000QSM1667)
Handcrafted • N/A
300QSM1647 • **Value $13**

(17) Football Beaver
Handcrafted • N/A
350QFM1829 • **Value $21**

(18) Fox
Handcrafted • N/A
350QFM1689 • **Value $13**

(19) Frog
Handcrafted • N/A
300QFM1729 • **Value $13**

(20) Gentle Pals Kitten
(2nd, *Gentle Pals*)
Handcrafted • N/A
350QFM1709 • **Value $20**

1991 COLLECTION

	Price Paid	Value of My Collection
1.		
2.		
3.		
4.		
5.		
6.		
7.		
8.		
9.		
10.		
11.		
12.		
13.		
14.		
15.		
16.		
17.		
18.		
19.		
20.		
PENCIL TOTALS		

1
Horse
(also avail. in Carousel Set, #2000QSM1667)
Handcrafted • N/A
300QSM1649 • **Value $25**

2
I Love Dad
Handcrafted • N/A
250QSM1657 • **Value $14**

3
I Love Mom
Handcrafted • N/A
250QSM1659 • **Value $14**

4
Indian Maiden
Handcrafted • N/A
250QFM1687 • **Value $14**

5
Irish Frog
Handcrafted • N/A
350QSM1539 • **Value $15**

6
Jingle Bell Santa
(2nd, *Jingle Bell Santa*)
Handcrafted • N/A
350QFM1717 • **Value $24**

7
Kitten
Handcrafted • N/A
300QFM1737 • **Value $13**

8
Lamb & Duck
Handcrafted • N/A
350QSM1569 • **Value $15**

9
Lion
(also avail. in Carousel Set, #2000QSM1667)
Handcrafted • N/A
300QSM1639 • **Value $18**

10
Mother Bunny
Handcrafted • N/A
300QSM1577 • **Value $17**

11
Mouse
Handcrafted • N/A
250QFM1789 • **Value $13**

12
Mummy
Handcrafted • N/A
250QFM1679 • **Value $15**

13
Music Makers Bear
(1st, *Music Makers*)
Handcrafted • N/A
300QFM1779 • **Value $23**

14
Pig
Handcrafted • N/A
300QFM1739 • **Value $15**

15
Puppy
Handcrafted • N/A
300QFM1727 • **Value $15**

16
Puppy
Handcrafted • N/A
300QFM1787 • **Value $14**

17
Puppy
Handcrafted • N/A
300QSM1529 • **Value $22**

18
Raccoon Thief
Handcrafted • N/A
350QSM1517 • **Value $13**

19
Skating Raccoon
Handcrafted • N/A
350QFM1837 • **Value $20**

20
Snow Bunny
Handcrafted • N/A
250QFM1749 • **Value $13**

1991 COLLECTION	
	Price Paid	Value of My Collection
1.		
2.		
3.		
4.		
5.		
6.		
7.		
8.		
9.		
10.		
11.		
12.		
13.		
14.		
15.		
16.		
17.		
18.		
19.		
20.		
PENCIL TOTALS		

MERRY MINIATURES

1 Snow Lamb *Handcrafted* • N/A 250QFM1759 • **Value $13**	**2** Snow Mice *Handcrafted* • N/A 250QFM1757 • **Value $13**

1
Snow Lamb
Handcrafted • N/A
250QFM1759 • **Value $13**

2
Snow Mice
Handcrafted • N/A
250QFM1757 • **Value $13**

3
Soccer Skunk
Handcrafted • N/A
300QFM1819 • **Value $20**

4
Teacher Raccoon
Handcrafted • N/A
350QFM1807 • **Value $11**

5
Turkey
(2nd, *Thankful Turkey*)
Handcrafted • N/A
350QFM1697 • **Value $22**

6
Turtle
Handcrafted • N/A
300QFM1747 • **Value $14**

1990

7
1st Christmas Together
Handcrafted • N/A
350QFM1686 • **Value $10**

1991 COLLECTION

	Price Paid	Value of My Collection
1.		
2.		
3.		
4.		
5.		
6.		

1990 COLLECTION

7.		
8.		
9.		
10.		
11.		
12.		
13.		
14.		
15.		
16.		
17.		
18.		
19.		

PENCIL TOTALS

8
Alligator
Handcrafted • N/A
300QSM1573 • **Value $12**

9
Artist Raccoon
Handcrafted • N/A
350QSM1543 • **Value $16**

10
Baby's 1st Christmas
Handcrafted • N/A
250QFM1683 • **Value $10**

11
Baby's 1st Easter
Handcrafted • N/A
300QSM1536 • **Value $14**

12
Baseball Bunny
Handcrafted • N/A
250QSM1576 • **Value $12**

13
Bear & Balloon
Handcrafted • N/A
300QFM1716 • **Value $11**

14
Birthday Clown
(1st, *Birthday Clowns*)
Handcrafted • N/A
350QFM1706 • **Value $20**

15
Boy Bunny
Handcrafted • N/A
350QSM1682 • **Value $12**

16
Bunny
Handcrafted • N/A
300QSM1593 • **Value $12**

17
Bunny in Tux
Handcrafted • N/A
300QFM1713 • **Value $12**

18
Candy Caboose
Handcrafted • N/A
350QFM1693 • **Value $16**

19
E-Bunny
Handcrafted • N/A
300QSM1726 • **Value $15**

1 Elephant
Handcrafted • N/A
350QSM1566 • **Value $12**

2 Gentle Pal – Lamb
(1st, *Gentle Pals*)
Handcrafted • N/A
350QFM1656 • **Value $21**

3 Get Well Puppy
Handcrafted • N/A
300QFM1703 • **Value $11**

4 Girl Bunny
Handcrafted • N/A
350QSM1675 • **Value $13**

5 Green Monster
Handcrafted • N/A
350QFM1613 • **Value $15**

6 Grey Mouse
Handcrafted • N/A
250QSM1533 • **Value $15**

7 Hippo Cupid
Handcrafted • N/A
350QSM1513 • **Value $20**

8 Indian Chipmunk
Handcrafted • N/A
300QFM1626 • **Value $16**

9 Jingle Bell Santa
(1st, *Jingle Bell Santa*)
Handcrafted • N/A
350QFM1663 • **Value $24**

10 Kangaroo
Handcrafted • N/A
350QFM1653 • **Value $11**

11 Kitten
Handcrafted • N/A
300QSM1516 • **Value $15**

12 Mama Polar Bear
Handcrafted • N/A
300QFM1666 • **Value $13**

13 Mouse
Handcrafted • N/A
250QSM1603 • **Value $15**

14 Mouse & Bunny
Handcrafted • N/A
350QSM1546 • **Value $16**

15 Owl
Handcrafted • N/A
300QSM1563 • **Value $19**

16 Papa Polar Bear & Child
Handcrafted • N/A
350QFM1673 • **Value $14**

17 Pig
Handcrafted • N/A
300QSM1526 • **Value $17**

18 Pilgrim Mouse
Handcrafted • N/A
250QFM1636 • **Value $14**

19 Pilgrim Squirrel
Handcrafted • N/A
300QFM1633 • **Value $15**

20 Puppy
Handcrafted • N/A
250QSM1583 • **Value $13**

1990 COLLECTION

	Price Paid	Value of My Collection
1.		
2.		
3.		
4.		
5.		
6.		
7.		
8.		
9.		
10.		
11.		
12.		
13.		
14.		
15.		
16.		
17.		
18.		
19.		
20.		
PENCIL TOTALS		

MERRY MINIATURES

① Raccoon
Handcrafted • N/A
350QSM1586 • **Value $14**

② Scarecrow
Handcrafted • N/A
350QFM1616 • **Value $15**

③ Snowman
Handcrafted • N/A
250QFM1646 • **Value $14**

④ Squirrel
Handcrafted • N/A
250QSM1553 • **Value $18**

⑤ Squirrel Caroler
Handcrafted • N/A
300QFM1696 • **Value $18**

⑥ Squirrel Hobo
Handcrafted • N/A
300QFM1606 • **Value $14**

⑦ Stitched Teddy
Handcrafted • N/A
350QSM1506 • **Value $28**

⑧ Teacher Mouse
Handcrafted • N/A
300QFM1676 • **Value $10**

1990 COLLECTION

	Price Paid	Value of My Collection
1.		
2.		
3.		
4.		
5.		
6.		
7.		
8.		
9.		
10.		

1989 COLLECTION

11.		
12.		
13.		
14.		
15.		
16.		
17.		
18.		
19.		

PENCIL TOTALS

⑨ Thankful Turkey
(1st, *Thankful Turkey*)
Handcrafted • N/A
350QFM1623 • **Value $24**

⑩ Walrus
Handcrafted • N/A
250QFM1643 • **Value $14**

1989

⑪ Baby Boy
Handcrafted • N/A
300QFM1585 • **Value $20**

⑫ Baby Girl
Handcrafted • N/A
300QFM1592 • **Value $20**

⑬ Baby's 1st Christmas
Handcrafted • N/A
300QFM1615 • **Value $16**

⑭ Bear
Handcrafted • N/A
250QSM1525 • **Value $20**

⑮ Bear Baker
Handcrafted • N/A
350QSM1522 • **Value $20**

⑯ Blue King
(also avail. in Nativity
Set, #3550QFM1685)
Handcrafted • N/A
300QFM1632 • **Value $22**

⑰ Bunny
Handcrafted • N/A
250QSM1512 • **Value $18**

⑱ Bunny
Handcrafted • N/A
300QFM1565 • **Value $14**

⑲ Bunny
Handcrafted • N/A
350QSM1552 • **Value $16**

1 Bunny & Skateboard
Handcrafted • N/A
350EBO3092 • **Value $29**

2 Bunny Caroler
Handcrafted • N/A
300QFM1662 • **Value $19**

3 Dog & Kitten
Handcrafted • N/A
350QSM1515 • **Value $31**

4 Elf
Handcrafted • N/A
300QFM1622 • **Value $16**

5 Grey Mouse
Handcrafted • N/A
250QSM1502 • **Value $22**

6 Joy Elf
Handcrafted • N/A
300QFM1605 • **Value $15**

7 Kitten
Handcrafted • N/A
250QSM1505 • **Value $23**

8 Lamb
Handcrafted • N/A
350QSM1545 • **Value $20**

9 Momma Bear
Handcrafted • N/A
350QFM1582 • **Value $17**

10 Mouse
Handcrafted • N/A
250QFM1572 • **Value $21**

11 Mouse Caroler
Handcrafted • N/A
250QFM1655 • **Value $20**

12 Mr. Claus
Handcrafted • N/A
350QFM1595 • **Value $16**

13 Mrs. Claus
Handcrafted • N/A
350QFM1602 • **Value $16**

14 Owl
Handcrafted • N/A
250QSM1555 • **Value $18**

15 Pink King
(also avail. in Nativity
Set, #3550QFM1685)
Handcrafted • N/A
300QFM1642 • **Value $12**

16 Raccoon
Handcrafted • N/A
350QFM1575 • **Value $14**

17 Raccoon Caroler
Handcrafted • N/A
350QFM1652 • **Value $17**

18 Teacher Elf
Handcrafted • N/A
300QFM1612 • **Value $15**

19 Train Car
Handcrafted • N/A
350QFM1562 • **Value $19**

20 Yellow King
(also avail. in Nativity
Set, #3550QFM1685)
Handcrafted • N/A
300QFM1635 • **Value $12**

1989 Collection

	Price Paid	Value of My Collection
1.		
2.		
3.		
4.		
5.		
6.		
7.		
8.		
9.		
10.		
11.		
12.		
13.		
14.		
15.		
16.		
17.		
18.		
19.		
20.		
PENCIL TOTALS		

MERRY MINIATURES

1988

1 Dog
Handcrafted • N/A
200GHA3524 • **Value $14**

2 Donkey
(also avail. in Nativity
Set, #3550QFM1685)
Handcrafted • N/A
225QFM1581 • **Value $11**

3 Indian Bear
Handcrafted • N/A
325QFM1511 • **Value $16**

4 Jesus
(also avail. in Nativity
Set, #3550QFM1685)
Handcrafted • N/A
250QFM1564 • **Value $22**

5 Joseph
(also avail. in Nativity
Set, #3550QFM1685)
Handcrafted • N/A
250QFM1561 • **Value $16**

6 Kitten in Slipper
Handcrafted • N/A
250QFM1544 • **Value $19**

7 Koala & Hearts
Handcrafted • N/A
200VHA3531 • **Value $12**

8 Koala & Lollipop
Handcrafted • N/A
200VHA3651 • **Value $21**

9 Koala & Ruffled Heart
Handcrafted • N/A
200VHA3631 • **Value $62**

10 Koala with
Bow & Arrow
Handcrafted • N/A
200VHA3624 • **Value $15**

11 Lamb
(also avail. in Nativity
Set, #3550QFM1685)
Handcrafted • N/A
225QFM1574 • **Value $27**

12 Mary
(also avail. in Nativity
Set, #3550QFM1685)
Handcrafted • N/A
250QFM1554 • **Value $17**

13 Mouse Angel
Handcrafted • N/A
250QFM1551 • **Value $30**

14 Mouse in Cornucopia
Handcrafted • N/A
225QFM1514 • **Value $15**

15 Mouse/Pumpkin
Handcrafted • N/A
225QFM1501 • **Value $52**

16 Owl
Handcrafted • N/A
225QFM1504 • **Value $18**

17 Penguin
Handcrafted • N/A
375QFM1541 • **Value $23**

18 Santa
Handcrafted • N/A
375QFM1521 • **Value $45**

19 Shepherd
(also avail. in Nativity
Set, #3550QFM1685)
Handcrafted • N/A
250QFM1571 • **Value $16**

1988 COLLECTION

	Price Paid	Value of My Collection
1.		
2.		
3.		
4.		
5.		
6.		
7.		
8.		
9.		
10.		
11.		
12.		
13.		
14.		
15.		
16.		
17.		
18.		
19.		
PENCIL TOTALS		

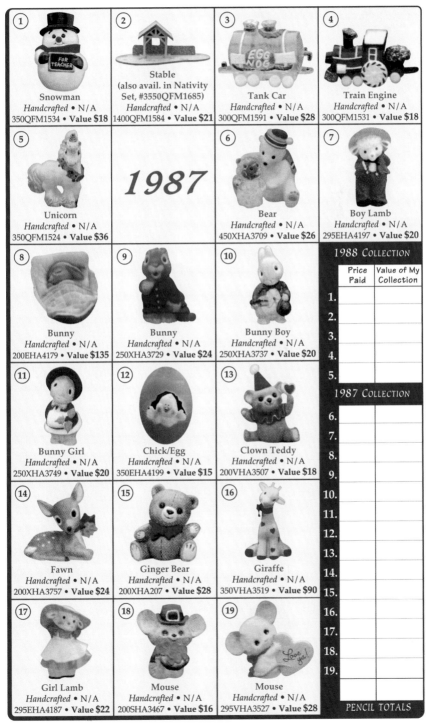

1. Snowman
Handcrafted • N/A
350QFM1534 • **Value $18**

2. Stable
(also avail. in Nativity Set, #3550QFM1685)
Handcrafted • N/A
1400QFM1584 • **Value $21**

3. Tank Car
Handcrafted • N/A
300QFM1591 • **Value $28**

4. Train Engine
Handcrafted • N/A
300QFM1531 • **Value $18**

5. Unicorn
Handcrafted • N/A
350QFM1524 • **Value $36**

1987

6. Bear
Handcrafted • N/A
450XHA3709 • **Value $26**

7. Boy Lamb
Handcrafted • N/A
295EHA4197 • **Value $20**

8. Bunny
Handcrafted • N/A
200EHA4179 • **Value $135**

9. Bunny
Handcrafted • N/A
250XHA3729 • **Value $24**

10. Bunny Boy
Handcrafted • N/A
250XHA3737 • **Value $20**

11. Bunny Girl
Handcrafted • N/A
250XHA3749 • **Value $20**

12. Chick/Egg
Handcrafted • N/A
350EHA4199 • **Value $15**

13. Clown Teddy
Handcrafted • N/A
200VHA3507 • **Value $18**

14. Fawn
Handcrafted • N/A
200XHA3757 • **Value $24**

15. Ginger Bear
Handcrafted • N/A
200XHA207 • **Value $28**

16. Giraffe
Handcrafted • N/A
350VHA3519 • **Value $90**

17. Girl Lamb
Handcrafted • N/A
295EHA4187 • **Value $22**

18. Mouse
Handcrafted • N/A
200SHA3467 • **Value $16**

19. Mouse
Handcrafted • N/A
295VHA3527 • **Value $28**

1988 Collection	Price Paid	Value of My Collection
1.		
2.		
3.		
4.		
5.		
1987 Collection		
6.		
7.		
8.		
9.		
10.		
11.		
12.		
13.		
14.		
15.		
16.		
17.		
18.		
19.		
PENCIL TOTALS		

MERRY MINIATURES

Value Guide – Merry Miniatures

① Puppy *Handcrafted* • N/A 200XHA3769 • **Value $21**	**②** Raccoon Witch *Handcrafted* • N/A 200HHA3487 • **Value $21**	**③** Santa *Handcrafted* • N/A 350XHA3717 • **Value $44**	**④** Sebastian *Handcrafted* • N/A 200EHA4167 • **Value $55**

⑤ Turkey
Handcrafted • N/A
375THA49 • **Value $19**

1986

⑥ Boy Bunny
Handcrafted • N/A
295EPF4133 • **Value $20**

⑦ Bunny
Handcrafted • N/A
350EHA3476 • **Value $20**

1987 COLLECTION

	Price Paid	Value of My Collection
1.		
2.		
3.		
4.		
5.		

1986 COLLECTION

6.		
7.		
8.		
9.		
10.		
11.		
12.		
13.		
14.		
15.		
16.		
17.		
18.		
19.		

PENCIL TOTALS

⑧ Bunny Girl
Handcrafted • N/A
295EPF4106 • **Value $20**

⑨ Cat
Handcrafted • N/A
200HHA3486 • **Value $22**

⑩ Duck
Handcrafted • N/A
295EHA3463 • **Value $15**

⑪ Duck Sailor
Handcrafted • N/A
295EPF4113 • **Value $17**

⑫ Girl Bunny
Handcrafted • N/A
200EHA3503 • **Value $32**

⑬ Goose
Handcrafted • N/A
200EHA3516 • **Value $16**

⑭ Katybeth
Handcrafted • N/A
200XHA3666 • **Value $47**

⑮ Mouse
Handcrafted • N/A
200XHA3533 • **Value $70**

⑯ Mr. Mouse
Handcrafted • N/A
200XHA3573 • **Value $30**

⑰ Mr. Squirrel
Handcrafted • N/A
200THA3403 • **Value $21**

⑱ Mrs. Mouse
Handcrafted • N/A
200XHA3653 • **Value $28**

⑲ Mrs. Squirrel
Handcrafted • N/A
200THA3416 • **Value $21**

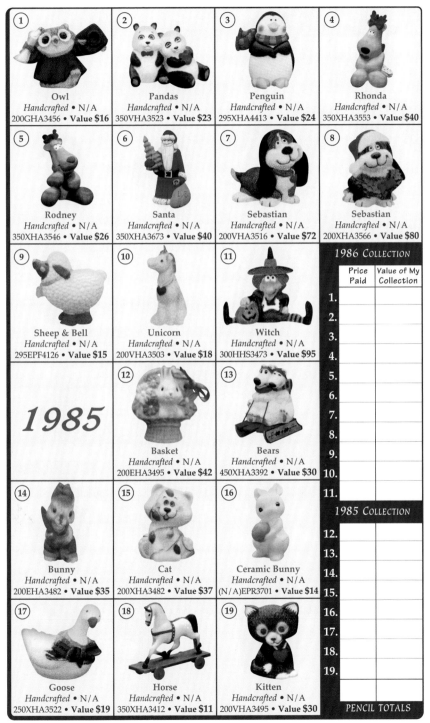

1 Owl
Handcrafted • N/A
200GHA3456 • **Value $16**

2 Pandas
Handcrafted • N/A
350VHA3523 • **Value $23**

3 Penguin
Handcrafted • N/A
295XHA4413 • **Value $24**

4 Rhonda
Handcrafted • N/A
350XHA3553 • **Value $40**

5 Rodney
Handcrafted • N/A
350XHA3546 • **Value $26**

6 Santa
Handcrafted • N/A
350XHA3673 • **Value $40**

7 Sebastian
Handcrafted • N/A
200VHA3516 • **Value $72**

8 Sebastian
Handcrafted • N/A
200XHA3566 • **Value $80**

9 Sheep & Bell
Handcrafted • N/A
295EPF4126 • **Value $15**

10 Unicorn
Handcrafted • N/A
200VHA3503 • **Value $18**

11 Witch
Handcrafted • N/A
300HHS3473 • **Value $95**

1985

12 Basket
Handcrafted • N/A
200EHA3495 • **Value $42**

13 Bears
Handcrafted • N/A
450XHA3392 • **Value $30**

14 Bunny
Handcrafted • N/A
200EHA3482 • **Value $35**

15 Cat
Handcrafted • N/A
200XHA3482 • **Value $37**

16 Ceramic Bunny
Handcrafted • N/A
(N/A)EPR3701 • **Value $14**

17 Goose
Handcrafted • N/A
250XHA3522 • **Value $19**

18 Horse
Handcrafted • N/A
350XHA3412 • **Value $11**

19 Kitten
Handcrafted • N/A
200VHA3495 • **Value $30**

1986 COLLECTION

	Price Paid	Value of My Collection
1.		
2.		
3.		
4.		
5.		
6.		
7.		
8.		
9.		
10.		
11.		

1985 COLLECTION

12.		
13.		
14.		
15.		
16.		
17.		
18.		
19.		
PENCIL TOTALS		

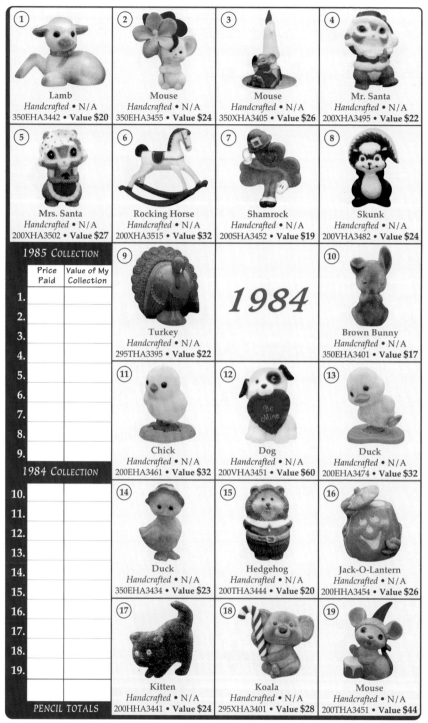

(1) Lamb
Handcrafted • N/A
350EHA3442 • **Value $20**

(2) Mouse
Handcrafted • N/A
350EHA3455 • **Value $24**

(3) Mouse
Handcrafted • N/A
350XHA3405 • **Value $26**

(4) Mr. Santa
Handcrafted • N/A
200XHA3495 • **Value $22**

(5) Mrs. Santa
Handcrafted • N/A
200XHA3502 • **Value $27**

(6) Rocking Horse
Handcrafted • N/A
200XHA3515 • **Value $32**

(7) Shamrock
Handcrafted • N/A
200SHA3452 • **Value $19**

(8) Skunk
Handcrafted • N/A
200VHA3482 • **Value $24**

(9) Turkey
Handcrafted • N/A
295THA3395 • **Value $22**

1984

(10) Brown Bunny
Handcrafted • N/A
350EHA3401 • **Value $17**

(11) Chick
Handcrafted • N/A
200EHA3461 • **Value $32**

(12) Dog
Handcrafted • N/A
200VHA3451 • **Value $60**

(13) Duck
Handcrafted • N/A
200EHA3474 • **Value $32**

(14) Duck
Handcrafted • N/A
350EHA3434 • **Value $23**

(15) Hedgehog
Handcrafted • N/A
200THA3444 • **Value $20**

(16) Jack-O-Lantern
Handcrafted • N/A
200HHA3454 • **Value $26**

(17) Kitten
Handcrafted • N/A
200HHA3441 • **Value $24**

(18) Koala
Handcrafted • N/A
295XHA3401 • **Value $28**

(19) Mouse
Handcrafted • N/A
200THA3451 • **Value $44**

1985 COLLECTION

	Price Paid	Value of My Collection
1.		
2.		
3.		
4.		
5.		
6.		
7.		
8.		
9.		

1984 COLLECTION

	Price Paid	Value of My Collection
10.		
11.		
12.		
13.		
14.		
15.		
16.		
17.		
18.		
19.		
PENCIL TOTALS		

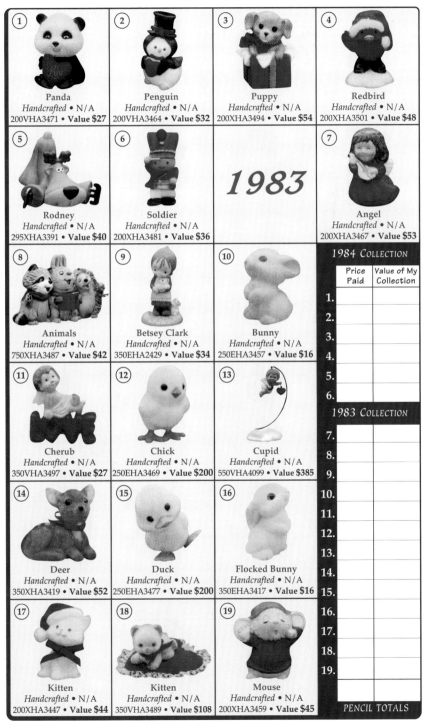

① **Panda**
Handcrafted • N/A
200VHA3471 • **Value $27**

② **Penguin**
Handcrafted • N/A
200VHA3464 • **Value $32**

③ **Puppy**
Handcrafted • N/A
200XHA3494 • **Value $54**

④ **Redbird**
Handcrafted • N/A
200XHA3501 • **Value $48**

⑤ **Rodney**
Handcrafted • N/A
295XHA3391 • **Value $40**

⑥ **Soldier**
Handcrafted • N/A
200XHA3481 • **Value $36**

1983

⑦ **Angel**
Handcrafted • N/A
200XHA3467 • **Value $53**

⑧ **Animals**
Handcrafted • N/A
750XHA3487 • **Value $42**

⑨ **Betsey Clark**
Handcrafted • N/A
350EHA2429 • **Value $34**

⑩ **Bunny**
Handcrafted • N/A
250EHA3457 • **Value $16**

⑪ **Cherub**
Handcrafted • N/A
350VHA3497 • **Value $27**

⑫ **Chick**
Handcrafted • N/A
250EHA3469 • **Value $200**

⑬ **Cupid**
Handcrafted • N/A
550VHA4099 • **Value $385**

⑭ **Deer**
Handcrafted • N/A
350XHA3419 • **Value $52**

⑮ **Duck**
Handcrafted • N/A
250EHA3477 • **Value $200**

⑯ **Flocked Bunny**
Handcrafted • N/A
350EHA3417 • **Value $16**

⑰ **Kitten**
Handcrafted • N/A
200XHA3447 • **Value $44**

⑱ **Kitten**
Handcrafted • N/A
350VHA3489 • **Value $108**

⑲ **Mouse**
Handcrafted • N/A
200XHA3459 • **Value $45**

1984 COLLECTION		
	Price Paid	Value of My Collection
1.		
2.		
3.		
4.		
5.		
6.		
1983 COLLECTION		
7.		
8.		
9.		
10.		
11.		
12.		
13.		
14.		
15.		
16.		
17.		
18.		
19.		
PENCIL TOTALS		

MERRY MINIATURES

1 Mouse
Handcrafted • N/A
350SHA3407 • **Value $21**

2 Penguin
Handcrafted • N/A
295XHA3439 • **Value $77**

3 Polar Bear
Handcrafted • N/A
350XHA3407 • **Value $230**

4 Santa
Handcrafted • N/A
295XHA3427 • **Value $47**

5 Shirt Tales
Handcrafted • N/A
295HHA3437 • **Value $43**

6 Snowman
Handcrafted • N/A
300XHA3479 • **Value $46**

7 Turkey
Handcrafted • N/A
295THA207 • **Value $45**

1982

8 Ceramic Bunny
Handcrafted • N/A
300EPF3702 • **Value $49**

9 Duck
Handcrafted • N/A
300EHA3403 • **Value $33**

10 Kermit
Handcrafted • N/A
395VHA3403 • **Value $32**

11 Kitten
Handcrafted • N/A
395HHA3466 • **Value $57**

12 Miss Piggy
Handcrafted • N/A
395VHA3416 • **Value $32**

13 Mouse
Handcrafted • N/A
450XHA5023 • **Value $67**

14 Pilgrim Mouse
Handcrafted • N/A
295THA3433 • **Value $219**

15 Rocking Horse
Handcrafted • N/A
450XHA5003 • **Value $98**

16 Santa (rigid)
Handcrafted • N/A
450XHA5016 • **Value $185**

17 Tree
Handcrafted • N/A
450XHA5006 • **Value $148**

18 Witch
Handcrafted • N/A
395HHA3456 • **Value $380**

1983 COLLECTION

	Price Paid	Value of My Collection
1.		
2.		
3.		
4.		
5.		
6.		
7.		

1982 COLLECTION

8.		
9.		
10.		
11.		
12.		
13.		
14.		
15.		
16.		
17.		
18.		
PENCIL TOTALS		

1981

1. Cupid
Handcrafted • N/A
300VPF3465 • **Value $58**

2. Ghost
Handcrafted • N/A
300HHA3402 • **Value $295**

3. Lamb
Handcrafted • N/A
300EPF402 • **Value $32**

4. Leprechaun
Handcrafted • N/A
300SHA3415 • **Value $50**

5. Penguin
Handcrafted • N/A
300XHA3412 • **Value $102**

6. Raccoon Pilgrim
Handcrafted • N/A
300THA3402 • **Value $54**

7. Redbird
Handcrafted • N/A
300XHA3405 • **Value $38**

8. Squirrel Indian
Handcrafted • N/A
300THA3415 • **Value $49**

9. Turkey
Handcrafted • N/A
300THA22 • **Value $50**

1980

10. Angel
Handcrafted • N/A
300XPF3471 • **Value $43**

11. Kitten
Handcrafted • N/A
300XPF3421 • **Value $40**

12. Pipe
Handcrafted • N/A
75SPF1017 • **Value $65**

13. Reindeer
Handcrafted • N/A
300XPF3464 • **Value $100**

14. Santa
Handcrafted • N/A
300XPF39 • **Value $35**

15. Sleigh
Handcrafted • N/A
300XPF3451 • **Value $50**

16. Turkey
Handcrafted • N/A
200TPF3441 • **Value $82**

17. Turtle
Handcrafted • N/A
200VPF3451 • **Value $53**

1981 Collection

	Price Paid	Value of My Collection
1.		
2.		
3.		
4.		
5.		
6.		
7.		
8.		
9.		

1980 Collection

10.		
11.		
12.		
13.		
14.		
15.		
16.		
17.		
PENCIL TOTALS		

MERRY MINIATURES

Value Guide – Merry Miniatures

1979

1 Bunny
Handcrafted • N/A
200EPF377 • **Value $90**

2 Duck
Handcrafted • N/A
200EPF397 • **Value $62**

3 Love
Handcrafted • N/A
150VPF1007 • **Value $124**

4 Mouse
Handcrafted • N/A
150XPF1017 • **Value $125**

1978

5 Joy Elf
Handcrafted • N/A
150XPF1003 • **Value $110**

6 Kitten
Handcrafted • N/A
150HPF1013 • **Value $28**

7 Mrs. Snowman
Handcrafted • N/A
150XPF23 • **Value $95**

8 Pilgrim Boy
Handcrafted • N/A
150TPF1003 • **Value $32**

9 Pilgrim Girl
Handcrafted • N/A
150TPF1016 • **Value $32**

10 Turkey
Handcrafted • N/A
150TPF12 • **Value $90**

1977

11 Barnaby
Handcrafted • N/A
125EPF12 • **Value $215**

12 Bernadette
Handcrafted • N/A
125EPF25 • **Value $215**

13 Chick
Handcrafted • N/A
125EPF32 • **Value $220**

14 Mouse
Handcrafted • N/A
125XPF122 • **Value $112**

15 Pilgrims
Handcrafted • N/A
150TPF502 • **Value $240**

16 Witch
Handcrafted • N/A
125HPF32 • **Value $185**

1979 Collection

	Price Paid	Value of My Collection
1.		
2.		
3.		
4.		

1978 Collection

5.		
6.		
7.		
8.		
9.		
10.		

1977 Collection

11.		
12.		
13.		
14.		
15.		
16.		
PENCIL TOTALS		

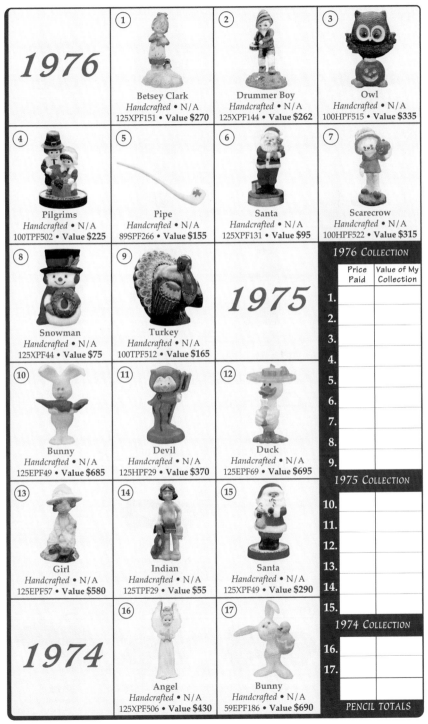

1976

① Betsey Clark
Handcrafted • N/A
125XPF151 • **Value $270**

② Drummer Boy
Handcrafted • N/A
125XPF144 • **Value $262**

③ Owl
Handcrafted • N/A
100HPF515 • **Value $335**

④ Pilgrims
Handcrafted • N/A
100TPF502 • **Value $225**

⑤ Pipe
Handcrafted • N/A
89SPF266 • **Value $155**

⑥ Santa
Handcrafted • N/A
125XPF131 • **Value $95**

⑦ Scarecrow
Handcrafted • N/A
100HPF522 • **Value $315**

⑧ Snowman
Handcrafted • N/A
125XPF44 • **Value $75**

⑨ Turkey
Handcrafted • N/A
100TPF512 • **Value $165**

1975

⑩ Bunny
Handcrafted • N/A
125EPF49 • **Value $685**

⑪ Devil
Handcrafted • N/A
125HPF29 • **Value $370**

⑫ Duck
Handcrafted • N/A
125EPF69 • **Value $695**

⑬ Girl
Handcrafted • N/A
125EPF57 • **Value $580**

⑭ Indian
Handcrafted • N/A
125TPF29 • **Value $55**

⑮ Santa
Handcrafted • N/A
125XPF49 • **Value $290**

1974

⑯ Angel
Handcrafted • N/A
125XPF506 • **Value $430**

⑰ Bunny
Handcrafted • N/A
59EPF186 • **Value $690**

1976 Collection	Price Paid	Value of My Collection
1.		
2.		
3.		
4.		
5.		
6.		
7.		
8.		
9.		
1975 Collection		
10.		
11.		
12.		
13.		
14.		
15.		
1974 Collection		
16.		
17.		
PENCIL TOTALS		

MERRY MINIATURES

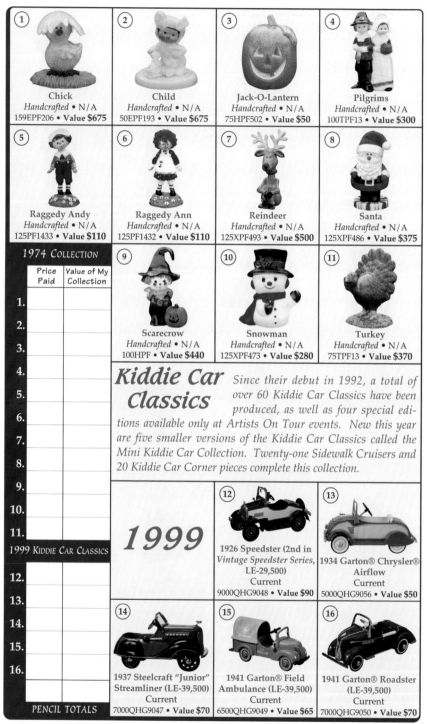

① Chick	② Child	③ Jack-O-Lantern	④ Pilgrims
Handcrafted • N/A	*Handcrafted* • N/A	*Handcrafted* • N/A	*Handcrafted* • N/A
159EPF206 • **Value $675**	50EPF193 • **Value $675**	75HPF502 • **Value $50**	100TPF13 • **Value $300**

⑤ Raggedy Andy	⑥ Raggedy Ann	⑦ Reindeer	⑧ Santa
Handcrafted • N/A	*Handcrafted* • N/A	*Handcrafted* • N/A	*Handcrafted* • N/A
125PF1433 • **Value $110**	125PF1432 • **Value $110**	125XPF493 • **Value $500**	125XPF486 • **Value $375**

1974 COLLECTION

⑨ Scarecrow	⑩ Snowman	⑪ Turkey
Handcrafted • N/A	*Handcrafted* • N/A	*Handcrafted* • N/A
100HPF • **Value $440**	125XPF473 • **Value $280**	75TPF13 • **Value $370**

	Price Paid	Value of My Collection
1.		
2.		
3.		
4.		
5.		
6.		
7.		
8.		
9.		
10.		
11.		

1999 KIDDIE CAR CLASSICS

12.		
13.		
14.		
15.		
16.		

PENCIL TOTALS

Kiddie Car Classics

Since their debut in 1992, a total of over 60 Kiddie Car Classics have been produced, as well as four special editions available only at Artists On Tour events. New this year are five smaller versions of the Kiddie Car Classics called the Mini Kiddie Car Collection. Twenty-one Sidewalk Cruisers and 20 Kiddie Car Corner pieces complete this collection.

1999

⑫ 1926 Speedster (2nd in Vintage Speedster Series, LE-29,500)	⑬ 1934 Garton® Chrysler® Airflow
Current	Current
9000QHG9048 • **Value $90**	5000QHG9056 • **Value $50**

⑭ 1937 Steelcraft "Junior" Streamliner (LE-39,500)	⑮ 1941 Garton® Field Ambulance (LE-39,500)	⑯ 1941 Garton® Roadster (LE-39,500)
Current	Current	Current
7000QHG9047 • **Value $70**	6500QHG9049 • **Value $65**	7000QHG9050 • **Value $70**

(1) 1941 Garton® Speed Demon
(4th in *Winner's Circle Collector's Series*)
Current
5500QHG9046 • **Value $55**

(2) 1949 Gillham™ Special
Don Palmiter Custom Collection
Current
5000QHG7108 • **Value $50**

(3) 1949 Gillham™ Sport
Don Palmiter Custom Collection
Current
6000QHG7109 • **Value $60**

(4) PHOTO UNAVAILABLE
1949 Gillham™ Sport with Golf Bag
(Artists On Tour Piece)
Current
(N/C) No stock # • **Value N/E**

(5) 1950 Holiday Murray® General
To Be Retired 1999
6000QHG9054 • **Value $60**

(6) 1950 Murray® General
Current
5000QHG9051 • **Value $50**

(7) Call Box & Fire Hydrant (set/2)
Current
2500QHG3618 • **Value $25**

(8) "Cinder" & "Ella" Dalmatians (set/2)
Current
1500QHG3619 • **Value $15**

(9) "Cinder Says . . ."
(3rd & final in *Bill's Boards Series*)
Current
3000QHG3621 • **Value $30**

(10) Corner Drive-In Sidewalk Signs (set/2)
Current
1500QHG3616 • **Value $15**

(11) Fire Station #1
(LE-39,500)
Current
7000QHG3617 • **Value $70**

(12) Flagpole
Current
2000QHG3620 • **Value $20**

(13) Table & Benches (set/3)
Current
2000QHG3615 • **Value $20**

(14) 1941 Murray® Pursuit Airplane
Current
2500QHG2203 • **Value $25**

(15) 1953 Murray® Dump Truck
Current
2500QHG2201 • **Value $25**

(16) 1955 Murray® Champion
Current
2500QHG2202 • **Value $25**

(17) 1955 Murray® Fire Truck
Current
2500QHG2204 • **Value $25**

(18) 1955 Murray® Tractor and Trailer
Current
2500QHG2205 • **Value $25**

(19) 1951 Hopalong Cassidy™ Velocipede (LE-24,500)
Current
4800QHG6325 • **Value $48**

1999 KIDDIE CAR CLASSICS		
	Price Paid	Value of My Collection
1.		
2.		
3.		
4.		
5.		
6.		
1999 KIDDIE CAR CORNER		
7.		
8.		
9.		
10.		
11.		
12.		
13.		
1999 MINI KIDDIE CAR COLLECTION		
14.		
15.		
16.		
17.		
18.		
1999 SIDEWALK CRUISERS		
19.		
	PENCIL TOTALS	

KIDDIE CAR CLASSICS

1998

1
1926 Steelcraft Speedster
by Murray® (1st in *Vintage
Speedster Series*, LE-29,500)
Retired 1998
9000QHG9045• **Value $98**

2
1929 Steelcraft Roadster
by Murray® (LE-39,500)
Retired 1998
7000QHG9040 • **Value $77**

3
1930 Custom Biplane
Don Palmiter Custom Collection
Current
5500QHG7104 • **Value $55**

4
1930 Spirit of Christmas
Custom Biplane
Don Palmiter Custom Collection
Retired 1998
6000QHG7105 • **Value $65**

5
1940 Custom Roadster
with Trailer (LE-39,500)
Don Palmiter Custom Collection
Current
7500QHG7106 • **Value $75**

6
1941 Steelcraft Chrysler
by Murray®
Current
5500QHG9044 • **Value $55**

7
1941 Steelcraft Fire
Truck by Murray®
Current
6000QHG9042 • **Value $60**

8
1941 Steelcraft Fire
Truck by Murray®
(Convention, silver)
Retired 1998
(N/C) No stock # • **Value N/E**

9
1950s Custom Convertible
Don Palmiter Custom Collection
To Be Retired 1999
6000QHG7101 • **Value $60**

10
1955 Custom Chevy®
Don Palmiter Custom Collection
Current
5000QHG7103 • **Value $50**

11
1958 Murray® Champion
Current
5500QHG9041 • **Value $55**

12
1960 Eight Ball Racer
(3rd in *Winner's Circle
Collector's Series*)
Current
5500QHG9039 • **Value $55**

13
1998 Nascar® 50th Anni-
versary Custom Champion
Don Palmiter Custom Collection
Current
6000QHG7110 • **Value $60**

14
Don's Street Rod
Don Palmiter Custom Collection
To Be Retired 1999
5500QHG7102 • **Value $55**

15
Car Lift and Tool Box
(set/2)
Current
2500QHG3608 • **Value $25**

16
Corner Drive-In
(LE-39,500)
Current
7000QHG3610 • **Value $70**

17
Famous Food Sign (2nd
in *Bill's Boards Series*)
Current
3000QHG3614 • **Value $30**

18
KC's Motor Oil
Current
1500QHG3609 • **Value $15**

19
Menu Station with
Food Trays (set/3)
Current
3000QHG3611 • **Value $30**

1998 KIDDIE CAR CLASSICS

	Price Paid	Value of My Collection
1.		
2.		
3.		
4.		
5.		
6.		
7.		
8.		
9.		
10.		
11.		
12.		
13.		
14.		
15.		
16.		
17.		
18.		
19.		

1998 KIDDIE CAR CORNER

PENCIL TOTALS

1. Newspaper Box & Trash Can Set (set/2)
Current
2000QHG3613 • **Value $20**

2. 1932 Keystone Coast-to-Coast Bus (LE-29,500)
Current
4500QHG6320 • **Value $45**

3. 1934 Mickey Mouse Velocipede
Current
4800QHG6316 • **Value $48**

4. 1937 De Luxe Velocipede
Current
4500QHG6319 • **Value $45**

5. 1960s Sealtest Milk Truck
Current
4000QHG6315 • **Value $40**

1997

6. 1937 GARTON® Ford (LE-24,500)
Retired 1997
6500QHG9035 • **Value $130**

7. 1938 GARTON® Lincoln Zephyr (LE-24,500)
Retired 1997
6500QHG9038 • **Value $140**

8. 1939 GARTON® Ford Station Wagon
Retired 1999
5500QHG9034 • **Value $60**

9. 1939 GARTON® Ford Station Wagon (Artists On Tour, brown)
Retired 1997
(N/C) No stock # • **Value N/E**

10. 1940 Gendron "Red Hot" Roadster (2nd in *Winner's Circle Collector's Series*)
To Be Retired 1999
5500QHG9037 • **Value $55**

11. 1941 Steelcraft Oldsmobile by Murray®
To Be Retired 1999
5500QHG9036 • **Value $55**

12. 1956 Murray® Golden Eagle (LE-29,500)
Retired 1997
5000QHG9033 • **Value $85**

13. 1941 Murray® Junior Service Truck
Retired 1999
5500QHG9031 • **Value $70**

14. KC's Garage (LE-29,500)
Retired 1997
7000QHG3601 • **Value $105**

15. Pedal Petroleum Gas Pump
Retired 1999
2500QHG3602 • **Value $35**

16. Pedal Power Premium Lighted Gas Pump
To Be Retired 1999
3000QHG3603 • **Value $30**

17. Sidewalk Sales Signs
To Be Retired 1999
1500QHG3605 • **Value $15**

18. Sidewalk Service Signs
To Be Retired 1999
1500QHG3604 • **Value $15**

19. Welcome Sign (1st in *Bill's Boards Series*)
To Be Retired 1999
3000QHG3606 • **Value $30**

1998 KIDDIE CAR CORNER

	Price Paid	Value of My Collection
1.		

1998 SIDEWALK CRUISERS

2.		
3.		
4.		
5.		

1997 KIDDIE CAR CLASSICS

6.		
7.		
8.		
9.		
10.		
11.		
12.		

1997 KIDDIE CAR CORNER

13.		
14.		
15.		
16.		
17.		
18.		
19.		
PENCIL TOTALS		

KIDDIE CAR CLASSICS

VALUE GUIDE — KIDDIE CAR CLASSICS

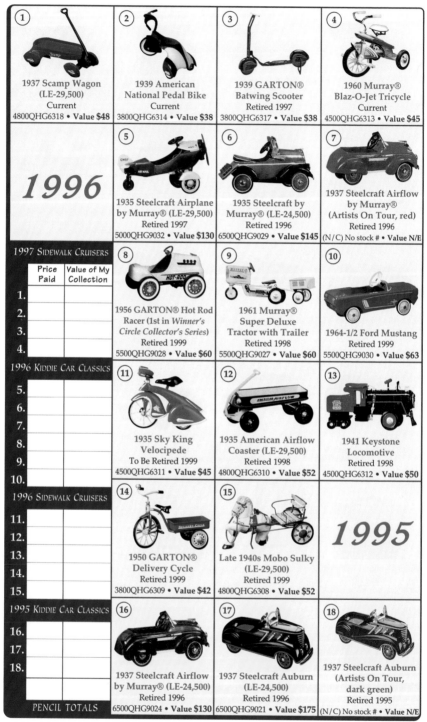

(1) 1937 Scamp Wagon (LE-29,500)
Current
4800QHG6318 • **Value $48**

(2) 1939 American National Pedal Bike
Current
3800QHG6314 • **Value $38**

(3) 1939 GARTON® Batwing Scooter
Retired 1997
3800QHG6317 • **Value $38**

(4) 1960 Murray® Blaz-O-Jet Tricycle
Current
4500QHG6313 • **Value $45**

1996

(5) 1935 Steelcraft Airplane by Murray® (LE-29,500)
Retired 1997
5000QHG9032 • **Value $130**

(6) 1935 Steelcraft by Murray® (LE-24,500)
Retired 1996
6500QHG9029 • **Value $145**

(7) 1937 Steelcraft Airflow by Murray® (Artists On Tour, red)
Retired 1996
(N/C) No stock # • **Value N/E**

1997 SIDEWALK CRUISERS

	Price Paid	Value of My Collection
1.		
2.		
3.		
4.		

1996 KIDDIE CAR CLASSICS

5.		
6.		
7.		
8.		
9.		
10.		

1996 SIDEWALK CRUISERS

11.		
12.		
13.		
14.		
15.		

1995 KIDDIE CAR CLASSICS

16.		
17.		
18.		

PENCIL TOTALS

(8) 1956 GARTON® Hot Rod Racer (1st in *Winner's Circle Collector's Series*)
Retired 1999
5500QHG9028 • **Value $60**

(9) 1961 Murray® Super Deluxe Tractor with Trailer
Retired 1998
5500QHG9027 • **Value $60**

(10) 1964-1/2 Ford Mustang
Retired 1999
5500QHG9030 • **Value $63**

(11) 1935 Sky King Velocipede
To Be Retired 1999
4500QHG6311 • **Value $45**

(12) 1935 American Airflow Coaster (LE-29,500)
Retired 1998
4800QHG6310 • **Value $52**

(13) 1941 Keystone Locomotive
Retired 1998
4500QHG6312 • **Value $50**

(14) 1950 GARTON® Delivery Cycle
Retired 1999
3800QHG6309 • **Value $42**

(15) Late 1940s Mobo Sulky (LE-29,500)
Retired 1999
4800QHG6308 • **Value $52**

1995

(16) 1937 Steelcraft Airflow by Murray® (LE-24,500)
Retired 1996
6500QHG9024 • **Value $130**

(17) 1937 Steelcraft Auburn (LE-24,500)
Retired 1996
6500QHG9021 • **Value $175**

(18) 1937 Steelcraft Auburn (Artists On Tour, dark green)
Retired 1995
(N/C) No stock # • **Value N/E**

(1) 1948 Murray® Pontiac
Retired 1998
5000QHG9026 • **Value $57**

(2) 1950 Murray® Torpedo
Retired 1996
5000QHG9020 • **Value $170**

(3) 1955 Murray® Royal Deluxe (LE-29,500)
Retired 1999
5500QHG9025 • **Value $65**

(4) 1959 GARTON® Deluxe Kidillac
Retired 1996
5500QHG9017 • **Value $125**

(5) 1961 GARTON® Casey Jones Locomotive
Retired 1996
5500QHG9019 • **Value $100**

(6) 1962 Murray® Super Deluxe Fire Truck
Retired 1997
5500QHG9095 • **Value $70**

(7) 1964 GARTON® Tin Lizzie
Retired 1997
5000QHG9023 • **Value $75**

(8) 1935 Steelcraft Streamline Velocipede by Murray®
Retired 1999
4500QHG6306 • **Value $50**

(9) 1937 Steelcraft Streamline Scooter by Murray®
Retired 1997
3500QHG6301 • **Value $47**

(10) 1939 Mobo Horse
Retired 1998
4500QHG6304 • **Value $50**

(11) 1940 GARTON® Aero Flite Wagon (LE-29,500)
Retired 1999
4800QHG6305 • **Value $52**

(12) 1958 Murray® Police Cycle (LE-29,500)
Retired 1999
5500QHG6307 • **Value $60**

(13) 1963 GARTON® Speedster
Retired 1999
3800QHG6303 • **Value $42**

(14) 1966 GARTON® Super-Sonda
Retired 1997
4500QHG6302 • **Value $55**

1994

(15) 1939 Steelcraft Lincoln Zephyr by Murray® (LE-24,500)
Retired 1996
5000QHG9015 • **Value $125**

(16) 1941 Steelcraft Spitfire Airplane by Murray® (LE-19,500)
Retired 1996
5000QHG9009 • **Value $190**

(17) 1955 Murray® Dump Truck (LE-19,500)
Retired 1996
4800QHG9011 • **Value $135**

(18) 1955 Murray® Fire Truck (LE-19,500, white)
Retired 1996
5000QHG9010 • **Value $290**

(19) 1955 Murray® Ranch Wagon (LE-19,500)
Retired 1996
4800QHG9007 • **Value $125**

1995 Kiddie Car Classics

	Price Paid	Value of My Collection
1.		
2.		
3.		
4.		
5.		
6.		
7.		

1995 Sidewalk Cruisers

8.		
9.		
10.		
11.		
12.		
13.		
14.		

1994 Kiddie Car Classics

15.		
16.		
17.		
18.		
19.		

PENCIL TOTALS

Kiddie Car Classics

1

1955 Murray® Red Champion (LE-19,500)
Retired 1996
4500QHG9002 • **Value $120**

2

1956 GARTON®
Dragnet® Police Car (LE-24,500)
Retired 1997
5000QHG9016 • **Value $80**

3

1956 GARTON®
Kidillac
Retired 1994
5000QHX9094 • **Value $85**

4

1956 GARTON®
Mark V (LE-24,500)
Retired 1997
4500QHG9022 • **Value $75**

5

1958 Murray® Atomic Missile (LE-24,500)
Retired 1997
5500QHG9018 • **Value $95**

6

1961 Murray® Circus Car (LE-24,500)
Retired 1997
4800QHG9014 • **Value $80**

7

1961 Murray® Speedway Pace Car (LE-24,500)
Retired 1997
4500QHG9013 • **Value $80**

1993

8

1955 Murray®
Fire Chief (LE-19,500)
Retired 1996
4500QHG9006 • **Value $125**

9

1968 Murray® Boat Jolly Roger (LE-19,500)
Retired 1996
5000QHG9005 • **Value $100**

1992

10

1941 Murray® Airplane (LE-14,500)
Retired 1993
5000QHG9003 • **Value $425**

11

1953 Murray® Dump Truck (LE-14,500)
Retired 1993
4800QHG9012 • **Value $310**

12

1955 Murray®
Champion (LE-14,500)
Retired 1993
4500QHG9008 • **Value $360**

13

1955 Murray® Fire Truck (LE-14,500)
Retired 1993
5000QHG9001 • **Value $380**

14

1955 Murray® Tractor and Trailer (LE-14,500)
Retired 1993
5500QHG9004 • **Value $385**

1994 Kiddie Car Classics

	Price Paid	Value of My Collection
1.		
2.		
3.		
4.		
5.		
6.		
7.		

1993 Kiddie Car Classics

| 8. | | |
| 9. | | |

1992 Kiddie Car Classics

10.		
11.		
12.		
13.		
14.		
PENCIL TOTALS		

Use these pages to record future Hallmark releases.

Future Releases	Material	Artist	Stock #	Price Paid	Value of My Collection
PENCIL TOTALS					
				Price Paid	Market Value

Value Guide — Future Releases

Use these pages to record future Hallmark releases.

Future Releases	Material	Artist	Stock #	Price Paid	Value of My Collection
			PENCIL TOTALS		
				Price Paid	Market Value

TOTAL VALUE OF MY COLLECTION

*Record the value of your collection here by adding the pencil totals
from the bottom of each Value Guide page.*

HALLMARK KEEPSAKE ORNAMENTS	Price Paid	Market Value
Page 47		
Page 48		
Page 49		
Page 50		
Page 51		
Page 52		
Page 53		
Page 54		
Page 55		
Page 56		
Page 57		
Page 58		
Page 59		
Page 60		
Page 61		
Page 62		
Page 63		
Page 64		
Page 65		
Page 66		
Page 67		
Page 68		
Page 69		
Page 70		
Page 71		
Page 72		
Page 73		
TOTAL		

HALLMARK KEEPSAKE ORNAMENTS	Price Paid	Market Value
Page 74		
Page 75		
Page 76		
Page 77		
Page 78		
Page 79		
Page 80		
Page 81		
Page 82		
Page 83		
Page 84		
Page 85		
Page 86		
Page 87		
Page 88		
Page 89		
Page 90		
Page 91		
Page 92		
Page 93		
Page 94		
Page 95		
Page 96		
Page 97		
Page 98		
Page 99		
Page 100		
TOTAL		

PAGE SUBTOTALS	PRICE PAID	MARKET VALUE

TOTAL VALUE OF MY COLLECTION

*Record the value of your collection here by adding the pencil totals
from the bottom of each Value Guide page.*

HALLMARK KEEPSAKE ORNAMENTS	Price Paid	Market Value
Page 101		
Page 102		
Page 103		
Page 104		
Page 105		
Page 106		
Page 107		
Page 108		
Page 109		
Page 110		
Page 111		
Page 112		
Page 113		
Page 114		
Page 115		
Page 116		
Page 117		
Page 118		
Page 119		
Page 120		
Page 121		
Page 122		
Page 123		
Page 124		
Page 125		
Page 126		
Page 127		
TOTAL		

HALLMARK KEEPSAKE ORNAMENTS	Price Paid	Market Value
Page 128		
Page 129		
Page 130		
Page 131		
Page 132		
Page 133		
Page 134		
Page 135		
Page 136		
Page 137		
Page 138		
Page 139		
Page 140		
Page 141		
Page 142		
Page 143		
Page 144		
Page 145		
Page 146		
Page 147		
Page 148		
Page 149		
Page 150		
Page 151		
Page 152		
Page 153		
Page 154		
TOTAL		

PAGE SUBTOTALS

	PRICE PAID	MARKET VALUE

TOTAL VALUE OF MY COLLECTION

*Record the value of your collection here by adding the pencil totals
from the bottom of each Value Guide page.*

HALLMARK KEEPSAKE ORNAMENTS	Price Paid	Market Value
Page 155		
Page 156		
Page 157		
Page 158		
Page 159		
Page 160		
Page 161		
Page 162		
Page 163		
Page 164		
Page 165		
Page 166		
Page 167		
Page 168		
Page 169		
Page 170		
Page 171		
Page 172		
Page 173		
Page 174		
Page 175		
Page 176		
Page 177		
Page 178		
Page 179		
Page 180		
Page 181		
TOTAL		

HALLMARK KEEPSAKE ORNAMENTS	Price Paid	Market Value
Page 182		
Page 183		
Page 184		
Page 185		
Page 186		
Page 187		
Page 188		
Page 189		
Page 190		
Page 191		
Page 192		
Page 193		
Page 194		
Page 195		
Page 196		
Page 197		
Page 198		
Page 199		
Page 200		
Page 201		
Page 202		
Page 203		
Page 204		
Page 205		
Page 206		
Page 207		
Page 208		
TOTAL		

PAGE SUBTOTALS

	PRICE PAID	MARKET VALUE

Total Value Of My Collection

*Record the value of your collection here by adding the pencil totals
from the bottom of each Value Guide page.*

Hallmark Keepsake Ornaments	Price Paid	Market Value
Page 209		
Page 210		
Page 211		
Page 212		
Page 213		
Page 214		
Page 215		
Page 216		
Page 217		
Page 218		
Page 219		
Page 220		
Page 221		
Page 222		
Page 223		
Page 224		
Page 225		
Page 226		
Page 227		
Page 228		
Page 229		
Page 230		
Page 231		
Page 232		
Page 233		
Page 234		
Page 235		
Page 236		
Page 237		
Page 238		
Page 239		
TOTAL		

Hallmark Keepsake Ornaments	Price Paid	Market Value
Page 240		
Page 241		
Page 242		
Page 243		
Page 244		
Page 245		
Page 246		
Page 247		
Page 248		
Page 249		
Page 250		
Page 251		
Page 252		
Page 253		
Page 254		
Page 255		
Page 256		
Page 257		
Page 258		
Page 259		
Spring Ornaments		
Page 260		
Page 261		
Page 262		
Page 263		
Page 264		
Page 265		
Page 266		
Page 267		
TOTAL		

Page Subtotals		
	Price Paid	Market Value

TOTAL VALUE OF MY COLLECTION

Record the value of your collection here by adding the pencil totals
from the bottom of each Value Guide page.

SPRING ORNAMENTS	Price Paid	Market Value
Page 268		
Page 269		
MERRY MINIATURES		
Page 270		
Page 271		
Page 272		
Page 273		
Page 274		
Page 275		
Page 276		
Page 277		
Page 278		
Page 279		
Page 280		
Page 281		
Page 282		
Page 283		
Page 284		
Page 285		
Page 286		
Page 287		
Page 288		
TOTAL		

MERRY MINIATURES	Price Paid	Market Value
Page 289		
Page 290		
Page 291		
Page 292		
Page 293		
Page 294		
Page 295		
Page 296		
Page 297		
Page 298		
Page 299		
KIDDIE CAR CLASSICS		
Page 300		
Page 301		
Page 302		
Page 303		
Page 304		
Page 305		
Page 306		
FUTURE RELEASES		
Page 307		
Page 308		
TOTAL		

PAGE SUBTOTALS		
	PRICE PAID	MARKET VALUE

GRAND TOTALS		
	PRICE PAID	MARKET VALUE

1998 YEAR IN REVIEW

With the 25th Anniversary Celebration of Hallmark Keepsake Ornaments, a new collection of Blown Glass pieces and many exciting additions to favorite series, 1998 made for an exciting year. So, CheckerBee Publishing polled retailers and collectors to find out what some of the top stories were in the year gone by. Here's what we found:

"The Grinch," based on the Dr. Suess Christmas story loved by children and adults alike, was without a doubt one of the most popular pieces for 1998. Other pieces based on classic television shows and movies also did well, including "Larry, Moe and Curly The Three Stooges™" and the Miniature Ornament "Glinda, The Good Witch™ Wicked Witch Of The West™ (set/2)."

The popular piece, "Stone Church," described by one collector as "heartwarming," was the first piece in the Magic series *Candlelight Services.* "Mistletoe Fairy," "Downhill Dash," "Santa's Deer Friend," and "Mop Top Wendy," rounded out the list of most coveted pieces.

For the series, *Frosty Friends* and *Fabulous Decade* (which will close this year), continued to be very popular among collectors, while *A Pony for Christmas* and *Snow Buddies* both had successful debuts with pieces of the same name. Both *Here Comes Santa* and *Merry Olde Santa* continued to thrive, while *Kiddie Car Classics* remained a favorite. And collectors grabbed up "Bright Sledding Colors," the 10th and final edition of the *CRAYOLA® Crayon* series, which will be sorely missed by many.

A Look Back At The 25th Anniversary Celebration

*O*n August 20, 1998 approximately 3,400 collectors flocked to Kansas City, Missouri to help Hallmark Keepsake Ornaments celebrate its 25th Anniversary.

In addition to meeting and reuniting with fellow collectors, attendees could choose from several activities and a variety of seminars in which to participate throughout the weekend. All of the Keepsake artists were on hand for signings, while shuttles ferried collectors to the Hallmark Visitors' Center for tours. An exhibit featuring several ornaments from noted historian Clara Johnson Scroggins was also on display.

WELCOME COLLECTORS

Seminars ranged from caring for your collection and decorating year-round to a history of the Hallmark line and discussions about Maxine, *Kiddie Car Classics* and other series. Many of the Keepsake artists led the seminars and even supplied numerous never-before-seen photos.

A highlight of the event came on Saturday, in the form of the Winter Wonderland Dinner. At the end of the evening, Keepsake artists Kristina Kline and Nello Williams performed a sentimental duet about collecting written by Williams that had many of the attendees in tears.

Collectors who attended the event were given three exclusive ornaments to commemorate the weekend's festivities: a pewter drummer boy upon registration, a crystal angel with lunch on Friday and a silver Snowflake, which represented the theme for the weekend, was a farewell gift presented at Saturday's reception.

SECONDARY MARKET OVERVIEW

Overview

*C*ollectors of Hallmark ornaments have taken on a challenging endeavor. Keepsake Ornaments are produced for one year, and once that time is up, the ornaments will, for the most part, never appear again. General releases can only be purchased for about half a year, usually from July to December. In other words, it takes a crafty collector to keep up with the movement of the Hallmark ornament market. If you find yourself in a bind, however, there is an alternative – the Hallmark secondary market.

WHAT IS THE SECONDARY MARKET?

The secondary market occurs once a Hallmark ornament has ceased production and retail stores have been depleted of their stock. Basically, if a piece is no longer available but collector demand is still high, those lucky enough to have purchased the piece at the retail level may be willing to part with it, provided the price is right. The secondary market is a valuable resource as it functions as a "meeting ground" of sorts where collectors can buy, sell and/or trade their ornaments. So, if you're looking for a specific ornament to add to your collection but you can't find it at your local Hallmark store, it's important not to give up – the piece you need may be literally right around the corner!

When shopping on the secondary market, it's important to remember that often there is a large demand for hard-to-find and popular pieces and their values may increase in response to this. So instead of paying $5 to $20 for an ornament, you may end up paying much more than that. In fact, some pieces on the secondary market can command hundreds of dollars!

WHERE IS THE SECONDARY MARKET?

So how do you go about finding a secondary market source? A good first step is to contact your local retailers, as they can often provide information on secondary market events slated for your area, or even put you in touch with other collectors. Sharing information with people who are on a similar hunt often leads to a great find.

Another option is to use a secondary market exchange service. These services publish newsletters which provide lists of pieces collectors are interested in buying or selling, as well as asking prices. Updates may be published on a monthly or weekly basis, and are often available through the mail. If you use an exchange, be prepared to pay a fee – usually between 10% and 20% percent – as the exchange takes a percentage for acting as the liaison.

If you're in the market solely for ornaments, you may want to try a secondary market dealer. These dealers usually specialize in one line of collectibles and are usually noted authorities. Often, they have their own price listings and can take away some of the guesswork you may encounter when you're dealing with exchanges as you can speak directly with the seller.

One of the most popular – and fastest growing – resources for collectors is the Internet. There are many sites dedicated to collectibles and they're all right at your fingertips. To locate such sites, try using keywords such as "Hallmark," "secondary market," "ornaments" or "collectibles." Also, to get general information about the line or for a history of Hallmark, don't forget to check out Hallmark's own web page at *www.hallmark.com*!

Many Internet sites you encounter may feature a bulletin board where you can "meet up" with other collectors. It's a great way to network, and it may just lead you to a sought-after piece. Other sites consist of pieces for sale, as well as the asking price. One of the benefits of using the Internet is its fast pace, as much of the information on the Internet is updated daily. If you do decide to use the Internet, however, be sure to proceed with caution to ensure the site you're dealing with is reputable.

If you don't have access to the Internet, you can always take advantage of print resources, such as newspapers or magazines. You may place an ad or register in the "swap & sell" section.

WHAT MIGHT AFFECT VALUES ON THE SECONDARY MARKET?

There are two major points to consider when buying and selling ornaments on the secondary market: packaging and condition. In the "real world," a box is just a box, but in the world of collectibles, boxes can have a significant effect on the secondary market value of an ornament. Also, always consider the condition of the piece you are about to purchase. Pieces that have sustained damage through the years will, for the most part, be valued at less than those in perfect or "mint" condition.

THE VALUE OF YOUR COLLECTION

While Hallmark ornaments mean different things to different collectors, most see them as a way to capture a little piece of a happy memory and keep it forever. So, whether your collection is valued in the thousands or includes only a few special pieces, always remember the reason you started in the first place – the joy they bring to your heart and home!

Let's Talk Hallmark

Knowing the "lingo" of the secondary market will keep collectors at the top of their game.

Here are some commonly used abbreviations:

MIB: mint in box

NB: no box

DB: damaged box

NT: no original price tag

EXCHANGES, DEALERS & NEWSLETTERS

The Baggage Car
Meredith DeGood
P.O. Box 3735
3100 Justin Drive, Suite B
Des Moines, IA 50322
515-270-9080

Christmas in Vermont
Kathy Parrott
51 Jalber Road
Barre, VT 05641
802-479-2024

The Christmas Shop
Shirley Trexler
P.O. Box 5221
Cary, NC 27512
919-469-5264

Collectible Exchange, Inc.
6621 Columbiana Road
New Middletown, OH 44442
800-752-3208
330-542-9646

Mary Johnson
P.O. Box 1015
Marion, NC 28752-1015
828-652-2910

Ron Kesterson
300 Camelot Court
Knoxville, TN 37922
423-675-7511

Morris Antiques
Allen and Pat Morris
2716 Flintlock Drive
Henderson, KY 42420
270-826-8378

New England Collectibles Exchange
Bob Dorman
201 Pine Avenue
Clarksburg, MA 01247
413-663-3643

The Ornament Trader Magazine
P. O. Box 469
Lavonia, GA 30553-0469
800-441-1551
770-650-2726

Twelve Months of Christmas
Joan Ketterer
P.O. Box 97172
Pittsburgh, PA 15229
412-367-2352

INSURING YOUR COLLECTION

*W*hen insuring your collection, there are three major points to consider:

KNOW YOUR COVERAGE: Collectibles are typically included in homeowner's or renter's insurance policies. Ask your agent if your policy covers fire, theft, floods, hurricanes, earthquakes and damage or breakage from routine handling. Also, ask if your policy covers claims at "current replacement value" – the amount it would cost to replace items if they were damaged, lost or stolen – which is extremely important since the secondary market value of some pieces may well exceed their original retail price.

> Many companies will accept a reputable secondary market price guide – such as the Collector's Value Guide™ – as a valid source for determining your collection's value.

DOCUMENT YOUR COLLECTION: In the event of a loss, you will need a record of the contents and value of your collection. Ask your insurance agent what information is acceptable. Keep receipts and an inventory of your collection in a different location, such as a safe deposit box. Include the purchase date, price paid, size, issue year, edition limit/number, special markings and secondary market value for each piece. Photographs and video footage with close-up views of each piece are good back-ups.

Collection Records

WEIGH THE RISK: To determine the coverage you need, calculate how much it would cost to replace your collection and compare it to the total amount your current policy would pay. To insure your collection for a specific dollar amount, ask your agent about adding a Personal Articles Floater or a Fine Arts Floater or "rider" to your policy, or insuring your collection under a totally separate policy. As with all insurance, you must weigh the risk of loss against the cost of additional coverage.

Biography

$\mathcal{C}$ lara Johnson Scroggins has been collecting Hallmark Ornaments for over 30 years and is considered to be the foremost authority on the subject. A lover of all ornament types, Clara has over 500,000 ornaments in her collection, including many one-of-a-kind pieces.

Clara was born and raised in Little Village, Arkansas. A member of a large family, she learned at an early age the importance of friends and relatives. As she grew older, Clara moved to Illinois and eventually

Clara with her husband, Joe

settled in Tampa, Florida where she lives today. Along with husband Joe Scroggins, Jr. (a member of President Clinton's administration), Clara has one son, Michael, three grandchildren and a great granddaughter.

Clara first began collecting ornaments in December 1972, soon after the death of her first husband. After weeks of depression, a friend convinced her to get out of the house for a while. Taking her advice, Clara went to a local mall where she noticed a silver cross ornament sparkling in the sunlight in a jewelry shop window. Clara was moved by the ornament's beauty and felt that the cross was a sign from her husband and God. Upon purchasing the

Clara's family

Reed & Barton ornament, she noticed that it was a second edition, and set out on a nationwide search for the first edition. In the process, Clara accumulated many additional ornaments that touched her heart and reminded her of the good times in her life. As she looks back now, Clara admits that her search for the first edition silver cross "literally saved my life."

Clara has become famous for her tradition of holiday decorating. Each year, she takes her ornaments out of the climate-controlled room in which they are stored, and displays them on numerous trees throughout her house. She likes to make decorating an interactive affair, and usually leaves a basket of ornaments under each tree, so that guests will be able to participate in the decorating tradition.

In addition to being a full-time collector, Clara has authored seven editions of the "Hallmark Keepsake Ornaments: A Collector's Guide" since 1980, including a new edition last year. Clara remembers the first time she called Hallmark to inquire about writing a book about the beloved collection of ornaments.

". . . ornaments should be used to help cherish, love and celebrate, as well as to decorate."

As she recalls, the people at Hallmark were very helpful, but "thought I was a little bit nuts." The young company, which was then called "Trim-A-Home," consisted of three artists, an office manager and a department manager, all crammed into three rooms over the parking garage at corporate headquarters.

Clara spends much of her time talking with collectors about her love of ornaments. Active on the lecture circuit, she spends a good deal of time traveling around the country to attend shows and has been interviewed by several newspapers and television shows nationwide.

In addition to ornaments, Clara collects nativities, antique sterling napkin rings, rare books, dolls and original artwork. She advises collectors to "collect what you love," and to keep in mind that "ornaments should be used to help cherish, love and celebrate, as well as to decorate."

*T*he Hallmark Keepsake Ornament Collector's Club, which was established in 1987, celebrates its 12th anniversary this year. With over 300,000 members nationwide, the club is a great way for collectors to meet new people with the same interests, attend exclusive collector events and, of course, receive exclusive ornaments!

For a membership fee of $22.50, collectors who join the club in 1999 will receive three complimentary Membership Ornaments sculpted by artists Robert Chad and Tammy Haddix.

"The Toymaker's Gift" shows Santa inspecting a newly created toy, while "Snowy Surprise" features a holiday jack-in-the-box created especially for Collector's Club members. "Arctic Artist" is an elf who is busy at work painting a soldier to be given to a good girl or boy on Christmas Eve.

Members who purchase a two or three year club membership will also receive the bonus ornament "Waiting for a Hug," which features an adorable teddy bear in an oversized elf hat.

In addition to the Membership Ornaments, 1999 Club members also have the opportunity to purchase three Club Edition Ornaments that are not available in stores:

"Snow Day – PEANUTS®" (set/2) is a set of ornaments that features Peppermint Patty and Marcie ice skating while Schroeder and Franklin work hard to build a snowman under Woodstock's supervision.

"1939 GARTON® Ford Station Wagon," crafted with wooden side panels, comes complete with a surfboard in the back. This piece complements the *Kiddie Car Classics* series.

"Based on the 1991 Happy Holidays® BARBIE™ Doll" is the fourth piece in the Club exclusive series. This piece complements the Keepsake Ornament *Holiday BARBIE®* series.

Each club member will also receive an official Club membership card, a one-year subscription to the *Collector's Courier*, the Club's official quarterly newsletter and a copy of the 1999 Hallmark Dream Book.

An additional benefit available to Hallmark Keepsake Ornament Collector's Club members is the opportunity to register to attend exclusive "Artists On Tour" events. The shows take place several times a year at various locations throughout the United States and allow club members the opportunity to meet with and receive signatures from Hallmark Keepsake Ornament artists.

Collectors interested in joining should contact their local retailer or the Club:

Hallmark Keepsake Ornament
Collector's Club
P.O. Box 419824
Kansas City, MO 64141-6824
(800) 523-5839

*W*hile many of the talented artists at the Hallmark Design Studio incorporate their childhood memories into the unique and expressive ornaments you see, there's in fact no telling where their inspiration may come from. However, aside from each artist's individual working style, the production process for producing each ornament is relatively similar.

Working at a minimum of two years in advance, all of the Hallmark artists have the opportunity to submit ideas for upcoming ornaments. Often, there are subjects such as classic movies that Hallmark wishes to reproduce in ornament form, so they will put forth the idea and request several drawings from each artist. Once all of the ideas are in, Hallmark Studio Managers work with the artists to decide which is the best representation; frequently working to incorporate several drawings into one piece.

A model, from which all other sculptures will be made, is then produced. The model is photographed and several pictures are given to the various sculptors so that at least seven duplicate sculptures can be made. Each of the sculptures serves a different purpose: some become the molds for the production process and others are used as models to display the options for color scheme. Once final decisions are made, the piece is then sent to the Hallmark production facility.

Over the years, the materials used to create Hallmark Ornaments have varied greatly. They are no longer just simple yarn figures; the options for designers have multiplied with advancing technology. Artists can incorporate a variety of materials into their work, including clay, porcelain, glass, pewter, plastic, wood and die-cast metal. To achieve the look they have envisioned, the artists may even choose a combination of materials, giving each piece in the collection its own individual style and beauty.

$\mathcal{F}$or Hallmark enthusiasts, ornament collecting is more than just a Christmas tradition. With over 3,000 Hallmark Keepsake Ornaments produced since 1973, there is a piece for every occasion, and for every room in the house. Here are eight tips to help you display your ornament collection year-round:

1. Countertops, bookshelves, curio cabinets and other flat surfaces can be dressed up with a creative display of Hallmark pieces. For example, the *Nostalgic Houses and Shops* series can be combined to create the look of a quaint, rural village. A pyramid of hat boxes makes for an innovative and original display area for your village scene, which can be viewed from all sides.

Shadowboxes also make great settings for Hallmark displays, while wicker baskets decorated with brightly colored flowers and filled with ornaments depicting nature scenes make a delightful centerpiece for any table.

2. Ornaments can be used as accessories for every room in your home. In the dining room, ball ornaments can be arranged in a decorated bowl to form a beautiful accent piece. In the living room and bedroom, ornaments can be attached to throw pillows, picture frames and mirrors. A decorative quilt with a holiday or seasonal theme can be transformed into a stunning wall hanging with the addition of Miniature Ornaments. For the best results, choose pieces with colors that will enhance the overall decorative theme of the room.

3. Miniature ornaments can look as great on you as they do on the tree! Attach your favorite pieces to your sweater, scarf or mittens for a fun alternative to jewelry. Ornaments such as those in the *Nature's Angels* series look great attached to a barrette, or used as earrings. Even sunglasses can be used to showcase your favorite ornaments!

4. Present newlyweds with a piece commemorating their "special day," such as "Our First Christmas Together" or "BARBIE™ and KEN™ Wedding Day" in the *BARBIE*™ series. For a great housewarming gift idea, give the new homeowners a basket full of goodies and ornaments. In addition to flowers, you can add freshly baked goods or gift certificates to local shops and include a few special ornaments, such as those in the *Welcome Friends* series to welcome newcomers into the neighborhood.

5. Intertwine strands of garland with strings of popcorn and dried cranberries then attach them to staircase banisters or braid them through the decorative rails. Use string or cord to hang ornaments from the garland and finish with festive bows and ribbons in colors to match your holiday decor.

6. Why not spread the joy that a traditional Christmas tree provides throughout the whole house? Many collectors these days are opting to decorate two, three or even more trees as a way to display their collections. A stunning way to welcome visitors to your home is to place a special tree in the main foyer by your front door. Another creative idea is to design themed trees for different rooms throughout the house. For instance, display the Child's Christmas and Disney pieces on a tree in a child's room, or showcase the sports-related pieces – such as the Collegiate, NFL and NBA Collections – on a tree in a den or recreation room.

DISPLAY TIPS

7. Decorative wreaths can be crafted for every season and holiday. A heart-shaped wreath covered in dried flowers and accentuated with heart-shaped ornaments makes a stunning Valentine's Day display. Racing fans may want to express their passion in a themed wreath using *Kiddie Car Classics* and *Stock Car Champions* pieces.

8. Birthdays are a great time to use Hallmark ornaments! Sports fans may enjoy a football-shaped cake decorated with their favorite *Football Legends,* while animal lovers may prefer cupcakes decorated with pieces from the *Cat Naps* and *Puppy Love* series. The lucky recipients will be thrilled to see the decorated cake, and even more excited to learn that they can keep the ornaments when the festivities are over!

9. Dress up your windows by stringing Hallmark Ornaments across the frame or on the cords of blinds. Mix them among suncatchers for a beautiful effect. The *Holiday Wildlife* and *Norman Rockwell* series are particularly good choices for this display.

10. Spice up your party with Hallmark Ornaments! Use ornaments as place settings, decorating the guests' places at the table with ornaments that features hobbies or activities that are interesting to them. When setting the table, attach ornaments to a piece of ribbon or fabric, and tie around napkins to form personalized napkin rings. As the hostess of a holiday party, you may be lucky enough to receive a gift of wine presented in a velvet sack, tied with a golden tassel and topped with a festive Santa ornament spreading good cheer to all!

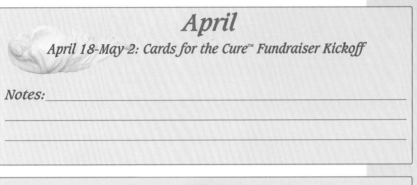

April

April 18-May 2: Cards for the Cure™ Fundraiser Kickoff

Notes:_____
_____
_____

May

New Kiddie Car Classics in stores now!

Notes:_____
_____
_____

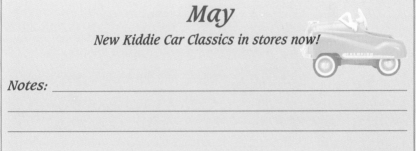

July

July 17: 1999 Keepsake Ornament Premiere
July 31: Artists On Tour – Milwaukee, Wisconsin
1999 Ornaments in stores now!
New Kiddie Car Classics in stores now!

Notes:_____
_____

August

August 7: Artists On Tour – Atlantic City, New Jersey
August 14: Artists On Tour – Oakland, California
August 28: Artists On Tour – Birmingham, Alabama
STAR TREK™ ornaments in stores now!

Notes:_____
_____

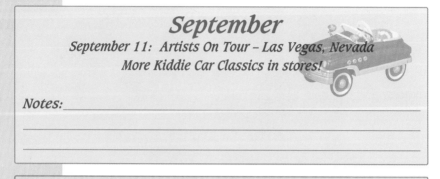

September

September 11: Artists On Tour – Las Vegas, Nevada
More Kiddie Car Classics in stores!

Notes:_____

_____

_____

October

October 16: Artists On Tour – Houston, Texas
"Angel of Hope," BARBIE™, Dr. Seuss™, Harley-Davidson®,
Sports Collection and Laser Creations in stores now!

Notes:_____

_____

November

November 13-14: Holiday Open House
"Millennium Princess BARBIE™" and "Christmas at Pooh's House"
in stores now!

Notes:_____

_____

_____

Local Events:_____

_____

_____

_____

_____

_____

ARTISTS ON TOUR—artist signing events held for Hallmark Keepsake Ornament Collector's Club members. Events are held across the country, and collectors can meet with artists, win prizes and purchase exclusive ornaments.

CLUB EDITION—ornaments which are made available for purchase only to members of the Hallmark Keepsake Ornament Collector's Club.

COLLECTIBLES—anything and everything that is "able to be collected." Figurines, dolls . . . or even *wooden decoys* can be considered a "collectible," but it is generally recognized that a true collectible should be something that increases in value over time.

COLLECTIBLE SERIES—a succession of ornaments released as annual editions (one ornament per year) over several years.

COLLECTION—several ornaments with a common theme that are released in one year (unlike a collectible series, which is spread over several years).

COLLECTOR'S CHOICE—title awarded each year by Hallmark Ornament historian Clara Johnson Scroggins. Ornaments chosen typically exemplify the spirit of Christmas or are "can't miss" ornaments.

COMMEMORATIVES—ornaments that celebrate special people (mother or sister) or special events (anniversaries or baby's first Christmas).

DAMAGED BOX (DB)—a secondary market term used when a collectible's original box is in poor condition, in most cases diminishing the value of the item.

DREAM BOOK—catalog issued by Hallmark debuting that year's ornaments and collectibles. The "Dream Book" contains color photographs and other information about the ornaments.

EDITIONS (ED.)—new ornaments released each year that belong to a new or ongoing series. For example, "Mop Top Wendy" is the 3rd edition in the Madame Alexander® series.

EXCHANGES—a secondary market service that lists pieces that collectors wish to buy or sell. The exchange works as a middleman and usually requires a commission.

GOLD CROWN STORE—Hallmark stores that meet certain criteria. Selected products (either entire lines or specific ornaments) are often available exclusively through such stores.

HANDCRAFTED—the manufacturing process of many Hallmark Ornaments where pieces are hand-assembled and hand-painted.

KEEPSAKE ORNAMENTS—brand name for Hallmark's line of ornaments, including miniature, light and motion and full-sized ornaments. The term "Keepsake" is also used to distinguish the regular ornament line from the Magic and Miniature lines.

Glossary

LIMITED EDITION—a piece scheduled for a predetermined production quantity or time period. Most ornaments are limited to one year of availability but can have varied production runs depending upon the demand for the ornament.

MAGIC ORNAMENTS—the Hallmark line of ornaments, first introduced in 1984, that incorporates features such as light, motion and sound.

MEMBERSHIP ORNAMENTS—exclusive ornaments given as gifts to Hallmark Keepsake Ornament Collector's Club members.

MINT IN BOX (MIB)—a secondary market term used when a collectible's original box is in "as good as new" condition, in most cases adding value to the item.

NO BOX (NB)—a secondary market term used when a collectible's original box is missing. For most collectibles, having the original box is a factor in its value on the secondary market.

ORNAMENT PREMIERE—Hallmark store event featuring the debut of that year's new ornaments. Some special pieces are available only at this event.

PERSONALIZED ORNAMENTS—ornaments offered through Gold Crown dealers between 1993 and 1995 that could be sent to Hallmark to be imprinted with personal messages.

PRIMARY MARKET—the conventional collectibles purchasing process in which collectors buy at issue price through retail stores, direct mail or home shopping networks.

ROOM HOPPING—the practice of going from one hotel room to another at a collectibles show to look at other attendees' collections or to see collectibles that guests are selling.

REACH PROGRAM—program that ran from 1989 to 1995 at selected retailers and featured promotional products available with a minimum Hallmark purchase.

SECONDARY MARKET—the source for buying and selling collectibles according to basic supply-and-demand principles. Pieces which are popular, retired or with low production quantities can appreciate in value far above the original retail issue price.

SHOWCASE ORNAMENTS—collection of ornaments that ran from 1993 to 1996 and featured traditional designs and materials, such as porcelain, die-cast metal and silver-plating.

TRIMMERS—tree decorations which are not part of the Keepsake Ornament Collection, are not boxed and are generally lower in price.

"UNANNOUNCED" SERIES—ornaments released in consecutive years that are not part of official series, but can be connected by theme. For example, the Tonka® vehicles from 1996, 1997 and 1998 are considered an "unannounced" series.

– Key –

All Hallmark Keepsake Ornaments, Spring Ornaments, Merry Miniatures and Kiddie Car Classics are listed below in alphabetical order. The first number refers to the piece's location within the Value Guide section and the second to the box in which it is pictured on that page.

ALPHABETICAL INDEX

ALPHABETICAL INDEX

ALPHABETICAL INDEX

ALPHABETICAL INDEX

ALPHABETICAL INDEX

Alphabetical Index

Alphabetical Index

ALPHABETICAL INDEX

ALPHABETICAL INDEX

ALPHABETICAL INDEX

Alphabetical Index

ALPHABETICAL INDEX

ALPHABETICAL INDEX

ALPHABETICAL INDEX

ALPHABETICAL INDEX

ALPHABETICAL INDEX

Alphabetical Index

ALPHABETICAL INDEX

ACKNOWLEDGEMENTS

CheckerBee Publishing would like to extend a special thanks to Clara Johnson Scroggins, Blanche Boisvert, Paula Fuller, Vicki Gilson, Wendy Leonard, Colleen Olbert, Tom Schmidt, Paula Sheridan and Diane Zimmer. Many thanks to the great people at Hallmark.

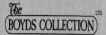

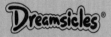

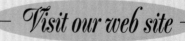